CHILE
AND EASTER ISLAND

CHILE
AND EASTER ISLAND

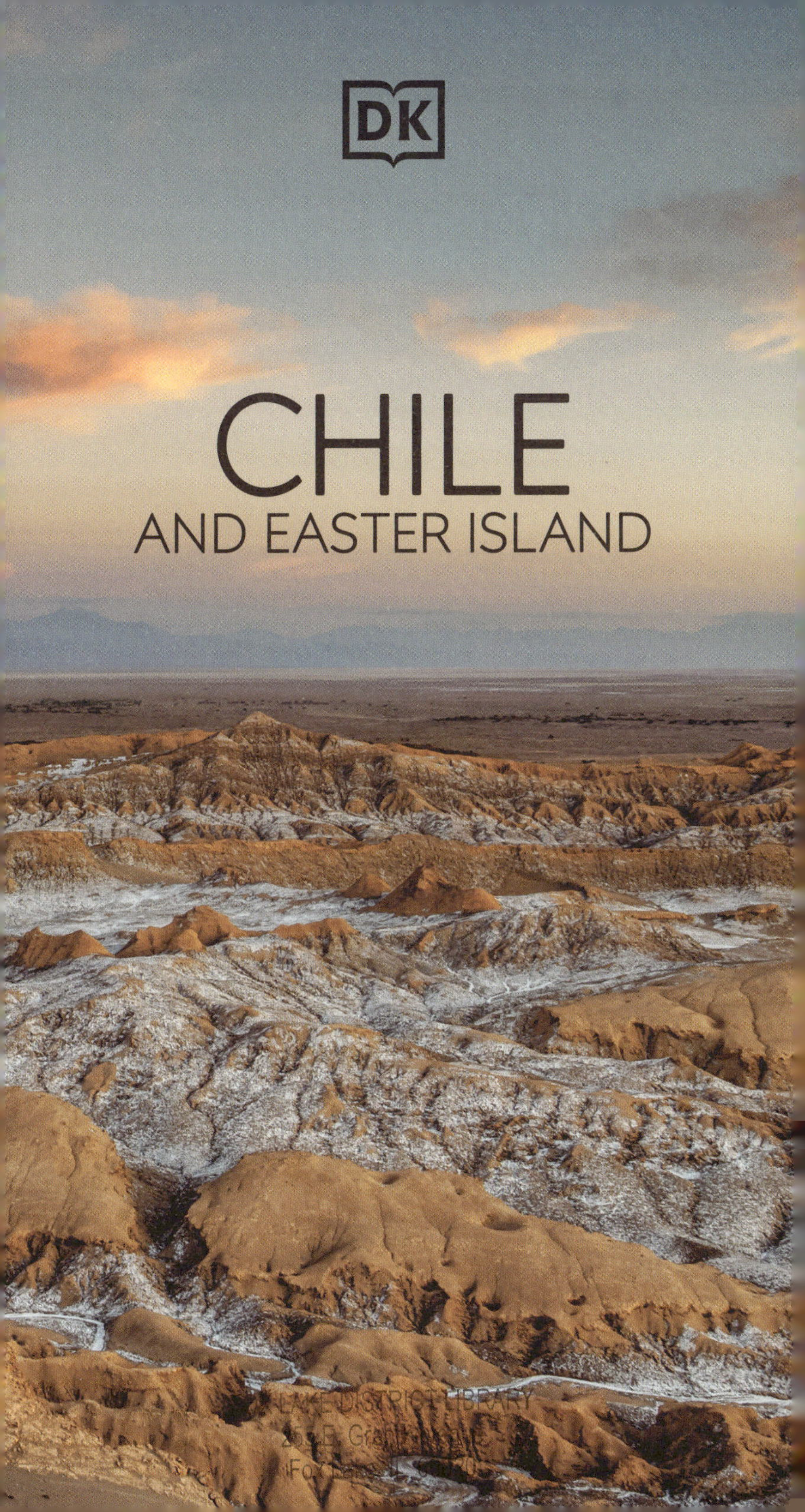

CONTENTS

DISCOVER 6

EXPERIENCE SANTIAGO 50

EXPERIENCE CHILE 112

NEED TO KNOW 280

Left: Vibrant apartments in Valparaíso
Previous page: Cordillera de la Sal in the Atacama Desert
Front cover: Los Cuernos towering above Lago Nordenskjold, Torres del Paine

DISCOVER

The sun cloaking the streets of Santiago

WELCOME TO CHILE AND EASTER ISLAND

From arid deserts to icy fjords, tropical beaches to snow-covered mountains, Chile's landscapes are diverse and beautiful. Yet the modern cities, provincial towns, and remote villages are also deserving of exploration. Whatever your dream trip entails, this DK travel guide is the perfect companion.

1 *Moai* statue facing inland on Easter Island.

2 Magellanic penguin on Isla Magdalena.

3 Hikers viewing the breathtaking Grey Glacier.

4 Colorful backstreet of Valparaíso.

Stretching more than 2,653 miles (4,270 km) north to south, with the Andes to the east and the Pacific to the west, the long and thin country of Chile has something for everyone. It is particularly famous for its dramatic scenery and myriad opportunities for hiking, rafting, diving, and other adventure sports. But the country also has a fascinating history, evident in its ancient sites, architecture, and impressive museums, not to mention fantastic seafood, world-class wine, and strong artistic, literary, and musical traditions.

Northern Chile is dominated by the volcanoes, lagoons, salt flats, and sand dunes of the dusty Atacama Desert, while in the heart of Chile, the endearingly cosmopolitan capital Santiago lies within striking distance of the bohemian port of Valparaíso and the vineyards of the fertile Central Valley. More than 2,182 miles (3,512 km) off the coast, the tiny and beautiful Easter Island is home to a dazzling array of monolithic statues. In the far south, meanwhile, Patagonia's many national parks rank among the world's finest places to hike.

With so much to see and do in Chile, it can be hard to know where to start. We've broken the country down into easily navigable chapters, with detailed itineraries, expert local knowledge, and colorful, comprehensive maps to help you plan the perfect visit. Whether you're staying for a week, a fortnight, or longer, this DK travel guide will ensure that you make the most of all that the country has to offer. Enjoy the book, and enjoy Chile.

REASONS TO LOVE CHILE AND EASTER ISLAND

Framed by the Andes, the Atacama Desert, and the Pacific Ocean, Chile's mesmerizing wild landscapes, captivating cities, and rich blend of cultures are just a few of the reasons to love the country. Here are our favorites.

1 PATAGONIA

Patagonia is home to endless plains, icy fjords, heaving glaciers, and raucous penguins, not to mention one of the world's great drives, the Carretera Austral *(p245)*.

VALPARAÍSO *2*

"Valpo" *(p118)* is spread across a multitude of hills overlooking the Pacific. It is blessed with beautiful architecture and an array of excellent places to eat, drink, and dance.

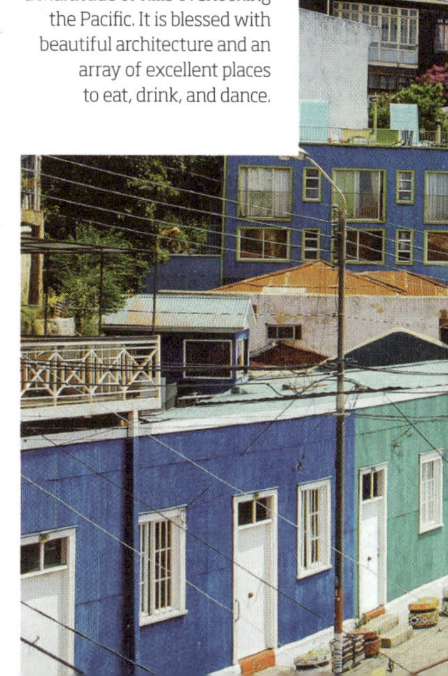

3 WHITE WATER RAFTING ON FUTALEUFÚ RIVER

The "Futa" *(p234)* is one of the best white water rafting rivers in South America, with more than 40 Class IV and V rapids, including the "Terminator" and the "Perfect Storm."

STARGAZING 4

Northern Chile's lack of light pollution and cloud-free days result in the clearest skies - the best places for stargazing are San Pedro de Atacama *(p158)* and the Valle de Elqui *(p172)*.

EASTER ISLAND 5

Easter Island *(p264)* - known locally as Rapa Nui - is one of the remotest inhabited places on earth, with a distinct Polynesian culture and many monolithic statues.

SOAK IN THE LAKE DISTRICT HOT SPRINGS 6

After a day's trekking, rafting, or kayaking in the adventure hub of Pucón *(p214)*, there are few better ways to relax than at one of the hot springs in the region.

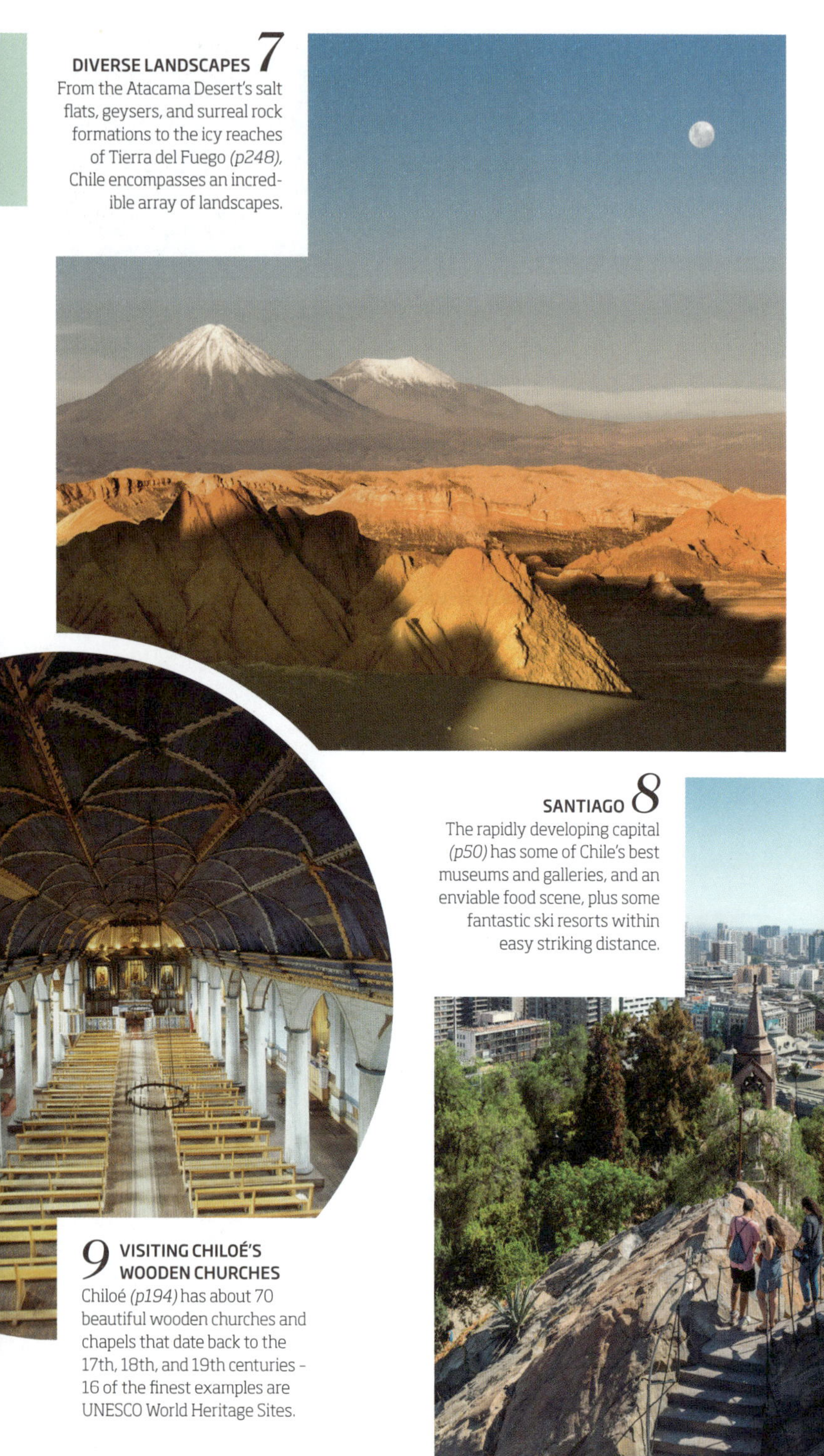

DIVERSE LANDSCAPES 7

From the Atacama Desert's salt flats, geysers, and surreal rock formations to the icy reaches of Tierra del Fuego *(p248)*, Chile encompasses an incredible array of landscapes.

SANTIAGO 8

The rapidly developing capital *(p50)* has some of Chile's best museums and galleries, and an enviable food scene, plus some fantastic ski resorts within easy striking distance.

9 VISITING CHILOÉ'S WOODEN CHURCHES

Chiloé *(p194)* has about 70 beautiful wooden churches and chapels that date back to the 17th, 18th, and 19th centuries – 16 of the finest examples are UNESCO World Heritage Sites.

10 SURFING IN PICHILEMU

A laid-back town on the Central Valley coast, Pichilemu *(p142)* is the best place in Chile to learn to surf, hone your skills, or simply kick back and watch the pros in action.

WINE TASTING IN CENTRAL VALLEY 11

Chilean wine has earned a world-class reputation. Many vineyards in the Central Valley *(p130)* offer tours and tasting sessions amid gorgeous rural scenery.

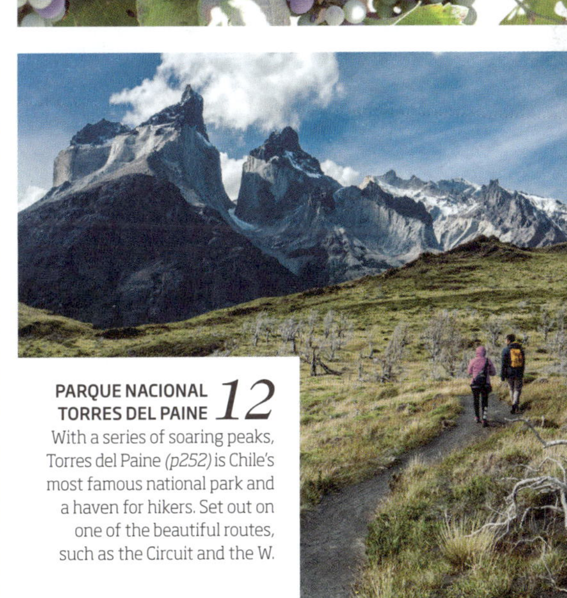

PARQUE NACIONAL TORRES DEL PAINE 12

With a series of soaring peaks, Torres del Paine *(p252)* is Chile's most famous national park and a haven for hikers. Set out on one of the beautiful routes, such as the Circuit and the W.

EXPLORE CHILE AND EASTER ISLAND

This guide divides Chile into seven color-coded sightseeing areas, as shown on this map. Find out more about each area on the following pages.

Pacific Ocean

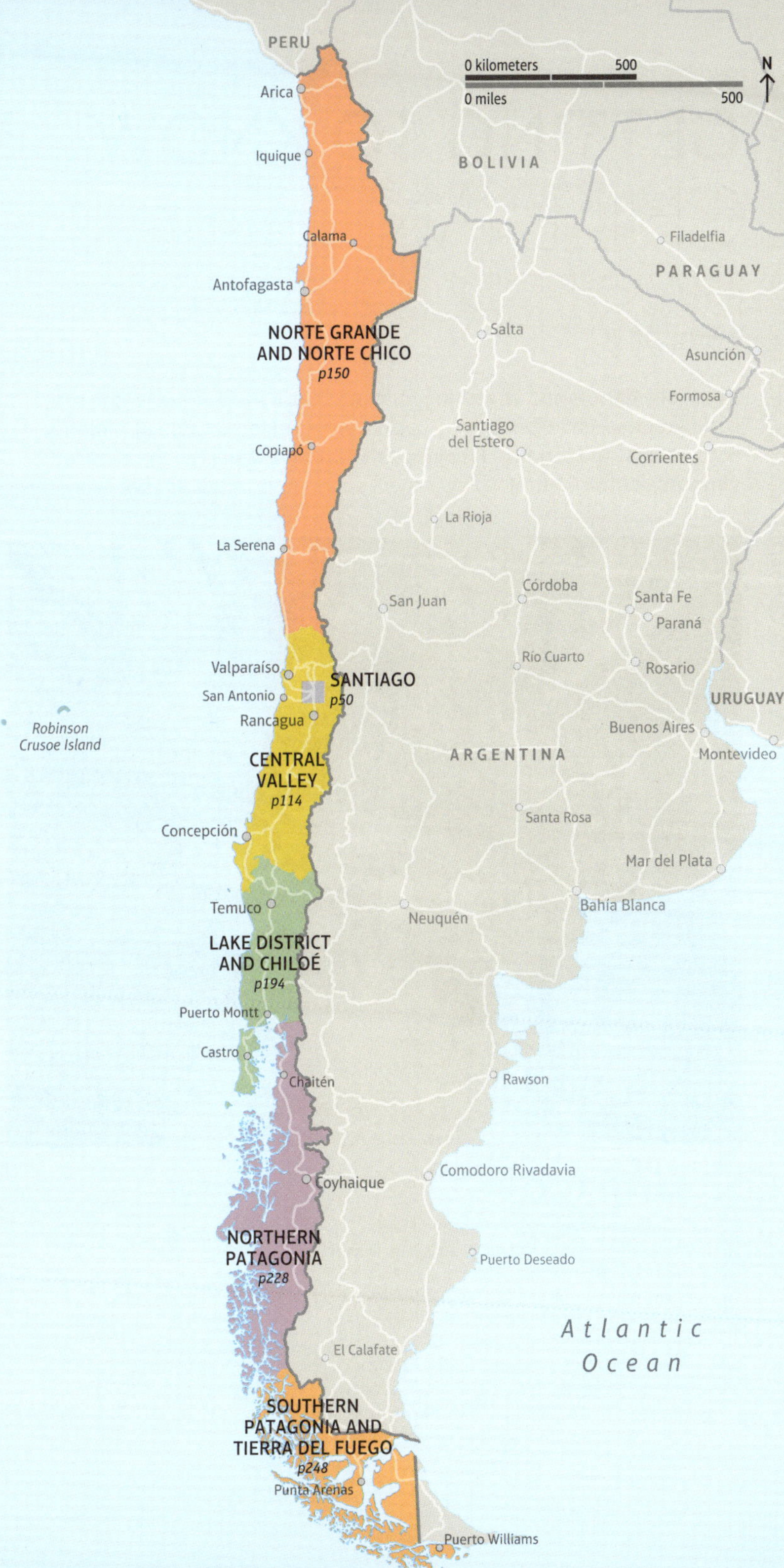

PERU
Arica
Iquique
Calama
Antofagasta
NORTE GRANDE AND NORTE CHICO
p150
Copiapó
La Serena
Valparaíso
San Antonio
SANTIAGO
p50
Rancagua
CENTRAL VALLEY
p114
Concepción
Temuco
LAKE DISTRICT AND CHILOÉ
p194
Puerto Montt
Castro
Chaitén
Coyhaique
NORTHERN PATAGONIA
p228
SOUTHERN PATAGONIA AND TIERRA DEL FUEGO
p248
Punta Arenas
Puerto Williams
Robinson Crusoe Island
0 kilometers 500
0 miles 500
N
BOLIVIA
Filadelfia
PARAGUAY
Salta
Asunción
Formosa
Santiago del Estero
Corrientes
La Rioja
Córdoba
San Juan
Santa Fe
Paraná
Río Cuarto
Rosario
URUGUAY
Buenos Aires
Montevideo
ARGENTINA
Santa Rosa
Mar del Plata
Bahía Blanca
Neuquén
Rawson
Comodoro Rivadavia
Puerto Deseado
El Calafate
Atlantic Ocean

GETTING TO KNOW CHILE AND EASTER ISLAND

Unusually narrow and stretching for more than a third of the length of Latin America, Chile is a country packed with a diverse range of climates, ecosystems, and terrains. From the arid Atacama Desert to the terraced vineyards of the Central Valley, expect superlative landscapes at every turn.

PAGE 50

SANTIAGO

The modern Chilean capital makes quite an impression. This buzzing metropolis is flanked in the east by the towering, snow-dusted Andes, while high-rise buildings in the financial district give way to forested hillsides. Locals flock to the bustling commerce of downtown or sip local wine in bars along tree-lined boulevards. Pulsing with a ceaseless energy, the city's keynotes include its thriving culinary scene that celebrates Indigenous gastronomy, and world-class museums that showcase the rich ancient cultures.

Best for
Museums, culture, food and drink

Home to
Museo Chileno de Arte Precolombino, Parque Quinta Normal, Parque Metropolitano de Santiago

Experience
Dining in some of Chile's finest restaurants

PAGE 114

CENTRAL VALLEY

The Pacific Ocean hugs sun-soaked, white-sand beaches along the full length of the Central Valley. The regional jewel is hillside Valparaíso, whose vibrant streets are a canvas for the country's finest artistic expression and accommodate rickety, turn-of-the-century funiculars and Nobel Prize-winning poets. Inland, fertile valley plains are dotted with pretty towns where vine-lined wineries tantalize the taste buds with Carménère and Cabernet Sauvignon wines. Eastward, the ever-present, snow-cloaked Andes promise high-adrenaline skiing and astonishing valley views.

Best for
Historic cities, wine tasting, skiing

Home to
Valparaíso, Casa Museo Isla Negra, Colchagua Valley wineries

Experience
Riding Valparaíso's funiculars

PAGE 150

NORTE GRANDE AND NORTE CHICO

The arid Atacama Desert spreads over the Chilean north, delivering stark, otherworldly landscapes. High-altitude plateaus, pitted with flamingo-flecked lagoons and geysers, are lit up at night by the dazzling arc of the Milky Way, while the wave-scoured beaches of Iquique offer visitors a place to surf huge, impressive waves. Further south, the calm, sweeping bay of picturesque La Serena has a swashbuckling legacy of pirates and privateers.

Best for
Otherworldly landscapes, stargazing, beaches

Home to
San Pedro de Atacama, Parque Nacional Lauca, Iquique, La Serena, Valle de Elqui

Experience
Stargazing in the Atacama Desert

→

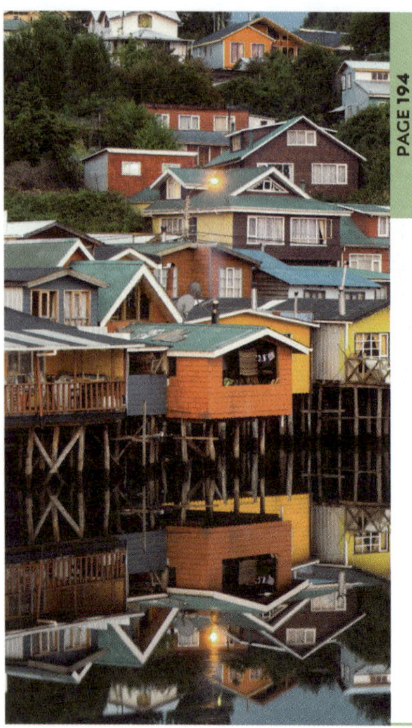

PAGE 194

LAKE DISTRICT AND CHILOÉ

Home to lush forests of *Araucaria araucana* (monkey puzzle trees) and towering *Fitzroya cupressoides* (alerce or Patagonian cypress), Chile's Lake District is an outdoor haven for adventure seekers. Hikers are lured to Pucón to trudge up snowcapped volcanic craters or sink into inviting thermal spring waters. Separated from mainland Chile by a narrow channel, the fishing villages of the bucolic Chiloé archipelago charm photographers and culture vultures. Here, find whimsical, technicolor-painted wooden churches and traditional seafood recipes.

Best for

National parks, sports, historic churches

Home to

Parque Nacional Conguillío, Parque Nacional Villarrica, Valdivia, Parque Nacional Vicente Pérez Rosales

Experience

Sampling curanto *in Chiloé*

PAGE 228

NORTHERN PATAGONIA

Careering through leafy temperate rainforests and glaciers that cling dizzyingly to cliffsides, the Carretera Austral extends through Northern Patagonia. Delving into the Patagonian hinterland, the mostly unpaved highway draws road-trippers and hikers. En route, the foam currents of the Río Futaleufú promise unparalleled white water rafting, while national parks are awash with wind-blasted steppes and cobalt-blue lakes. Head here to see the country's most mesmerizing terrain.

Best for

Dramatic Andean scenery, epic drives, white water rafting

Home to

Parque Nacional Pumalín Douglas Tompkins, Futaleufú, Parque Nacional Queulat, Parque Nacional Laguna San Rafael

Experience

Driving the Carretera Austral

PAGE 248

SOUTHERN PATAGONIA AND TIERRA DEL FUEGO

The three granite towers of the Torres del Paine soar into the clouds, casting a spell on every visitor to Southern Patagonia. Excursions by boat into the pristine channels of the fjords stippling the coast reveal just some of the region's secrets. Hikers are guaranteed lofty mountains and glistening glaciers, while photographers and wildlife lovers revel in glimpses of guanaco, chattering penguins, and even puma.

Best for
Glaciers and mountains, trekking, wildlife

Home to
Parque Nacional Torres del Paine, Punta Arenas, Puerto Williams

Experience
Sailing in the awe-inspiring Beagle Channel, home to sea lions and birdlife

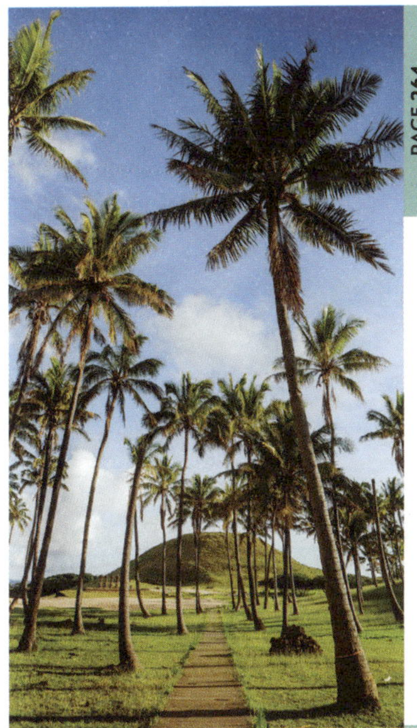

PAGE 264

EASTER ISLAND AND ROBINSON CRUSOE ISLAND

A far-flung outpost some 2,300 miles (3,700 km) west across the Pacific, Easter Island is best known for stoic *moai*, who stare across the ages from their plinths.On the streets of Hanga Roa, modern Rapa Nui culture pulses through rhythmic dance and grueling sporting festivals. Closer to mainland Chile, Robinson Crusoe and the Juan Fernández Islands harbor a World Biosphere Reserve with humming birds and rare endemic animals.

Best for
Ancient sites, Indigenous cultures, diving

Home to
Ahu Tongariki, Rano Raraku, Rano Kau and Orongo

Experience
The bustling Tapati Rapa Nui festival

1

2

3

4

1 A hiker enjoying the vast expanse of Valle de la Luna.

2 The sun setting on the Tahai ceremonial site.

3 Bustling *marisquerías* at Mercado Central, Santiago.

4 Soaking at Termas Baños de Puritama.

Chile is remarkably diverse. Spend your time hiking one of the world's driest deserts, visiting the icy expanses of Patagonia, and wandering around crowded and creative cities. Here we select some of the highlights to help you plan your stay.

2 WEEKS

Day 1

On the first day in San Pedro de Atacama you can take a guided tour of the Salar de Atacama *(p185)*, a vast, gleaming salt flat that contains glorious lakes, including the flamingo-populated Laguna Chaxa. The *salar* can be combined with several other sites, such as the beautiful Miscanti, Miñiques, and Lejía *lagunas*, and the scenic villages of Toconao, Peine, and Socaire. In the evening, head over to Adobe *(p159)* for dinner.

Day 2

Get up in the early hours for another full-day guided tour around San Pedro de Atacama. The first stop is the Géiseres del Tatio *(p184)*, the world's highest geothermal field, excursions to which are often combined with a dip in a hot spring, such as the Termas Baños de Puritama *(p183)*. Tours also include visits to places like the oasis villages of Caspana and Chiu-Chiu, and the pre-Inca ruins of the Pukará de Lasana *(p182)*. Back in San Pedro de Atacama, try Tierra Todo Natural *(p159)* for dinner and then Chelacabur *(p161)* for drinks.

Day 3

In the morning, take a guided tour of the ALMA Observatory *(p160)*, the world's biggest astronomical project. After lunch, visit Pukará de Quitor *(p160)*, a ruined pre-Inca fortress, and watch the sunset in the otherworldly Valle de la Luna *(p184)*. Then go for an early dinner at Tierra Todo Natural *(p159)* before taking a stargazing tour *(p160)*.

Day 4

Drive or take the bus for roughly an hour from San Pedro de Atacama to the city of Calama and catch a flight to Santiago. In the afternoon, look round the city center and the Museo Chileno de Arte Precolombino *(p66)*, one of the finest museums on the continent. In the evening, head over to the Lastarría neighborhood *(p79)* for dinner and drinks at Bocanáriz *(p78)*.

Day 5

In your first morning in Santiago, look round the Museo de la Memoria y los Derechos Humanos *(p90)*, which offers a powerful insight into the human rights abuses of the Pinochet dictatorship. After, reflect on your visit in the neighboring Parque Quinta Normal *(p88)*. For lunch, try one of the *marisquerías* (fish and seafood restaurants) at the Mercado Central *(p81)*, such as Richard El Rey Del Mariscal *(p69)*. In the afternoon, take the funicular to the summit of Cerro San Cristóbal *(p102)* and enjoy the vistas. Try traditional fare for dinner at Boragó *(p109)* or El Huerto *(p109)*.

1

2

3

Day 6

In the morning, take a flight to Easter Island, which will take five hours. After looking around the town of Hanga Roa *(p274)*, stroll to the Museo Antropológico Sebastián Englert for an introduction to Rapa Nui history and culture. Then find a vantage point near the Tahai ceremonial site *(p276)* and enjoy the sunset. Finish the day with dinner at Au Bout du Monde *(p275)*.

Day 7

Take a guided tour to Ahu Tongariki *(p272)* and watch the sun rise behind 15 monumental *moai*. Head to Rano Raraku *(p268)*, where the island's statues were carved. In the afternoon, swim, sunbathe, and stroll at Anakena beach *(p276)*, where the first settlers are believed to have landed. In the evening, head to Te Moana *(p275)*, a prime spot for drinks and dinner.

Day 8

Spend the day hiking up to the staggering Rano Kau *(p274)* volcanic crater and looking round the ruins of Orongo village *(p274)*, which was closely associated with the Birdman cult. In the evening, watch one of the cultural shows in Hanga Roa, which often feature a traditional feast of *curanto* (meat, fish, and vegetables baked over hot rocks).

Day 9

Fly back to Santiago first thing. In the late afternoon, head to the upmarket Las Condes district for a well-mixed cocktail and panoramic views at the W hotel's swish rooftop bar *(p111)*. Then go for dinner in one of nearby Providencia's many restaurants, such as Liguria *(p58)*.

Day 10

Drive or take the bus to one of the Casablanca Valley wineries *(p130)* for a tour, tasting session, and lunch. Head on to Valparaíso *(p118)* and spend the afternoon exploring the city's most atmospheric *cerros* (hills), Concepción and Alegre. Both are covered with cobbled streets and historic, colonial townhouses and churches, as well as

1 Restaurants of Providencia, Santiago, illuminated at night.

2 A hiker looking out at the Rano Kau crater, Easter Island.

3 Vibrant street art in Valparaíso.

4 Soaring peaks of the Torres del Paine.

5 Casablanca wineries.

6 Hikers at the foot of the Valle del Francés.

plenty of places to eat, drink, and enjoy the sweeping views. For dinner, try El Peral *(p121)* or Maralegre *(p121)*, followed by an *helado* (ice cream) at Amor Porteño *(p121)*.

Day 11

Look around the crumbling architecture of the Barrio Puerto, before taking the *ascensor* (funicular lift) up to the Museo Marítimo Nacional *(p118)*, which offers an insight into Chile's turbulent history. After lunch at Bar La Playa *(p120)*, take bus "0" *(p118)* up to Nobel Prize-winning poet Pablo Neruda's former home, La Sebastiana, which is now a museum *(p125)*. Check out Valparaíso's innovative street art scene at the Museo a Cielo Abierto *(p126)*. After dinner at Casa Altamira *(p121)*, head down to Bar Liberty *(p125)* for drinks and live music.

Day 12

Drive, catch the bus, or take a taxi to Santiago airport for a flight to Puerto Natales *(p258)*. Take it easy in the afternoon by exploring the town center and the Museo Histórico Municipal, which offers a snapshot of Puerto Natales' history. Then stop off at The Singular *(p257)* for gourmet dishes of king crab or Patagonian roast lamb.

Day 13

Get up early and drive, catch the bus, or take an organized tour to Parque Nacional Torres del Paine *(p252)*. Spend the day hiking along one of the park's trails, for example to Mirador las Torres *(p254)*, which takes you to views of the park's iconic peaks. Stay at the campgrounds or *refugios* (huts that offer intriguing dorm-like accommodation), or splash out on a luxury lodge, such as Tierra Patagonia *(p255)*.

Day 14

Spend your final day in the park soaking up the dramatic Patagonian landscapes of mountains, glaciers, waterfalls, and lagoons at Parque Nacional Torres del Paine. Two good trails to attempt are the ones to Mirador Cuernos and Mirador Ferrier *(p254)*.

1

2

3

7 DAYS
in Southern Patagonia

Day 1

Spend the first day exploring Punta Arenas, the largest city in Chile's far south *(p256)*. Start in the main square, Plaza Benjamín Muñoz Gamero, which has as its centerpiece a statue of Ferdinand Magellan. Then look round the Palacio Sara Braun and the Museo Regional de Magallanes, both of which provide a glimpse into the city's heyday in the late 19th and early 20th centuries. After lunch at one of the cafés in the city center, visit the Museo Naval y Marítimo to see fascinating exhibits on Chile's naval history. Then meander around the Cementerio Municipal Sara Braun. Afterward, head for dinner at Damiana Elena *(p257)*.

Day 2

Begin the day by joining a guided tour to the Isla Magdalena *(p257)*, a small island reserve northeast of the Punta Arenas that is home to a colony of 100,000 Magellanic penguins. Then head back to the center of Punta Arenas for a delicious lunch and take a trip south to Puerto Hambre (Port Hunger; *p256*), site of one of the earliest Spanish settlements on the Magellan Strait. In the evening, have some drinks at the charming Taberna Club de la Unión *(p257)*; if you fancy staying for dinner, it also serves up tasty Chilean dishes.

Day 3

In the morning, head to Puerto Natales *(p258)*. After lunch, drive, take a taxi, or go on a tour to the Cueva del Milodón *(p258)*, a massive cave north of Puerto Natales in which the remains of the giant sloth were discovered in 1890. Cueva del Milodón also provided inspiration for English writer Bruce Chatwin's famous travelog, *In Patagonia* (1977). As well as exploring the wonderful *cueva*, visitors can check out displays on some of the interesting prehistoric creatures of Patagonia. Finish off with some dinner at Cangrejo Rojo *(p257)*.

Day 4

Drive or take the bus to reach the spectacular Parque Nacional Torres del Paine *(p252)*, a UNESCO World Biosphere Reserve and a trekker's paradise. Check

4

6

5

1 Plaza Benjamín Muñoz Gamero, Punta Arenas.

2 Sunset over Punta Arenas.

3 Magellanic penguins.

4 View from the Cueva del Milodón.

5 The ice-blue Grey Glacier.

6 Horseback riding in Parque Nacional Torres del Paine.

into the luxurious Explora Patagonia *(p255)*, an upmarket hotel that offers spectacular views of the park's soaring granite peaks. Enjoy a light lunch in the restaurant, then make your first foray into the park on one of the hotel's horse-back riding tours. Spend the rest of your afternoon trotting past aquamarine lakes and though ancient beech woods, keeping your eyes peeled for a glimpse of the region's diverse wildlife, including condors and guanacos.

Day 5

Rise early and grab a big breakfast in the hotel – you'll need it to tackle one of the park's best day hikes, which ends at the base of the granite needles known as Las Torres (The Towers). This route – which is, in fact, the first section of the popular multi-day W trek – meanders through varied scenery, including grass-lands, forests, and scrubland, passing by teal-hued lakes and sheer-sided mountains. Eventually, your legs tired, you'll reach *Las Torres*, whose shard-like prongs pierce the sky above. Take a minute to soak in this magnificent sight, before heading back to your hotel for an evening of well-deserved relaxation in the spa.

Day 6

Explore Lago Grey, one of the most beautiful lakes in the park. It is bordered to the north by a mighty glacier and to the east by the rugged peaks of the Cordillera del Paine. Paddle over its ice-berg-filled expanse on a kayaking trip with the excellent Kayak en Patagonia *(kayakenpatagonia.com)*, whose full-day tours let you explore both the lake and gently winding Rio Grey. After a day in the great outdoors, head to Cangrejo Rojo *(p257)* for a delicious seafood dinner.

Day 7

In the morning, travel back to Puerto Natales and spend the rest of the day looking around the town. Make sure to stop off at Museo Histórico Municipal *(p258)*, which showcases some of Puerto Natales' pioneering history. Finish with drinks at Last Hope Distillery.

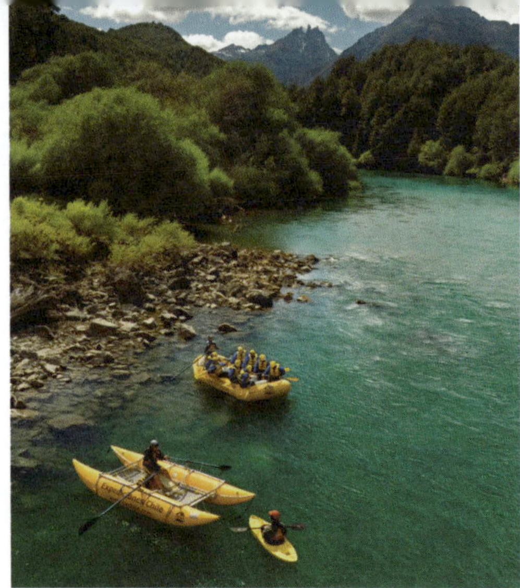

Grab a Paddle

The many rivers, channels, lagoons, and fjords of the Lake District and Patagonia are best explored in a raft or a kayak. Río Futaleufú *(p234)* is particularly good for those interested in white water rafting. A less adrenaline-charged but equally memorable experience is kayaking across the waterways of Parque Nacional Laguna San Rafael *(p238)* amid icebergs, glaciers, and sea lion colonies.

Rafters enjoying a rare calm spot on the Río Futaleufú

CHILE AND EASTER ISLAND FOR THRILL SEEKERS

Chile's reputation as an adventure-sports hub is well deserved. There is a multitude of electrifying activities to try throughout the country, including some truly epic paddles, climbs, dives, and glides.

Head to the Skies

On the arid coast of northern Chile, the city of Iquique *(p162)* has the ideal combination of geographic and climatic conditions for paragliding: the sun shines year round, it rarely rains, the skies are largely cloud free, and air currents whistle off the Pacific. Moreover, the views from the air - notably of Cerro Dragón *(p162)*, the huge sand dune that looms over the city - are superb. Puro Vuelo *(purovuelo.cl)* is a popular local paragliding operator.

INSIDER TIP
Where to Stay

Calling all outdoor enthusiasts. Not sure where to stay? The Lake District town of Pucón *(p214)* is the country's adventure-sport capital. Here you'll find various companies offering sports and excursions, including skydiving and white water rafting.

Landing in the desert just outside the town of Iquique, northern Chile

↑ Hiking the impressive Villarrica, and *(inset)* the volcano from afar

Scale a Volcano

Chile has more than 2,900 volcanoes, and several agencies offer guided hikes, ranging from day trips to technical climbs for experienced mountaineers. In the Lake District, &Beyond (*andbeyond.com*) takes hikers up Villarrica and Ascension, all in Parque Nacional Villarrica *(p202)*. Soaring above Parque Nacional Vicente Pérez Rosales *(p204)*, snowy Volcán Osorno can be explored with Huella Andina Expeditions *(huellandina.com)*.

Dive into the Blue

Two of the world's largest marine reserves surround Easter Island *(p264)* and Robinson Crusoe Island *(p278)*. The former protects around 140 species and offers the chance to see underground caves and a submerged replica of a *moai* statue, while the latter has a similarly rich marine life. Mike Rapu *(mikerapudivingcenter.cl)* is a dive center in Hanga Roa *(p274)* and Refugio Náutico Eco Lodge *(islarobinson crusoe.cl)* arranges trips on Robinson Crusoe Island.

→ Snorkeling in waters near Ahu Tongariki, Easter Island

Culinary Cities

Santiago is fast becoming one of the continent's most delectable spots, with many of its restaurants ranking high among the world's best places to eat. Don't miss Boragó *(p109)*, an innovative restaurant focused on sourcing Indigenous ingredients, or Bocanariz *(bocanariz.cl)*, whose menu complements its extensive collection of Chilean wines. Beyond the capital, Valparaíso beckons gourmets with inventive restaurants; try Maralegre *(p121)*, a stylish spot serving creative seafood dishes.

→

One of the many inventive restaurants found in Valparaíso

CHILE AND EASTER ISLAND FOR FOODIES

Compared to other countries in Latin America, notably Peru and Mexico, Chile's cuisine remains under the radar. But with some of the world's finest fish and seafood, a burgeoning wine industry, an array of traditional dishes, and fabulous restaurants, Chile has plenty to offer the foodie traveler.

Sweet and Sour

From wine to *pisco* (a fruity brandy, *p175*), Chilean drinks are famous around the world. Central Valley has vineyards offering tours and tasting sessions; many have been linked into wine routes, including in the Casablanca *(p130)* and Colchagua *(p148)* valleys. Although not as well-known as Chilean wine, *pisco* is not to be missed. It's often served in a *pisco* sour, where it's mixed with lemon, bitters, and sugar, and topped with egg whites. Valle de Elqui *(p172)* in Norte Chico is the heart of the *pisco* industry. Distilleries are open to visitors *(p173)*.

Pisco sour, an unmissable and delicious South American cocktail

Lush and Local

Although separated by more than 2,180 miles (3,508 km), Chiloé *(p220)* and Easter Island *(p264)* have a delicious dish in common: *curanto*. Traditionally, curanto is made by digging a pit, filling it with hot rocks, layering on fish, shellfish, meat, and starchy vegetables (and dumplings in Chiloé), covering everything with leaves, and allowing it to slow-cook for hours or even days. The result is worth the wait. As well as playing a key role in curanto, fish and seafood are staples throughout Chile. The Littoral Central (Central Coast) is known for its *marisquerías* (fish and seafood restaurants): keep an eye out for razor clams topped with a cheesy crust, conger eel stew, and super-fresh ceviche.

Curanto cooking amid hot rocks in the ground

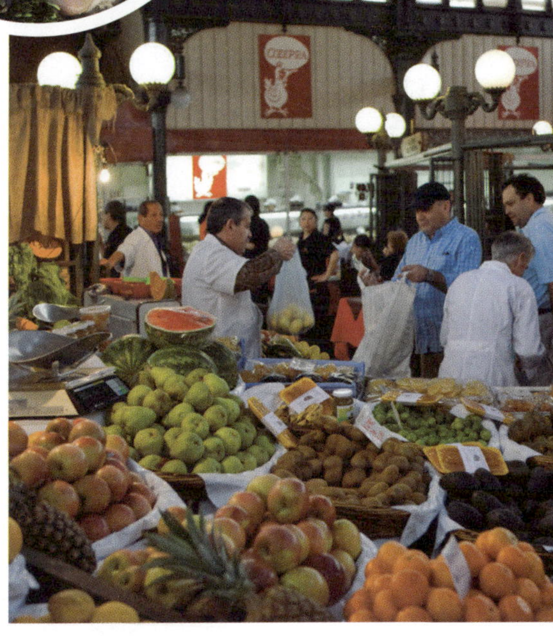

Bustle and barter at Santiago's Mercado Central

TOP 5 CHILEAN DISHES NOT TO MISS

Asado
A barbecue featuring a variety of cuts of beef (or lamb in the south), sausages, and sides.

Pastel de choclo
A minced-meat pie with a blitzed-corn topping.

Cazuela
A soupy stew with vegetables and a piece of meat on the bone.

Humitas
Steamed corn cakes.

Chorrillana
A heaped plate of strips of steak, eggs, onions, and French fries.

Tale of Two Markets

It's easy to lose yourself for a few hours in either of Santiago's bustling markets: the Mercado Central *(p81)*, which is housed in an elegant building that dates back to the mid-1800s, and the more rustic and less touristy La Vega, a few blocks away *(p106)*. Both are buzzing hives of activity, with stalls piled high with fresh produce from across the country. They are also home to an array of low-cost fish and seafood restaurants.

Mapuche funerary statues at the Museo Chileno de Arte Precolombino

CHILE AND EASTER ISLAND FOR ART LOVERS

From ancient crafts dating back thousands of years to cutting-edge fashion, Indigenous jewelry to hard-hitting street art, Chile has something to suit every artistic taste.

Hit the Streets

With a long tradition of creative, large-scale, and often highly political street art, murals, and graffiti, Chile has been called a "nation of muralists." The scenes in Santiago *(p50)* and Valparaíso *(p118)* are particularly interesting. Bellavista, Brasil, and Yungay neighborhoods in the capital are excellent places to start. Valparaíso, meanwhile, is home to the Museo a Cielo Abierto *(p126)*, an open-air gallery of works by some of Chile's best-known street artists. A number of agencies, such as Santiago Street Art Tours *(stgostreetart.com)*, offer tours, which are worth taking as works are often left unsigned.

Modern Art in Santiago

Chile's capital is home to one of South America's finest museums, the Museo Chileno de Arte Precolombino *(p66)*, which has a remarkable and extensive range of exhibits. The Museo Nacional de Bellas Artes *(p79)*, a fine arts museum featuring predominantly Chilean artists, also impresses, as does the Museo de Arte Contemporáneo *(p80)*. Other venues include the Estación Mapocho *(p80)*, a former railroad station turned into a cultural venue, and the Museo de la Moda *(p110)*, a fashion museum with a collection of more than 10,000 pieces.

← Exterior of the Museo Chileno de Arte Precolombino

TOP 5 ARTISTS TO LOOK OUT FOR

Roberto Matta
Seminal figure in 20th-century surrealism and abstract expressionism.

Rebeca Matte Bello
Sculptor particularly known for her work *Icarus and Daedalus.*

Carlos Sotomayor
Leader of Neo-Cubism in South America.

Gracia Barrios
Painter who developed a style known as "informal realism."

Nemesio Antúnez Zañartu
Painter, engraver, and founder of Workshop 99.

INSIDER TIP
Bellas Artes

Fine art meets street art at Bellas Artes subway station. Check out well-known street artist Inti's work before heading to the Museo Nacional de Bellas Artes *(p79)*.

A Mapuche person working on beautiful textiles ↑

↑ A colorful mural showing Santiago's vibrant street art scene

Indigenous Art

The Mapuche people *(p207)* are Chile's largest Indigenous group: roughly 10 per cent of the population have Mapuche heritage. In the face of long-standing discrimination, they have retained a distinct culture and way of life. From an artistic perspective, the Mapuche people are known for impressive textiles, metalwork, and silver jewelry. Museums in the Lake District, the Museo de los Volcanes *(p215)* and the Museo Regional de la Araucanía *(p207)*, have collections of Mapuche artworks and jewelry.

ROUTE OF PARKS

Launched in 2018 following a donation of land from Tompkins Conservation *(p232)* to the Chilean state, the spectacular Ruta del los Parques (Route of Parks; *rutadelos parques.org*) stretches 1,700 miles (2,736 km) from Puerto Montt to Cape Horn and connects 17 parks. It aims to use sustainable tourism to drive conservation efforts in Patagonia and Tierra del Fuego - including significant rewilding schemes - and provide various economic opportunities for what are often remote and underserved communities.

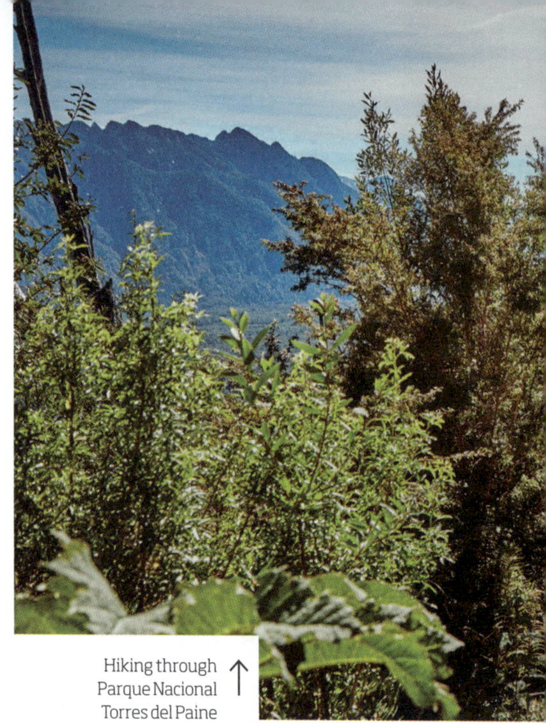

Hiking through Parque Nacional Torres del Paine ↑

CHILE AND EASTER ISLAND FOR HIKERS

Few countries can compare with Chile when it comes to hiking. Its many national parks - which cover landscapes as diverse as deserts, rainforests, and ice fields - are home to a wide range of trails, with options to suit virtually every traveler, regardless of levels of fitness and aptitude.

Multi-Day Treks

Chile's two best-known multi-day treks can be found in Parque Nacional Torres del Paine *(p252)*: the W and the Circuit. Both routes showcase the park's three iconic peaks, and are extremely popular, which means you need to book accommodation in advance. South of Parque Nacional Torres del Paine, Puerto Williams *(p261)* - the southernmost town on earth - is the jumping-off point for the Dientes de Navarino circuit, a tough but truly spectacular four- or five-day expedition through the majestic mountain wilderness of Tierra del Fuego.

Grey Glacier in Parque Nacional Torres del Paine ↓

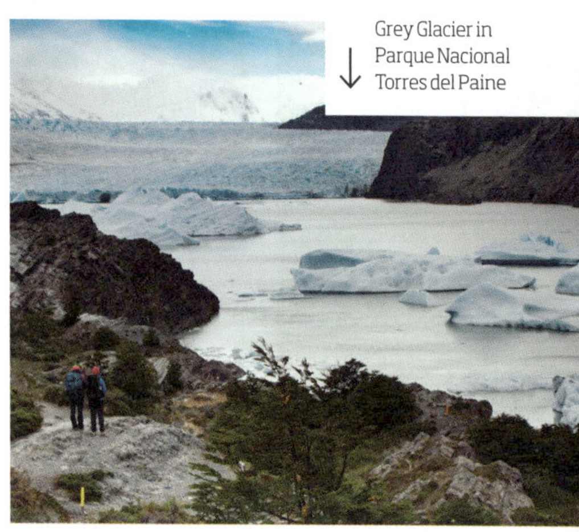

Hiking for Beginners

After a simple stroll? Parque Nacional Pumalín Douglas Tompkin *(p232)* has the answer, with a wide range of short hikes, including the Sendero Laguna Tronador, with views of the Michinmahuida volcano. Parque Nacional Queulat *(p236)* offers the 2-mile (3-km) Sendero Ventisquero Colgante hike, while Parque Nacional Patagonia *(p243)* has walks that take half a day or less. On Easter Island *(p264)*, hike up Rano Kau crater and the ruined Orongo village *(p274)*.

TOP 4 WAYS TO HIKE RESPONSIBLY

Plan ahead
Ensure that you have equipment suited to the environment.

Respect wildlife
Do not touch or approach the animals.

Dispose of waste
Retain garbage and use the appropriate disposal points.

Leave what you find
Do not take what belongs to nature.

Andean gull on the rocks in Parque Nacional Lauca

Resting by a lake in the spectacular Parque Nacional Lauca

One-Day Hikes

Cochamó Valley in the Lake District has many trails that take a day or less. The 7-mile (12-km) La Junta trek follows an old logging route and passes through rainforest. The Norte Grande's Parque Nacional Lauca *(p166)* is a high-altitude region of volcanoes, brightly colored lakes, herds of vicuñas, and more than 140 species of birds. There are several one-day trails in the park. Before setting off, take time to acclimatize properly.

Chill with Penguins

From November to March, Isla Magdalena *(p257)* in the Strait of Magellan is home to a rookery of penguins. Day trips to the island run from Punta Arenas. In Chiloé, Monumento Natural Islotes de Puñihuil *(p220)* is home to a rare mixed colony of Megallanic and Humboldt penguins. Alternatively, head for Bahia Inutil in Tierra del Fuego to see king penguins or Reserva Nacional Pingüino de Humboldt *(p191)* in the Norte Chico, which has Humboldt penguins.

King penguins socializing in Tierra del Fuego

CHILE AND EASTER ISLAND FOR WILDLIFE

From raucous penguin rookeries in Patagonia to skittish herds of camelids in the Atacama Desert, not to mention circling condors in the Lake District and breaching whales in the Strait of Magellan, Chile simply abounds with wildlife. Here we round up some of the most characterful critters.

Catch Sight of Condors

The sight of an Andean condor high in the sky against a backdrop of Andean peaks lives long in the memory. One of the world's largest flying birds, with a wingspan of 10 ft (3 m), they are found in many of the Lake District's national parks, including Conguillío *(p198)* and Tolhuaca *(p208)*. Chile's national bird can also be spotted in places like Termas de Cauquenes *(p138)*, the Reserva Nacional Altos de Lircay *(p143)*, and the Parque Nacional Laguna del Laja *(p147)*, as well as in Parque Nacional Pan de Azúcar *(p189)* in the Norte Chico.

Male Andean condor cruising over southern Patagonia, Chile

Go Whale-Watching

The Strait of Magellan *(p260)*, which separates Southern Patagonia from Tierra del Fuego and links the Pacific to the Atlantic, is a breeding ground for an array of marine species, including humpback whales. To get the chance to catch a glimpse of these majestic creatures, take a boat trip on the waters of Parque Marino Francisco Coloane; Punta Arenas-based operator Far South Expeditions *(farsouth exp.com)* runs tours to an eco-camp inside the reserve on Isla Carlos III. Blue whales, the world's largest mammals, can be seen off Melinka *(p240)* in Northern Patagonia, and in Reserva Nacional Pingüino de Humboldt *(p191)*, where sperm and humpback whales also visit.

← Humpback whale jumping in Parque Francisco Coloane Marino

↑ An inquisitive guanaco in the arid Atacama Desert

Keeping up with the Camelids

Four species of camelids - llamas, alpacas, guanacos, and vicuñas - can be spotted in Chile, predominantly in the high Andean regions. All four are found in Parque Nacional Lauca *(p166)* in the Norte Chico; the shy, elegant vicuña tends to be the most elusive. Also keep an eye out for the vizcacha, a long-tailed member of the chinchilla family seen in Parque Nacional Nevado Tres Cruces *(p190)* and Parque Nacional La Campana *(p137)*.

SAVING THE BLUE WHALE

Chile has a truly impressive track record when it comes to protecting endangered marine life, especially its approach to saving the blue whale. The world's largest animal was close to extinction and so it was with much excitement that a blue whale nursery was discovered off the coast of Chiloé, in 2003. In 2008, Chile decided to ban whale hunting along its entire coast, and then, in 2014, the country set up a sanctuary for declining marine life. This protected area is the size of Santiago and further welcomes dolphins and endangered otters. Chile now has 31 marine parks covering a huge collective expanse.

Step Back in Time
Some of Chile's finest architecture dates back to the Spanish era, between the 17th and 19th centuries. Santiago offers plenty of examples: highlights include the Palacio de la Real Audiencia and the Catedral Metropolitana *(p68)*. Similarly impressive are Chiloé's Jesuit churches *(p224)*. All the surviving churches are built from wood, and 16 of them have been named UNESCO World Heritage Sites.

→ Interior of Iglesia de Achao, one of Chile's 16 UNESCO World Heritage Sites

CHILE AND EASTER ISLAND FOR ARCHITECTURE

Encompassing desert ghost towns and late 19th-century mansions, churches dating back more than 400 years and brightly colored fishers' houses raised on stilts, the architecture in Chile is vibrant and diverse.

Picturesque Palafitos
Castro, capital of the Chiloé archipelago, is home to some beautiful *palafitos (p222)*, colorfully painted wooden homes raised above water. Many *palafitos* were destroyed in the 1960 Valdivia earthquake, but fortunately some survived. In the last few years, *palafitos* have been turned into guesthouses, hostels, and restaurants.

→ Vibrant and charming *palafitos* in Castro

Valparaíso's Heyday

Spread across Valparaíso's many rolling *cerros* (hills) are wonderful examples of late 19th- and early 20th-century architecture, testament to a period in which the city was a commercial hub. Cerro Alegre and Cerro Concepción are the most attractive areas, once home to a community of European traders and businessmen. They lined the steep, cobbled streets with townhouses with bucolic gardens - many are now hotels or restaurants - as well as sober churches and promenades with views out to the Pacific.

ALEJANDRO ARAVENA

Founder of the architecture firm Elemental, Aravena (born 1967) is Chile's most famous contemporary architect. Known for his pioneering work on social housing across Latin America, he won the prestigious Pritzker Architecture Prize in 2016 for his work reinventing low-cost housing.

↑ Hotel in Valparaíso built from shipping containers

Like a Ghost Town

In the 19th century, huge nitrate reserves made the Atacama Desert one of the most profitable places on earth. Echoes of the period reverberate around two former nitrate oficinas, Humberstone and Santa Laura *(p178)*, now atmospheric ghost towns. The crumbling machinery of the former seems straight out of a steampunk novel, while the latter is more intact, with abandoned houses, a theater, church, and hotel.

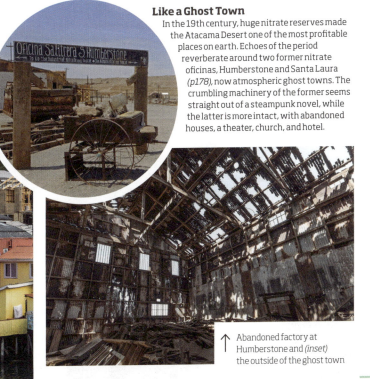

↑ Abandoned factory at Humberstone and *(inset)* the outside of the ghost town

The Craft of Neruda

"He who does not travel, who does not read, who does not listen to music, who does not find grace in himself... dies slowly," wrote Pablo Neruda, who remains one of Chile's most significant writers. He was just 19 when his second poetry collection was published. It sold more than 20 million copies and won him the Nobel Prize for Literature. Three of Neruda's homes - La Chascona *(p105)* in Santiago, La Sebastiana *(p125)* in Valparaíso, and Isla Negra *(p128)* in the place of the same name - are now museums.

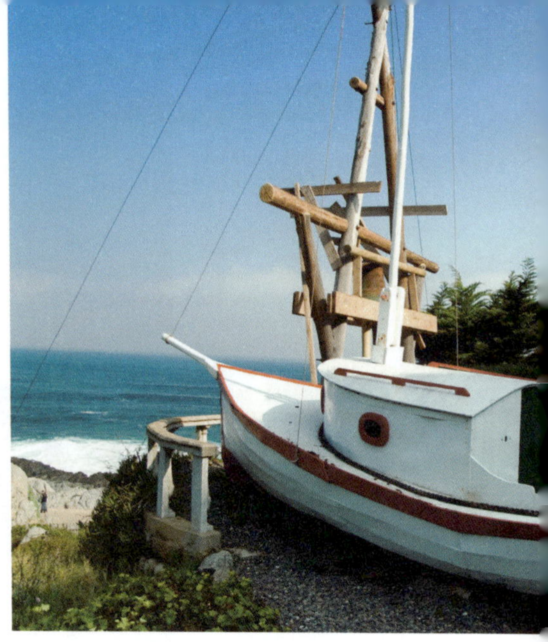

Isla Negra, the Central Valley home of Pablo Neruda

CHILE AND EASTER ISLAND FOR BOOKWORMS

With a pair of Nobel Prize-winning poets and some of the most influential Latin American novelists of the 20th and early 21st centuries, Chile punches well above its weight in literary terms. The country has also inspired groundbreaking works by eminent scientists and travel writers.

The Magic of Gabriela Mistral

The first Latin American to win a Nobel Prize for Literature, Gabriela Mistral's poetry was deeply influenced by the beautiful Valle de Elqui *(p172)*, which she described as a "heroic slash in the mass of mountains." She was born in this very valley, in the town of Vicuña, today home to a wonderful museum dedicated to her life and work. Mistral later moved to the village of Montegrande; seek out her tomb on a peaceful hillside just south of the village.

Chilean Nobel Prize-winning poet Gabriela Mistral

Follow in Bruce Chatwin's Footsteps

Southern Chile features heavily in Bruce Chatwin's seminal travelog *In Patagonia*. His quixotic journey was strangely inspired by a giant sloth skin that was found in the Cueva del Milodón *(p258)* near Puerto Natales. As well as exploring the cave, Chatwin also visited Punta Arenas *(p256)*, where his distant relative Charlie Milward lived. In his collection *What Am I Doing Here?* Chatwin writes about the wooden churches, the rain-soaked landscapes, and the "tormented mythologies" of the archipelago of Chiloé *(p220)*.

← Eminent travel writer Bruce Chatwin

TOP 4

LITERARY WORKS

The House of the Spirits, Isabel Allende (1982)
A family struggles through Chile's political upheavals.

The Motorcycle Diaries, Che Guevara (1992)
An account of Guevara's travels through South America.

The Savage Detectives, Roberto Bolaño (1998)
A riotous chase through literary South America in pursuit of a lost poet.

Pinochet in Piccadilly, Andy Beckett (2002)
The book unpicks the arrest of the dictator in London, in 1998.

Retrace the Route of Charles Darwin

In the course of his journey on HMS *Beagle*, Darwin explored many parts of Chile, including the San Rafael glacier *(p238)*, Chiloé *(p220)*, Concepción *(p146)*, and Valparaíso *(p118)*. He climbed the trail up the northern flank of Cerro La Campana and later wrote: "We spent the day on the summit, and I never enjoyed one more thoroughly. Chile, bounded by the Andes and the Pacific, was seen as in a map."

→ Viewing breathtaking Glacier Alley, once visited by Charles Darwin

Browsing an exhibit at the Museum of Memory and Human Rights

CHILE AND EASTER ISLAND FOR HISTORY BUFFS

Chile's myriad historic sites, museums, and ruins take visitors on a journey through 8,000 years of human history. The country is home to the oldest mummies ever discovered, pioneering Patagonian settlements, and 450-year-old cities, to mention just a few of its historical attractions.

Historic Cities

La Serena *(p168)*, Chile's second-oldest city, is home to some truly beautiful churches, including the soaring Neo-Classical Catedral de La Serena and eye-catching Iglesia Santo Domingo. The city of Valdivia *(p200)*, founded eight years after La Serena in 1552, is also worth a visit; stroll along its riverside to spy spectacular 19th-century Teutonic architecture. Don't forget to admire the ruins of three epic forts – Fuerte de Niebla, Fuerte de Mancera, and Fuerte de Corral – found just outside of the city.

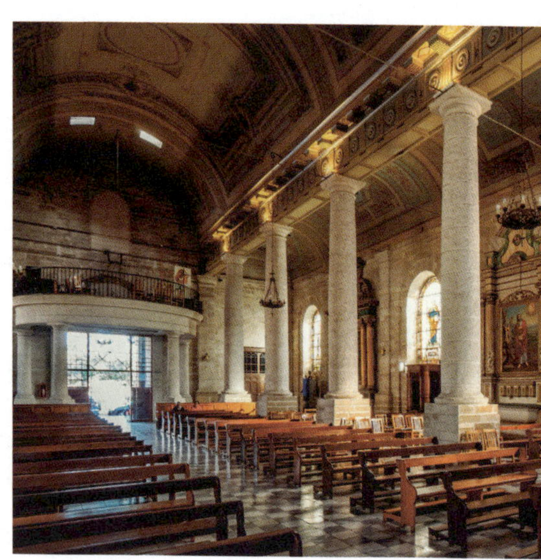

Beautiful interior of the Catedral de La Serena

Museums of Memory

Santiago is home to a pair of groundbreaking museums that rank among the finest on the continent. In the city center, the Museo Chileno de Arte Precolombino *(p66)* has a vast collection of artifacts from pre-Hispanic and Indigenous cultures across Latin America. West of the center, in a glass building, the Museo de la Memoria y los Derechos Humanos *(p90)* uses multimedia, personal items, poetry, and other exhibits to tell the stories of some of the estimated 3,000 people who were killed or "disappeared" under the Pinochet dictatorship.

← Museum of Memory and Human Rights

GEOGLYPHS

Geoglyphs are formed by elements of the landscape, such as clastic rocks, trees, or earth. Ancient geoglyphs carry cultural significance and give visitors a glimpse into the past. They are often shrouded in mystery, leading to theories regarding origin. Chile hosts some of the world's most famous geoglyphs, including the Atacama Giant, the largest prehistoric anthropomorphic figure in the world.

INSIDER TIP

Ride Around

A bike path runs through vibrant La Serena, passing by its many historic churches and cathedrals. Rent a bike from one of the city's guesthouses and get exploring.

Chinchorro mummies at the Museo Arqueológico San Miguel de Azapa ↑

Mummies Return

Chinchorro people (6000–2000 BCE) used various complex techniques to mummify the dead, who were at the time buried in collective tombs in the Atacama Desert. Some of the mummies survived and are now considered the oldest examples of the process on earth, predating even the more famous examples from ancient Egypt. The Museo Arqueológico San Miguel de Azapa *(p156)*, just outside the city of Arica, provides a home to some of the Chinchorro mummies.

A YEAR IN CHILE AND EASTER ISLAND

JANUARY

△ **Festival Internacional Teatro a Mil** *(Jan–early Feb)*. A major theater, dance, and performing arts festival that takes place in Santiago every year. It is the country's largest festival and aims to promote arts in Chile.

FEBRUARY

△ **Tapati Rapa Nui** *(early Feb)*. A two-week celebration of Rapa Nui (Easter Island) culture.

Festival Costumbrista Chilote *(mid-Feb)*. A celebration of Chiloé's culture, folklore, and traditional cuisine.

MAY

△ **Glorias Navales** *(May 21)*. Military ceremonies commemorate the 1879 Battle of Iquique. Expect parades and speeches.

JUNE

△ **Fiesta de San Pedro** *(Jun 29)*. Fishers take statues of their patron saint out to sea to wish for good fortune.

Pride *(mid/late Jun)*. Chile's biggest LGBTQ+ Pride march held in Santiago.

SEPTEMBER

△ **Fiestas Patrias** *(Sep 18)*. Chile's Independence Day sees various celebrations, including street parties, dancing, music, and plenty of eating and drinking.

Festival de Cine Internacional *(mid-Sep)*. Viña del Mar's film festival.

OCTOBER

Festival de los Mil Tambores *(first weekend in Oct)*. The arrival of spring is marked by Valparaíso's Thousand Drums Festival.

Día de la Raza *(Oct 12)*. Once commemorating the "discovery" of the Americas by Columbus, the festival now celebrates Chile's Indigenous peoples.

△ **El Ensayo** *(late Oct/early Nov)*. An important horse race at Santiago's Club Hípico.

APRIL

Semana Santa *(Mar/Apr)*. Holy Week (Easter) features church services and vibrant street processions, as well as huge numbers of Chileans heading off for a much-deserved weekend away.

△ **Fiesta de Cuasimodo** *(first Sun after Easter)*. After mass, priests travel in beautifully decorated carts, motorbikes, or bikes, accompanied by *huasos* (cowboys).

MARCH

△ **Festival de la Vendimia** *(throughout Mar)*. The grape harvest is marked in many of the wine regions with tastings, grape-crushing, and various other events. The festival is hugely popular with visitors.

Lollapalooza *(mid-Mar)*. The popular music festival comes to Chile, with celebrations taking place in Santiago's Parque Bicentenario.

JULY

△ **Festival de la Tirana** *(Jul 12–16)*. Honors the Virgen del Carmen in a major fiesta that blends pre-Columbian and Catholic traditions.

Fiesta de la Virgen del Carmen *(Jul 16)*. Military parades celebrate armed forces, the independence struggle, and the patron saint.

Carnaval de Invierno *(third weekend)*. Punta Arenas' carnival has parades and fireworks.

AUGUST

La Asunción de la Virgen *(Aug 15)*. Celebrates the Assumption of the Virgin Mary and is one of the most important religious events of the year.

△ **Jesús Nazareno de Caguach** *(Aug 21–31)*. One of Chiloé's key religious festivals, featuring rowing competitions, church services, and processions.

NOVEMBER

△ **Día de Todos los Santos** *(Nov 1)*. Chileans tend to family graves on All Saints' Day.

Feria del Libro *(early Nov)*. Book festival at Santiago's Centro Cultural Estación Mapocho, with various exhibits and readings from writers from across the continent and beyond.

DECEMBER

△ **Fiesta Grande de la Virgen del Rosario** *(late Dec)*. Thousands travel to Andacollo to worship the patron saint of mining.

Noche Buena *(Dec 24)*. Chileans meet extended families for dinner and midnight mass.

Navidad *(Dec 25)*. Christmas Day is typically spent at home with the family.

Fin de Año/Año Nuevo *(Dec 31)*. Firework displays mark the end of the year.

A BRIEF HISTORY

It was a rocky road to becoming South America's most stable economy and democracy. Ferocious earthquakes, violent clashes between Indigenous peoples, colonizing empires, and a 17-year dictatorship have left their mark on what is now a modern and culturally rich country.

The First Pioneers

Excavations at Monte Verde, just north of Puerto Montt in the Lake District, date the arrival of humans to Chile around 15,000 years ago. These pioneers crossed the Bering Strait 2,000 years before, finding their way overland or by boat south through the Americas. Over the next 10,000 years, these semi-nomadic, hunter-gatherer cultures domesticated native camelids for transportation and practiced complex funerary rites; the Chinchorro began mummifying their dead around 7,000 years ago. South in the hinterlands of Patagonia, canoe-faring cultures used bone harpoons and vegetable fiber nets to hunt.

1 An early map of Chile. ↑

2 Pioneers approaching the shores.

3 *A View of the Monuments of Easter Island* by William Hodges.

4 Portrait of Ferdinand Magellan.

Timeline of events

13,000 BCE

Establishment of Monte Verde, Chile's first-known settlement.

1200

Polynesians settle on Easter Island.

1520

Magellan reaches Tierra del Fuego and the Strait of Magellan.

1528

Francisco Pizarro and Diego de Almagro first land in Peru.

2

3 4

The Polynesian Colonizers

Hotu Matu'a and his people – Polynesians from the now unknown land of Hiva – sailed 1,200 miles (1,930 km) and settled in Rapa Nui (Easter Island), landing in 1200 CE. An organized society soon emerged, based on kinship and ancestor worship, with Hotu Matu'a as the *ariki mau* (supreme chief or king). The next 550 years were spent carving monolithic stone statues, before clan warfare and deforestation sent the island into disarray.

The Arrival of the Europeans

The first European to discover Chile – reaching the archipelago of Tierra del Fuego – was Portuguese explorer Ferdinand Magellan in 1520. A couple of decades later, in 1541, a Spanish expedition from newly colonized Peru, led by Pedro de Valdivia, brought Chile under Spanish control, founding Santiago as capital. But the Indigenous Mapuche prevented Spanish forces from penetrating south beyond the Río Biobío in a 350-year conflict, with sporadic fighting lasting into the 18th century. Failing to make fortunes, the Spanish divided Central Valley into *encomiendas*, enslaving the Indigenous population.

INDIGENOUS CULTURE AND HERITAGE IN CHILE

Chile is home to a rich array of Indigenous cultures. The Mapuche is the largest, with 1,745,000 Chileans identifying as Mapuche today. Many Mapuche still live in small patrilineal communities.

1541

Pedro de Valdivia founds city of Santiago.

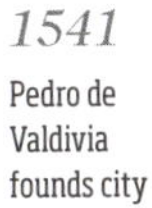

1574

Juan Fernández discovers islands in the Pacific Ocean.

1704

Alexander Selkirk, the inspiration for *Robinson Crusoe*, is marooned on uninhabited Juan Fernández Island.

1722

Jacob Roggeveen is the first European to land on Rapa Nui, reaching there on Easter Sunday.

1774

Captain James Cook visits Rapa Nui.

1

2

The Battle for Independence

As the long, narrow territory of Chile was being brought under central rule, the ties that bound the colony with the Spanish Crown were weakening. When Napoleon marched into Spain in 1808, Chile's independence campaign began in earnest. Spearheaded by Chilean Congressman and wealthy landowner Bernardo O'Higgins, the bitter and furious display of arms between republicans and royalists lasted until 1818, when O'Higgins was installed as the first head of state of an independent Chile.

↑ Horace Castelli's depiction of boats near Easter Island

The War of the Pacific

The nation's economy grew rapidly over the next century. Mining camps in the Norte Chico produced vast quantities of copper, making Chile the largest global producer. In 1879, an argument about Chilean investors paying export taxes for the nitrate deposits in the Atacama Desert – a region owned by Peru and Bolivia – provoked the three-year-long War of the Pacific. Chile emerged victorious, expanding its territory by one third to include the lucrative nitrate fields.

Timeline of events

1808

Napoleon invades Spain.

1818

Chile declares independence after ten years of conflict between royalists.

1826

Remaining Spanish troops in Chiloé surrender, ending Spanish presence.

1834

Charles Darwin sails along Chile's coast aboard HMS *Beagle*.

Indigenous Repression

Two years later, the country expanded further, this time into the south. The Indigenous Mapuche had fiercely resisted Spanish rule since the 1500s. This came to a head between 1861 and 1883, when the government launched an offensive known as the Pacification of the Araucanía. Some 100,000 Mapuche – around 90 per cent of the population – were killed and most Mapuche ancestral lands were ceded to the Chilean government.

The Annexation of Easter Island

In 1888, Chile annexed Easter Island. The population had been devastated by smallpox, which was introduced by European explorers, and by Peruvian slave raiders who had abducted 1,500 Rapa Nui – around 50 per cent of the islanders at the time. Over the next 50 years, the Scottish-owned Williamson-Balfour Company turned the island into a sheep ranch, confining the Indigenous population to its eastern corner. This continued until 1954, when the island came under the control of the Chilean Navy. It took another 12 years before the Rapa Nui were given citizenship and the right to vote in mainland elections.

1 Clashes during the Battle of Independence. ↑

2 The three-year-long War of the Pacific.

3 A Mapuche village.

Did You Know?

"Chile" most likely comes from the Mapuche word "chili," which means "where the land ends."

1849

California Gold Rush, with Valparaíso a key port.

1879

War of the Pacific begins as Chileans occupy the port city of Antofagasta.

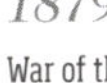

1883

The Pacification of Araucanía forces the Mapuche people from their lands.

1888

Easter Island annexed by Chile.

1

2

Economic Turbulence and Salvador Allende

By the mid-1900s, economic woes threatened stability. The Chilean nitrate industry collapsed, while copper prices hit rock bottom. In 1970, socialist Salvador Allende was elected president. He nationalized copper and confiscated land for redistribution. Strikes, runaway inflation, and shortages of basic commodities brought the country into chaos. On September 11, 1973, army commander-in-chief Augusto Pinochet launched a military coup. As the air force began bombing the presidential palace in Santiago, Allende killed himself rather than surrender.

The Pinochet Dictatorship

The following 17 years saw political parties banned and over 80,000 political opponents imprisoned, tortured, and executed. The economy was transformed using free-market strategies; regulations were eliminated and state assets sold off, while a new constitution expanded Pinochet's powers. But protests forced a plebiscite in 1988, with the electorate voting emphatically against Pinochet. In 1989, center-left politician Patricio Aylwin became the first president of a newly democratic Chile.

1 Salvador Allende delivering a speech. ↑

2 Protests against Augusto Pinochet.

3 Michelle Bachelet, Chile's first female president.

1945

Gabriela Mistral is the first Latin American and the fifth woman to win the Nobel Prize for Literature.

Timeline of events

1966

The Rapa Nui are granted full Chilean citizenship and the right to vote.

1970

Salvador Allende elected as president.

1973

Military coup deposes Allende.

1988

Pinochet loses plebiscite; Chile starts returning to democracy.

2006

Michelle Bachelet elected president; Pinochet dies in December.

3

The After-Effects of Dictatorship

After the return to democracy, center-left presidents continued Pinochet's economic course, which created a stable economy but expanded the wealth divide. Over these years, there were national and international calls to investigate the human rights abuses of the dictatorship. When Pinochet visited the UK in 1998, Spanish judge Baltasar Garzón filed to extradite him. Pinochet was put under house arrest until 2001. On his return to Chile he was charged with crimes against humanity.

Chile Today

In 2006, history was made when Michelle Bachelet was elected as Chile's first female president. In March 2010, right-wing billionaire Sebastián Piñera replaced her as president. He returned for a second term in 2018, which witnessed widespread protests over Indigenous rights and rising inequality *(p106)*, prompting a referendum to rewrite the constitution. This was followed by the election of former student leader and left-wing politician Gabriel Boric as president in 2022. However, despite Boric's support, referendum voters rejected the idea of a new constitution.

MICHELLE BACHELET (1951-)

Born into a military family, Bachelet was detained by Pinochet's secret police in 1975 because her father had worked for Allende. She went into exile in Australia, returning to Chile in 1979. In power, she was lauded for her progressive political stance and, in 2018, she was appointed to the position of UN High Commissioner for Human Rights.

2010

Sebastián Piñera elected president; central Chile struck by a major earthquake.

2010

A billion people watch the rescue of 33 Chilean miners.

2019

Over a million Chileans protest against the government over inequality and high living costs.

2025

President Gabriel Boric becomes the first head of state to visit the South Pole.

EXPERIENCE SANTIAGO

Relaxing in the Providencia district

GOOSE
ISLAND

EXPLORE SANTIAGO

This guide divides Santiago into three sightseeing areas, as shown on the map below. Find out more about each area on the following pages.

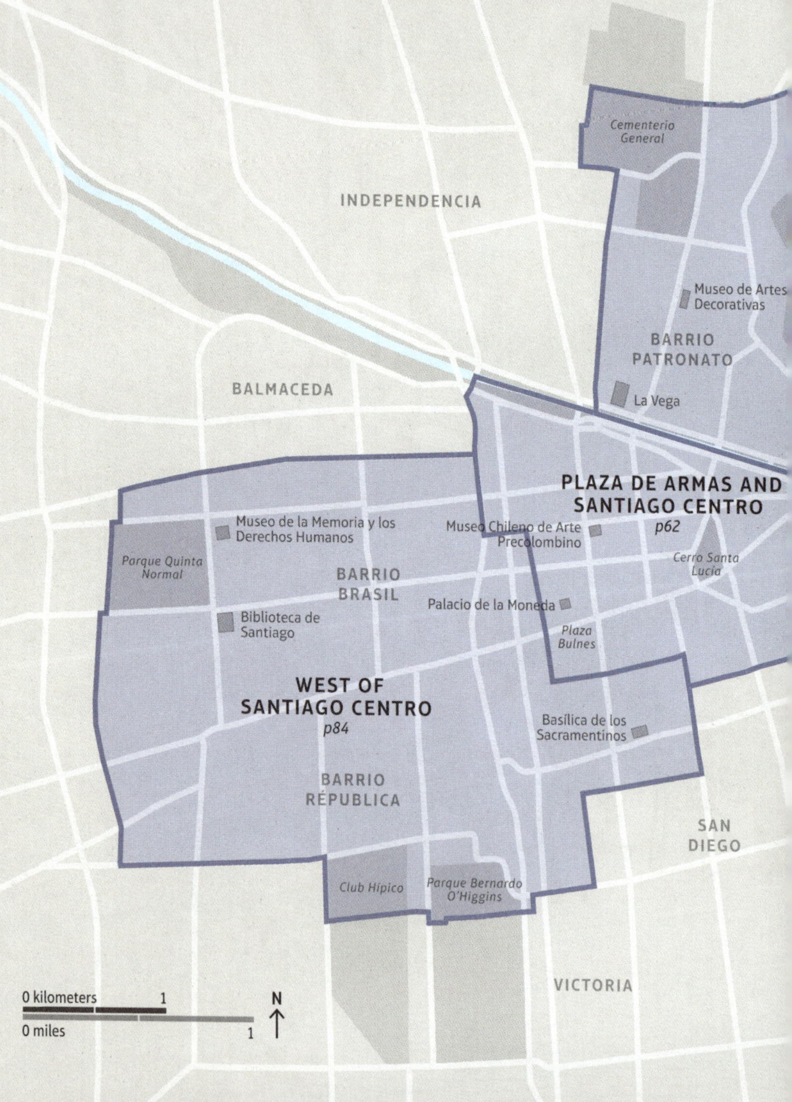

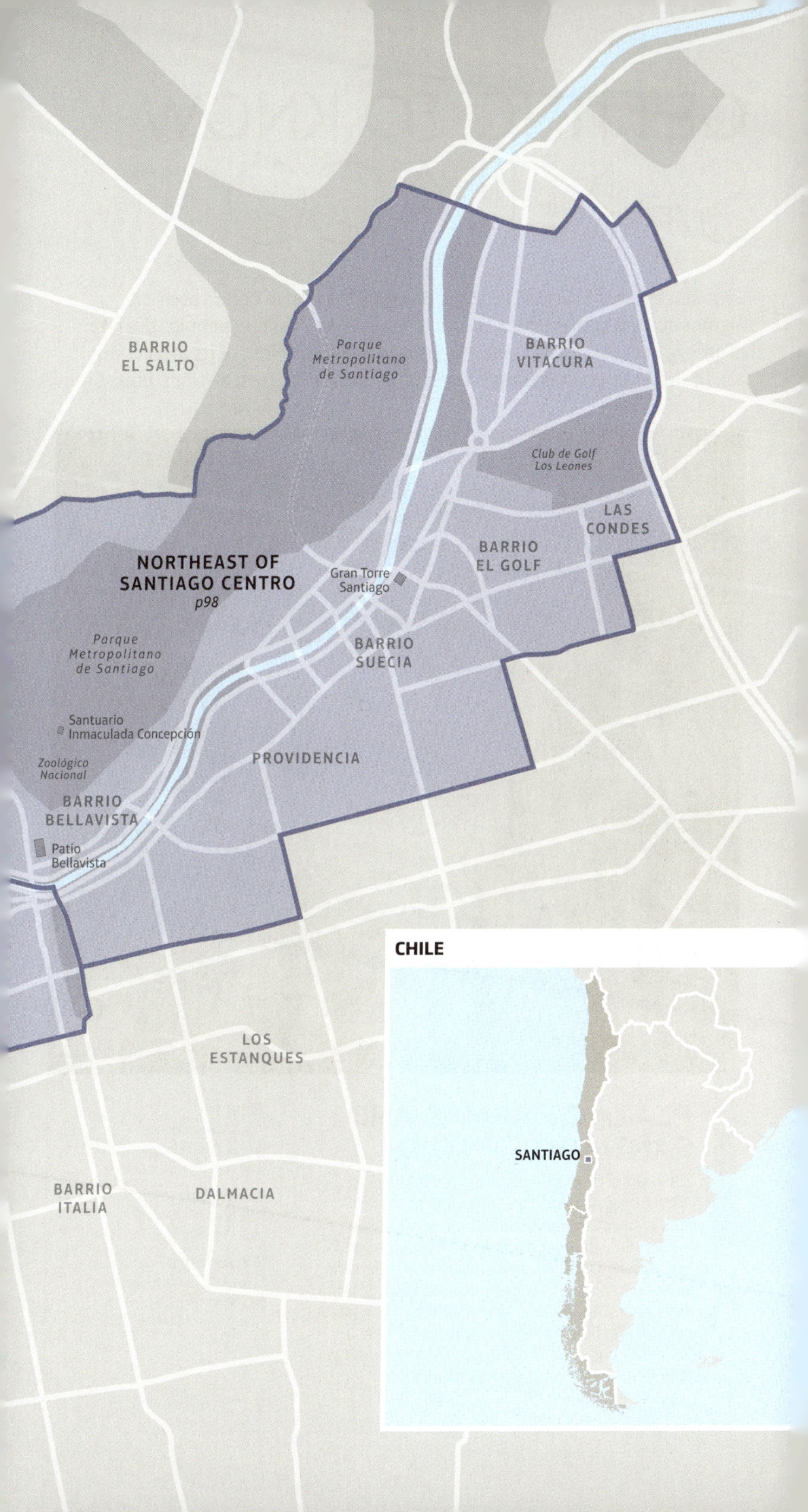

BARRIO
EL SALTO
Parque
Metropolitano
de Santiago
BARRIO
VITACURA
Club de Golf
Los Leones
LAS
CONDES
BARRIO
EL GOLF
NORTHEAST OF
SANTIAGO CENTRO
p98
Gran Torre
Santiago
BARRIO
SUECIA
Parque
Metropolitano
de Santiago
Santuario
Inmaculada Concepción
PROVIDENCIA
Zoológico
Nacional
BARRIO
BELLAVISTA
Patio
Bellavista
LOS
ESTANQUES
BARRIO
ITALIA
DALMACIA
CHILE
SANTIAGO

GETTING TO KNOW SANTIAGO

Ever since it was founded in 1541, Santiago has been Chile's political, economic, and cultural hub. Home to more than 7 million people, the city is green, well connected, and constantly evolving. Most of its attractions are found in three main areas, each of which has its own distinct vibe.

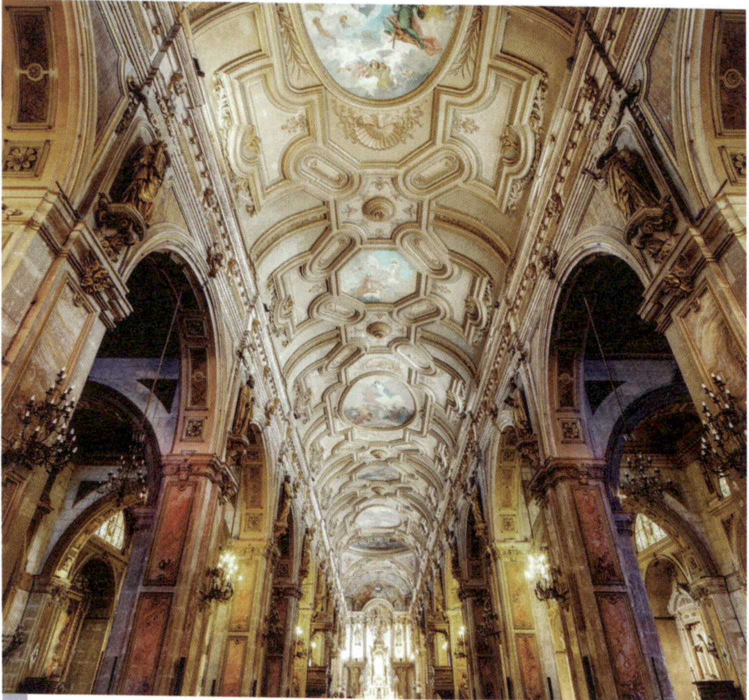

PAGE 62

PLAZA DE ARMAS AND SANTIAGO CENTRO

The heart of downtown Santiago, the Plaza de Armas is a wonderful place for an idle stroll and a spot of people-watching. The surrounding area is an architectural treasure trove, with the cathedral and the presidential palace among its many emblematic buildings. Another must-see is the captivating Museo Chileno de Arte Precolombino, which has a remarkable collection of Indigenous Latin American art. For a change of pace from the museum, visit the bustling shopping streets and lively food markets.

Best for
Historic architecture, world-class museums, and colorful food markets

Home to
The Museo Chileno de Arte Precolombino

Experience
A seafood lunch at one of the marisquerías in the Mercado Central

PAGE 84

WEST OF SANTIAGO CENTRO

After a long period of decline, the area west of the city center has been rejuvenated. Historic and beautiful neighborhoods such as Brasil, Yungay, and Concha y Toro have blossomed into trendy and hip places to live, socialize, and have fun, while many opulent *palacios*, once the homes of Santiago's elite, have been restored to their previous glory. The area also has several worthwhile museums, notably the powerful Museo de la Memoria y Derechos Humanos.

Best for
Elegant palacios, *hip neighborhoods, and insightful museums*

Home to
Parque Quinta Normal

Experience
Learning about the victims of the oppressive Pinochet regime at the Museo de la Memoria y Derechos Humanos

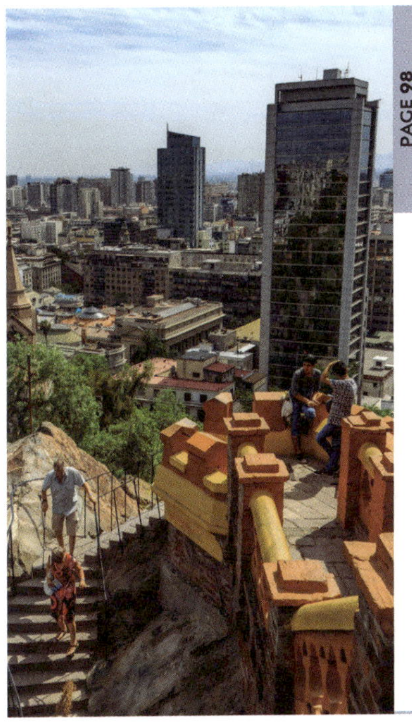

PAGE 98

NORTHEAST OF SANTIAGO CENTRO

As it stretches toward the foothills of the Andes, Santiago becomes greener, more modern, and residential. Much of the city's middle- and upper-classes live in this area, which is also home to Parque Metropolitano de Santiago, one of the world's largest urban green spaces, and the Gran Torre Santiago, the tallest skyscraper in South America. It is well-known for its array of restaurants, bars, and clubs, many of them located in buzzing Bellavista.

Best for
A vibrant culinary scene and expansive green spaces

Home to
Parque Metropolitano de Santiago

Experience
Immersing yourself in the city's street art scene on a guided graffiti tour

←

1 Santiago as seen from Cerro San Cristóbal.

2 Statue at the center of Plaza de Armas.

3 Food from one of Mercado Central's *marisquerías*.

4 Vibrant buildings in the Bellavista neighborhood.

Chile's capital and biggest city offers visitors an appealing mix of architectural gems, insightful museums, peaceful green spaces, and top-class restaurants. Here we pick a few of the highlights to help you plan a two-day stay.

2 DAYS

in Santiago

Day 1

Morning After breakfast, walk over to the Plaza de Armas *(p62)*, Santiago's main square and the perfect place to start an exploration of the city's historic core. Keep an eye out for impressive buildings, such as the Catedral Metropolitana and the Ex Congreso Nacional, which was formerly home to the Chilean Congress. Make sure to also take a stroll down the pedestrian Ahumada, Bandera, and Huérfanos streets, bustling places lined with stores, arcades, and cafés.

Afternoon For an atmospheric lunch, head over to the Mercado Central *(p81)*, which is home to numerous *marisquerías* (fish and seafood restaurants), including Richard El Rey del Mariscal *(p69)*. Then walk back into the city center and spend the rest of the afternoon in the Museo Chileno de Arte Precolombino *(p66)*. This excellent museum has an exhaustive collection of artifacts from Latin America's pre-Columbian cultures. If you are looking for an afternoon snack, try a freshly baked empanada from nearby El Rápido *(p69)*.

Evening Head over to the lively, cosmopolitan Lastarría neighborhood *(p79)*, just east of downtown, for an evening stroll before drinks and dinner at Bocanáriz *(p78)*. Finish the night with an ice cream from Emporio La Rosa *(p69)*.

Day 2

Morning Start the day by heading west of the city center to the thought-provoking Museo de la Memoria y los Derechos Humanos *(p90)*, which commemorates the thousands of victims of the brutal Pinochet dictatorship. Afterward take a stroll in the neighboring Parque Quinta Normal *(p88)*, one of the most tranquil green spaces in the city.

Afternoon For lunch, head over to the Bellavista neighborhood, a short walk west of downtown and home to scores of restaurants, such as Liguria *(p58)*. Next, visit the wonderful La Chascona *(p105)*, one of Nobel Prize-winning poet Pablo Neruda's former homes, which has now been turned into a quirky museum. Then take the funicular up to the summit of Cerro San Cristóbal for superb, sweeping views of the city and the Andes beyond. If the weather proves hot, take a dip in one of the two swimming pools that can be found on the hilltop.

Evening Take the subway or jump in a taxi to the fantastic Providencia neighborhood for drinks at Baco *(p109)*. Afterward, stay for dinner at Le Flaubert *(leflaubert.cl)* or take a taxi to Boragó *(p109)*.

Livin' La Vida Local

No visit to Santiago is complete without sampling some of the country's favourite dishes. El Rápido *(p69)* serves the best empanadas (deep-fried, filled pastries) in the city, while Liguria offers up classics like *pastel de choclo* (beef pie with a corn crust). One must is Confitería Torres *(p92)*, birthplace of the *barros luco*, a steak-and-cheese sandwich loved by the former president of the same name.

→ The *chacarero* sandwich, filled with steak, tomatoes, and green beans

SANTIAGO FOR FOODIES

With historic food markets, world-famous wineries, local joints serving Chilean classics, and swish restaurants that rank among the best in Latin America, Santiago is a wonderful place to eat and drink.

EAT

Liguria

This iconic restaurant, dressed up as a 1920s bistro, is set inside a Neo-Baroque building and features dazzling interiors. It specializes in delicious classic Chilean fare, such as *cazuelas* (stews) and *carne mechada* (braised beef).

Providencia Avenida 1353 Sun liguria.cl

$$$

Onces in a Lifetime

Chile's version of afternoon tea, *onces* is typically eaten between 5 and 7pm. At home, it is a simple affair, consisting of tea or coffee, toast, and perhaps a cookie. *Onces* at a *salón de té*, however, are fancy occasions, with sandwiches, cakes, and pastries - head to Liguria or Le Flaubert *(Orrego Luco 125)* to indulge.

→ Vintage prints and posters adorn the walls of Liguria

Pinot and Pisco

On the outskirts of Santiago are some of Chile's oldest vineyards, most of which offer tours and tastings, such as Viña Cousiño-Macul *(cousinomacul.com)*. Closer to the city is Baco *(p109)*, perhaps the best wine bar in Santiago. For something different, head to El Hoyo *(p91)* for a *terremoto* (earthquake), an earth-shaking blend of sweet, fermented pipeño wine and pineapple ice cream.

→

A selection of red wines at Concha y Toro

Santiago in Style

The city's culinary scene is fast gaining global renown, with many of its restaurants regarded as the best in Latin America. One highlight is Boragó *(p109)*, which offers locally sourced dishes that draw on Chile's Indigenous culture. Another is Ambrosia *(ambrosia.cl)*, whose menu is inspired by the continent's diverse cuisines.

←

Plate of food at Boragó, one of Chile's most prestigious restaurants

Fish and Fruit

Dating back to 1872, Mercado Central *(p81)* is home to *marisquerías* (fish and seafood restaurants), which serve mouthwatering dishes such as ceviche and *paila marina* (traditional seafood soup). Nearby La Vega *(p106)* is the city's main fruit-and-vegetable market. It offers a truly eclectic experience, with simple restaurants providing hearty meals, such as *cazuela*, a stew packed with vegetables and a piece of meat on the bone.

→

Plenty of fresh produce on offer at La Vega market

Showtime in Santiago

There are countless places in Santiago to watch a show, concert, or performance, from Neo-Classical *teatros* to indie venues. The Teatro Municipal *(p76)* is the city's premier theater and opera house, while the Centro Cultural Gabriela Mistral *(p79)* has an innovative program of dance, theater, and music events, as well as film screenings and art exhibitions. Other notable venues include Matucana 100 *(p92)*, a multifunctional arts complex, and the Centro Cultural Estación Mapocho *(p80)*, which hosts everything from theater to film.

Former railroad station Estación Mapocho, refitted for cultural events

SANTIAGO FOR CULTURE

From art-filled museums and kaledoscopically colorful graffiti tours to independent film screenings and energetic live performances, Chile's capital has a thriving art and cultural scene.

Writing on the Wall

Santiago street art is some of the best in the world. Works can be found throughout the city, but the Bellavista and Yungay neighborhoods have strong reputations. Check out San Miguel, home to the Museo a Cielo Abierto, a collection of 40 murals. Take a guided tour with an agency such as Santiago Street Art Tours *(p107)* to learn about the artists and the complex political, social, and historical background of the art.

Vibrant street art on a wall in Bellavista

Art for Art's Sake

Santiago is awash with incredible artworks. The Museo Nacional de Bellas Artes *(p79)* and the Museo de Arte Contemporáneo *(p80)* might both be based in the same building - a spectcular Art-Nouveau *palacio* overlooking the Parque Forestal - but they have very different focuses. Head to the former to admire a wealth of art, including religious-focused works from around the 16th and 17th centuries, 19th-century paintings of landscapes and historical themes, and 20th-century pieces by Surrealists such as Roberto Matta. If you're after modern art, head to the latter - which is commonly known as MAC - to see works by members of the influential Grupo Signo and Generación del Trece movements. It also hosts temporary exhibitions, often by successful Latin American artists.

←

Experimental pieces at the Museo de Arte Contemporáneo

TOP 4 CHILEAN MOVIES

El Chacal de Nahueltoro, 1969
Directed by Miguel Littín, this movie tracks a farmer's horrific crimes.

Bear Story, 2014
Animated movie about a lonely bear, directed by Pato Escala Pierart and Gabriel Osorio Vargas.

A Fantastic Woman, 2017
Sebastián Lelio directed this Oscar-winning movie about a woman accused of murder.

The Settlers, 2023
Felipe Gálvez's movie about the genocide of the Indigenous peoples of Tierra del Fuego.

Silver Screen

Chile - and Santiago - has a strong cinematic tradition, and its movie-makers are increasingly making an impact on the international stage. In 2017, *A Fantastic Woman* - filmed in Santiago - became the first Chilean movie in history to win the Best Foreign Language Film Oscar. But Santiago isn't just a filming location; if you're visiting in October, you'll see movie stars descend for the Santiago Festival Internacional de Cine (SANFIC). Want to catch a movie showing instead? The city has some impressive movie theaters, including the striking Matucana 100 *(p92)*.

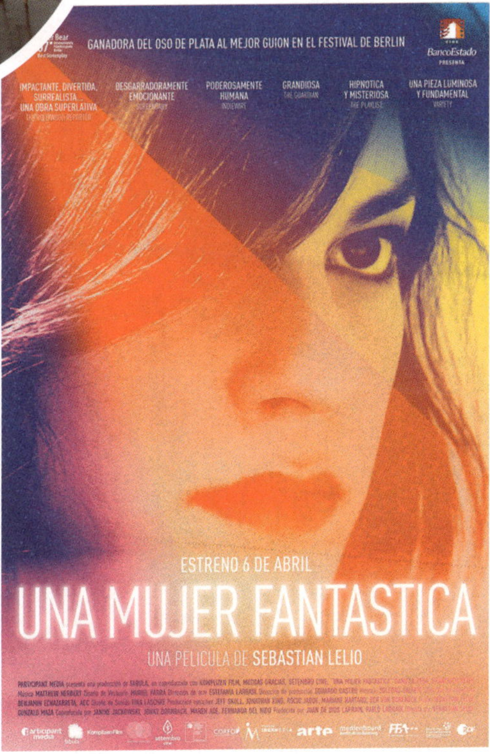

→

Poster for the award-winning film *A Fantastic Woman*

The magnificent interior of Catedral Metropolitana

PLAZA DE ARMAS AND SANTIAGO CENTRO

The Plaza de Armas, Santiago's bustling main square, has always been the focal point of the city. It dates back to 1541, when Santiago was founded by conquistador Pedro de Valdivia. The cathedral, the governor's palace, the court of law, and several luxurious mansions were swiftly built around the plaza, which has since played host to everything from public executions and bullfights to markets and festivals. Many of the original buildings fell victim to earthquakes or fires, with those that remain dating largely from the 18th and 19th centuries. Nevertheless, the palm-lined square and the blocks that fan out around it remain the most historic part of Santiago, with locals and visitors enjoying the vibrant atmosphere, and the city's most famous shopping streets.

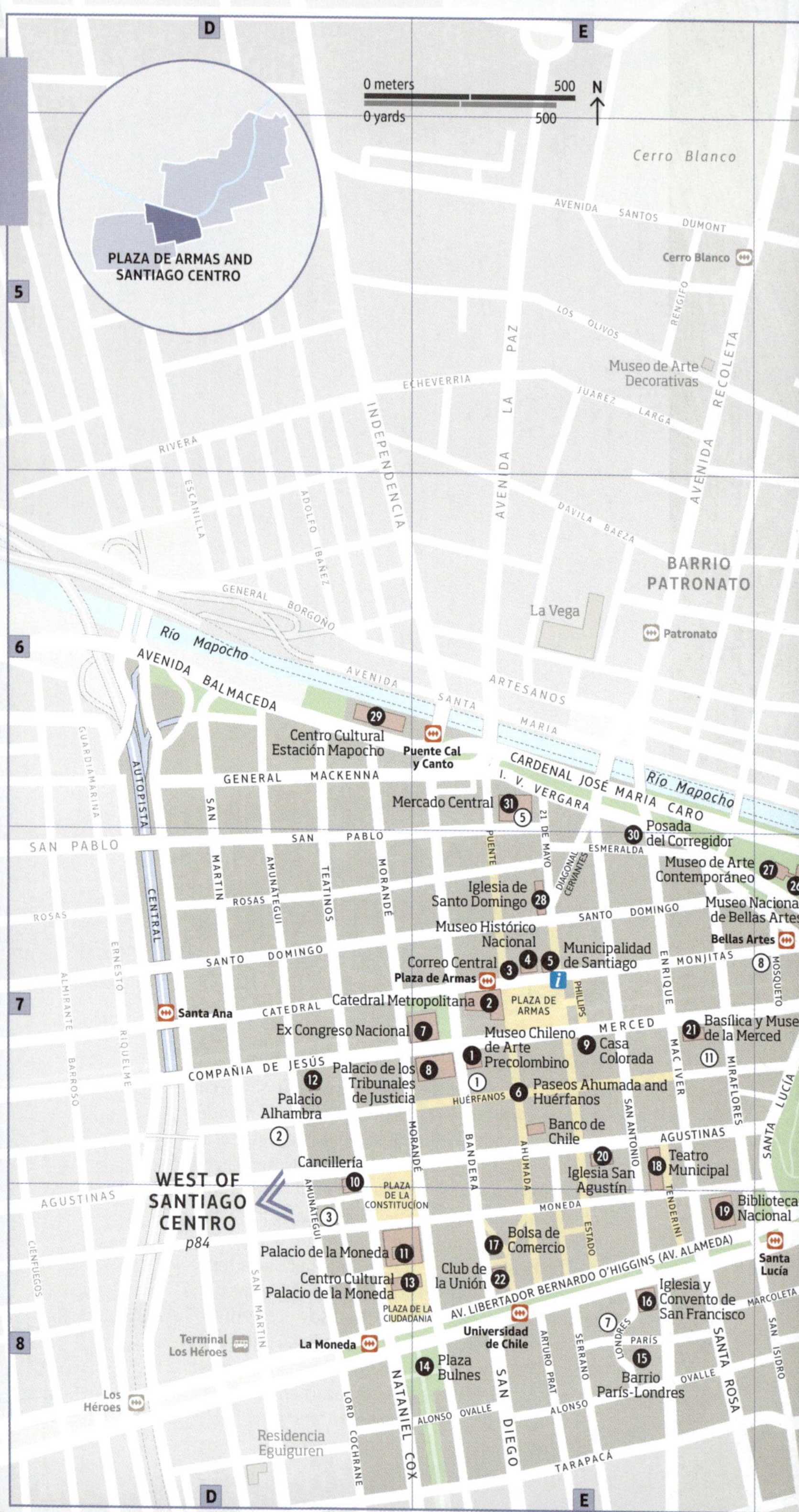
PLAZA DE ARMAS AND SANTIAGO CENTRO
0 meters 500
0 yards 500
N
D
E
5
6
7
8
Cerro Blanco
Avenida Santos Dumont
Cerro Blanco
Museo de Arte Decorativas
Barrio Patronato
La Vega
Patronato
Río Mapocho
Avenida Balmaceda
Avenida Santa María
Artesanos
Centro Cultural Estación Mapocho
Puente Cal y Canto
Cardenal José María Caro
Mercado Central
Posada del Corregidor
Museo de Arte Contemporáneo
Museo Nacional de Bellas Artes
Bellas Artes
Iglesia de Santo Domingo
Museo Histórico Nacional
Municipalidad de Santiago
Correo Central
Plaza de Armas
Catedral Metropolitana
Plaza de Armas
Santa Ana
Ex Congreso Nacional
Museo Chileno de Arte Precolombino
Casa Colorada
Basílica y Museo de la Merced
Palacio de los Tribunales de Justicia
Palacio Alhambra
Paseos Ahumada and Huérfanos
Banco de Chile
Cancillería
Iglesia San Agustín
Teatro Municipal
WEST OF SANTIAGO CENTRO p84
Plaza de la Constitución
Biblioteca Nacional
Bolsa de Comercio
Palacio de la Moneda
Club de la Unión
Centro Cultural Palacio de la Moneda
Santa Lucía
Iglesia y Convento de San Francisco
Plaza de la Ciudadanía
Av. Libertador Bernardo O'Higgins (Av. Alameda)
Universidad de Chile
Terminal Los Héroes
La Moneda
Plaza Bulnes
Barrio París-Londres
Los Héroes
Residencia Eguiguren

PLAZA DE ARMAS AND SANTIAGO CENTRO
Must See
1 Museo Chileno de Arte Precolombino
Experience More
2 Catedral Metropolitana
3 Correo Central
4 Museo Histórico Nacional
5 Municipalidad de Santiago
6 Paseos Ahumada and Huérfanos
7 Ex Congreso Nacional
8 Palacio de los Tribunales de Justicia
9 Casa Colorada
10 Cancillería
11 Palacio de La Moneda
12 Palacio Alhambra
13 Centro Cultural Palacio de la Moneda
14 Plaza Bulnes
15 Barrio París-Londres
16 Iglesia y Convento de San Francisco
17 Bolsa de Comercio
18 Teatro Municipal
19 Biblioteca Nacional
20 Iglesia San Agustín
21 Basílica y Museo de la Merced
22 Club de la Unión
23 Cerro Santa Lucía
24 Museo de Artes Visuales
25 Barrio Lastarría
26 Museo Nacional de Bellas Artes
27 Museo de Arte Contemporáneo
28 Iglesia de Santo Domingo
29 Centro Cultural Estación Mapocho
30 Posada del Corregidor
31 Mercado Central
Eat
① El Rapido
② Romasanta
③ Blue Jar
④ Emporio la Rosa
⑤ Richard El Rey del Mariscal
Drink
⑥ Bocanáriz
Stay
⑦ Hotel Vegas
⑧ Merced 88
⑨ Río Amazonas
⑩ Luciano K
Shop
⑪ Libreria Inglesa
F
5
6
7
8
G
H
AVENIDA PERÚ
TABARE
DOMINICA
HUMORISTA CARLOS HELO
LORETO
BELLAVISTA
CARDENAL JOSÉ MARIA CARO
Parque Forestal
MONJITAS
MERCED
PLAZA MULATO GIL DE CASTRO
Museo de Artes Visuales
ROSAL
VILLAVICENCIO
LASTARRIA
Barrio Lastarría
Iglesia de la Vera Cruz
Castillo Hidalgo
Cerro Santa Lucía
Universidad Católica
Museo Violeta Parra
RAMÓN CORVALÁN
AVENIDA VICUÑA MACKENNA
Baquedano
ARTURO BURHLE
EULOGIA SANCHEZ
RAMON CARNICER
AVENIDA GENERAL BUSTAMANTE
Museo de Tajamares
NORTHEAST OF SANTIAGO CENTRO
p98
MARIA LUISA SANTANDER
AVENIDA SALVADOR
RANCAGUA
SEMINARIO
Parque San Borja
PORTUGAL
Universidad de Chile
LIRA
MARCOLETA
DIAGONAL PARAGUAY
CURICO
Parque Bustamante
AVENIDA CONDELL
AVENIDA ITALIA
CARMEN
BLAS CANAS
GENERAL JOFRÉ
MARÍN
ROOT
Santa Isabel
SANTA ISABEL

MUSEO CHILENO DE ARTE PRECOLOMBINO

E7 Bandera 361 Plaza de Armas 10am-6pm Tue-Sun
museo.precolombino.cl

This Aladdin's cave of curiosities is arguably one of the city's – and the country's – best museums. The encyclopedic Museo Chileno de Arte Precolombino is dedicated to the artistic and symbolic legacy of cultures throughout Chile and Latin America, housing all manner of items and relics relating to the Incas, Aztecs, Mayans, and other ancient peoples.

Inaugurated in 1981, the museum is housed in the impressive Neo-Classical Palacio de la Real Aduana, which was built between 1805 and 1807 as the Royal Customs House, and which later served as the National Library and Court of Law. The museum housed 1,500 exhibits when it opened – today it's double this number.

The first floor's three temporary exhibition halls feature in-depth displays which focus on particular cultures. Galleries on the museum's second floor feature fascinating collections divided into cultural areas across Mesoamerica, Intermediate era, Amazonian, the Caribbean, and Central and Southern Andes. Of special interest is the valuable collection of textiles and excellent ceramics. There is a café and a space for outdoor events at the museum's entrance patio. Tours are also available by prior arrangement.

HIDDEN GEM
Cut from the Same Cloth

Don't miss the Sala Textil (Textile Gallery), which has some remarkable exhibits from across Latin America. In its holdings is a scrap of cloth from the Chavín culture (from what is now Peru) that is almost 3,000 years old.

SERGIO LARRAÍN GARCÍA-MORENO

Hailed as a visionary advocate of Latin American and European art, Sergio Larraín García-Moreno (1905-99) was the founder of the Museo Chileno de Arte Precolombino. An architect with a passionate interest in archaeology and ancient American cultures, Larraín traded modern art to buy pre-Columbian relics. He convinced the Santiago Municipality and the city mayor to let him convert the old, fire-damaged Royal Customs House into a museum, and employed experts to procure artifacts from private collections located across Europe and the Americas.

The museum's collection of *chemamulles* - wooden funerary statues

1 A colorful woolen hat, which was worn by the Aymara people of the Altiplano region.

2 The striking exterior of the museum. The building was originally built as a customs house in the 19th century.

3 A Mayan ceramic vase. It dates from around 600-900 CE.

EXPERIENCE MORE

Catedral Metropolitana

E7 Plaza de Armas Plaza de Armas 11am-7pm Tue-Sat, 9am-7pm Sun catedraldesantiago.cl

Set on the western side of the Plaza de Armas, the Catedral Metropolitana was inaugurated in 1775 and is the fourth church to be built on this site, after previous structures were destroyed by earthquakes. The cathedral is considered the most important in Chile, and is the seat of the Archdiocese of Santiago de Chile. The original design was conceived by Bavarian Jesuits, whose influence can still be seen in the cathedral's imposing woodwork, despite the church having undergone an endless series of restorations.

The grand interior is 295-ft- (90-m-) long and divided into three naves. The right nave holds an urn that guards the hearts of soldiers who fought in the Battle of La Concepcion during the War of the Pacific (1879–83). Highlights in the central nave include the organ, imported from London in 1850; the cathedral's original 18th-century pulpit; and the central altar, constructed in Munich in 1912. Behind the altar is the crypt where Chile's former cardinals and archbishops are buried. The left nave is the Iglesia del Sagrario (Tabernacle Church), a national monument and site of the first parish that was founded in the country. Crafted by Jesuits, the cathedral's Capilla del Santísimo Sacramento (Chapel of the Blessed Sacrament) is covered in beautiful silver work.

In the same complex is the Museo de Arte Sagrado (Museum of Sacred Art), which houses the cathedral's Jesuit artwork.

Correo Central

E7 Plaza de Armas 989 Plaza de Armas 9am-6:30pm Mon-Fri, 9am-1pm Sat correos.cl

Historically known as the site of the first house built in early Santiago, the Correo Central (Central Post Office) was initially the residence of the city's founding father, Pedro de Valdivia. Later it served as the Governing Council, and then as the presidential residence until 1846. In 1881, a fire destroyed part of the edifice. Soon after, the government planned a grand post office on the Plaza de Armas, enlisting the help of architect and musician Ricardo Brown, who adapted his design using parts of the existing building. In 1908, architect Ramón Ferham rebuilt the facade in Renaissance style.

Today, the Correo Central has a small postal museum and stamp collection on the first floor to memorialize the history of the Correos de Chile (Post Office of Chile).

Museo Histórico Nacional

E7 Plaza de Armas 951 Plaza de Armas 10am-5:30pm Tue-Sun mhn.gob.cl

Built between 1804 and 1808, the Neo-Classical

The Catedral Metropolitana, fronted by the bustling Plaza de Armas

INSIDER TIP
Plaza Life

Although busy during the day, the Plaza de Armas really comes alive in the early evening. To see how the locals live, arrive early, grab a seat on one of the benches, and settle down for a spot of people-watching.

Palacio de la Real Audiencia has been witness to some of the most important events in Chile. In 1811, the palace was the site of Chile's first National Congress, and later it housed the governmental offices of Chile's first president and liberator, Bernardo O'Higgins. During the 20th century, the edifice also housed the City Hall.

Located in this old palace, the Museo Histórico Nacional charts Chile's history through a chronological display of exhibits from the colonial period (1541–1818) to the military coup of 1973. Exhibit rooms are spread around a central courtyard and feature rare 18th-century paintings and furniture, such as a sacristy wardrobe. Reproductions of home interiors depict daily life in colonial Chile, as do traditional clothing and agricultural instruments. There are also sections dedicated to transportation and education. The temporary exhibit hall, called Sala Plaza de Armas (Heritage Square), features displays about Chilean culture and customs.

Municipalidad de Santiago

E7 Plaza de Armas 451 Plaza de Armas To the public munistgo.cl

Although Santiago's municipal building is closed to the public, its exterior architecture is easily appreciated from the Plaza de Armas. Originally founded in 1578 as the *cabildo*, or town hall, this was also the site of the city's first jail. Three buildings on the site were destroyed by earthquakes or fire. In 1785, Italian architect Joaquín Toesca, who had already put his signature Neo-Classical stamp on many of Santiago's buildings, rebuilt the city hall.

The city hall offices were expanded in 1883, following the transfer of the jail to modern premises, but within a decade the edifice succumbed to a major fire. Restorations began apace and by 1895 the Santiago Municipality was installed in the restored building. The reconstruction still maintained the previous structure's Neo-Classical style, but now displayed touches of Italian Renaissance, in the form of arched doorways and three enormous frontal windows framed by columns. Today, the front facade bears a coat of arms given by Spain.

An old piece of machinery on display in the Museo Histórico Nacional

EAT

El Rápido

A wallet-friendly joint with a concise menu. The freshly baked empanadas are delicious.

E7 Bandera 347 Sun elrapido.cl

Romasanta

This lively spot in the city center serves staples like churrasco grilled meat, *albóndigas* (meatballs), and salads.

D7 Huérfanos 1454 (056) 9422 64166 Sat & Sun

Blue Jar

This café-restaurant is good for coffee, light meals, and alcoholic drinks. The reservation-only dinner on the first Thursday of each month is superb.

D8 Profesora Amanda Labarca, 102 Sat & Sun bluejar.cl

Emporio la Rosa

A delightful ice cream parlor with an inventive range of flavors.

F7 Merced 291 emporiolarosa.cl

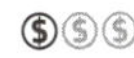

Richard El Rey del Mariscal

One of Mercado Central's best *marisquerías* (seafood restaurants), with great service.

E6 Mercado Central, San Pablo 943 (02) 2269 6255 Mon

$$$

Paseos Ahumada and Huérfanos

E7 Plaza de Armas

Pedestrianized in 1977, Paseo Ahumada and Paseo Huérfanos are two walkways flanked by numerous shopping galleries, restaurants, electronics stores, and commercial businesses. Catering to a bustling downtown population, the *paseos* take on a lively ambience, with thousands of people walking to and fro all day. Street performers add to the excitement of a stroll here.

Paseo Ahumada stretches from Avenida del Libertador Bernardo O'Higgins, popularly called Avenida Alameda, to the Mercado Central *(p81)*. It is cut across by a number of streets, most notably by Agustinas, whose junction with Ahumada is the site of the former Hotel Crillón. The first story of this edifice is occupied by Galería Crillón, one of many downtown *galerías* – labyrinthine shopping malls brimming with stores selling everything from handicrafts to designer wear.

Paseo Huérfanos runs parallel to Agustinas and crosses Paseo Ahumada near the historic Banco de Chile. Built in 1921–25 by Viennese architect Alberto Siegel, the bank features ornate interiors and old-fashioned teller windows that are worth a look.

Ex Congreso Nacional

E7 Catedral 1150 Plaza de Armas 10am-5:30pm Mon-Fri senado.cl

The Ex Congreso Nacional, an imposing Neo-Classical structure with massive columns, was designated a National Monument in 1976. Beginning in 1858, the building's construction experienced a series of delays and was only completed in 1876, under the direction of architect Manuel Aldunate. In 1895, the building nearly burned to the ground and was rebuilt by architect Emilio Doyère in 1901.

Congressional sessions were held in this building until the dissolution of the Congress by former dictator Augusto Pinochet in 1973. Today, it houses the Santiago offices of the Senate as well as the Chamber of Deputies.

The edifice is surrounded by lush, enchanting gardens that are open to the public. The statue of the Virgin that dominates the grounds was placed in memory of the 2,000 people who were killed in a fire at the Iglesia Compañía de Jesús in 1863, which was located nearby.

SHOP

Libreria Inglesa

Stock up on reading material for your travels at this bookstore, which has a small (and slightly pricey) range of English-language titles. There are also a couple of other branches dotted around the city.

E7 Huérfanos 669 Sun libreriainglesa.cl

Palacio de los Tribunales de Justicia

D7 Compañía de Jesús, 1140 (02) 2412 5700 Plaza de Armas 8am-2pm Mon-Fri (IDs to be left at the front desk)

Constructed between 1905 and 1930, the Palacio de los Tribunales de Justicia (Supreme Court) exhibits both Neo-Classical and Greco-Roman features. The colossal building stretches from calles Morandé to Bandera, covering an area of around 43,000 sq ft (4,000 sq m). Designed by the French architect Emilio Doyère, the building is entered through a marble stairway that is flanked by two fine caryatids. Although the edifice has a somber facade, its interior offers a stunning example of 20th-century architecture. An open three-story central hall is encircled with wraparound interior balconies and topped with a vaulted glass-and-metal ceiling. Located above the entrance is a bas-relief of a condor clutching a book inscribed with the letters LEX, the Latin term for Law.

Today, the palace houses Chile's Supreme Court, the Court of Appeals, the Military and Police Courts, as well as the Supreme Court Library.

The Ex Congreso Nacional, set amid immaculately landscaped gardens

Casa Colorada

E7 Merced 860 Plaza de Armas 10am-6pm Tue-Fri, 10am-2pm Sat munistgo.cl/casacolorada

The Casa Colorada (Red House) is regarded as a pristine example of colonial architecture designed for the bourgeoisie of Chile. Built in 1770, it was the home of Don Mateo de Toro y Zambrano (1727–1811), a wealthy entrepreneur and the first Count of the Conquest, who served as a senior military leader and Royal Governor during Spanish rule. On September 18, 1810, he was elected the first president of the newly formed government junta during Chile's struggle of Independence. In 1817, after the Battle of Chacabuco, revolutionaries José San Martín and Bernardo O'Higgins stayed at the Casa Colorada, followed by Lord Cochrane.

↑ Casa Colorada's front, dotted with wrought-iron balconies

The Casa Colorada is exceptional in that it has two floors, which was unusual at the time. The family originally lived on the second floor, while the rooms on the first floor were used as Don Mateo's offices. With its red-brick facade (hence the name), the building is now home to a museum dedicated to Santiago's history, tracing the city's development from Pre-Hispanic times to the present.

METROARTE

Santiago is known for its street art, and now there's more of it to explore underground. The city's MetroArte project has transformed subway stations into open-air galleries. Of the 81 artworks on display, the most famous is Mario Toral's enormous mural Memoria Visual de una Nación. Found at the Universidad de Chile stop, it depicts Chilean history in all its bloody detail.

↑ The stately, white-pillared facade of the Cancillería

Cancillería

D7 Teatinos 180 La Moneda minrel.gob.cl

Chile's Ministry of Foreign Relations, or Cancillería, is located in an impressive 17-story building that was formerly the Hotel Carrera. Open from 1940 to 2003, this was the grandest hotel of its time. It was designed by architect Josué Smith Solar, who was already well known for his design of the Club Hípico *(p96)*. The hotel's guests included Fidel Castro, Henry Kissinger, Charles de Gaulle, Nelson Rockefeller, and Neil Armstrong.

The hotel was most famous for its proximity to the Palacio de la Moneda during the 1973 coup d'état, when it acted as a temporary home for nearly every international journalist reporting in the country. Most of the images of the presidential building being bombarded were taken from the hotel's windows and rooftop. The hotel itself was slightly damaged by the shelling.

In 2004, the hotel was sold for US$24 million and revamped to accommodate the Ministry of Foreign Relations. Today, most of the building's interiors, other than the lobby, are unrecognizable from its hotel era. The lobby features beautiful marble columns and a striking mural made of opal glass – a depiction by Spanish artist Luis Egidio Meléndez of the discovery of the Americas.

Did You Know?

New Year's Eve fireworks take place at the Torre Entel, near the Palacio de la Moneda.

Palacio de la Moneda

D8 Avenida Alameda, between calles Morandé & Teatinos La Moneda 9am-5pm daily visitaspatrimonio.presidencia.cl

The immaculately preserved Palacio de la Moneda is Chile's presidential headquarters. Built between 1784 and 1799 by the Spanish, it was inaugurated in 1805 as the Casa de Moneda, the nation's mint. From 1845, it housed the republican government offices, and also served as the presidential residence until 1958. The palace was the largest building erected in any of Spain's colonies during the 18th century, and is considered one of Chile's finest examples of Neo-Classical architecture.

At its northeastern side is the Plaza de la Constitucíon, an expansive grassy space crisscrossed by walkways. Visitors can present their passports here to enjoy a stroll through the palace's patios (although you must also email in advance). The plaza was designed in the 1930s to create Barrio Cívico, the country's administrative and political center. At the plaza's southern corner is a statue of Chile's former president Salvador Allende, who perished here during the coup d'état of 1973. A ceremonial changing of the guard takes place at the plaza at 10am every other day. Visitors can also enter the palace's interior courtyards that comprise the Patio de los Cañones – named for the two 1778 cannons on display here – and the Patio de los Naranjos, named for its pleasant orange trees.

Palacio Alhambra

D7 Compañia de Jesús 1340 (9) 9432 8982 La Moneda Until further notice, call for details

This extraordinary architectural gem stands out in a neighborhood dominated chiefly by Neo-Classical structures and modern storefronts. It was built in 1860–62 by the architect Manuel Aldunate, who traveled to Granada, Spain, to study the original Alhambra Palace. Upon his return, he

created a smaller version of it with elaborate plaster ceilings and a replica lion fountain. Following the original owner's death, the *palacio* was bought by Don Julio Garrido Falcón, a wealthy Chilean philanthropist, who donated it to the National Society of Fine Arts in 1940.

Today the palace is closed, awaiting funding for much-needed restoration work.

Palacio Alhambra stands out in a neighborhood dominated chiefly by Neo-Classical structures and modern storefronts.

Centro Cultural Palacio de la Moneda

D/E8 Plaza de la Ciudadanía 26 La Moneda 10am-7pm daily cclm.cl

A pet project of former president Ricardo Lagos, the cutting-edge Centro Cultural Palacio de la Moneda was inaugurated in 2006 as part of the 2010 Bicentennial Project that introduced latest museums and improved road infrastructure in Santiago. It is located in what once served as the Palacio de la Moneda's basement. Designed by noted Chilean architect Cristián Undurraga, the center features three subterranean floors that surround a spacious central hall. Three large salons host international traveling expositions and shows by well-known Chilean artists. The Centro Cultural also accommodates the Arts Documentation Center library; the National Film Archive; a number of cafés and restaurants; and a superb *artesanía* store that showcases arts and crafts from the length of Chile. The Plaza de la Ciudadanía, landscaped with walkways and reflecting pools, acts as the roof for the center.

Plaza Bulnes

E8 Northern end of Paseo Bulnes La Moneda

Plaza Bulnes was the site of military and patriotic celebrations during the years of the Pinochet dictatorship, as well as a center for dissident protests that continued long after the return to democracy.

In 1975, General Pinochet established the controversial Eternal Flame of Liberty at the plaza. The flame was regarded by many as a visible monument to the dictatorship, and dissidents regularly attempted to extinguish it in protest.

In 1979, the remains of Chile's first president, Bernardo O'Higgins *(p259)*, were moved from the Cementerio General *(p104)* to the plaza by the Pinochet regime, in an attempt to create a patriotic altar that symbolized a return to traditional historical values.

Plaza Bulnes was rebuilt in 2005 and now features an underground crypt holding the remains of O'Higgins that can be viewed through a glass window. The Eternal Flame of Liberty was finally put out during the restorations.

↑ Centro Cultural Palacio de la Moneda's cavernous main hall

STAY

Hotel Vegas
Conveniently located in the quaint París-Londres neighborhood, this mid-range hotel does the basics well: well-equipped rooms, competitive prices, and efficient service.

E8 Calle Londres 49 hotelvegassantiago.com

Merced 88
In addition to large four- to ten-bedroom dorms, this smart hostel, set in a 1920s mansion, has private bedrooms, a games room, and a sunny communal roof terrace.

F7 Merced 88 merced88.cl

Río Amazonas
Located just 10 minutes from Bellavista, this delightful guesthouse is a place for travelers of all ages. There's a great vibe and lots of information on offer.

G7 Vicuña Mackenna 47 hostalrioamazonas.cl

Luciano K
This boutique hotel is an architectural gem, with gorgeous 1920s Art-Deco fittings, generous en suites, and a superb restaurant-bar on the roof terrace.

F7 Merced 84 lucianokhotel.com

$$$

15 

Barrio París-Londres

E8 Londres and París (02) 2325 037 Universidad de Chile

With small, artful mansions, the tiny neighborhood of Barrio París-Londres (because the two neighborhoods intersect) is an architectural oasis. Laid out in 1922, the *barrio* was constructed over the gardens of the Convento de San Francisco. It was conceived by the architect Ernesto Holzmann, who believed that downtown Santiago lacked attractive neighborhoods within walking distance of services and stores. After purchasing the gardens of the Convento de San Francisco, he enlisted architects to create what he envisioned as a "model block residence."

Today, the neighborhood is well preserved, with an elegant ambience, courtyards, and cafés. Within a four-block radius of winding, cobblestone streets are styles such as French Neo-Classical (Londres 70), and Italian Renaissance and Neo-colonial (Londres 65).

The museum at **Londres 38** was infamous during the dictatorship years (1973–90) as a torture center. Visitors can explore the exhibits pertaining to the repressions of the Pinochet years here.

Londres 38
8331009 Santiago, Región Metropolitana
11am-1:30pm & 3-5:30pm Tue-Fri londres38.cl

16 

Iglesia y Convento de San Francisco

E8 Avenida Libertador Bernardo O'Higgins 834 Universidad de Chile 10am-2pm & 3-5pm Mon-Fri, 10am-2pm Sat & Sun museosanfrancisco.com

This church, which is the oldest surviving building in Santiago, is a national monument with

1951

The year that the Iglesia y Convento de San Francisco became a national monument.

A pretty street in the Barrio París-Londres neighborhood

distinct architectural details from various eras. Pedro de Valdivia first erected a chapel here in the 16th century in honor of the Virgen del Socorro, whose image he had brought with him and who, he believed, had protected the conquistadores against attacks. In 1618, the Franciscan Order established a church of stone walls and coffered ceilings, expanding the complex to include cloisters, gardens, and an infirmary. With the exception of the church's bell towers, the structure survived two major earthquakes. The current tower was designed by Fermín Vivaceta in 1857 in Neo-Classical style.

The giant stones used to build the walls of the original church are still visible, as are the nave's intricately carved woodwork and the grand doors carved from cedar. The convent's lush and tranquil patio and tiled roofs are early examples of the traditional architecture of Chile *(p36)*. Set in the church is the **Museo San Francisco**, with an extremely valuable series of 17th-century paintings that narrate the life of St. Francis of Assisi. Also on display are antique locks; paintings representing the life of the Virgen del Socorro; a graph indicating the lineage of the Franciscans; and the Salon Gabriela Mistral, which houses the poet's Nobel Prize medal *(p38)*.

Museo San Francisco
Alameda 834
9:30am-2pm & 3-5pm Mon-Fri, 9:30am-2pm Sat
museosanfrancisco.com

17

Bolsa de Comercio

E8 La Bolsa 64
Universidad de Chile
Mar-Oct: 9:30am-4pm Mon-Fri; Nov-Feb: 9:30am-5pm Mon-Fri
bolsadesantiago.com

Launched in 1884 with only 160 incorporated companies, Chile's stock market expanded rapidly to include twice the number of companies within a decade. The early years of the 20th century continued to be a time of tremendous good fortune for the Chilean economy, mostly due to the boom in metal and nitrate mining in the northern deserts.

Today this area – the financial nerve center of the capital – is a micro-district comprising charming cobblestone streets and historic buildings. At the heart of this economic hub is the Bolsa de Comercio, Santiago's lively stock exchange. It is housed in a French Renaissance-style triangular structure, with Roman pillars and a slate roof with a cupola. This elegant old building was built in 1917 by Emilio Jéquier, who was already famous for his design of the Museo Nacional de Bellas Artes *(p79)*.

Although there has been considerable modern technology installed, the interiors of the Bolsa de Comercio retain their original splendor.

The striking Bolsa de Comercio, housing Santiago's stock exchange

↑ The gleaming marble interiors of the Teatro Municipal

18  

Teatro Municipal

E7 Agustinas 794 Universidad de Chile municipal.cl

Built between 1853 and 1857, the Teatro Municipal is Chile's most important venue for classical music, opera, and theater. The theater was originally designed by architect Claude François Brunet de Baines in an elegant, French Neo-Classical style with a lovely symmetrical facade. Its first-ever performance was an Italian production of Verdi's *Ernani*. Soon the theater became the cultural and social center of Santiago's elite, who contributed heavily to the production of important opera performances. In 1870, a raging fire nearly razed the theater. However, architect Lucien Hénault successfully restored the building to its earlier splendor, and it was reopened in 1873.

The theater foyer, La Capilla, features two sculptures by Nicanor Plaza – *Prólogo* and *Epílogo*. The main concert hall has a capacity of 1,500, not including the private Sala Arrau salon, which has space for 250. The interior hall was designed after the Paris Opera house with lateral viewing boxes and a large ceiling cupola, whose grand crystal chandelier dates from 1930. Throughout the theater there are costume workshops, rehearsal studios, dressing rooms, and set design studios. The Philharmonic Orchestra, Santiago Ballet, and Municipal Theater Chorus are all permanent residents. Many great artistes have graced this stage, including Igor Stravinsky, Anna Pavlova, and Chilean pianist Claudio Arrau.

Tours take place Mondays, Thursdays, and Saturdays.

19 

Biblioteca Nacional

E8 Avenida Alameda 651 Santa Lucía 9:15am-6pm Mon-Thu, 9:15am-5pm Fri bibliotecanacional.cl

An imposing building that occupies a whole city block, the Biblioteca Nacional was built between 1914 and 1927 by architect Gustavo García Postigo in the style of the French Academy in Paris. Its interiors have marble staircases, bronze balustrades, painted murals, and carved wood detail in a highly ornamental style, unusual in a 20th-century building. The library is home to one of Latin America's most valuable collections of colonial-era literary works – it is estimated that 60 per cent of everything printed during this period can be found in the second-floor Medina Library. Key works include *Mística Teología* from Mexico (1547), *La Doctrina Cristina* from Peru (1584), and chronicles of explorers such as Sir Francis Drake.

Iglesia San Agustín

E7 Agustinas 828 Universidad de Chile 9am-6pm Mon-Fri iglesiadesantiago.cl

The construction of the Iglesia San Agustín, formerly known as Templo de Nuestra Señora de Gracia, marked the founding of the Catholic Augustinian mission in Chile. Reaching Chile from Peru in 1595, Augustinians erected their first church here in 1625. In 1647, an earthquake destroyed the church, along with most of the city. After being rebuilt in 1707, the church was toppled by another earthquake in 1730. It was restored by architect Fermín Vivaceta, who added columns to the facade and bell towers.

A curious aspect of San Agustín is the *Cristo de Mayo* statue. After the

Soon the Teatro Municipal became the cultural and social center of Santiago's elite, who contributed heavily to the production of important opera performances.

HIDDEN GEM
Mystery Tablet

The Basílica y Museo de la Merced contains some remarkable Easter Island exhibits, such as a rare tablet covered with the undeciphered *rongorongo* script - a system of glyphs used by the Rapa Nui.

1647 earthquake, priests salvaged the intact statue to find that Christ's crown of thorns had fallen around his neck, which seemed miraculous given that the diameter of the crown was smaller than that of the head. Priests paraded through the rubbled streets of Santiago to celebrate this event, and in the ensuing decades the commemoration of May 13 grew into the city's most venerable religious festival. Today, followers still celebrate May 13, but on a much smaller scale.

Basílica y Museo de la Merced

E7 Mac Iver 341 Plaza de Armas 10am-1pm & 3-7:30pm Mon-Fri mercedarios.cl

Established by the Order of the Blessed Mary of Mercy – who arrived with the first expedition to Chile – the Basílica y Museo de la Merced was built in 1566. During the city's early years, it was patronized by the elite, some of whom are buried within its walls. These include Governor Rodrigo de Quiroga and his wife Inés de Suarez, the first Spanish woman to arrive in Chile. The present-day basilica was built in 1760 and later adorned with Neo-Classical touches by architect Joaquín Toesca. On the second floor of the basilica is the Museo de la Merced, a collection of Easter Island artifacts, colonial art, and 18th-century figurines.

Club de la Unión

E8 Avenida Alameda 1091 Universidad de Chile clubdelaunion.cl

The exclusive Club de la Unión is an architectural gem. It was constructed between 1917 and 1925 by noted Chilean architect Alberto Cruz Montt (1879–1955) in French Neo-Classical style. Inside, the club's gleaming marble walls and antique furnishings line spacious dining rooms, halls, and a private art gallery. The club also houses the longest carved oak bar in the country. It operated as a men's-only association until 2006, when it invited its first female member.

The club's on-site restaurant is open to non-members, though visitors should be aware that entry to the club itself is by invitation only.

The Basílica y Museo de la Merced, standing in a leafy square ↓

Cerro Santa Lucía

F7 Avenida Alameda 499 Santa Lucía 9am-8pm daily

Rising above the bustle of Santiago, the Santa Lucía hill is a lush park that was once the strategic defense point for conquistador Pedro de Valdivia, who founded Santiago at this very spot in 1541. Following the conquest, local Mapuches named the hill Huelén, meaning Sadness or Pain. In 1871, Mayor Benjamin Vicuña Mackenna transformed the 226-ft (69-m) denuded outcrop into a veritable Eden, with dense foliage, Gothic-style iron balustrades, stone walkways, statuary, fountains, and lookout points. Vicuña was buried here in the tiny chapel, Capilla la Ermita. Other historical curiosities include a 6-ft- (2-m-) high stone carved with a passage chronicling the land features of Chile, which was taken from a letter sent to Charles V, Holy Roman Emperor, by Pedro de Valdivia. A statue commemorates dissenters – those who were non-Catholics or had died by suicide – who were once buried at Cerro Santa Lucía. At the summit sits Castillo Hidalgo, built by Royalists in 1816 during the Chilean War of Independence.

The principal access point to the hill from Avenida Alameda is at the monumental Plaza Neptuno staircase, or up a cobblestone road across from Calle Agustinas. Visitors can also take the glass elevator from Calle Huérfanos, but that only operates occasionally. There is a cannon boom at noon every day, a tradition dating from the 18th century.

Museo de Artes Visuales

F7 José Victorino Lastarría 307 Universidad Católica 10am-6pm Tue-Sun mavi.uc.cl

Opened in 1994, the Museo de Artes Visuales is the ideal place to view contemporary Chilean sculpture, painting, photography, and conceptual art. The museum's permanent collection comprises more than 1,500 works by artists such as Samy Benmayor, a Neo-Expressionist painter; Gonzalo Cienfuegos, who uses a variety of media, including oil and acrylic; and Rodrigo Cabezas, best known for his three-dimensional assemblies. Located on the second floor, the Museo Arqueológico de Santiago is a compact salon

DRINK

Bocanáriz

This is the city's best dedicated wine bar, with hundreds of bottles, and dozens available by the glass. It also has a good food menu, friendly French ownership, and pleasant, contemporary surroundings.

F7 Lastarría 276
bocanariz.cl

↓ The ornate Plaza Neptuno staircase, on Cerro Santa Lucía

with over 3,300 artifacts from pre-Columbian Chile, including a Chinchorro mummy, hallucinogenic tablets from Atacama, everyday utensils and tools, and decorative finery from the Aymara, Mapuche, Fueguino, and Rapa Nui cultures.

Barrio Lastarría

F7 José Victorino Lastarría Universidad Católica barriolastarria.com

Also known as Barrio Parque Forestal, the charming Barrio Lastarría is a fashionable neighborhood for artists, actors, and other young creatives. On Calle Lastarría and the narrow streets that branch off it, there are cafés, restaurants, high-end *artesanía* stores, galleries, bookstores, and a couple of boutiques, which together provide a wonderful atmosphere for shopping and strolling. In the middle of Calle Lastarría is the serene and sober Iglesia de la Vera Cruz, dating from 1858.

Barrio Lastarría's prime attraction is the tiny **Plaza Mulato Gil de Castro**. Named for the famed 19th-century portrait painter José Gil de Castro who lived in the *barrio* (neighborhood), the plaza was once the patio of a former house. A small, outdoor book and antiques fair is held here Thursday through Saturday.

The **Centro Gabriela Mistral** art center, named for the first Latin American Nobel Prize winner for literature, regularly hosts concerts, theater and dance performances. It is set in a remarkable building and is a maze of little plazas and cafés. The center also has airy exhibition spaces on the first floor where Chilean artists display their works. Free tours in Spanish can be requested at the information desk.

HIDDEN GEM
Visual Artistry

South of Barrio Lastarría is the intriguing Museo Violeta Parra, which celebrates the first Chilean artist to have a Louvre exhibition *(museovioletaparra.cl)*.

Attractive interiors and vaulted glass ceiling of the Museo Nacional de Bellas Artes

Plaza Mulato Gil de Castro
Mecred, Lastarría
11am-midnight Mon-Fri

Centro Gabriela Mistral
Avenida O'Higgins 227
9am-5pm daily (to 10pm Mon-Thu, Sat & Sun) gam.cl

Museo Nacional de Bellas Artes

F7 Palacio de Bellas Artes, Parque Forestal Bellas Artes 10am-6:30pm Tue-Sun mnba.cl

First established in 1880 as the Museo de Pintura Nacional and housed in the Parque Quinta Normal *(p88)*, the Museo Nacional de Bellas Artes is the oldest and one of the most important art museums in South America. The lovely palace in which it is housed today was built to celebrate Chile's centennial in 1910. It was designed by French-Chilean architect Emilio Jéquier, who created a French Neo-Classical edifice with Art-Nouveau details, including a facade modeled after the Petit Palais in Paris. In front of the museum is a large bronze sculpture by Chilean artist Rebeca Matte, *Unidos en la Gloria y la Muerte* (United in Glory and Death), from 1922.

The museum's collection numbers 2,700 works and is divided according to aesthetic, historic, and thematic criteria. Early works include colonial art – which principally centered on religious themes and the fusion of Spanish and Indigenous cultures; 19th-century paintings of landscapes; and portraits of major figures in Chilean history, the most famous of which are by José Gil de Castro. The most valuable paintings here are by Roberto Matta, the 20th-century Surrealist. Since 1990, the museum has drawn major traveling expositions from artists including Damien Hirst and David Hockney.

↑ Exhibits within Santiago's Museo de Arte Contemporáneo

27 

Museo de Arte Contemporáneo

F7 Palacio de Bellas Artes, Parque Forestal Bellas Artes 10:30am-5:30pm Tue-Sat mac.uchile.cl

The Museo de Arte Contemporáneo (MAC) is housed in the Palacio de Bellas Artes, but is accessed via a separate western entrance. The museum, along with its auxiliary branch at Parque Quinta Normal, features over 2,000 works in its permanent collection, and there are also monthly exhibits highlighting international and local artists. The collection features Latin American art, including works by members of Chilean artists' collective groups Generación del Trece and Grupo Signo. The influence of Europe in the creation of Chilean artwork is vividly apparent, though the art features Indigenous viewpoints. This is seen in the work of Chilean Hugo Marín, who has melded European technique with pre-Columbian influences. The grounds house a sculpture by famous Colombian artist Fernando Botero.

Iglesia de Santo Domingo

E7 Santo Domingo 961 Plaza de Armas iglesiadesantiago.cl

The present-day Iglesia de Santo Domingo is the fourth church of the Dominican Order to be built on this site. The existing building was designed by architect Juan de los Santos Vasconcelos. Its construction began in 1747 in a Doric Neo-Classical style that is distinct from other structures in downtown Santiago. In 1795–99, Italian architect Joaquín Toesca intervened to complete the church's interiors and added Bavarian Baroque brick towers. The church was finally inaugurated in 1808. Today, worshippers pray to the Virgin of Pompeii, whose statue occupies the central altar.

29   

Centro Cultural Estación Mapocho

D6 Plaza de la Cultura s/n, Balmaceda and Independencia Cal y Canto 11am-8pm daily estacionmapocho.cl

Now a cultural center, Estación Mapocho was built in 1913 as a grand terminal for trains that connected Santiago to northern Chile and Argentina. The station was designed by renowned French-Chilean architect Emilio Jéquier, who had studied in France and returned greatly influenced by the Beaux-Arts movement and the teachings of Gustave Eiffel, architect of Paris's Eiffel Tower. The Beaux-Arts style can be readily appreciated in the details of the station's stunning facade and the columns in the access hall. The station's vast steel roof and skeleton were produced in Belgium, and its interior vaults were designed by a Paris-based company. All were later shipped to Chile and assembled there.

Estación Mapocho was one of several public works projects to celebrate the country's centennial in 1910, and construction lasted from 1905 to 1912. It was declared a national monument in 1976. The station closed in 1987 when train services were suspended. Abandoned, the building fell into disrepair. Eventually, the government converted it into a cultural center, and it reopened as the Centro Cultural Estación Mapocho in 1994.

During the restoration, architects rescued the station's facade and preserved most of the edifice's ornate details, so visitors today can marvel at the splendor of its architecture and decor. The center now hosts all manner of events, including music concerts,

→ Packed restaurants in the beautiful Mercado Central

theater performances, and cinema. Many of the original salons have been converted into galleries, but the building is worth a visit in its own right.

The signature event at the center is the austral spring's Feria Internacional del Libro de Santiago. Held in October or November, this fortnight-long book fair attracts Chilean and foreign authors from throughout the Spanish-speaking world and beyond. See camaradellibro.cl for up-to-date information on forthcoming book fair events.

Posada del Corregidor

E7 Esmeralda 749 Bellas Artes 10am-1pm & 2-5pm Mon-Fri (book ahead) santiago cultura.cl

A national landmark dating from 1750, the Posada del Corregidor is one of the few colonial adobe buildings left in Santiago. Its thick walls, stone foundations, and second-story wraparound balcony are outstanding examples of urban architecture in 18th-century Chile. In the 1920s, the *posada* became a social center for Santiago's bohemian set.

Today, it operates as an art gallery featuring exhibits of emerging artists, but it once served as a dance hall of dubious reputation known as the Filarmónica. The *posada* suffered significant damage in the 2010 earthquake, but has since been restored.

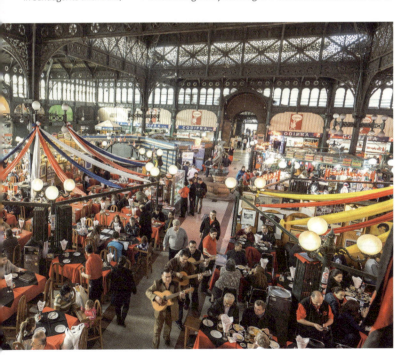 

Mercado Central

E6 San Pablo 967 7:30am-5pm daily (to 8pm Fri & to 7pm Sat)

Built in 1872 for the National Exposition in Chile, Mercado Central (Central Market) stands on the site of the burned ruins of Plaza de Abastos, which had been set up in the early 1800s. Designed by self-taught architect Fermín Vivaceta, the market is considered one of the most beautiful public structures of its era.

After the 1872 Exposition, Mercado Central became Santiago's major wholesale fish and vegetable market. Although it has since moved elsewhere, the Mercado is still an important commercial center. It is popular with both locals, who come to see and buy fresh produce, and tourists, who visit to eat lunch at one of its many atmospheric seafood restaurants. The Mercado Central was declared a national monument in 1984 .

HIDDEN GEM
Empanadas

If you're heading for the Mercado Central, and hankering for an empanada, try Zunino. The family business has been running since 1930 and they've perfected their recipe *(emporiozunino.cl)*.

A SHORT WALK
PLAZA DE ARMAS

Distance 1 mile (1.5 km) **Time** 20 minutes
Nearest subway Bellas Artes

The symbolic heart of Santiago, the Plaza de Armas (Arms Plaza) was designed to suit the Spanish norm of leaving one block of a city grid empty for use as a parade ground. Government offices ringed the plaza during the colonial years, and in the 17th century it became a thriving commercial area with shopping galleries stretching around the perimeter. In 2000, the square was cleared to create more open spaces. Today, it is a vibrant social center, drawing people who come here to rest on park benches, play chess, or enjoy the lively atmosphere and street performances.

The venerable **Ex Congreso Nacional** *(p70) edifice was constructed between 1858 and 1876 in the Neo-Classical style, with striking Corinthian columns.*

Chile's Supreme Court, **Palacio de los Tribunales de Justicia** *(p71), occupies a Neo-Classical building with French influences. Its vaulted glass-and-metal ceiling runs the length of the edifice.*

Housed in the Palacio de la Real Aduana, the **Museo Chileno de Arte Precolombino** *(p66) highlights the arts and symbols of pre-Columbian cultures in the Americas.*

Paseos Ahumada *and* **Huérfanos** *are lined with shopping malls, cafés, and restaurants.*

←
Neo-Classical facade of Palacio de los Tribunales de Justicia

↑ The vibrant colors and lively atmosphere of Plaza de Armas

Locator Map

For more detail see p64

Consecrated in 1775, **Catedral Metropolitana** (p68) *is the fourth church to be built on this site. It was designed by Jesuits, but received a Neo-Classical makeover from 1780 to 1789.*

Chile's **Correo Central** *(Post Office,* p68*) occupies a French Neo-Classical edifice built in 1882 on the site of Pedro de Valdivia's residence.*

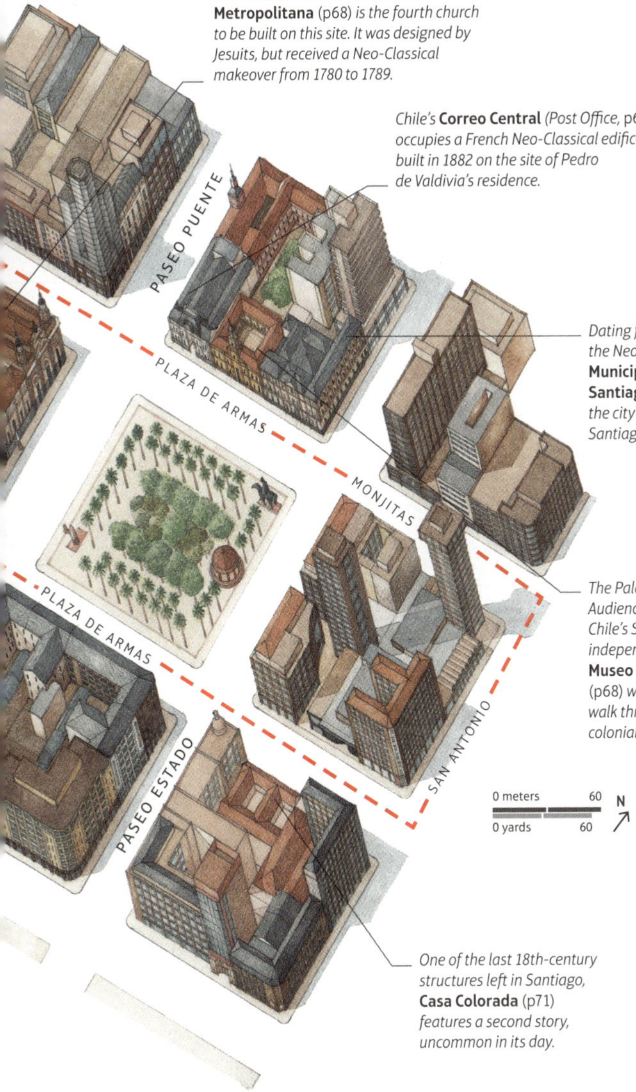

Dating from 1785, the Neo-Classical **Municipalidad de Santiago** (p69) *served as the city jail before housing Santiago's municipality.*

The Palacio de la Real Audiencia served as Chile's Supreme Court until independence in 1810. The **Museo Histórico Nacional** (p68) *within offers a walk through Santiago's colonial past.*

One of the last 18th-century structures left in Santiago, **Casa Colorada** (p71) *features a second story, uncommon in its day.*

Street artist Payo's work on display in Brasil neighborhood

WEST OF SANTIAGO CENTRO

Stretching west from Santiago Centro to verdant Parque Quinta Normal are some of the city's oldest residential neighborhoods, notably *barrios* Brasil, Concha y Toro, Yungay, and Dieciocho. This was once where the city's wealthier classes lived, as the opulent Neo-Classical and French-style *palacios* on and around the Alameda testify. As the 20th century wore on, however, the area fell into serious decline, as many residents decided to leave for the fast-developing, more suburban neighborhoods northeast of the city center. Over the last 20 years, the situation has changed. The area has become increasingly gentrified, with *barrios* such as Brasil and Yungay now among the hippest in the city.

Few Spanish-era buildings have survived, but there is an array of handsome 19th- and early-20th-century architecture, much of it rebuilt and home to various restaurants, bars, and boutique hotels. Founded in 1841 to cultivate a variety of plants, the Parque Quinta Normal now provides an open green space for visitors to relax in the heart of the city.

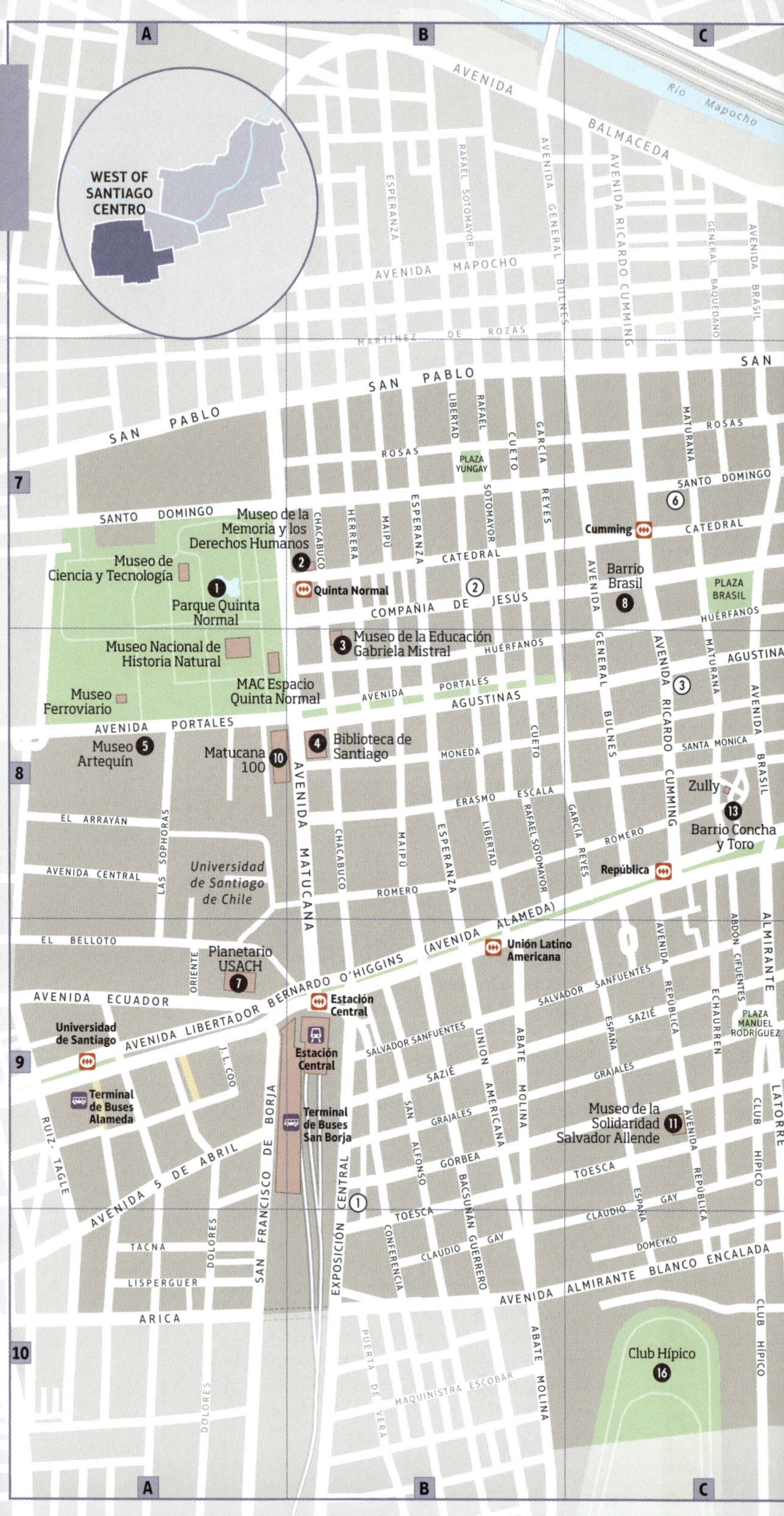

WEST OF SANTIAGO CENTRO
Museo de la Memoria y los Derechos Humanos
Museo de Ciencia y Tecnología
Parque Quinta Normal
Quinta Normal
Museo de la Educación Gabriela Mistral
Museo Nacional de Historia Natural
MAC Espacio Quinta Normal
Museo Ferroviario
Museo Artequín
Matucana 100
Biblioteca de Santiago
Universidad de Santiago de Chile
Planetario USACH
Estación Central
Universidad de Santiago
Terminal de Buses Alameda
Terminal de Buses San Borja
Unión Latino Americana
República
Cumming
Barrio Brasil
Plaza Brasil
Zully
Barrio Concha y Toro
Plaza Manuel Rodríguez
Museo de la Solidaridad Salvador Allende
Club Hípico
Plaza Yungay
Río Mapocho
Avenida Balmaceda
Avenida Mapocho
Martínez de Rozas
San Pablo
Rosas
Santo Domingo
Catedral
Compañía de Jesús
Huérfanos
Agustinas
Avenida Portales
Moneda
Santa Monica
Erasmo Escala
Romero
El Arrayán
Avenida Central
El Belloto
Avenida Ecuador
Avenida Libertador Bernardo O'Higgins (Avenida Alameda)
Avenida 5 de Abril
Salvador Sanfuentes
Sazié
Grajales
Gorbea
Toesca
Claudio Gay
Domeyko
Avenida Almirante Blanco Encalada
Maquinista Escobar
Tacna
Lisperguer
Arica
Avenida Matucana
Avenida Ricardo Cumming
Avenida General Bulnes
Avenida Brasil
Exposición Central
San Francisco de Borja
Abate Molina
Club Hípico
Almirante Latorre
Echaurren
Abdón Cifuentes
Chacabuco
Herrera
Maipú
Esperanza
Libertad
Rafael Sotomayor
Cueto
García Reyes
Maturana
General Baquedano
Las Sophoras
Oriente
J. L. Coo
Ruiz-Tagle
Dolores
San Alfonso
Conferencia
Bacsuñán Guerrero
Unión Americana
España
Avenida República
Puerta de Vera
A
B
C
7
8
9
10

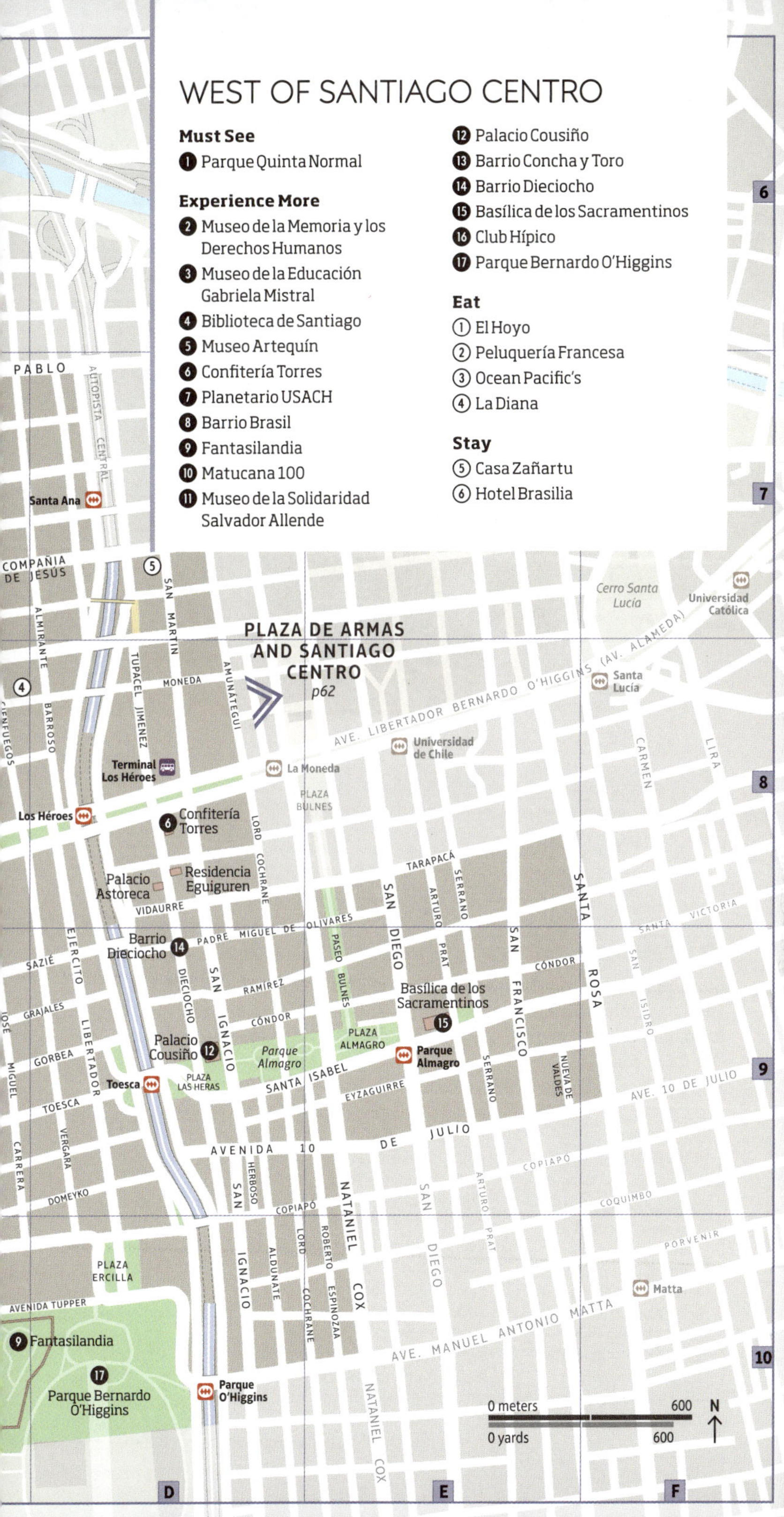

WEST OF SANTIAGO CENTRO
Must See
1 Parque Quinta Normal
Experience More
2 Museo de la Memoria y los Derechos Humanos
3 Museo de la Educación Gabriela Mistral
4 Biblioteca de Santiago
5 Museo Artequín
6 Confitería Torres
7 Planetario USACH
8 Barrio Brasil
9 Fantasilandia
10 Matucana 100
11 Museo de la Solidaridad Salvador Allende
12 Palacio Cousiño
13 Barrio Concha y Toro
14 Barrio Dieciocho
15 Basílica de los Sacramentinos
16 Club Hípico
17 Parque Bernardo O'Higgins
Eat
① El Hoyo
② Peluquería Francesa
③ Ocean Pacific's
④ La Diana
Stay
⑤ Casa Zañartu
⑥ Hotel Brasilia
PLAZA DE ARMAS AND SANTIAGO CENTRO
p62
Santa Ana
Terminal Los Héroes
Los Héroes
La Moneda
Universidad de Chile
Santa Lucía
Universidad Católica
Cerro Santa Lucía
Confitería Torres
Palacio Astoreca
Residencia Eguiguren
Barrio Dieciocho
Palacio Cousiño
Basílica de los Sacramentinos
Parque Almagro
Plaza Almagro
Toesca
Plaza Las Heras
Plaza Bulnes
Plaza Ercilla
Fantasilandia
Parque Bernardo O'Higgins
Parque O'Higgins
Matta
AVE. LIBERTADOR BERNARDO O'HIGGINS (AV. ALAMEDA)
AVENIDA 10 DE JULIO
AVE. 10 DE JULIO
AVE. MANUEL ANTONIO MATTA
AVENIDA TUPPER
0 meters 600
0 yards 600
N
6
7
8
9
10
D
E
F

Colorful pedal boats at the lake in Parque Quinta Normal

1

PARQUE QUINTA NORMAL

A7 Avenida Matucana 520 (02) 2689 0119 7am–8:30pm Tue–Sun

Stroll alongside beautiful trees, take a pedal boat around an artificial lake, picnic on expansive lawns, explore fascinating museums, or listen to soapbox rants – experience all this and so much more at Parque Quinta Normal.

HISTORY IN THE PARK

Quinta Normal has long been associated with learning. It hosted the Chilean International Exhibition in 1875–76, an event that featured scientific, artistic, and agricultural exhibits. One venue built for the fair was turned into the Museo Nacional de Historia Natural.

Set up in 1842 to propagate foreign plants, Parque Quinta Normal is famous for its wide number of tree species. Many of the different varieties of trees were planted by French naturalist Claudio Gay, whose extensive pioneering studies of Chilean flora and fauna gave birth to the city's Museo Nacional de Historia Natural and to the actual park itself. In its early years, Parque Quinta Normal was also used for agricultural studies and in 1928 it was incorporated into the University of Chile as the School of Agronomy and Veterinary Sciences. Today, the park is only a mere fraction of its earlier size, but it nonetheless remains popular owing to its large and expansive lawns, and its mature and beautiful trees. The park is also home to a handful of scientific museums, an art museum, picnic areas, and an artificial lake. In the summer months, it's quite common for the residents of Santiago to enjoy barbecues at the standing grills located at the back of the park.

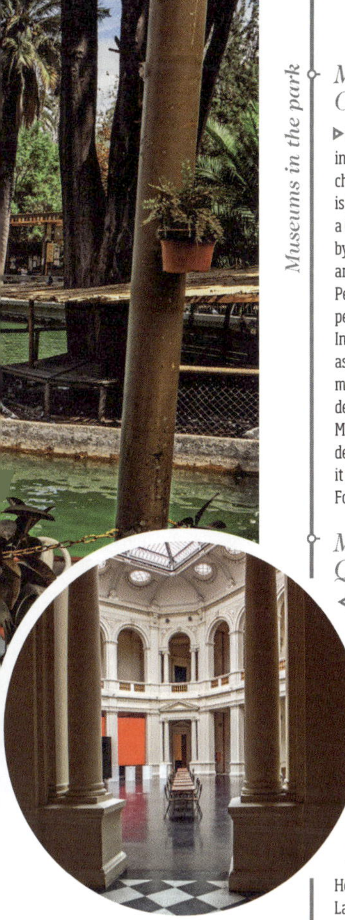

Museo de Ciencia y Tecnología

▶ Set up in 1985, the Museo de Ciencia y Tecnología was the first interactive museum in Chile designed to engage children in science and technology. The museum is housed in a building called the Parthenon, a Greco-Roman-style edifice built in 1884 by Naples-born artist Alejandro Cicarelli and inaugurated by Chilean painter Pedro Lira, who sought to create a permanent exhibition hall for art. Interactive displays are offered on astronomy, geology, technology, and many more subjects. In 1887, the Unión de Arte opened the city's first Fine Arts Museum here. It later became the Museo de Arte Contemporáneo (MAC), then in 1974 it was transferred to its current location in Parque Forestal, in the center of Santiago.

MAC Espacio Quinta Normal

◀ Housed in the Neo-Classical Palacio Versailles, built in the early 1900s, and declared a national monument in 2004, Espacio Quinta Normal is a branch of MAC *(p80)*. In 2005, MAC briefly relocated here while its salons in the Palacio de Bellas Artes were renovated. Since then, this building has been retained by MAC for shows. With 12 spacious salons surrounding a central plaza, the museum hosts large expositions of up-and-coming national artists and large international expositions such as Germany's Fluxus and the São Paulo Biennial.

Museo Ferroviario

Housing one of the most important collections of steam locomotives in Latin America, the Museo Ferroviario is spread across 5 acres (2 ha) in the southwest corner of the Quinta Normal. On display are 16 locomotives and three wagons. Locomotive type 20, made by the now defunct Sociedad de Maestranza y Galvanizaciones from Caleta Abarca, is a pristine example of a locally built machine. Also on display is a Kitson-Meyer locomotive built in 1909 in Leeds, UK. This served the Ferrocarril Transandino that, until 1971, connected Los Andes *(p135)* in Chile with Mendoza in Argentina - a distance of 154 miles (248 km) across the precarious peaks of the Andes. In all, there were nine locomotives used for the Andean passage, of which only two remain. Visitors can also view the restored 1923 presidential carriage used by former presidents Arturo Alessandri (1868-1950) and Carlos Ibáñez del Campo (1877-1960).

Museo Nacional de Historia Natural

▶ Santiago's museum of natural history was built in 1875 for the city's first International Exposition. The main hall is dominated by the skeleton of a juvenile fin whale. Displays are divided into 12 categories, including insects and flora. There is a salon dedicated to the native forests of Chile, with wood slabs showing the age of such giants as alerce, the world's second-oldest tree. The building was restored after it was damaged in the 2010 earthquake.

TOP 3 ACTIVITIES FOR KIDS

Museo de Ciencia y Tecnología
Offers plenty of child-friendly, hands-on exhibits, experiments, and activities.

Pedal Boats
Rent one of the retro pedal-powered boats and head out for an adventure on the lake.

Open-Air Pools
Go for a swim in the park's open-air *piscina* (swimming pool) or splash around in the fountains.

EXPERIENCE MORE

Museo de la Memoria y los Derechos Humanos

B7 Matucana 501 Quinta Normal 10am-6pm Tue-Sun mmdh.cl

The Museum of Memory and Human Rights opened in 2010 as a memorial to the victims of Chile's brutal military dictatorship (1973–90), during which an estimated 3,000 people were killed or "disappeared," and many others were tortured, detained, or exiled. Among the items on display are personal letters, official documents, and government propaganda, alongside information on torture methods and some of the implements used, offering grisly testimony to the horrors of the time, as well as the historical background that led to the rise of the dictatorship.

The vast, spacious glass building utilizes its interior for multimedia exhibits on the notorious regime and its survivors, with the objective of encouraging reflection and debate on human rights. Although sobering, a visit here is essential for anyone who wants to gain an understanding of Chile's past and present.

Museo de la Educación Gabriela Mistral

B8 Compañía 3150 Quinta Normal 10am-5pm Mon-Fri, 10am-4pm Sat museodelaeducacion.gob.cl

Housed in the Escuela Normal Brígada Walker, the Museo de la Educación Gabriela Mistral tracks the history and development of education in Chile. The museum is named for Nobel laureate and literary artist Gabriela Mistral *(p38)*, who was an educator throughout most of her life in spite of having left school at the age of 12. Self-taught and born with a natural verbal dexterity, Mistral became an advocate for education in response to the lack of opportunities for schooling in Chile.

This education museum was launched in 1941 as an exposition by the Museo Nacional de Bellas Artes *(p79)* to celebrate Santiago's 400th anniversary. Its exhibitions explored the history of education from the colonial period onward. Following the popular success of the exposition, director Carlos Stuardo combed through grade schools and even industrial and mining schools in search of material and furniture to establish a permanent collection. Today, the exhibits consist of more than 6,500 historical pieces, including antique maps, school desks, skills-based teaching apparatus such as sewing machines, abacuses, and more. There is also an extensive library of some 40,000 texts covering education, as well as a photo library of 6,000 digitalized images that track the history of education in the country.

↑ Examining an exhibit at the Museo de la Memoria y los Derechos Humanos

↑ The colorful Pabellón París, housing the cool Museo Artequín

Biblioteca de Santiago

B8 Avenida Matucana 151 Quinta Normal 11am-7:15pm Tue-Fri, 11:30am-5pm Sat & Sun bibliotecasantiago.cl

Opened in 2005, this was Chile's first major public library. It was built near Quinta Normal *(p88)* in an effort to create a center of cultural and educational development. Housed in a 1930s warehouse, the Biblioteca has given the people of Santiago access to a vast range of literature, lectures, and children's books.

Museo Artequín

A8 Avenida Portales 3530 Quinta Normal 9am-2pm Mon, 9am-5pm Tue-Fri, 11am-6pm Sat & Sun Feb artequin.cl

This offbeat museum features reproductions of the world's greatest painters. It is located in the gorgeous Pabellón París, which was designed to represent Chile at the 1889 Universal Exposition in Paris. The Pabellón's Art-Nouveau facade and interiors are the work of French architect Henri Picq, who used iron, steel, and zinc in a clear reference to the Industrial Revolution. Built in Paris, taken apart, and then reassembled at Parque Quinta Normal, the Pabellón housed a museum, and also featured works by contemporary figures such as writer and artist Pedro Lira (1845–1912). It became a national monument in 1986, and in 1992, the Pabellón was rebuilt and reopened as the present-day Museo Artequín. The purpose of the museum is to inspire and educate visitors about art through physical copies of the world's best paintings. On display are prints of some of the world's greatest artists, each represented by a piece for which he or she is best known. Among the most recognizable international names are Goya, Dalí, Kahlo, and Kandinsky.

> **The Biblioteca has given the people of Santiago access to a vast range of literature, lectures, and children's books.**

EAT

El Hoyo

This restaurant may look modest, but it delivers delicious dishes. To drink, try the *terremoto* (earthquake), a potent Chilean cocktail mix of white wine and pineapple ice cream served in a glass pitcher.

B9 San Vicente 375 Sun elhoyo.cl

Peluquería Francesa

A restaurant with an attached barbershop sounds unlikely, but it works at Peluquería Francesa. The menu has specialties such as *confit de pato a la naranja* (orange duck confit), and there's often live music, too.

B7 Compañía 2789 Mon peluqueríafrancesa.com

$$$

Ocean Pacific's

Decked out with maritime memorabilia and waiters dressed as sailors, Ocean Pacific's serves delicious fish and seafood. The restaurant can get very busy, so try to book ahead.

C8 Agustinas 2267 oceanpacifics.cl

$$$

La Diana

This kitschy restaurant specializes in seafood. It adjoins an iconic amusement arcade.

C8 Arturo Prat 435 ladiana.cl

$$

↑ White tablecloths and a checkered floor inside the Confitería Torres

6  

Confitería Torres

D8 Avenida Alameda 1570 Quinta Normal 10am–8pm Mon–Wed, 10am–9pm Thu & Fri confiteriatorres.cl

The Confitería Torres opened in 1879 and is Santiago's oldest café. Located close to the government buildings of the Palacio de la Moneda *(p72)*, the café served the capital's politicians, intellectuals, and elite society when the Barrio Dieciocho area was still considered fashionable. After a period of declining popularity, lengthy restoration began in 2002, which salvaged the old red-leather booths, French doors, and long oak bar, and the café reopened in 2004 with its antique ambience still quite palpable. The Confitería has produced several emblematic elements of Chile's culinary repertoire. Perhaps the most famous item on the café's menu is the *barros luco*, a beef sandwich with melted cheese that is named after former president Ramón Barros Luco, who ordered one every time he visited. The *cola de mono* aperitif of alcoholic *aguardiente*, with milk and coffee was also invented here. The restaurant can be particularly popular at lunchtime, so it's best to book in advance.

7  

Planetario USACH

A9 Avenida Alameda 3349, Estación Central Estación Central 11am–5pm Tue–Sun planetariochile.cl

The University of Santiago's planetarium is one of Latin America's most prominent astronomy education centers. Its projection dome, the Sala Albert Einstein, has an unusual conical design. Made of copper, it is 72 ft (22 m) in diameter, and has a Carl Zeiss model VI projector that uses 160 lenses, allowing visitors to observe the moon and the solar system, and over 5,000 stars in both hemispheres. Of particular interest are the special expositions that highlight discoveries by Chile's top astronomical observatories. The planetarium offers workshops, audiovisual salons, and exhibitions for both children and adults.

Barrio Brasil

C7 Cumming, Santa Ana

During the early 20th century, Barrio Brasil was a posh residential neighborhood. By the 1940s, wealthy residents began migrating eastward, toward the Andes. Later, the construction of the Norte-Sur Highway severed the neighborhood from the rest of the city, and Barrio Brasil was by and large forgotten. Thanks to this, the area escaped development and many of its grand early 20th-century Gothic and Neo-Classical mansions have been left intact. As a result, Barrio Brasil is now one of the most picturesque areas in Santiago. It has also experienced a cultural and architectural resurgence, due to the presence of many universities nearby. Artists and musicians have moved in, drawn by the neighborhood's eclectic ambience. Today, trendy lofts and funky restaurants sit alongside traditional *picadas* and bars.

The streets of nearby Barrio Yungay are especially well preserved, with two of the most beautiful being Pasaje Adriana Cousiño

Pool floats taking visitors up on a slide in Fantasilandia

between Huérfanos and Maipú, and Pasaje Lucrecia Valdés off Compañía between Esperanza and Maipú. Both are cobblestone walkways that exude a strong European feel. Other vestiges of Barrio Yungay's past can be seen at the restaurant Peluquería Francesa *(p91)*.

Fantasilandia

C10 Beaucheff 938
Parque O'Higgins
Noon-8pm daily
fantasilandia.cl

The third-largest amusement park in South America, Fantasilandia is sometimes dubbed the Chilean Disneyland. It opened in 1978 as the brainchild of entrepreneur Gerardo Arteaga, who felt that Santiago had grown insufferably boring for families who were seeking amusement during their spare time.

The park offers plenty of knee-trembling rollercoasters and stomach-churning rides such as Xtreme Fall, Raptor, and Boomerang. There are also more tranquil attractions for younger children, including a carousel, the Kids' Zone, and water attractions like the Mini Splash ride. The amusement park is set in lush green surroundings and a variety of dining options are available.

Matucana 100

A8 Avenida Matucana 100, Estación Central
Quinta Normal 10am-5pm Mon-Fri (performance times vary, check website)
m100.cl

Matucana 100 is set in a huge brick warehouse built in 1911 for the state railroad company. The gallery was designed in 2001 to create a space in which a variety of art forms could participate simultaneously – whether cinema, theater, artwork, photography, or music. Over time, the center has grown to include a large art gallery and a concert hall. It now focuses solely on contemporary works principally by national artists.

TOP 5 RIDES AT FANTASILANDIA

Tsunami
You'll definitely get soaked on this giant wave-themed ride.

Boomerang
A stomach-churning rollercoaster that features a "cobra roll" and a "vertical loop."

Xtreme Fall
This ride lifts you up to a great height, lets you stew for a few moments, and then plunges you back to earth.

Kamikaze
Passengers are spun back and forth to build up momentum before some 360-degree spins.

Raptor
A classic, fast-paced rollercoaster with multiple loops.

11 

Museo de la Solidaridad Salvador Allende

C9 República 475 República 10am-6pm Tue-Fri, 11am-6pm Sat & Sun mssa.cl

Set in the former headquarters of DINA, the secret police during the Pinochet military dictatorship *(p48)*, the Museo de la Solidaridad is the only museum in Latin America that consists entirely of works donated by artists. In an act of solidarity with the government of Salvador Allende *(p48)*, artists in 1971 founded this museum with a collection of more than 400 pieces by such names as Joan Miró, Alexander Calder, Víctor Vasarely, and Roberto Matta. After Salvador Allende was overthrown in the 1973 coup d'état, however, the works were hidden in the Museo de Arte Contemporáneo *(p80)*. The museum's administration moved to Paris, where artists continued to donate until the collection reached some 1,500 pieces. The works date from 1950 to 1980, and many of them evoke the social struggle of Latin Americans. In 2005 the Fundación Allende bought and remodeled this townhouse, where the works are now displayed.

12  

Palacio Cousiño

D9 Calle Dieciocho 438 Toesca 9:30am-4:30pm Tue-Fri, 10am-1pm Sat (book ahead) santiagocultura.cl/palacio-cousino

Built between 1870 and 1878, the Palacio Cousiño was Santiago's most extravagant mansion of the day. It was designed by French architect Paul Lathoud for the Cousiño family, who had made a fortune in mining and shipping. The Cousiños imported many of their materials from Europe: walnut and mahogany parquet floors, brocade tapestries, Italian marble, and French embroidered curtains. They also employed some European artisans to install these fineries.

The mansion also housed the country's first electric fittings and included the first elevator in Chile. The palace was auctioned off to Santiago's mayor in 1940, who donated it to the city. Subsequently, the building was used to house visiting dignitaries such as Golda Meir, Charles de Gaulle, and Belgian king Baudouin. In 1968, the mansion was converted into a museum, which preserved the house as it was during the 19th century.

Following the restorations after the 2010 earthquake, Palacio Cousiño is now

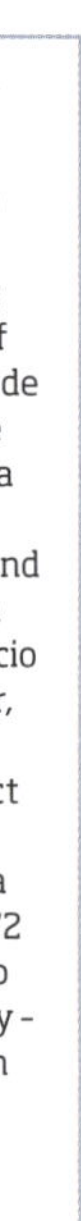

CITY CENTER PALACIOS

As well as the Palacio Cousiño, there are several other historic *palacios* in this part of Santiago. These include Edificio Íñiguez at the corner of the Alameda and Calle Dieciocho, which dates to 1908 and houses the Confitería Torres *(p92)*. The Palacio Irarrázabal, next door, was built two years later and has a distinct French style. Palacio Errázuriz, at Alameda 1656, was built in 1872 and was once home to the Brazilian embassy - extensive restoration work has returned the palace to its former glory.

restored and holds exhibitions throughout the year. The palace's former wine cellar also functions as a gallery for temporary exhibitions.

Barrio Concha y Toro

C8 República

Dating from the 1920s, Barrio Concha y Toro is one of Santiago's best-preserved neighborhoods, comprising mansions built by the flourishing upper class in the early 20th century. The area was initially owned by engineer-entrepreneur Enrique Concha y Toro and his wife Teresa Cazotte, who reaped a fortune in mining in the late 1800s. They sought to replicate European towns with sinuous cobblestone streets, closely grouped buildings behind a continual facade, and a plaza. The best Chilean architects of the time – Larraín Bravo, Siegel, González Cortés, Machiacao, and Bianchi – were entrusted with the design. They created a cohesive style that incorporated influences such as Neo-Gothic, Neo-Classical, Baroque, and even Bauhaus. Highlights include the Teatro Carrera, built in 1926 by Gustavo Monckeberg. The former home of poet Vicente Huidobro can also be found here. The picturesque Plazoleta de la Libertad de Prensa, often used as a set for television productions, was named in 1994 in honor of the World Press Freedom Day.

Barrio Dieciocho

D9 Los Héroes

During the turn of the 20th century, Santiago's upscale neighborhood was centered around Calle Dieciocho. Wealthy families erected opulent mansions here as a means of flaunting their new-found fortunes from shipping and mining. The constructions clearly reflect the influence of European styles, principally French.

Santiago's elite has since moved uptown but the architectural gems their ancestors built can still be seen, in spite of the fact that the neighborhood now looks a little worse for wear. Among its best are the Subercaseaux Mansion at No. 190, Residencia Eguiguren at No. 102, and the Palacio Astoreca at No. 121. The grand buildings are now occupied by university groups, libraries, and other similar associations.

Did You Know?

In the 16th century Santiago comprised just 200 houses, and only became a city 200 years later.

↓ The stately exterior of Palacio Cousiño, and *(inset)* the intricate detail of the gate

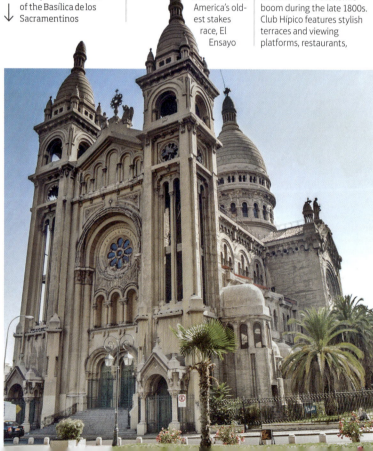

Basílica de los Sacramentinos

E9 Arturo Prat 485 (02) 2638 3189 Toesca 10am-7pm daily

Designed by architect Ricardo Larraín Bravo, the Basílica de los Sacramentinos was built as an imitation of the Sacré-Coeur in Paris, between 1919 and 1931. The church is notable for its Roman Byzantine architecture and a 4,925-ft- (1,500-m-) long burial chamber that runs underneath. The parquet floors are the first of their kind to be made in Chile. The wooden pulpit, confessionals, and seats were all hand-carved by Salesians, a Roman Catholic order. Also of interest are the French stained glass and the organ, which was imported from Germany. The church suffered significant damage in the 2010 earthquake, but has since been restored. The exterior is also striking, and made more pleasant by Parque Almagro, which stretches out before it.

Club Hípico

C10 Avenida Almirante Blanco Encalada 2540 Unión Latinoamericana For races; schedules vary, check website clubhipico.cl

Founded in 1870, Club Hípico is Chile's preeminent racetrack and home to South America's oldest stakes race, El Ensayo *(p42)*, which takes place in late October/early November every year. It is part of the Triple Corona together with Hipódromo Chile and Valparaíso Derby.

The current racetrack was designed by architect Josué Smith and opened in 1923, the previous track house having succumbed to fire in 1892. The club building is a fine example of early 20th-century architectural grandeur, a result of Chile's economic boom during the late 1800s. Club Hípico features stylish terraces and viewing platforms, restaurants,

Did You Know?

An unknown species of dinosaur was discovered in Santiago in 2015, and named the "Chilesaurus."

↓ The splendid exterior of the Basílica de los Sacramentinos

formal gardens, and a picnic area, set amid the faded elegance of the old República neighborhood. In the distance, the looming bulk of the Andes provides a backdrop to the racetrack.

In total, there are about 1,500 races held here annually, including the famed Alberto Vial Infante and the Arturo Lyon Peña. The club has also hosted major music concerts, including performances by Iron Maiden and Linkin Park. Despite the racetrack's roots as an elite social club, it is now visited by people from all backgrounds.

↑ Pedaling along one of the wide avenues in Parque Bernardo O'Higgins

Parque Bernardo O'Higgins

D10 Between Avenida Beaucheff & Autopista Central Parque O'Higgins 9am-8pm daily

The capital's second-largest park is a popular recreation area for families and a major staging area for the Fiestas Patrias celebrations *(p42)*. The park was inaugurated in 1873, at which time it was originally named Parque Cousiño after the Chilean millionaire Luis Cousiño who commissioned it. Some 100 years later the park's name was changed to honor Bernardo O'Higgins, one of Chile's founding fathers. Sprawling Parque Bernardo O'Higgins is home to a skate park, picnic areas, tennis courts, soccer fields, an artificial lake, Santiago's largest indoor music stadium, and a public pool. Perhaps the most curious aspect of the park is the Campo de Marte, a gigantic strip of concrete that resembles a landing strip. Military parades take place here every September 19 – known as the Day of the Glories of the Army – which draw thousands of spectators.

Among the park's attractions is El Pueblito, a mock Spanish-era village. There is also a museum located here. The Museo de Insectos y Caracoles houses a collection of butterfly and insect displays. There are also artisan workshops and fairs held here. During the Fiestas Patrias, the grounds are bloated to capacity with revelers who come for the *fondas*, or festival centers tents – a hallmark of this popular park. For days, a veritable patriotic bacchanal takes over the park with non-stop *cueca* music, smoking barbecues, and excessive drinking. The park also hosted Lollapalooza Chile for several years – a hugely busy event and the first version of the popular Chicagoan festival to take place outside the United States. The event has since moved to Parque Bicentenario *(p111)*.

Sprawling Parque Bernardo O'Higgins is home to tennis courts, soccer fields, an artificial lake, Santiago's largest indoor music stadium, and a public pool.

STAY

Casa Zañartu

This swish hotel is housed in an attractive 19th-century mansion that belonged to Don Miguel Zañartu, a signatory of the Chilean declaration of independence. It has large bedrooms, original tiled floors, a shaded patio, and antique furniture. The location in the hip Barrio Brasil neighborhood is excellent.

D7 Compañía de Jesús 1520 casazanartu.cl

Hotel Brasilia

This hotel makes for a comfortable stay with its modern bedrooms, ample parking, and great location in the heart of Barrio Brasil.

C7 2228 Santo Domingo hotel brasiliasantiago.com-hotel.com

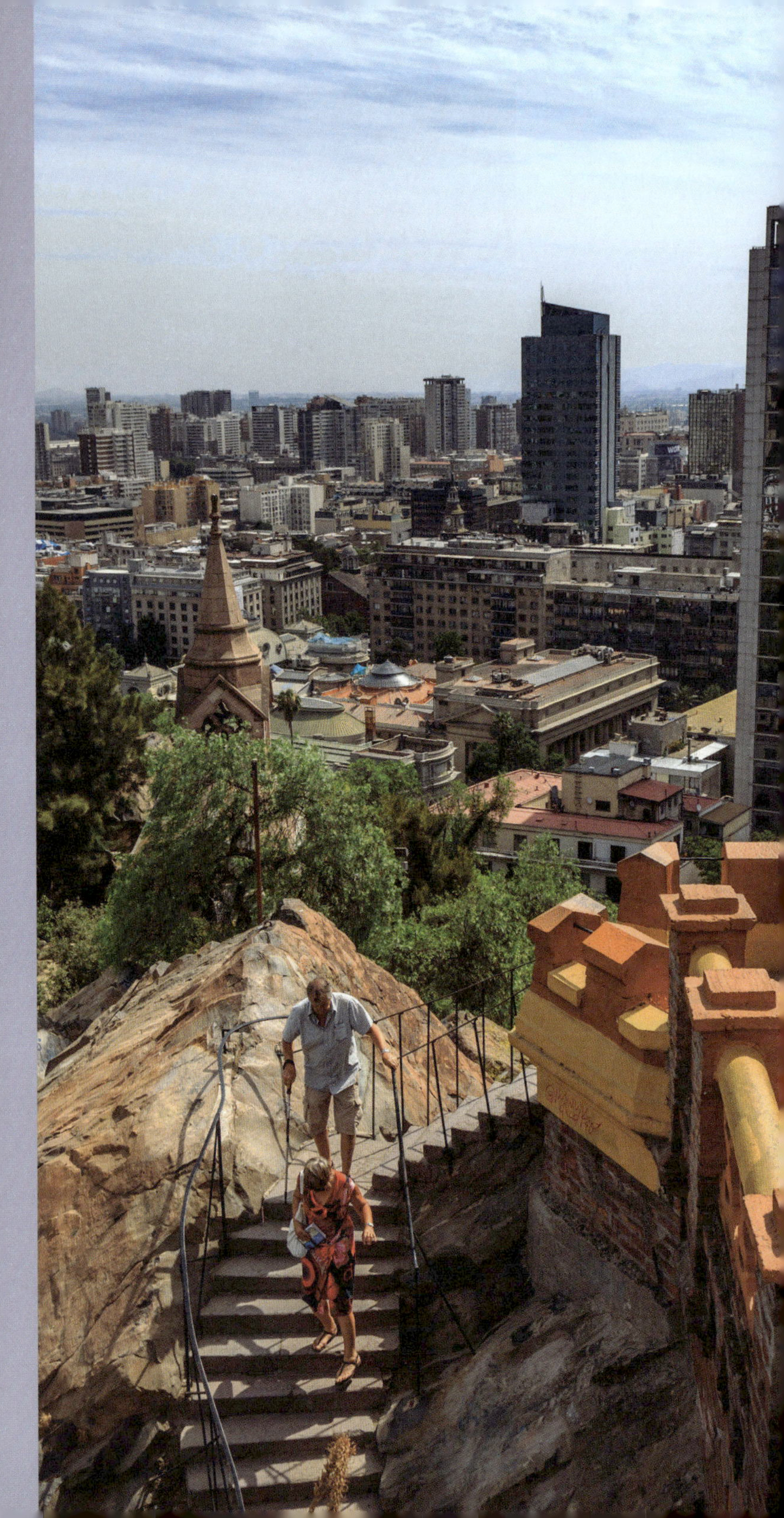

Northeast Santiago as seen from the Santa Lucía hill

NORTHEAST OF SANTIAGO CENTRO

For the first 400 years of Santiago's existence, the area northeast of the city center was largely undeveloped, home to only a scattering of country houses surrounded by large plots of land, as well as a number of more deprived areas. Things started to change in the 1950s, as Santiago's population grew and many middle- and upper-class residents abandoned neighborhoods like Brasil, Concha y Toro, and Yungay, and headed toward the foothills of the Andes. They settled first in Providencia – which includes the alternative Barrio Bellavista at the foot of Cerro San Cristóbal – and slowly pushed east. Today, leafy Providencia has a thriving dining scene and an exciting selection of buzzing bars, though it is relatively short on tourist attractions. To the northeast are the skyscrapers of Las Condes, home to the city's financial district,high-end restaurants, and luxury apartments, while to the north is the similarly exclusive but more residential neighborhood of Vitacura.

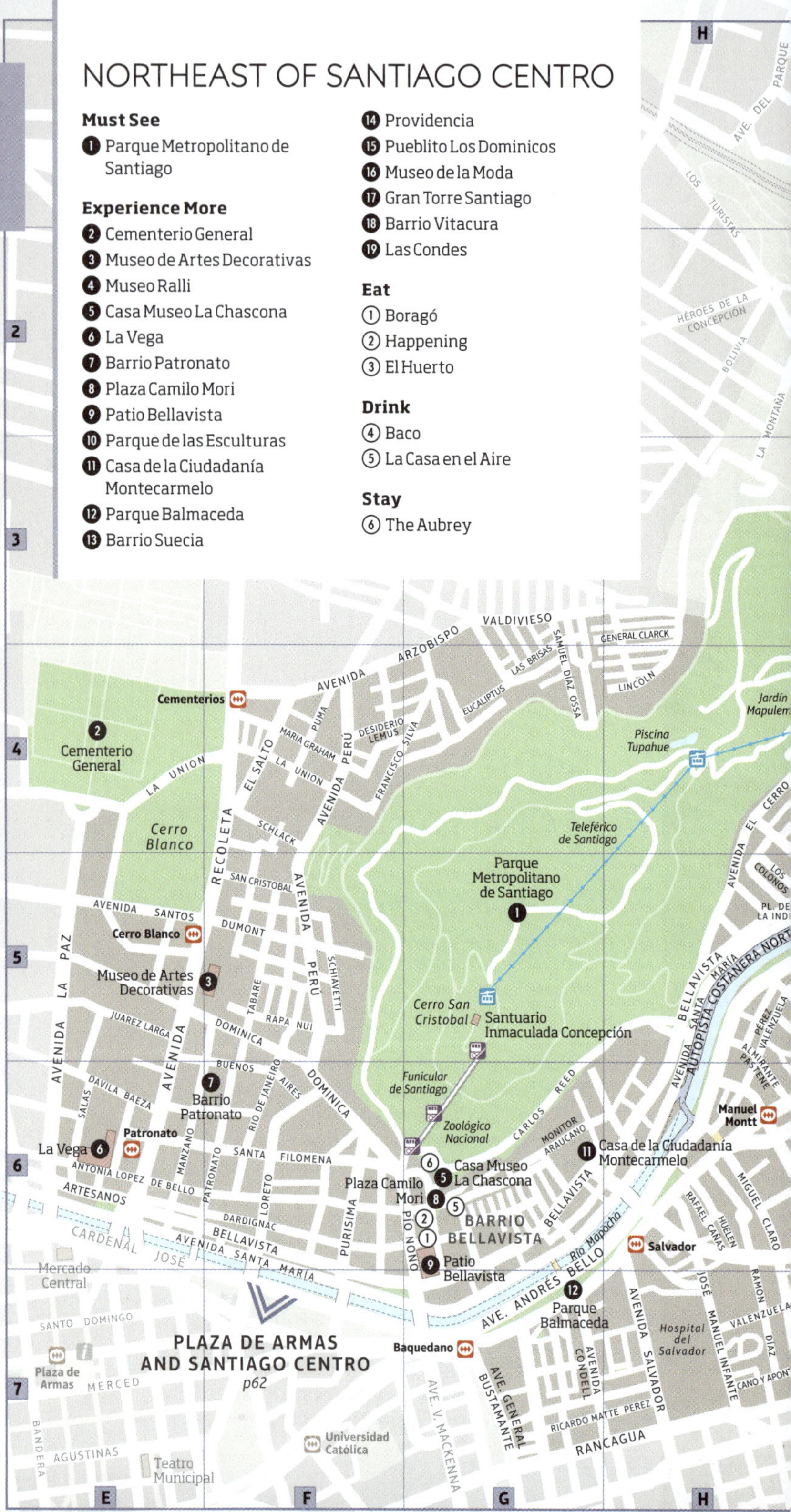
NORTHEAST OF SANTIAGO CENTRO
Must See
1 Parque Metropolitano de Santiago
Experience More
2 Cementerio General
3 Museo de Artes Decorativas
4 Museo Ralli
5 Casa Museo La Chascona
6 La Vega
7 Barrio Patronato
8 Plaza Camilo Mori
9 Patio Bellavista
10 Parque de las Esculturas
11 Casa de la Ciudadanía Montecarmelo
12 Parque Balmaceda
13 Barrio Suecia
14 Providencia
15 Pueblito Los Dominicos
16 Museo de la Moda
17 Gran Torre Santiago
18 Barrio Vitacura
19 Las Condes
Eat
① Boragó
② Happening
③ El Huerto
Drink
④ Baco
⑤ La Casa en el Aire
Stay
⑥ The Aubrey
H
2
3
4
5
6
7
E
F
G
AVE. DEL PARQUE
LOS TURISTAS
HÉROES DE LA CONCEPCIÓN
BOLIVIA
LA MONTAÑA
VALDIVIESO
AVENIDA ARZOBISPO
SAMUEL DÍAZ OSSA
LAS BRISAS
GENERAL CLARCK
LINCOLN
EUCALIPTUS
Cementerios
Cementerio General
LA UNION
MARIA GRAHAM
PUMA
DESIDERIO LEMUS
FRANCISCO SILVA
AVENIDA PERU
EL SALTO
RECOLETA
SCHLACK
Cerro Blanco
SAN CRISTOBAL
AVENIDA SANTOS
DUMONT
Cerro Blanco
Museo de Artes Decorativas
AVENIDA LA PAZ
TABARE
PERU
SCHIAVETTI
RAPA NUI
JUAREZ LARGA
DOMINICA
BUENOS AIRES
AVENIDA
Barrio Patronato
DAVILA BAEZA
SALAS
RIO DE JANEIRO
Patronato
La Vega
MANZANO
SANTA FILOMENA
ANTONIA LOPEZ DE BELLO
ARTESANOS
PATRONATO
LORETO
DARDIGNAC
BELLAVISTA
CARDENAL JOSÉ
AVENIDA SANTA MARÍA
Mercado Central
PURISIMA
PIO NONO
Jardín Mapulemu
Piscina Tupahue
Teleférico de Santiago
Parque Metropolitano de Santiago
Cerro San Cristobal
Santuario Inmaculada Concepción
Funicular de Santiago
Zoológico Nacional
CARLOS REED
MONITOR ARAUCANO
Casa de la Ciudadanía Montecarmelo
Casa Museo La Chascona
Plaza Camilo Mori
BARRIO BELLAVISTA
Patio Bellavista
BELLAVISTA
Río Mapocho
AVE. ANDRÉS BELLO
Parque Balmaceda
AVENIDA EL CERRO
LOS COLONOS
PL. DE LA INDI
AUTOPISTA COSTANERA NORT
AVENIDA SANTA MARÍA
BELLAVISTA
PÉREZ VALENZUELA
ALMIRANTE PASTENE
Manuel Montt
MIGUEL CLARO
RAFAEL CAÑAS
HUELEN
Salvador
RAMON
JOSÉ MANUEL INFANTE
VALENZUELA
DIAZ
CANO Y APONT
Hospital del Salvador
AVENIDA SALVADOR
AVENIDA CONDELL
AVE. GENERAL BUSTAMANTE
RICARDO MATTE PEREZ
RANCAGUA
SANTO DOMINGO
Plaza de Armas
MERCED
PLAZA DE ARMAS AND SANTIAGO CENTRO
p62
Baquedano
AVE. V. MACKENNA
Universidad Católica
BANDERA
AGUSTINAS
Teatro Municipal

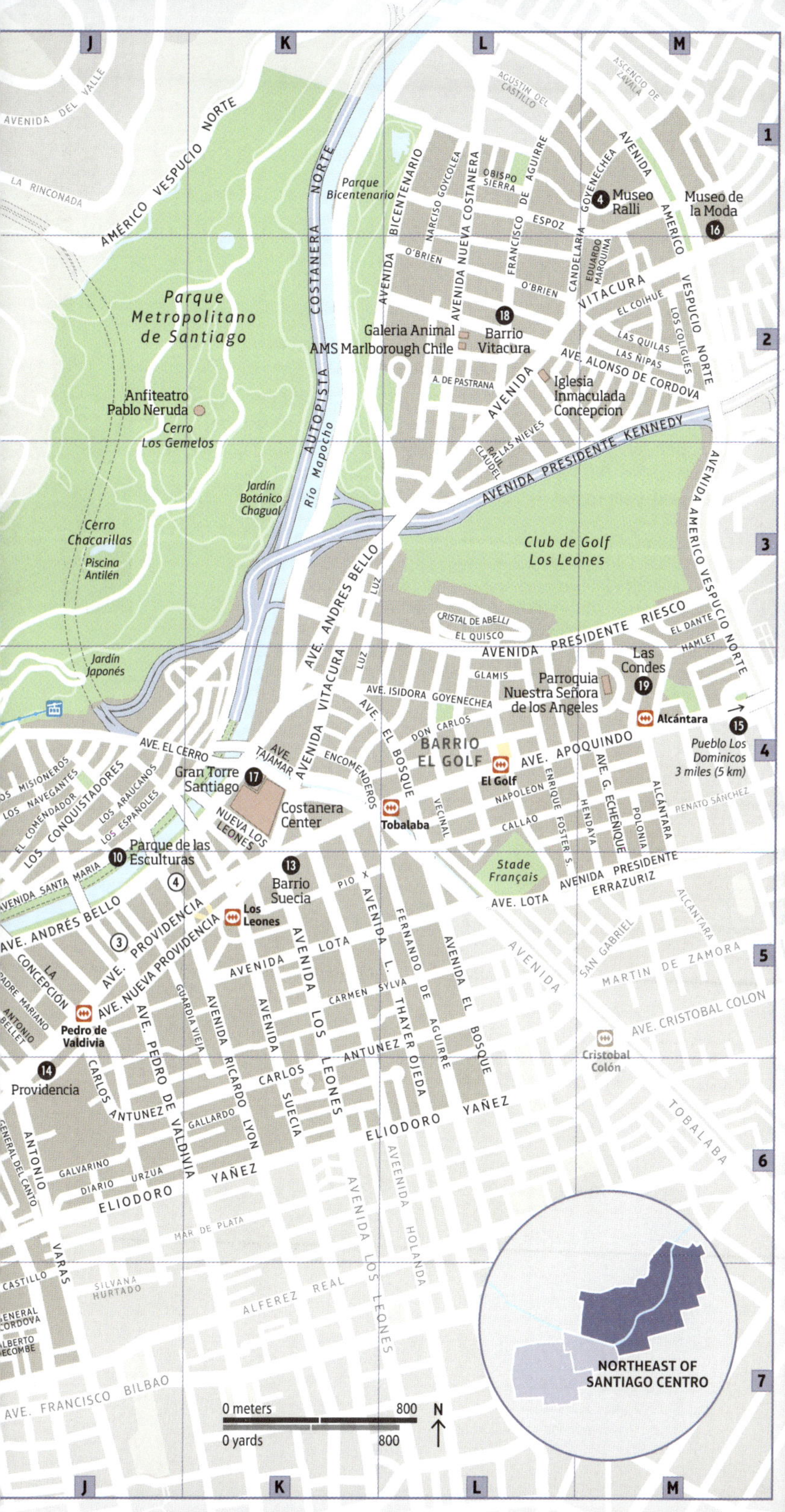

Parque Metropolitano de Santiago
Anfiteatro Pablo Neruda
Cerro Los Gemelos
Jardín Botánico Chagual
Cerro Chacarillas
Piscina Antilén
Jardín Japonés
Parque Bicentenario
Río Mapocho
Museo Ralli
Museo de la Moda
Barrio Vitacura
Galeria Animal
AMS Marlborough Chile
Iglesia Inmaculada Concepcion
Club de Golf Los Leones
Las Condes
Parroquia Nuestra Señora de los Angeles
Alcántara
Pueblo Los Dominicos 3 miles (5 km)
BARRIO EL GOLF
El Golf
Gran Torre Santiago
Costanera Center
Tobalaba
Parque de las Esculturas
Barrio Suecia
Los Leones
Stade Français
Pedro de Valdivia
Providencia
Cristobal Colón
NORTHEAST OF SANTIAGO CENTRO
0 meters 800
0 yards 800
N

1

PARQUE METROPOLITANO DE SANTIAGO

G5 Pedro de Valdivia Norte (02) 2730 1331 Baquedano
6am-6pm daily (summer: to 9pm) parquemet.cl

With the National Zoo leading conservation efforts for endangered Chilean species, cable cars climbing the summit of San Cristóbal, and open-air swimming pools providing respite from the heat, it is no surprise that Parque Metropolitano de Santiago attracts visitors all year round.

Covering 3 sq miles (7 sq km) of vegetation-clad slopes, the Parque Metropolitano de Santiago was developed between 1903 and 1927 as the lungs of Santiago, encompassing the hills San Cristóbal, Pirámide, Bosque, and Chacarillas. Previously bare and dry, the park was reforested with native plants and trees and further developed with trails, picnic areas, swimming pools, a cultural center, and a cable car. It is now the city's recreational center and home to the Zoológico Nacional, and offers sweeping views of Santiago and the Andes.

Did You Know?

The Statue of the Virgin is believed to be a reproduction of the "Virgin of Rome."

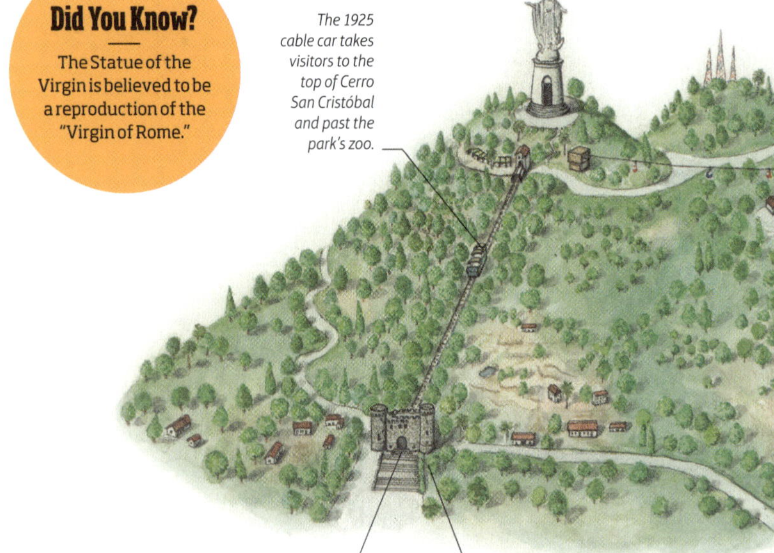

The 45-ft- (14-m-) high Statue of the Virgin was donated by France in 1904. It can be seen from most of Santiago Centro.

The 1925 cable car takes visitors to the top of Cerro San Cristóbal and past the park's zoo.

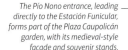

The Pío Nono entrance, leading directly to the Estación Funicular, forms part of the Plaza Caupolicán garden, with its medieval-style facade and souvenir stands.

The funicular station at Plaza Caupolicán is the main entry point to the park.

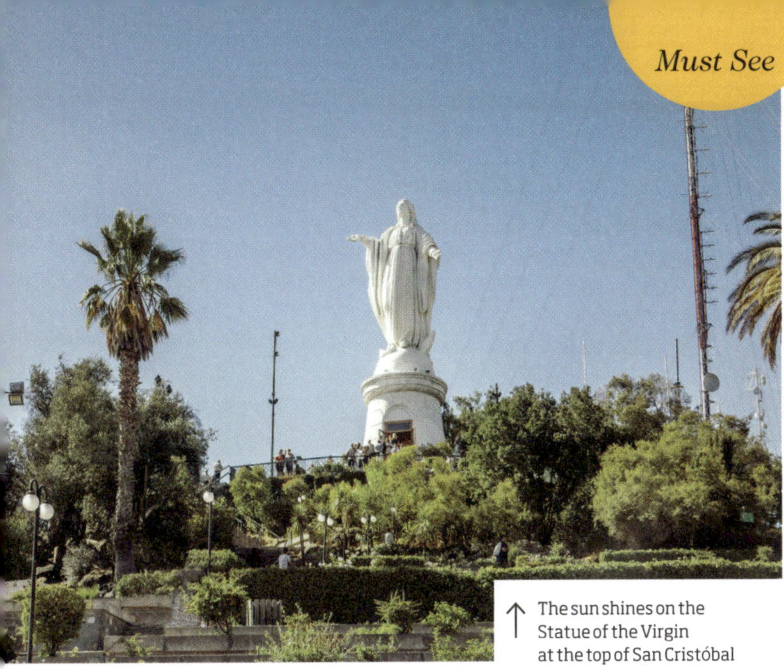

↑ The sun shines on the Statue of the Virgin at the top of San Cristóbal

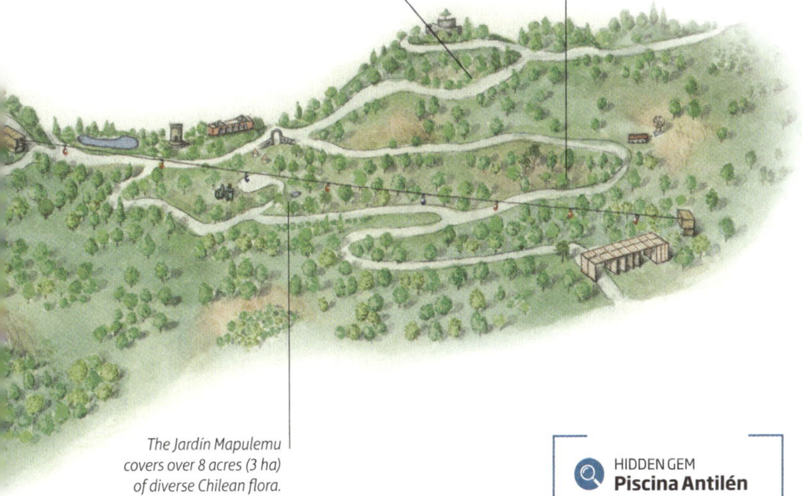

With beautiful views of the city, Piscina Antilén is Santiago's highest swimming pool and offers great respite from the summer heat.

Inaugurated in 1997 by Prince Hitachi of Japan, the Jardín Japonés features a lotus pond, waterwheel, cherry trees, and Japanese maples.

The Jardín Mapulemu covers over 8 acres (3 ha) of diverse Chilean flora.

↑ Illustration of Parque Metropolitano de Santiago showing the main sights

HIDDEN GEM
Piscina Antilén

For a "swim with a view," head for a dip in the Antilén and Tupahue pools, located on the summit of Cerro San Cristóbal.

EXPERIENCE MORE

Cementerio General

E4 Avenida Alberto Zañartu 951 Cementerios 8:30am-6pm daily cementeriogeneral.cl

Most of the nation's past presidents are buried here, including Salvador Allende, whose remains were moved to this site from Viña del Mar *(p130)* in 1990. The cemetery opened in 1821 and was inaugurated by Chile's first president, Bernardo O'Higgins, who now rests in a crypt at Plaza Bulnes *(p73)*. The area was designed as a "city" for the dead, with tree-lined streets and elaborate mausoleums. These run the gamut of styles from Gothic to Egyptian to Greek.

Among those buried here are legendary folk singer Violeta Parra; former Senator and leftist Orlando Letelier, who was assassinated in Washington, DC; noted poet and singer Victor Jara, tortured and shot dead by the Pinochet regime in 1973; and, more recently, the Communist Party leader Gladys Marín. There is also a monument to the dictatorship era *(p48)* – a mural by sculptor Francisco Gazitúa called *Rostros* (Heads) – which lists the Chileans who were executed. On the west of the cemetery is the Dissenters' Patio, a burial sector for the Protestants, who had been moved from their earlier burial site at Cerro Santa Lucía *(p78)* in the late 1800s. In 2018, the Mausoleo Trans was created to bury members of the trans-gender community. It is the first of its kind in Latin America.

Museo de Artes Decorativas

E/F5 Avenida Recoleta 683 Cerro Blanco 10am-5pm Tue-Fri, 10am-2pm Sat artdec.gob.cl

In 1982, the very valuable Coleccion Garcés was donated to the Chilean government and established as the Museo de Artes Decorativas. The pieces here (more than 2,500) are divided into 20 thematic displays and include beautiful examples of 18th- and 19th-century porcelain, crystal glasses and vases, ornate silverwork, marble and ceramic objects, jewelry, and Greek, Roman, and Latin American art.

The center houses two other collections of interest. The Museo Histórico Dominico displays 18th- and 19th-century religious objects, while the Biblioteca Patrimonial

STAY

The Aubrey

Housed in a wonderfully restored mansion, this hotel combines modern conveniences with magnificent 1920s details. The lively Barrio Bellavista neighborhood is mere steps away.

G6 Constitución 317 theaubrey.com

$$$

An Egyptian-style tomb in Santiago's Cementerio General

Recoleta Domínica is one of the largest private libraries in Latin America, with 115,000 historically important books, maps, and investigative papers covering science and religion.

Museo Ralli

M1 Alonso de Sotomayor 4110 Mar-Dec: 10:30am-5pm Mon-Sat (Jan: Sat & Sun only) Feb rallimuseums.com

One of Santiago's lesser-known museums, the Museo Ralli has a small yet impressive collection of Latin American and European art, which includes a handful of works by Salvador Dalí, Marc Chagall, and Joan Miró. This transnational museum – there are other branches in Spain, Uruguay, and Israel – was founded in 1992 by Harry Recanati, an art collector and retired banker who shunned any profit from it. The museum is spread across 32,290 sq ft (3,000 sq m) and is located on a residential street, where it occasionally hosts temporary exhibits by contemporary European and Latin American artists.

Casa Museo La Chascona

G6 Fernando Márquez de la Plata 192 Baquedano 10am-6pm Tue-Sun (Jan & Feb: to 7pm) fundacionneruda.org

Built in 1953 on a steep slope of Cerro San Cristóbal in the Bellavista neighborhood, the entrancing Museo La Chascona is one of 20th-century poet Pablo Neruda's three homes. The home was named La Chascona (Woman with Unruly Hair) for Matilde Urrutia, Neruda's secret mistress, who lived here alone for a year; they eventually married in 1966. Neruda eschewed many of his architect's designs for the home, and instead used a deeply personal and notably whimsical layout, filled with winding staircases and secret doors. His love of the sea is evident in the house's maritime-influenced details, such as porthole windows, a dining area that was once fronted by a stream to give the illusion of sailing, and a living room that resembles a lighthouse. The interiors exhibit Neruda's vast collection of art and artifacts, bought during his travels around the world.

Neruda was both a friend of former president Salvador Allende and a Communist. After the Pinochet-led coup of 1973, military vandals damaged the house, and while it was declared that the poet's funeral would not be a public event, Chileans took to the streets in his memory nonetheless. The Fundación Pablo Neruda later restored La Chascona to its original state. It now contains household items rescued from the house, as well as furniture and personal objects from Neruda's office in France, where he served as ambassador between 1970 and 1973. The library holds Neruda's famous Nobel Prize medal along with various letters, photographs, books, and other publications. Audio-guided tours are available on a first-come, first-served basis.

↑ Street art by Gabriel Maulen outside Casa Museo La Chascona

PABLO NERUDA

Chile's most beloved poet was born Neftalí Ricardo Reyes Basoalto in 1904 *(p38)*. He took his pen name from Czech poet Jan Neruda, in part to hide his earliest works from his father, who did not consider writing a suitable career choice. Neruda found early success with the collection *Twenty Poems of Love and a Song of Despair*, after which he undertook a series of diplomatic posts abroad. He wrote his opus *Canto General* in 1950, and won the Nobel Prize for Literature in 1971, but died two years later.

La Vega

E6 Dávila Baeza 700 Cal y Canto, Patronato 7am-4pm daily (to 5pm Mon-Fri) vegacentral.cl

Located just across from Mercado Central (*p81*), La Vega is the city's principal fruit and vegetable market and a must-see for foodies. Amid its chaos of crates and stalls, and the buying and negotiating, La Vega offers an earthy and colorful experience. The market occupies a purpose-built structure that covers several city blocks and is surrounded by 100 or more vendors selling items such as shoes, electronics, and pet food. At the center are the food stalls that sell inexpensive meals such as chicken soup *cazuela*. This is an ideal place to look out for local fruits such as *chirimoya* (a custard apple), *tuna* cactus fruit, and *lucuma*, a butterscotch-flavored fruit used in desserts like ice cream.

Barrio Patronato

F6 Between Loreto, Bellavista, Domínica, and Recoleta sts Patronato Stores: 10am-7:30pm Mon-Fri, 10am-5:30pm Sat tiendaspatronato.cl

Occupying over a dozen blocks, Barrio Patronato is a bustling shopping area dominated by clothing stores and small places to eat operated in large part by immigrants from Korea, China, and the Middle East. During the colonial period, the *barrio* was a poor residential neighborhood. It was then called La Chimba, which means Other Side of the River. The area continues to be populated by the working class and many of the neighborhood's original adobe houses still stand.

During the late 19th century, Arab immigrants from Syria, Lebanon, and especially Palestine settled in the Patronato neighborhood. They established the city's principal textile commercial center here, selling imported clothing and fabrics, as there was little national production of textiles at the time. Today, Patronato heaves with more than 10,000

Creative stores, bars, and restaurants in Patio Bellavista

THE 2019 PROTESTS

The biggest anti-government protests since the fall of the Pinochet dictatorship broke out in the city in late 2019. Though sparked by an increase in subway fares, the protests were the result of discontent over inequality, the high cost of living, and inadequate health and social care. President Piñera declared a state of emergency and deployed the army, which resulted in more than 30 people being killed, hundreds injured, and thousands arrested. On 25 October 2020, a referendum to decide whether to rewrite the constitution was held, with 78 per cent voting in favor, but the proposed changes were rejected in 2023.

shoppers per day, who pack the streets searching for T-shirts, shoes, ball gowns, suits, and trendy clothing at dirt-cheap prices.

Plaza Camilo Mori

G6 Constitución, Antonia López de Bello Baquedano

Located in the heart of the Bellavista neighborhood, Plaza Camilo Mori is named for the well-known Chilean painter whose house and studio stood here. The triangular plaza is dominated by the Castillo Lehuedé, a striking mansion popularly known as the Casa Rosa (Red House), which is now a boutique hotel. This beautiful stone edifice was built in 1923 by architect Federico Bieregel for entrepreneur Pedro Lehuedé. The plaza is also home to trendy boutiques and restaurants, as well as the Centro Mori, which hosts offbeat theater performances.

INSIDER TIP
Walking Street Art

Bellavista is well known for its impressive array of street art. Several agencies offer guided walking tours that take in some of the finest examples, including Santiago Street Art Tours (*stgostreetart.com*).

Patio Bellavista

G6 Constitución 30-70 Baquedano 10-1am daily (to 3am Thu-Sat) patiobellavista.cl

Inaugurated in 2006 as an urban renewal project, the charming Patio Bellavista is a large collection of stores and restaurants that are spread around an interior square. This central plaza was originally a *cité* – a housing facility for the working class in the 19th century. Today, well restored, Patio Bellavista features over 80 stores selling high-end *artesanía*, or crafts, around two dozen restaurants and bars, bookstores, art galleries, and jewelry shops. For those souvenir shopping, this is an excellent place to pick up some jewelry featuring lapis lazuli – a blue, semi-precious stone. Pretty pieces are sold by many of the stores and stalls in Bellavista.

There are a number of excellent outdoor cafés here too, which are popular with both locals and visitors. Patio Bellavista also hosts a variety of open-air cultural programs that include dance performances, live music shows, as well as rotating exhibitions of paintings and photography.

TOP 3 LGBTQ+ VENUES IN BELLAVISTA

Fausto
Avenida Santa María 832
fausto.cl
A popular club that's been running for over 30 years. Expect great live music and a slightly more mature crowd.

Limón
Dardignac 142
One of the few local joints open throughout the week, this place has inexpensive drinks and a wide-ranging playlist.

Illuminati
Antonia López de Bello 131
This cool and welcoming bar/club draws a varied crowd, and is a great place for drinks and a dance.

Parque de las Esculturas

J5 Avenida Santa María 2205, between Avenida Pedro de Valdivia & Padre Letelier (02) 2335 1832 Los Leones 8am-7pm daily

Laid out after a massive flooding of Río Mapocho in 1982, Parque de las Esculturas was a creative response to the need to reinforce this area of the river shore. The park was landscaped between 1986 and 1988 by architect Germán Bannen, and offers views of the snowcapped Andes. Serene walking paths meander through the area, which is dotted with sculptures by Chilean and international artists, including *Libre Albedrío* by Alicia Larraín and *Oda al Aire* by Ignacio Bahna.

> **Serene walking paths meander through Parque de las Esculturas, which is dotted with sculptures by Chilean and international artists.**

Casa de la Ciudadanía Montecarmelo

G6 Bellavista 594 Salvador 9am-5pm Mon-Thu, 9am-4pm Fri, 10am-6pm Sat cultura providencia.cl

Barrio Bellavista's primary cultural center, the Casa de la Ciudadanía Montecarmelo, is located in the building of the former Montecarmelo Convent. In the late 19th century the covent belonged to the nuns of Carmelitas de Santa Teresa – an order that was known for its humility, with its members being referred to as *descalzos* (barefoot). The convent's doors reopened as a beautifully rebuilt cultural space in 1991, and today the center – operated by the Corporación Cultural de Providencia – conducts workshops and classes in music, photography, art, and dance. There is an impressive year-round calendar of concerts, cinematic events, and theater productions that take place on an outdoor stage, surrounded by the picturesque brick walls of the old convent. Montecarmelo also provides a place for Chilean authors to showcase their works of fiction and poetry.

Parque Balmaceda

G7 Avenida Providencia, between Baquedano & Del Arzobispo Baquedano, Salvador

Built in 1927 following the canalization of Río Mapocho, Parque Balmaceda is named for José Manuel Balmaceda, Chile's former president and a central figure in the country's short-lived Civil War of 1891. A statue commemorating this national figure stands at the western end of the park.

Parque Balmaceda's central attraction is the Fuente Bicentenario – a fountain shooting out graceful arcs of water that are lit up at night in a rainbow of colors. Standing at the foot of the fountain is the Monumento de Aviación, an abstract sculpture installed during the Pinochet dictatorship.

The park's western edges at Plaza Baquedano became the focal point of Santiago's 2019 protests *(p106)*, and even now demonstrations take place here every Friday afternoon. Due to this, the once manicured plaza is now a dusty, graffitied shadow of its former self.

← A sculpture in the Parque de las Esculturas, with the Gran Torre Santiago glinting behind

Barrio Suecia

K5 Avenida Suecia, Avenida Providencia Los Leones

A bold and brash micro-neighborhood, Barrio Suecia is jam-packed with largely character-free, US-style restaurants, bars, pubs, and nightclubs, all competing for the attention of customers. A few decades ago, Barrio Suecia was still considered one of the city's most popular spots for nightlife, offering a unique vibe and more than 60 places to eat, drink, and dance. These days, however, many of the old places have closed down, the vibe has changed, and the focus for nightlife has moved to other areas across the city, such as Bellavista. Despite this, many young travelers and office workers continue to flock to the neighborhood for the innumerable happy-hour specials, no-frills restaurants offering decent *menús del día* (fixed-price lunch menus), and rowdy clubs, which remain open well until the early hours of the morning.

Providencia

J6 Avenida Providencia Baquedano, Salvador, Manuel Montt, Pedro de Valdivia, & Los Leones

The pleasant, leafy district of Providencia is a good place for visitors to base themselves. Although there is only a handful of tourist attractions, there are many mid-range hotels, an array of cafés and restaurants, and a lively nightlife scene, including the popular craft brewery Krossbar Orrego Luco. Good transport connections also make it easy to travel to the rest of the city.

↑ Relaxing at a café in the lovely neighborhood of Providencia

EAT

Boragó

Explore the unique flavors of Chile with a world-class tasting menu here.

G6 Avenida San José María Escrivá de Balaguer 5970 Sun & Mon borago.cl

$$$

Happening

This Argentine steakhouse serves juicy *entraña* (skirt steak), a prized beef cut.

G6 Avenida Apoquindo 3090 Sun happening.cl

$$$

El Huerto

One of the city's best vegetarian restaurants, with plenty of vegan options and a tempting array of desserts.

J5 Orrego Luco 54 elhuerto.cl

$$$

DRINK

Baco

Baco serves Chilean and international wines by the glass, as well as French-inspired food.

J5 Nueva de Lyon 113 baco.cl

La Casa en el Aire

Taking its name from one of Pablo Neruda's verses, The House in the Air is an excellent spot for a drink.

G6 Antonia López de Bello 125 lacasaenelaire.cl

Shopping along the tree-lined Pueblito Los Dominicos

15   

Pueblito Los Dominicos

M4 Avenida Apoquindo 9085 (22) 8969844 Los Dominicos 10:30am-8pm daily

One of Santiago's best shopping areas for local arts and crafts, the Pueblito Los Dominicos is a rustic complex housed within the former grounds of the neighboring Iglesia Los Dominicos. In 1982, the *pueblo* was expanded and landscaped to resemble a traditional Chilean village with whitewashed, low-slung adobe buildings. The area was originally a Mapuche settlement headed by chief Apoquindo, whose name was given to the grand avenue that ends here.

Today, the *pueblo* offers 160 small stores to independent artisans for selling wares such as ceramics, leather goods, jewelry, folk art, textiles, and even animals such as rabbits and birds. The stores double as workshops, allowing a glimpse of the artistic process.

The ambience is truly idyllic, enhanced by trickling creeks and the sound of flute music wafting through the village. Saturday and Sunday are the best days to come here, when the Iglesia Los Dominicos holds Mass. The church is featured on the Chilean 2,000 peso bill and is a historical monument that provided shelter to revolutionaries during the nation's battle for independence in the 1810s.

16   

Museo de la Moda

M1 Avenida Vitacura 4562 For restoration museodelamoda.cl

Built to honor a family legacy and love of fashion, the Museo de la Moda was established in 2007 by Jorge Yarur, who converted his parents' Modernist home into one of the most important fashion museums in the world. Yarur scoured the globe for a decade in order to compile a nearly encyclopedic collection of more than 10,000 pieces of clothing. These range from the 18th century to modern day, from classic couture gowns by Chanel and Lanvin to modern frocks by Gaultier and celebrity memorabilia such as Madonna's cone bra and John Lennon's jacket from 1966. The utterly stylish museum rotates its collections in themes, with a special wing devoted to tennis, Yarur's sport of choice. The museum is also a tour through his family home, preserved as it was in the 1960s and 1970s and with clothing once owned by Yarur's mother, Raquel Bascuñán, on display. There is also a restaurant occupying the family's former garage.

17   

Gran Torre Santiago

K4 Avenida Andrés Bello Tobalaba 10am-10pm daily skycostanera.cl

This is the tallest building in Chile – and in South America – at 984 ft (300 m) high. It was designed by the Argentinian architect César Pelli (of Malaysia's Petronas Towers fame) and can be seen from almost every point in the city. On a clear day there are panoramic views of the capital and the Andes from the Sky Costanera viewing platform.

Did You Know?

The Sky Costanera within the soaring Gran Torre is the highest observatory in Latin America.

18

Barrio Vitacura

L2 vitacura.cl

Named for the Mapuche chief Butacura (Big Rock) who lived here with his clan at the time of the conquistadores' arrival, Barrio Vitacura was expropriated in the mid-1500s as an *asentamiento* – Spanish settlements on Indigenous land and developed into haciendas.

Today, Vitacura is the residential neighborhood of the affluent. Lying under the shadow of the rocky mountain Cerro Manquehue, the area is characterized by towering condominiums and upscale stores and restaurants.

The borough, which includes Parque Bicentenario, a grassy expanse with lagoons and trails, has undergone a colossal urban renewal. The banks of Río Mapocho have been rebuilt as well. Its now the location for Lollapalooza Chile – the first version of the popular Chicagoan music festival to take place outside the United States. Lollapalooza Chile mixes Chilean acts with international headliners, and takes place annually in late March.

Barrio Vitacura is also Santiago's epicenter of highbrow art galleries, with more than two dozen venues highlighting Chile's finest artists. Sala de Arte CCU has built up a collection of around 600 pieces since it opened in 1993. It focuses on contemporary Chilean artists working in sculpture, painting, photography, installation, and video. Several heavyweight galleries are open to the general public, including the transnational AMS Marlborough Chile, Isabel Aninat (known especially for new talent), Artespacio, Eduardo Lira, and Patricia Ready.

GREAT VIEW
Sky-High Sips

For some of the finest views in the city - with drinks and music to match - head to the rooftop bar at the W hotel *(marriott.com)* in Las Condes.

19

Las Condes

M4 Avenida Apoquindo & Avenida Las Condes El Golf, Alcántara, Tobalaba, & Escuela Militar

East of Providencia *(p109)* is Las Condes, a large, upscale area home to many of the city's wealthier residents, foreign embassies, and the offices of major Chilean corporations. Tourist attractions are thin on the ground, but there are many four- and five-star hotels, plenty of good (though pricey) restaurants and bars, and several shopping malls. Within Las Condes and bordering Providencia, the micro-neighborhood of El Golf is often referred to as "Sanhattan," thanks to its glitzy skyscrapers and North American feel.

↑ Gran Torre Santiago, towering above the skyscrapers of the Las Condes neighborhood

EXPERIENCE CHILE

Hiking across the Perito Moreno Glacier

Looking out over the Viña Santa Cruz vineyard

CENTRAL VALLEY

Inhabited since pre-Columbian times, Central Valley is considered Chile's oldest region and a bastion of its traditions. Its original settlers were the Mapuche, who resisted assimilation into the Inca Empire. The Spanish arrived in 1541, founding Santiago at the foot of the Andes, Valparaíso on the coast, and, later, towns across the valley floor. Central Valley became the center of colonial Chile: the womb from which the country's north and south grew, its wealthiest area, and the political hub. The hacienda system, by which old families controlled vast tracts of land, evolved around Central Valley, spawning Chile's legendary *huasos* (cowboys). Mining of silver, nitrates, and copper brought later wealth.

Agriculture, in particular viticulture, remains the greatest source of income, the dry climate and long summers making the region ideal for the production of award-winning fine wines. The valley's world-class wineries, open for tours and tastings, are part of a tourism sector that offers an array of other activities to locals and visitors alike. The cities still have well-preserved haciendas and mines, and Spanish-era towns.

CENTRAL VALLEY

Must Sees

1. Valparaíso
2. Casa Museo Isla Negra

Experience More

3. Casablanca Valley
4. Viña del Mar
5. Sewell
6. Cartagena
7. Quintay
8. Algarrobo
9. Cachagua
10. Papudo
11. Zapallar
12. Los Andes
13. Cristo Redentor
14. Portillo
15. Termas de Jahuel
16. Rancagua
17. Parque Nacional La Campana
18. El Teniente
19. Valle de Cachapoal
20. Termas de Cauquenes
21. Cajón del Maipo
22. Hacienda Los Lingues
23. Reserva Nacional Río de los Cipreses
24. Valle de Curicó
25. Santa Cruz
26. Pichilemu
27. Termas de Panimávida
28. Maule
29. Reserva Nacional Altos de Lircay
30. Parque Nacional Radal Siete Tazas
31. Lago Vichuquén
32. Chillán
33. Nevados de Chillán
34. Saltos del Laja
35. Concepción
36. Parque Nacional Laguna del Laja
37. Lota
38. Tomé

Pacific Ocean

NORTE GRANDE AND NORTE CHICO
p150
VALPARAÍSO
METROPOLITAN
LIBERTADOR
MAULE
BIOBÍO
ARGENTINA
1 VALPARAÍSO
2 CASA MUSEO ISLA NEGRA
3 CASABLANCA VALLEY
4 VIÑA DEL MAR
5 SEWELL
6 CARTAGENA
7 QUINTAY
8 ALGARROBO
9 CACHAGUA
10 PAPUDO
11 ZAPALLAR
12 LOS ANDES
13 CRISTO REDENTOR
14 PORTILLO
15 TERMAS DE JAHUEL
16 RANCAGUA
17 PARQUE NACIONAL LA CAMPANA
18 EL TENIENTE
19 VALLE DE CACHAPOAL
20 TERMAS DE CAUQUENES
21 CAJÓN DEL MAIPO
22 HACIENDA LOS LINGUES
23 RESERVA NACIONAL RÍO DE LOS CIPRESES
24 VALLE DE CURICÓ
25 SANTA CRUZ
26 PICHILEMU
27 TERMAS DE PANIMÁVIDA
28 MAULE
29 RESERVA NACIONAL ALTOS DE LIRCAY
30 PARQUE NACIONAL RADAL SIETE TAZAS
31 LAGO VICHUQUÉN
32 CHILLÁN
33 NEVADOS DE CHILLÁN
34 SALTOS DEL LAJA
35 CONCEPCIÓN
36 PARQUE NACIONAL LAGUNA DEL LAJA
37 LOTA
38 TOMÉ
Ingeniero Santa María
Río del Sobrante
Petorca
La Ligua
Quintero
Concón
San Felipe
Quilpué
Colina
El Colorado
Curacaví
Santiago International Airport
Santiago
San Antonio
Talagante
Puente Alto
San José de Maipo
Melipilla
Paine
Navidad
Río Rapel
Vila Ahué
Litueche
Rengo
Cahuil
Paredones
San Fernando
Chimbarongo
Teno
Volcán Tinguiririca 14,107 ft (4,299 m)
Licantén
Curicó
Los Queñes
El Sosneado
Molina
Huaquén
Carrizal
Lagunas de Teno
Cumpeo
Constitución
Talca
Malargüe
Lago Colbún
San Javier
Chanco
Sauzal
Pelluhue
Linares
Cerro Campanario 13,284 ft (4,048 m)
Bardas Blancas
Cauquenes
Laguna del Maule
Río Melado
Cobquecura
Parral
Camelia
Quirihue
Vegas de Itata
San Carlos
Coelemu
San Fabián de Alico
Talcahuano
Carriel Sur International Airport
Pinto
Bulnes
Recinto
Barrancas
Chiguayante
Volcán Chillán 10,538 ft (3,211 m)
Coronel
Pemuco
Golfo de Arauco
Yumbel
Río Laja
Yungay
Andacollo
Llico
Polcura
Arauco
Laja
Río Biobío
Laguna de la Laja
Antuco
Chos Malal
Nacimiento
Los Ángeles
Lebu
Los Álamos
Santa Barbara
Cañete
Mulchén
Cayucupil
Río Renaico
Ralco
Volcán Copahué 9,776 ft (2,979 m)
Lago Lanalhue
Río Biobío
Lago Lleulleu
Quidico
LAKE DISTRICT AND CHILOÉ
p194
0 kilometers 60
0 miles 60
N

Panoramic view of the colorful Valparaíso skyline and coast

VALPARAÍSO

B7 75 miles (120 km) NW of Santiago
Plaza Sotomayor 233, piso 1; 9am-4:30pm Mon-Fri; vlpo.cl

Founded in 1543, the city of Valparaíso covers over 45 steep hills, each a jumble of winding streets lined with colorful houses and 19th-century museums. It is a UNESCO World Heritage Site, and much of its rich architecture is beautifully preserved.

Edificio de la Aduana

Plaza Wheelwright 144
9am-5pm Mon-Fri
aduana.cl

Built in 1855, the pink-painted Edificio de la Aduana (Customs Building) is a rare example of post-colonial architecture. The institution's most famous employee was the Nicaraguan Modernist poet Rubén Darío, who worked here in the 1880s while writing his seminal work, *Azul* (1888). Edificio de la Aduana overlooks Plaza Wheelwright, named for American industrialist William Wheelwright, who played a major role in building Chile's railroads and steamship fleet. His statue, raised in 1877, adorns the plaza.

INSIDER TIP
City Tour

For an inexpensive sightseeing tour of the city, catch public bus "0" (also known as the "612"), which takes a scenic route from the port and winds its way up to La Sebastiana.

Plaza Echaurren

Calle Cochrane 253, Calle Serrano

The birthplace and historic heart of Valparaíso, Plaza Echaurren marks the spot where Spanish explorer Juan de Saavedra first made landfall in 1543. Today, it is fronted by crumbling yet elegant mid-19th-century structures. The beautiful old market building of Mercado Puerto is a prime example, and has been fully restored to house crafts stalls, an art gallery, and a wine boutique.

Overlooking the plaza is the Iglesia de la Matriz, notable for its octagonal steeple. This edifice was built in 1837 on the site of the city's first church.

3   

Museo Marítimo Nacional

Paseo 21 de Mayo 45, Cerro Artillería 10am-6pm daily museo maritimo.cl

Chile's excellent Museo Marítimo Nacional is housed in a building dating from 1893, which offers great views of the city from its front lawns. It has 17 exhibition rooms, including salons dedicated to Chile's foremost naval figures – Lord Thomas Cochrane, Arturo Prat, and Bernardo O'Higgins – and to Chile's key 19th-century naval battles. Exhibits include antique sabers and swords, pocket revolvers, bayonets, military plans, and models of battleships. Items salvaged from Prat's schooner, *Esmeralda*, such as the clock which stopped at the precise time the ship sank during the Battle of Iquique (1879), are also displayed.

The museum also has an interesting display that explores the remarkable rescue of 33 San José miners who were trapped underground for 69 days in 2010. The story of these miners was widely covered on international news and watched around the world.

Children will also love the large replica pirate ship in the Sala Hermandad de la Costa. Surrounding the ship are flags from countries all around the world.

THE TROLEBUSES

Valparaíso imported a fleet of electric *trolebuses* from the US between 1946 and 1952. This includes the world's oldest trolleybuses in service. Trolleybus systems had deteriorated under the Pinochet regime, but in 1982 city businessmen acquired and renovated them. Today, they ply between Avenida Argentina and Edificio de la Aduana. Low on noise and air pollution, they offer an easy and charming way to see the city.

FUNICULARS OF VALPARAÍSO

Valparaíso's funiculars are the cheapest, easiest, and most fun way of traveling between the city's residential hillsides and the port and financial districts of its El Plan (Lower Town). The funiculars were introduced between 1883 and 1912, and only 11 are currently still in service, with Ascensor Concepción being the oldest. They rattle up and down Valparaíso's steep hills and spill out onto dramatic promenades with beautiful city and ocean vistas. Many also access historic sights and tourist attractions.

Bar La Playa

Blanco 44 (9) 9961 2207 11am-7pm Mon-Thu

Bar La Playa continues to evoke Valparaíso's halcyon days as the greatest port city in the South Pacific. It was opened in 1908 in the city's old port area as a meeting spot for sailors and ship-workers, who passed time here between shifts. Today, it is in a different location but remains one of the most atmospheric places in the city to drink. There is a polished mahogany bar, strings of international flags, black-and-white photos from Valparaíso's heyday, and plenty of nautical knick-knacks strewn about the place. Pub grub-style food is also on offer, though the quality can be variable.

Muelle Prat

Avenida Errázuriz, in front of Plaza Sotomayor

A bustling and busy pier, Muelle Prat is the departure point for half-hour tours of Valparaíso's bay by water-taxi. Vendors on the pier are set up with various offerings, including small pieces of jewelry, face painting, and temporary tattoos. There are dozens of bobbing *lanchas* (small and often colorful boats) that are dwarfed by the much larger cargo ships in the area. The bobbing ships are often used to call out the departure times for the next tour that is leaving the pier. There are plenty of tours available, which offer tremendous views of Valparaíso's hillsides, densely built up with rows of brightly colored houses. Boats wind a sinuous trail between gigantic cruise ships docked in the bay and the Chilean navy's battleships stationed offshore, before stretching out onto the open water. If you are very lucky, you may even get a close-up view of a sea lion colony. The port has a large amount of history and remains a significant and active commercial port today.

Palacio de Justicia

Plaza Justicia
To the public

Built in 1939, the Palacio de Justicia is Valparaíso's appeals court. The imposing edifice has a sober, rectilinear facade, with a 10-ft- (3-m-) high statue of Justitia (Lady Justice) at its entrance. The figure is curiously anomalous in that she wears no blindfold, her customary symbol of objectivity, and her scales of truth dangle forlornly at her side,

Plaza Sotomayor is centered around the Monumento a los Héroes de Iquique, raised in memory of the crew of the *Esmeralda*, killed in the 1879 Battle of Iquique.

People resting on benches in the vast Plaza Sotomayor ↑

rather than at the end of her outstretched arm. According to legend, it was an angry merchant who had the statue placed here to protest against a perceived injustice, though the statue has been the subject of many different myths.

Plaza Sotomayor

Calle Cochrane, Avenida Tomás Ramos

Valparaíso's main square is the stately Plaza Sotomayor, a large open space that holds parades on Glorias Navales or Navy Day *(p42)*. The plaza is centered around the Monumento a los Héroes de Iquique, raised in memory of the crew of the *Esmeralda*, killed in the 1879 Battle of Iquique. The battle saw *Esmeralda*, the Chilean navy's oldest ship, fight the Peruvian fleet's most powerful vessel, *Huáscar*, for four hours.

Although the former was sunk, and her captain, Arturo Prat, killed, the battle was a turning point in the War of the Pacific *(p46)*. Prat's bronze effigy crowns the monument and his body also lies buried in a crypt here. Towering far above the southern end of Plaza Sotomayor is the unique and elaborate facade of the Neo-Gothic Comandancia en Jefe de la Armada. Built in 1910, its design was inspired by the Hôtel de Ville in Paris, and its interiors were multi-functional, serving both as a summer residence for various of Chile's former presidents and as the office of many of the city's mayors and regional governors. Expropriated by the Chilean navy in the mid-1970s, it has since functioned as Chile's naval headquarters.

The Ministry of Culture, a Modernist building which dates back to 1936, is open daily to the public and hosts various displays and art exhibitions. Adjacent to this edifice, the Compañía de Bomberos, which was built in 1851, is the site of the oldest volunteer fire service in Latin America, still helping across Valparaíso to the present day.

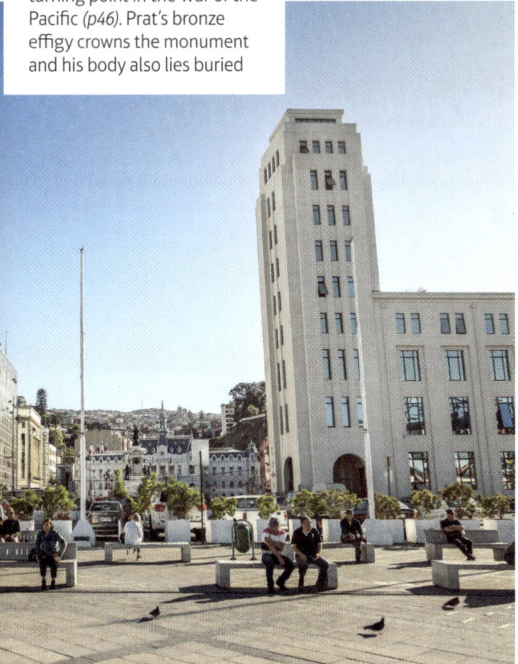

EAT

Amor Porteño

Come to this charming Argentine-style ice-cream parlor and coffee shop for a sundae, churros, or a *medialuna* (a sweet, doughy croissant).

Almirante Montt 418, Cerro Concepción
(032) 2216 253

El Peral

A shady terrace with great harbor views complements the menu of fresh seafood at El Peral. Don't miss the *ostiones gratinados* (parmesan oysters).

El Peral 182, Cerro Alegre
(569) 2829 3900

Casa Altamira

This brewery serves burgers and pizzas made with beer-infused dough. There is live music on most evenings.

Elías 126
cerveceraaltamira.cl

Maralegre

A classy restaurant, Maralegre has a small but perfectly created menu specializing in seafood and steaks. Book ahead for a spot on the sunny terrace.

Calle Higuera 133, Cerro Alegre
maralegre.cl

STAY

Palacio Astoreca
This historic hotel is the result of a Francophile union of two former residences. The rooms and restaurant all feature contemporary decor.

Montealegre 149, Cerro Alegre
hotelpalacioastoreca.com

Hotel Somerscales
Experience history at this boutique hotel, which was once home to British-Chilean artist Thomas Somerscales.

San Enrique 446, Cerro Alegre
hotelsomerscales.cl

Hostal Po
An attractive graffitied hostel in a great location, Po has spacious dorms and private rooms, plus a rooftop seating area.

Urriola 379, Cerro Concepción
(569) 5403 7766

$$$

Calle Prat

A narrow thoroughfare through the city's financial district, Calle Prat links Plaza Sotomayor and the monumental 1929 Reloj Turri (Turri Clock Tower), the city's Big Ben. Looming over both sides of the road are grand buildings of stone and black marble, constructed at the turn of the 20th century. Many of the buildings include columns and pediments. Among these is the old Bank of London building, today the Banco de Chile (No. 698), which houses a monument built to commemorate the British soldiers that were killed in World War I. Another evocative edifice here is Valparaíso's stock exchange, La Bolsa de Valores, the oldest stock exchange in South America. The old bidding wheel still stands inside the building's cavernous, domed interior.

Plaza Aníbal Pinto

End of Calle Esmeralda

Uniting Valparaíso's financial district and the commercial downtown area, Plaza Aníbal Pinto is a small, chaotic square fronted by beautiful buildings. The plaza is a busy spot, situated right on the edge of the historic district. On one side is the striking Librería Ivens building. Founded in 1891, it is one of the city's oldest bookstores. At the entrance to this building is the plaza's attractive public artwork – a street fountain that was sculpted as Neptune in 1892.

The fountain sculpture of Neptune in Aníbal Pinto Square

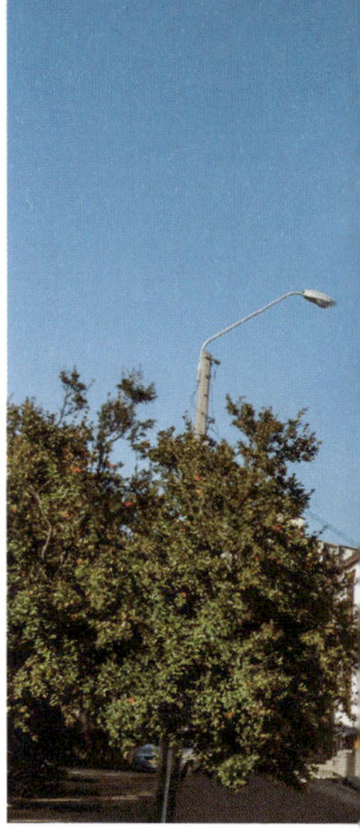

The attractive exterior of Palacio Baburizza, now a historic monument

Calle Esmeralda

An extension of Calle Prat, Calle Esmeralda starts at the Turri Clock Tower, which is close to Ascensor Concepción (*p120*), and ends at Plaza Aníbal Pinto. The street's most beautiful construction is the El Mercurio building, which has housed the popular *El Mercurio de Valparaíso* newspaper since 1901. The ornate exterior of the edifice is crowned by an incredible bronze statue of Mercury pointing skyward. Adjacent to El Mercurio, a stairway climbs up to the mystical Cueva Chivito, a natural rock cave, which according to local folklore and legend was formed and once inhabited by the devil.

Palacio Baburizza

Paseo Yugoslavo s/n, Cerro Alegre Ascensor El Peral 10am-7pm Tue-Sun museobaburizza.cl

This elegant Art-Nouveau mansion was constructed in 1916 for Italian saltpeter tycoon Ottorino Zanelli. It was subsequently purchased by Pascual Baburizza, a Croatian immigrant and nitrates magnate, in 1925. Today, the structure houses Valparaíso's fine arts museum, which displays the Baburizza family's personal collection of 19th- and 20th-century European art.

Did You Know?

In the 1800s, Valparaíso was the first port of call for ships around Cape Horn.

The palace is situated on the summit of Cerro Alegre, from where it overlooks the lovely Paseo Yugoslavo. A leafy promenade and viewing point, the street offers breathtaking vistas of neighboring hillsides, the city's port, financial districts, and the blue Bahía de Valparaíso.

Now reopened after having been restored to something that perhaps even exceeds its original elegance, the museum features a wing that showcases Chilean landscapes as depicted by expatriate painters. It also includes original furnishings and an extraordinary Art-Deco bathroom. The collection has been being gathered since 1895, and is considered to be one of the country's most important. It includes works by national and European artists and is best visited with a 45-minute tour or using the free English audio guide available at the entrance. The garden annex includes a café that serves snacks and drinks and a museum shop.

Paseo Gervasoni

Cerro Concepción Ascensor Concepción

Spilling out on to Paseo Gervasoni at the top of Cerro Concepción, this cobbled promenade edged with wildflowers affords splendid views across the Bahía de Valparaíso to Viña del Mar in the north. Along the street are the elegant Café Turri, the old Danish consulate building dating from 1848, and **Casa Mirador de Lukas**. The last is a 1900 house with a museum dedicated to the life and works of Chile's best-loved cartoonist, Renzo Antonio Pecchenino Raggi (1934–88), popularly known as Lukas.

Casa Mirador de Lukas

Paseo Gervasoni 448, Cerro Concepción (032) 2221 344 10:30am-6:30pm Tue-Fri, 11am-7pm Sat & Sun

The striking Iglesia Luterana de la Santa Cruz with its towering steeple

A must-see for devotees of Pablo Neruda, La Sebastiana is the last of three houses that were bought by the poet in Chile.

Iglesia Anglicana San Pablo

Pilcomayo 566, Cerro Concepción 10:30am-1pm Mon-Fri saintpaulchile.cl

The Neo-Gothic Iglesia Anglicana San Pablo was built in 1858 by British engineer William Lloyd. This church was established by Valparaíso's English community, but only after the city's Catholic archbishop imposed many conditions on what he considered a temple to a rival faith. Among the most curious was that this church's doors be smaller than those of the city's Catholic churches – and to this day visitors enter not via a grand portal, but by one of the two small side doors. The church's simple stone and wood interior houses a pipe organ, which was donated in memory of Britain's Queen Victoria in 1903.

Iglesia Luterana de la Santa Cruz

Abtao 689, Cerro Concepción 10:30am-1pm Mon-Fri iluterana.cl

Built by the city's German community in 1898, the Iglesia Luterana de la Santa Cruz was South America's first Protestant church to be allowed a steeple and bell tower. Its beautifully austere facade tapers upward toward a slender, 115-ft (35-m) high steeple, which crowns Cerro Concepción and is visible from the city's lower sections. Inside, the nave fills with natural light and a sculpture of Christ on the cross, which is carved from a single pine trunk, hangs above the altar. A grand organ, which was brought over from England in 1884, stands opposite the altar.

Cementerios Católico and Disidentes

Dinamarca s/n, Cerro Panteón Cementerio Católico: 9am-1pm & 3-5pm daily; Cementerio de Disidentes: 9am-1pm, 3-5pm Mon-Sat, 9am-12:45pm Sun

Spectacularly located high up on an overhanging hillside, the Cementerio Católico and Cementerio de Disidentes are poignant evocations of this port city's halcyon days in the 1800s as a melting pot of different cultures and creeds. The Cementerio de Disidentes is the site of the simple, sometimes austere, graves of the city's non-Catholic communities, including American Mormons, English Anglicans, and

EL MERCURIO DE VALPARAÍSO

The oldest newspaper in continuous circulation in the entire Spanish-speaking world, *El Mercurio de Valparaíso* was founded in 1827 by Chilean journalist Pedro Félix Vicuña and the American typographer Thomas G. Wells. Since the 1880s, it has been under the uninterrupted stewardship of Chile's eminent Edwards-Ross family, who continue to aspire to the newspaper's founding ideal that it be "adequate enough to moderate the extreme passions that divide men."

German Lutherans. Many of the gravestones are engraved with tales of war and shipwreck. Opposite the Cementerio de Disidentes, a grand portal enters the Cementerio Católico, otherwise known as Cementerio N°1. Valparaíso's most illustrious sons and daughters lie here in grand, marbled mausoleums. Among the luminaries buried are members of the Edwards-Ross family, owners of the *El Mercurio de Valparaíso* newspaper; José Francisco Vergara, founder of the town Viña del Mar; and Renzo Pecchenino, a popular Chilean cartoonist.

DRINK

Bar Liberty
Valpo's oldest bar draws a loyal crowd. Expect live *cueca* music Thursday through Saturday and pitchers of deliriously sweet *pipeño* (unfiltered wine).

Almte. Riveros 9

16

La Sebastiana

Ferrari 692, Cerro Florida Ascensor Espíritu Santo 10am-6pm Tue-Sun fundacionneruda.org

A must-see for devotees of Pablo Neruda *(p38)*, La Sebastiana is the last of three houses that were bought by the poet in Chile. Neruda and two of his friends acquired the shell of this house in 1961 and named it for its architect and first owner, Sebastian Collado. The house was unfinished and had been abandoned for many years after the death of Don Sebastian in 1949. Neruda made extensive renovations to the structure, which resulted in an anarchic but interesting architecture that mirrored the city itself – the house became a jumble of narrow, twisting stairways and myriad nooks and crannies, painted in a range of colors.

In 1991, the structure was restored and converted into a museum that preserves the house as it was when Neruda lived there. It also contains a number of strange and wonderful objects bought by the poet, such as a Parisian carousel pony in the living room and an unfitted wash-basin from England in the study. Pablo Neruda's rich imagination is also evident in the American oakwood stairway, which was rescued from a demolition site, and a floor mosaic of uncut pebbles shaped into an antique map of Patagonia and Antarctica.

As with Neruda's other houses in Santiago and Isla Negra, La Sebastiana is open for audio-guided tours, which are available in a range of languages and on a first-come, first-served basis. There is no need to book in advance.

The interesting interior of Pablo Neruda's house, La Sebastiana, and *(inset)* the colorful exterior ↓

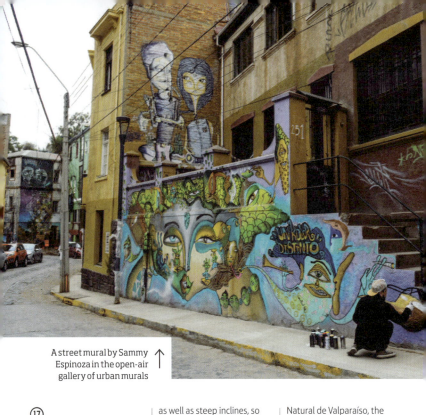

A street mural by Sammy Espinoza in the open-air gallery of urban murals

Museo a Cielo Abierto

Cerro Bellavista
Ascensor Espíritu Santo

A fascinating outdoor museum on Cerro Bellavista, the Museo a Cielo Abierto comprises a maze of winding streets and passageways painted with giant, colorful street murals by some of Chile's best-known contemporary artists. There are about 20 murals, ranging from highly abstract works to humorous depictions of daily life in the city, and a self-guided tour takes about an hour. There are many steps along the way, as well as steep inclines, so be sure to wear comfortable shoes. The greatest concentration of murals are on Calle Ferrari and on Pasaje Santa Lucía. The latter is a steeply stepped passageway and a whirl of kaleidoscopically vibrant motifs and figures.

The museum features works by Chilean artists, including surrealist Roberto Matta, Gracia Barrios of the Grupo Signo, and Nemesio Antúnez, founder of Taller 99, an artists' collective.

Unfortunately, weather and vandalism have damaged many of the works, but they are undergoing restoration.

Did You Know?

Museo a Cielo Abierto began in 1973 but was completed in 1991 after the fall of Pinochet.

18

Palacio Lyon

Museo de Historia Natural de Valparaíso: Condell 1546 10am–5:30pm Tue–Fri, 11am–4pm Sat (book ahead) mhnv.cl

Built in 1887, Palacio Lyon houses the Museo de Historia Natural de Valparaíso, the city's natural history museum and Chile's second-oldest state museum. Built of stone, cast iron, and glass, this edifice evokes the 19th century as an age of exploration, scientific discovery, and public education. Displays include exhibits from the early 1900s that feature Chile's marine flora and fauna, stuffed animals from around the world, and rows of curiosities, including bovine conjoined twins conserved in tanks of formaldehyde. The crypt in the basement features contemporary artworks by Chile's finest artists.

Iglesia de los Sagrados Corazones

Avenida Independencia 2086 (032) 2746 728 Daily

Dating from 1874, the impressive Iglesia de los

Sagrados Corazones was the first church built in the Americas for the French Order of the Sacred Hearts. Inside the church, a Gothic style predominates. Most of its striking architectural elements, including the elegant clock tower, the wooden altar, pulpit, and confessional boxes, were brought over from France. There is a stunning pipe organ that was made by Aristide de Cavaillé-Coll, the most famous French organ maker of the time. Stained glass, a replica of the glass found in the Church of Saint Gudula in Belgium, adorns the church's upper reaches and there are thousands of tiny, gold-painted stars decorating its vaulted ceiling. The church was declared a national monument in 2003.

Adjacent to the church, the Colegio de los Sagrados Corazones dates from 1837 and is Chile's oldest private high school. Several former presidents were educated here.

Iglesia y Convento de San Francisco

Blanco Viel s/n, Cerro Barón 10am-8pm daily

Established in 1846, the Iglesia San Francisco is one of Chile's most impressive examples of redbrick architecture. The church, designated a national monument in 1983, features an ornate facade topped with a distinct, rising bell tower, which used to be illuminated at night to guide ships to Valparaíso's port. The interior of the church is a study in beautiful simplicity, comprising modest whitewashed walls and a Spanish-tiled floor beneath an arched, dark-wood ceiling.

Entered from the side of the church, the Convento de San Francisco was established as a boarding house for visiting priests. In 2013, as both church and convent were under-going a restoration, a fire broke out. Restoration work was eventually completed in 2024.

Congreso Nacional

Avenida Pedro Montt s/n 9:30am-12:30pm & 3-5pm Mon-Fri (reserve 30 days in advance) camara.cl

In 1988, General Pinochet was obliged to return the country to democracy after 14 years of dictatorship *(p48)*. In doing so, Pinochet chose Valparaíso, rather than Santiago, as the seat of the country's then new National Congress. Two years later, the starkly modern Congreso Nacional building, built on the site of one of Pinochet's boyhood homes, was inaugurated. The structure has been met with divided opinion ever since its construction – some see it as a powerful and vital symbol of democracy and of decentralized political power, while other people question its general aesthetic appeal.

Tours of its halls and salons guide visitors through the rich allegory and symbolism of this building's spectacular architecture. The tours, which are given in both Spanish and English, cover the National Senate, the Deputy chambers, and the Salón de Honor – the ceremonial hall where international statesmen, such as Mikhail Gorbachev and Bill Clinton, former Russian and US presidents respectively, have given speeches to dignitaries.

VALPO'S BEST STREET ART

Valparaíso is famous for its array of street art and graffiti, much of it political in nature and highly creative. The Museo a Cielo Abierto (Open Air Museum) on Cerro Bellavista is the best place to start: it has a collection of murals by some of the city's best-known street artists. For a deeper dive into the scene, head out for a guided walk with local agency Valpo Street Art Tours (*valpo streetart.com*).

Dating from 1874, the impressive Iglesia de los Sagrados Corazones was the first church built in the Americas for the French Order of the Sacred Hearts.

2

CASA MUSEO ISLA NEGRA

B6 56 miles (90 km) S of Valparaíso; Poeta Neruda s/n, Isla Negra 10am-6pm Tue-Sun (Jan-Feb: to 7pm) fundacionneruda.org

Steeped in literary history, Museo Isla Negra offers visitors a charming insight into the life of Nobel Prize-winning author Pablo Neruda. Isla Negra is home to thousands of unique and eccentric objects collected by Chile's most famous writer, including figureheads, retort of sails, whale teeth, antique shoes, and smoking pipes.

Attracted by its location facing the Isla Negra beach, Pablo Neruda bought the original building from a Spanish sailor in 1939. Neruda extended the house, creating a structure whose long, thin shape mirrored the geography of Chile, and filled it with over 3,500 weird and wonderful objects from across the globe. Today, the house is a museum and remains exactly as it was when the poet lived here with his third wife, Matilde Urrutia, prior to his death in 1973.

Dining room

Neruda's bedroom

Ship figureheads, stained glass, and wooden angels adorn the living room. Neruda encrusted its floor with seashells to massage his feet.

The house bar conserves Neruda's comprehensive collection of surreal bottles. An array of colors, shapes, and sizes are displayed.

Named for its isolation and wild black rocks, Isla Negra beach is associated with the poet's love for the sea.

Did You Know?

Isla Negra gets heavy rains in winter, which inspired Neruda to write "Ode to the Storm."

Illustration of Pablo Neruda's house turned museum, Casa Museo Isla Negra ↑

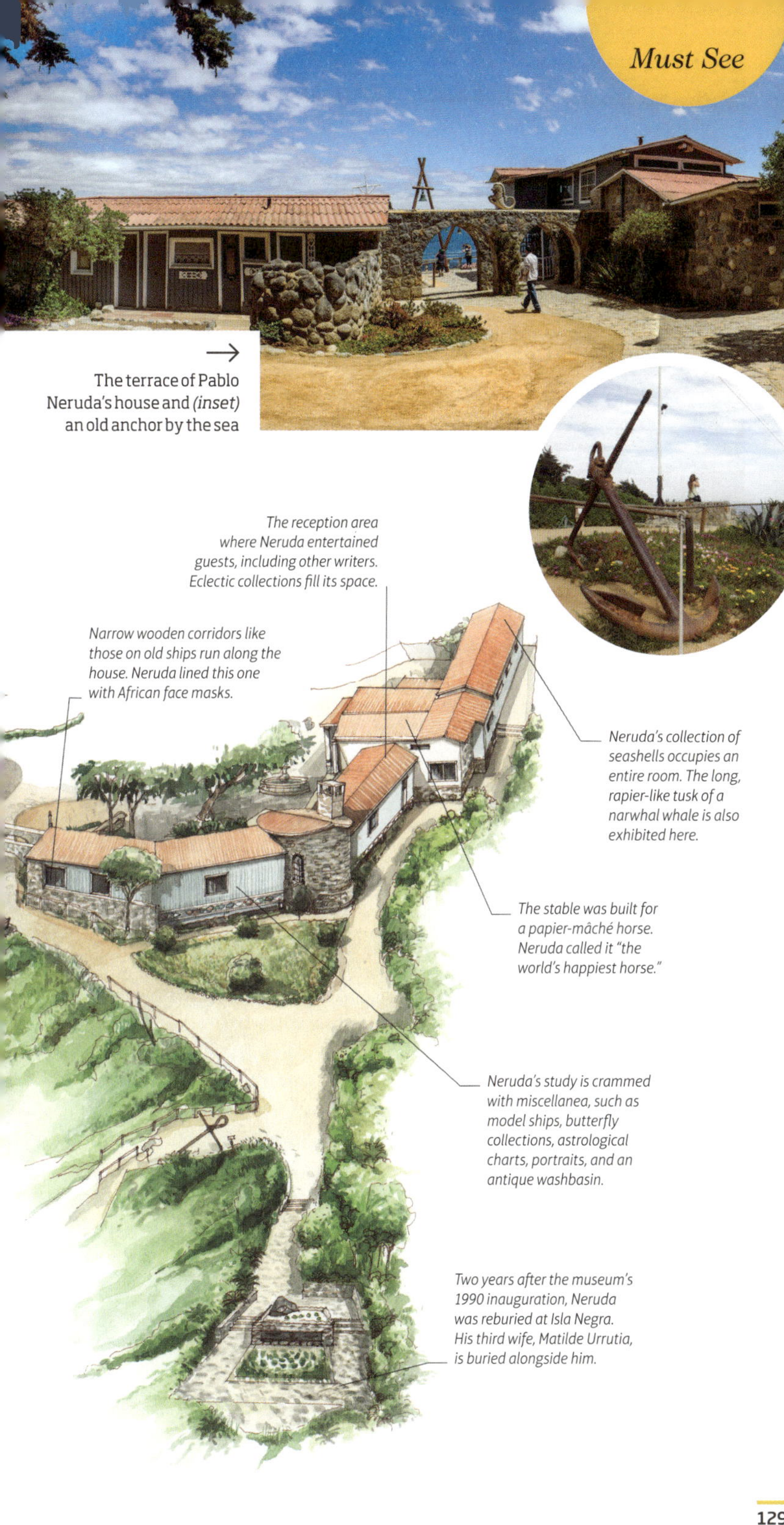

The reception area where Neruda entertained guests, including other writers. Eclectic collections fill its space.
Narrow wooden corridors like those on old ships run along the house. Neruda lined this one with African face masks.
Neruda's collection of seashells occupies an entire room. The long, rapier-like tusk of a narwhal whale is also exhibited here.
The stable was built for a papier-mâché horse. Neruda called it "the world's happiest horse."
Neruda's study is crammed with miscellanea, such as model ships, butterfly collections, astrological charts, portraits, and an antique washbasin.
Two years after the museum's 1990 inauguration, Neruda was reburied at Isla Negra. His third wife, Matilde Urrutia, is buried alongside him.

→ The terrace of Pablo Neruda's house and *(inset)* an old anchor by the sea

↑ Vineyards rolling across the hills of Casablanca Valley

EXPERIENCE MORE

3

Casablanca Valley

**B6**

Located between Santiago and Valparaíso, the Casablanca Valley is home to a string of vineyards whose maritime-influenced climates produce crisp, refreshing white wines. Overlooked by the snow-topped Andes, most of the wineries offer tours, tasting sessions, and accommodation. Many are easy to visit independently by taking a taxi from the town of Casablanca, or a trip can be booked with the excellent Valparaiso Wine Tours agency *(valparaiso winetours.com)*.

HIDDEN GEM

Reloj de Flores

Planted in 1962 on a grassy slope facing the ocean, the Reloj de Flores (Flower Clock) symbolizes Viña del Mar's status as the "Garden City." The dial is a circular flower bed set with bright flowers.

4

Viña del Mar

B6  **5 Norte 901; visitavina.munivina.cl**

Founded in 1874, Viña del Mar (Vineyard of the Sea) has its origins in a hacienda whose vineyards faced the ocean. The area became a city after the 1906 earthquake compelled Valparaíso's elite to relocate here. Its flatter topography was ideal for building the French-style garden palaces that were then fashionable and the town became a resort for the rich. Today, it is Chile's Ciudad Jardín (Garden City), with green spaces, great beaches, and fine palaces housing stunning museums.

Viña del Mar's elegant central square, Plaza José Francisco Vergara, is named for the city's founder, whose bronze statue stands on a marble plinth in one corner. The plaza is dotted with pools, statues, fountains, and shady trees, as well as impressive buildings. Also of note is the **Palacio Vergara**, which houses the Museo Municipal de Bellas Artes. It is home to over 150 artworks. Surrounding the palace are the parklands of the Quinta Vergara, which are planted with many introduced species. Dominating the grounds, the Anfiteatro de la Quinta Vergara is a modern

amphitheater that hosts the Festival de Cine Internacional *(p42)*.

Castillo Wulff, located on the city's coastal avenue, was constructed in 1908. A national monument and architectural landmark, it is built in the style of a typical medieval castle, with turrets, ramparts, a round tower, and a central courtyard. The courtyard stairs offer great ocean vistas, while the tower out the back has a fantastic view of the sea through its glass floor.

The **Museo de Arqueología e Historia Francisco Fonck** features displays of pre-Hispanic objects collected from across Chile and Latin America. Its standout collection was brought from Easter Island *(p264)* in 1951. Constructed after the 1906 earthquake, the **Palacios Rioja and Carrasco** are national monuments. The former was inspired by Versailles and is now a decorative arts museum that conserves the Rioja family home as it was a century ago. The Palacio Carrasco was built between 1912 and 1923 in the Beaux-Arts style, and houses the city's cultural center. The **Jardín Botánico Nacional** is located 5 miles (8 km) southeast of the city. The park is home to more than 3,000 plant species.

Palacio Vergara
Errázuriz 596
(563) 2218 5651
10am-1:30pm & 3-5:30pm Tue-Sun

Castillo Wulff
Avenida Marina 37
(563) 2218 5751

Museo de Arqueología e Historia Francisco Fonck
4 Norte N 784
10am-6pm Tue-Sat, 10am-2pm & 3-6pm Mon, 10am-2pm Sun
museofonck.cl

Palacios Rioja and Carrasco
Palacio Rioja: Quillota 214; Palacio Carrasco: Avenida Libertad 250
(032) 218 4690
10am-1:30pm & 3-5:30pm Tue-Sun

Jardín Botánico Nacional
5 miles (8 km) SE of Viña del Mar
9am-6pm daily
jbn.cl

EAT

Los Roldán

This takeout-only bakery specializes in delicious, freshly made empanadas. Try the delectable scallop or razor clam.

B6 Avenida Borgono 14777, Viña del Mar
(032) 3114 779

$

Divino Pecado

This upmarket spot offers Italian-influenced fish and seafood dishes in sophisticated surroundings. It's popular, so book ahead.

B6 San Martín 180, Viña del Mar
divinopecado.cl

$$$

Gulls flying above the shoreline in Viña del Mar

5 

Sewell

C7 46 miles (75 km) SE of Santiago; Carretera al Cobre Hours vary, check website fundacion sewell.org

Clinging to Cerro Negro at 7,215 ft (2,200 m) above sea level, Sewell – the City of Stairs – was established by the American Braden Copper Company in 1905 as a camp for workers of the nearby El Teniente mine. By 1960, it was a thriving town, with around 15,000 inhabitants, a bank, a courthouse, a town hall, recreational clubs, and Chile's most advanced hospital. Sewell was slowly abandoned from the 1970s to 1999, but was declared a UNESCO World Heritage Site in 1998, and now remains an eerily beautiful preserved city of multistoried wooden buildings. A steep central staircase, the Escalera Central, is the backbone of the abandoned city. Access paths and secondary stairs stem from it in a herringbone pattern. The Museo de la Gran Minería del Cobre, occupying the Modernist building of the old Industrial School, displays historical and geological exhibits from Sewell's past.

6

Cartagena

B6 62 miles (100 km) S of Valparaíso  Municipalidad, Plaza de Armas

The delightful hillside town of Cartagena has narrow winding streets and colorful houses hanging from a hilltop overlooking a bay. The best time to visit is late spring or early fall, when the beaches are not as crowded as they are during summer.

From the palm-shaded Plaza de Armas in Cartagena's upper town, twisting streets and stairways wend their way down to Playa Chica, south of the plaza, and to Playa Grande, north of the plaza. Set on a hillside east of Playa Chica is the home and tomb of Vicente Huidobro (1893–1948), a great Chilean poet who lived for several years in Cartagena. Though it's sadly run down, the spot is still a popular point of pilgrimage for Chilean poets and artists. The house is under private ownership and closed to public view.

Did You Know?

A group of Humboldt penguins in water is known as a "raft," and on land, they're called a "waddle."

7

Quintay

B6 29 miles (47 km) S of Valparaíso 

The fishing village of Quintay is an idyllic spot. Buses drop off visitors at its small plaza, from where sandy lanes wend down to the *caleta*. This is a horseshoe-shaped fishermen's harbor edged by a rocky beach and weatherboard seafood restaurants. Sea otters and birds congregate on the beach and fishermen unload their catch here from wooden boats.

Overlooking the *caleta* is the **Ballenera de Quintay**, Chile's biggest whaling station until its closure in 1967. Now a

whaling museum, it includes the station's old and somewhat eerie whaling platform onto which the carcasses of 1,600 blue whale – the world's largest animal – were dragged year after year.

Quintay has two main beaches. From the plaza a ten-minute walk through cool pine and eucalyptus forest leads to the breathtakingly picturesque Playa Chica, a wave-pummeled beach ringed by high, rugged cliffs and wildflowers. North of the town center, Playa Grande is a long stretch of golden sand, spoiled slightly by condominiums. For activities in Quintay, diving schools at the *caleta* run scuba-diving and kayaking excursions.

Ballenera de Quintay
Caleta de Quintay
Jan-Mar: 11am-7pm Tue-Sun (Apr-Dec: to 6pm Thu-Sun) fundacionquintay.com

Algarrobo

B6 43 miles (70 km) S of Valparaíso

The largest town along the section of Pacific coast south of Valparaíso, Algarrobo is a family-oriented resort that gets crowded in summer with families arriving from Santiago. This town has excellent tourist services as well as some 14 separate beaches where activities include scuba-diving, windsurfing, and horseriding. Its most popular beach, Playa San Pedro, is close to the town center and faces calm waters, ideal for swimming. Playa Grande is a more dramatic, big-wave beach. South of the town center is Playa El Canelo, a stretch of fine sand washed by aquamarine waters, which backs onto thick pine forest. Playa El Canelillo, meanwhile, is secluded and quieter. Reached by boat from Algarrobo, the Isla de Pájaros Niños is a rocky islet visited each September to April by nesting colonies of Humboldt penguins. Boats skirt the islet's shore, moving past birdlife such as pelicans, cormorants, and gulls.

A small fishing harbor in Quintay, with traditional boats lining the sands

Humboldt penguins perched on the rocky islet of nature reserve Cachagua

Cachagua

B6 45 miles (73 km) N of Valparaíso

A beautiful, rustic beach-town, Cachagua arrives as a welcome change along a stretch of coastline dominated by upscale resorts and condominiums. The town has a eucalyptus-shaded plaza from which sandy lanes flanked by thatched houses descend to the long, dramatic Playa Grande, Cachagua's main beach. Horseriding and surfing are popular activities here.

Visible from Playa Grande, the Monumento Natural Isla Cachagua is a rocky islet that is refuge for a wide variety of birdlife, including nesting colonies of Humboldt penguins from September to April. Boat trips take visitors near the islet and offer a chance to observe this rare birdlife from a close range. Also of interest at Cachagua is Playa Las Cujas, a sheltered, rocky beach that is popular with divers and anglers.

STAY

Hotel Isla Seca
Despite sitting on the busy coastal highway, this Zapallar hotel is a quiet place, with most rooms facing the Pacific. It has a good seafood restaurant, too.

B6 Camino Costero F-30-E No. 31, Zapallar hotelislaseca.cl

El Copihué
The smartest option in the area, El Copihué is a great base for exploring Parque Nacional La Campana *(p137)*. You'll find comfy rooms, a decent restaurant, and a spa.

B6 Diego Portales 2203, Olmué copihue.cl

$$$

→

Chalet Recart towering over beachgoers enjoying the Papudo seaside

Papudo

B6 56 miles (91 km) N of Valparaíso municipalidadpapudo.cl

Less exclusive than the neighboring beach-towns of Zapallar and Cachagua, Papudo is a small and unpretentious seaside town with great walks. A sweeping coastal boulevard runs parallel to the two main beaches: Playa Grande, a long, open beach popular with surfers, and the smaller, sheltered Playa Chica, which is frequented by families. A number of attractive seaside walks strike out from both beaches, crossing sections of cliffs along the coast that are pitted with caves and caverns. On fine days, horses are available for those who wish to ride along the shoreline.

Among the buildings that line the main coastal boulevard, visitors will find the Iglesia Nuestra Señora de las Mercedes, a church and national monument that was built in 1918. Farther on, the honey-colored Chalet Recart, site of Papudo's town hall, is one of several alpine-chalet buildings that front the coast here.

Zapallar

B6 50 miles (80 km) N of Valparaíso Municipalidad, Germán Riesgo 399

An exceptionally picturesque coastal town and an erstwhile high-end destination, Zapallar is small, secluded, and ringed by steeply forested coastal mountains. The town sits on a wooded hillside that sweeps dramatically down to rocky cliffs and a half-moon-shaped sandy beach. A number of weatherboard holiday villas dot the coastal mountains around Zapallar.

Since the late 19th century, this town has been a favorite summer destination for the wealthy citizens of Santiago, and today Zapallar is only a two-hour drive from the capital along fast-moving freeways. From Zapallar's beach a 4-mile (6-km) coastal path skirts clifftops and has wide ocean vistas. Boat launches make daily departures in summer, taking birdwatchers and vacationers southward to the Monumento Natural Isla Cachagua *(p133)*.

A sandy path up the hillside from the beach leads to Zapallar's white-sand plaza, which is fronted by a clapboard theaterhouse. This dates from 1908 and was originally the town church. From the plaza,

Did You Know?

La Ligua, just inland from Papudo, was home to La Quintrala, an infamous Chilean serial killer.

a number of lanes climb uphill to Zapallar's commercial center, which is filled with stores, places to eat, and tourist information.

Los Andes

B6 87 miles (141 km) NE of Valparaíso Avenida Santa Teresa 333

Ringed by the vineyards of Aconcagua valley, at the foot of the Andean cordillera (mountain ranges), Los Andes was founded in 1791 as a staging post on a colonial trade route. Today, it is the first stop for many travelers making the road crossing of the Andes from Argentina to Chile's Central Valley. There's not a huge amount to see in the town itself, but there are two museums of interest here. The first, the **Museo Arqueológico de los Andes** is a small house with well-kept pre-Columbian displays. The **Museo del Antiguo Convento del Espíritu Santo** is a convent building dedicated to Santa Teresa de Los Andes, Chile's first saint. Visitors can wander about the convent's old workrooms, sleeping quarters, cloistered courtyard, and orchard. Next door, the Capilla Espíritu Santo is a Neo-Gothic chapel and shrine to the saint, who was a novice nun in Los Andes during her short life.

Also of note are the Neo-Classical headquarters of the regional government, which were built between 1888 and 1891 and overlook Los Andes' pretty colonial plaza. At the edge of town, the Cerro de la Vírgen is a hilltop lookout point with fine views.

Museo Arqueológico de los Andes
Avenida Santa Teresa 398 10am-2pm & 3-5:30pm Wed-Fri museolosandes.cl

Museo del Antiguo Convento del Espíritu Santo
Avenida Santa Teresa 389 (034) 2421 765 9:30am-1pm, 3-6pm Mon-Fri, 10am-5:30pm Sat & Sun

Cristo Redentor

C6 130 miles (210 km) E of Valparaíso; Camino Cristo Redentor Dec-Mar

The gigantic Cristo Redentor (Christ the Redeemer) marks one of the world's great frontier passes: the crossing of the central Andes between Chile and Argentina. Set against a backdrop of the snow-swathed Andes, the figure stands at a dizzying 12,539 ft (3,823 m) above sea level. The 23-ft- (7-m-) tall statue of Christ is set on a 20-ft (6-m) granite plinth weighing 8,800 lb (4,000 kg). Sculpted in 1904 in Buenos Aires, the Cristo Redentor was conveyed by train to the foot of the Andes, dismantled into various parts, and hauled up the mountains by mules. Its erection marked a historic signing of peace between Chile and Argentina, following decades of border disputes that pushed both countries to the brink of war. Tour buses and private cars that pass the Chilean customs post reach the monument by taking the Camino Cristo Redentor, a gravel turnoff en route to the Túnel del Cristo Redentor, a 2-mile- (3-km-) long tunnel crossing of the Andes.

EAT

El Chiringuito

With fishermen hauling in skiffs within sight of the restaurant, this spot provides some of the freshest seafood in Chile. There are great views from the terrace, but take care that the seabirds overhead don't steal your lunch.

B6 Avenida Zapallar 151, Zapallar (033) 2741 024

$$$

Taking photographs of the Cristo Redentor against its mountainous backdrop

Ski slopes of Portillo, where *(inset)* competitions take place

Portillo

C6 126 miles (203 km) E of Valparaíso; Renato Sánchez 4270, Las Condes Mid-Jun-Sep skiportillo.com

Spectacularly located at 10,000 ft (3,000 m) above sea level, Portillo is South America's oldest ski resort. It has 17 runs for skiers and snowboarders of all levels. Expert and extreme skiers will find fantastic opportunities on slopes that descend from an altitude of 10,900 ft (3,270 m). Challenges include 50-degree descents, countless off-piste routes, heli-skiing and night-skiing. Views from the slopes are tremendous, embracing surrounding peaks and the Laguna del Inca, a lake that freezes in winter. The ski center is a self-contained resort with packages that include hotel lodging, lift tickets, and facilities such as a movie theater and a heated outdoor pool. Visitors can also choose to stay in cheaper mountain lodges or backpackers' lodges. There is a lively après-ski scene and excellent family-oriented services, including day care for children aged four to six years.

Termas de Jahuel

B6 87 miles (140 km) NE of Valparaíso; Jahuel s/n, San Felipe jahuel.cl

Set on the slopes of the arid Andean foothills, overlooking the fertile Aconcagua Valley, Termas de Jahuel is a modern, luxurious spa retreat that accepts both day and overnight guests. Sophisticated natural therapies are on offer; the spa's signature massage treatment is an olive-oil therapy that uses organically grown plants. There is also an outdoor pool edged by palms and jasmine.

Jahuel's thermal properties were recognized by the travelers crossing the Andes who came to rest here. Today, guests reside in a pavilion or an exclusive boutique hotel with en-suite thermal baths, and activities include mountain biking and horseback riding. Trails climb to a plateau with fine views of the high-altitude Aconcagua Valley wine district. Facilities include children's playrooms, tennis courts, and a good range of restaurants.

Rancagua

B7 54 miles (87 km) S of Santiago Germán Riesgo 350; rancagua.cl

Founded in 1743, Rancagua lies deep in *huaso* (cowboy) country and hosts the Campeonato Nacional de Rodeo each year. Steeped in history, the city was the site of one of Chile's bloodiest conflicts – the 1814 Battle of Rancagua, in which the patriot militia led by Bernardo O'Higgins *(p259)* fought against Spanish forces. The Monumento a Bernardo O'Higgins dominating the city's central plaza is an equestrian memorial honoring Chilean soldiers who were killed at this spot.

Just north of the plaza, the Iglesia de la Merced is an adobe church built in 1778. O'Higgins directed his troops from its bell tower, which was rebuilt in 1857. It suffered further damage in the earthquake of 2010. Located south of the plaza, the Paseo del Estado is an old street lined with fine historic structures. The highlight here is the **Museo Regional de Rancagua**, housed in two buildings that date from 1790 and 1800. The museum has engaging exhibits on religious art and on the Central Valley's weaving traditions and mining heritage. It also re-creates typical colonial-era living quarters. At the southern end of Paseo del Estado, another large colonial building houses Rancagua's **Casa de la Cultura**. Built in the early 1700s, it was the base for Spanish forces during the Battle of Rancagua. Today it is a cultural center, fronted by shaded gardens.

Museo Regional de Rancagua
Calle del Estado 685 10am-5:45pm Tue-Thu, 10am-4:45pm Fri, 10am-1:45pm Sat museo rancagua.cl

Casa de la Cultura
Avenida Cachapoal 90 (072) 222 6076 10am-6pm daily (to 7pm Mon-Fri) rancagua cultura.cl

A lofty Chilean wine palm in the Parque Nacional La Campana

Parque Nacional La Campana

B6 37 miles (60 km) E of Valparaíso; Paradero 43, Avenida Granizo 9137 8:30am-5:30pm Tue-Sun (book ahead) conaf.cl

A UNESCO-recognized area, La Campana harbors a wilderness habitat that is considered exceptional for its biodiversity. The park's signature flora is a relict population of Chilean wine palms *(Jubaea chilensis)*, the world's southernmost palm. The birdlife here is rich, while among mammals and reptiles, there is the vizcacha, a large burrowing rodent, as well as iguanas, snakes, and lizards. The park is named for its dominant natural feature, Cerro La Campana (Bell Peak).

From the entrance in the Granizo sector, Sendero El Andinista is a popular 9-mile (14-km) day hike that reaches the summit of this peak. Less visited, the park's northern Ocoa sector has its largest, densest concentrations of Chilean palms, which may live for several hundred years. This sector is accessed via the 5-mile (7-km) Sendero Amasijo, which is connected to the Sendero Los Peumos.

DARWIN AND LA CAMPANA

In August 1834, English naturalist Charles Darwin began a two-night ascent of Cerro La Campana on foot and horseback. With two cowboys, Darwin climbed the hill's northern flank and made camp at the Agua del Guanaco spring. Writing later in *The Voyage of the Beagle*, he noted, "the atmosphere was so clear the masts at anchor in the Bay of Valparaíso... could be distinguished as little black streaks." The group summited on the second morning, where a plaque commemorates their ascent.

18  

El Teniente

C7 49 miles (79 km) SE of Santiago; Carretera al Cobre vts.cl

The biggest subterranean copper mine in the world, El Teniente comprises over 2,700 miles (4,500 km) of underground tunnels. In operation since the early 1800s, the mine produces around 485,000 tons (440,000 tonnes) of copper-ore each year. Guided tours take visitors through a maze of tunnels, past giant ore-crushing machinery and an underground cave of crystal that miners discovered while digging for copper.

19  

Valle de Cachapoal

B7 60 miles (96 km) S of Santiago winesofchile.org

Located in Chile's agricultural heartland, Valle de Cachapoal is renowned for its production of two excellent red wine grapes, the Cabernet Sauvignon and the distinctive Carménère. Most of the valley's wineries are nestled in its cool eastern sector and are open for tours and tastings. Viña San Pedro dates back to 1865. In 2002, it founded a winery that specializes in collection wines and uses gravity to make wine rather than pumps. It also offers tastings. More traditional wineries include the Spanish-style Viña Chateau Los Boldos.

Valle de Cachapoal lies in prime *huaso* territory and customized wine tours here include rodeo shows and horseback rides through the mountains. Although the valley can be covered on a day trip from nearby Rancagua, overnight travelers can find accommodation at Hacienda Los Lingues *(p140)*.

20  

Termas de Cauquenes

C7 73 miles (117 km) S of Santiago 9am-6:30pm Thu-Sun htdc.cl

Nestled in the Andean foothills, Termas de Cauquenes has entertained such luminaries as English naturalist Charles Darwin and revered Chilean Bernardo O'Higgins. This historic spa complex is set amid dense eucalyptus forests with numerous guided walks to an appealing lookout, from where condors can be seen circling in the sky. The 19th-century bathhouse of the spa is cathedral-like in size and ambition, with a soaring ceiling, stained-glass walls, and a mosaic floor between rows of private bathrooms. Overnight guests are housed in a hotel that is constructed around a Spanish courtyard.

The resort also welcomes day visitors, who can luxuriate in the spa's thermal baths and enjoy a range of relaxing therapeutic treatments. Facilities include a heated outdoor pool, a children's playground, and a lovely gourmet restaurant.

ANTIQUE WINERIES OF PIRQUE

In the Pirque area of the Maipo Valley are two of Chile's oldest wine estates. The Viña Cousiño-Macul, founded in 1856, is the oldest family-run bodega in Chile. The estate has a museum and offers tastings in a candlelit 19th-century cellar. Viña Concha y Toro, meanwhile, is the biggest winery in Chile. Established in 1883, it is the largest exporter of wine in Latin America.

Cajón del Maipo

C6 20 miles (33 km) SE of Santiago Comercio 19788, San José del Maipo; cajondelmaipo.com

Offering a gamut of outdoor activities, Cajón del Maipo is a popular weekend destination from Santiago. Independent visitors usually make their base at San José del Maipo, the largest of several small towns in the area. Founded in 1791, the town is an attraction in its own right for its church and adobe houses.

Southwest of Cajón del Maipo is **Reserva Nacional Río Clarillo**, an area of stunning natural beauty. It is ideal for hiking, bird-watching, horseback riding, and rafting excursions.

The ski resort of **Lagunillas** has 13 slopes attracting skiers of all levels during the winter months. It is also one of the few ski centers where night-skiing is possible.

An adventure-tourism resort and sanctuary, **Santuario de la Naturaleza Cascada de las Ánimas** protects an area of rugged mountains, rivers, and waterfalls, and lures visitors with adrenaline-charged activities such as white water rafting, hiking and horseback riding, and zip-lining. Accommodation options include log cabins set in the forest, domes, and a scenic campground.

Monumento Natural El Morado embraces the 16,597-ft (5,060-m) high Cerro El Morado. This snowcapped peak is best viewed on the park's three-hour trek to Laguna El Morado, an alpine lake from where a trail reaches the base of the Glaciar San Francisco. The Baños Morales area has hot-spring pools that attract weekenders from Santiago.

Sun beaming on a vineyard in Cachapoal Valley

↑ The pretty, pink-painted church in Cajón del Maipo

The rustic hot-springs resort of **Termas Valle de Colina** sits at the eastern end of Cajón del Maipo. It comprises a series of natural clay pools that bubble and steam on the slopes of a mountain overlooked by snowcapped peaks. Access to the pools is difficult, as the road to the resort is closed to public transportation; however, Santiago-based Expediciones Manzur runs round trips over weekends. Visitors can hire horses at the resort, and rides to the Argentine border can be arranged in advance.

Reserva Nacional Río Clarillo
25 miles (40 km) SW of San José del Maipo 8:30am-5pm daily (last entry 1pm; book ahead) conaf.cl

Lagunillas
11 miles (17 km) NE of San José del Maipo Jun-Oct skilagunillas.cl

Santuario de la Naturaleza Cascada de las Ánimas
9 miles (14 km) SE of San José del Maipo; 31087 Camino al Volcán, San Alfonso cascadadelasanimas.cl

Monumento Natural El Morado
26 miles (43 km) E of San José del Maipo 8:30am-12:30pm Thu-Sun (book ahead) conaf.cl

Termas Valle de Colina
37 miles (60 km) SE of San José del Maipo 8am-5pm daily termasvallecolina.cl

STAY

Cascada de las Ánimas

A base from which to explore Cajón del Maipo, this lodge has camping, domes, and private rooms. Horseback-riding and hiking are popular from here, with trails along short nature paths and tours through the mountains.

C6 Camino al Volcán N° 31087, San Alfonso cascadadelasanimas.cl

$$$

22    

Hacienda Los Lingues

B7 78 miles (125 km) S of Santiago; Panamericana Sur km 124.5, San Fernando Daily loslingues.com

One of Chile's oldest and most prestigious estates, Hacienda Los Lingues dates from the end of the 16th century when it was gifted by King Philip III of Spain to Don Melchor Jufré del Águila. For over four centuries, it has remained in this Spanish nobleman's family, the current generation of which lives on the hacienda.

Overnight guests stay in traditional rooms that preserve the original architecture and furnishings. Antique family portraits hang from walls, and the sensation of staying at an old aristocratic home rather than simply a luxury hotel is tangible – although contemporary amenities, such as a pool, have been added.

Visitors can also opt for the more economical day tour of the hacienda, which takes in the courtyard, parks, wine cellar, stables, and 1790-built chapel. Dating from 1760, the impressive stables breed gorgeous thoroughbred Aculeo horses, whose lineage can be traced back to Moorish Spain. Day tours also feature a delicious gourmet lunch, rodeo show, and even horseback rides.

The hotel is situated near the wine valleys of Cachapoal *(p138)* and Colchagua *(p148)*, making it a perfectly placed stop-off for wine-tasting novices and oenophiles alike.

TOP 3 LOCAL SKI CENTERS

El Colorado
elcolorado.cl
A popular, economical option, within easy reach of Santiago.

La Parva
laparva.cl
Caters to both beginners and experts, offering good off-piste skiing.

Valle Nevado
vallenevado.com
Chile's biggest, most modern ski center, with heli-skiing and a snowboard park.

↑ Workers harvesting grapes in the vineyards of Los Lingues

23  

Reserva Nacional Río de los Cipreses

C7 81 miles (131 km) S of Santiago; Camino Chacayes s/n 8:30am-5:30pm daily (book ahead) conaf.cl

Created in 1985, Reserva Nacional Río de los Cipreses protects over 142 sq miles (367 sq km) of Andean wilderness, comprising river canyons and forests of mountain cypress. The reserve's popular northern sector has an administration center with displays on the area's wildlife. Starting at the center, paths cross the scenic Cajón Alto Cachapoal, from where the short Sendero Tricahues trail leads to a wildlife observation point. Here, colonies of the burrowing parrot, loro tricahue, can be seen nesting in the canyon wall.

The reserve's less-visited central and southern sectors can be reached by longer hikes and horseback rides that depart from the administration

Smaller than most other wine valleys of central Chile, the Valle de Curicó carries one significant advantage for wine enthusiasts - personalized, unhurried tours and tastings hosted by wine experts.

center. These trace the Cajón Río Cipreses that forms the spine of the reserve. Along the way, visitors traverse cypress forests and pass grazing guanaco herds. It is also possible to see pre-Hispanic petroglyphs and enjoy dramatic Andean vistas, including views of the soaring 15,941-ft- (4,860-m-) high Volcán Palomo.

Valle de Curicó

B7 37 miles (60 km) S of Santa Cruz; Curicó

While smaller than most other wine valleys of central Chile, the Valle de Curicó carries one significant advantage for wine enthusiasts – personalized, unhurried tours and tastings hosted by wine experts. Valle de Curicó produces fine white wines, especially sauvignon blanc, as well as Cabernet Sauvignon reds – some from 80-year-old vines. Its wineries (many of which are relatively small and family-owned) include the Spanish-owned Miguel Torres estate, the San Pedro, and Millamar vineyards. The wineries are visited on customized tours arranged by **Ruta del Vino Curicó**, which also organizes private tours. In the third week of March each year, the Fiesta de la Vendimia Curicó is held here – a unique celebration that elects a Queen of the Harvest alongside many wine-themed activities. The festival has been running since 1991.

Ruta del Vino Curicó
Prat 301-A, Curicó
9am-2pm & 3:30-6pm Mon-Fri rutadelvinocurico.cl

Santa Cruz

B7 113 miles (182 km) SW of Santiago Plaza de Armas s/n

One of the larger towns of the Colchagua Valley *(p148)*, Santa Cruz was founded in the 19th century. The town's most notable building is the Municipalidad (town hall), a reddish arcaded house. The undoubted highlight of Santa Cruz is the private **Museo de Colchagua**, owned by alleged arms dealer Carlos Cardoen. It houses over 5,000 objects relating to Chilean history. Displays range from rare objects that belonged to former president Bernardo O'Higgins to the Gran Rescate exhibit, which showcases objects relating to the rescue of 33 miners trapped in San José in August 2010.

Santa Cruz is the starting point for winery tours to Colchagua. A popular tour option is via the wine-themed 1920s steam train **Tren Sabores del Valle**. The train leaves from Santiago's Estación Central and terminates at San Fernando in the valley's north, from where visitors can depart for a winery coach tour to Valle Colchagua.

Museo de Colchagua
Avenida Errázuriz 145 10am-6:30pm daily museocolchagua.cl

Tren Sabores del Valle
Plaza de Armas 298
Sat efe.cl

CHILE'S RODEO

The rodeo arose in the 16th century, when cattle were gathered together and branded as a means of identification, before it evolved into Chile's national sport. Today *huasos* - or cowboys - steer the horses around a *medialuna*, a half-moon arena, in an attempt to pin down a calf. The sport is an integral part of Chilean life, but it is highly controversial and some organizations continue to seek a ban similar to the bullfighting ban in Catalonia, Spain.

↑ An antique horse carriage displayed at the Museo de Colchagua in Santa Cruz

EAT

La Casa Verde
After a busy day of surfing, relax at this restaurant with scrumptious sandwiches and vegetarian burgers, best enjoyed on the terrace with views of the beach.

B7 Millaco 451, Pichilemu (9) 2093 6331

Pichilemu

B7 161 miles (259 km) SW of Santiago Angel Gaete 365; pichilemu.cl

Central Valley's surf capital, Pichilemu is a haven for surfers, bodyboarders, and hippies. Before the boarders arrived, Pichilemu was a luxury coastal resort, built in the 1900s by Chilean speculator Agustín Ross-Edwards. It was the site of Chile's first casino, but went into decline with the rise of Viña del Mar *(p130)* in the north. Pichilemu retains many charming vestiges of its aristocratic past, however. The old casino building is now occupied by a cultural center.

Today, Pichilemu is a small laid-back town with several beaches, including the main Las Terrazas stretch, which has surf schools and is popular with novice boarders owing to its small waves. About 4 miles (6 km) south of the town center, the Punta de Lobos beach's long, 8-ft- (2.5-m-) high leg breaks attract expert surfers. A stop on the international surfing circuit, Punta de Lobos has an excellent infrastructure. Located between the two is Infernillo, with its extremely dangerous lefts. It is recommended only for experienced surfers.

27   

Termas de Panimávida

B7 55 miles (88 km) SE of Talca; Panimávida s/n, Linares 10am-8pm daily termasde panimavida.cl

Set in pastoral farmlands in the Andean foothills, this spa resort occupies an old colonial-style edifice surrounded by statue-dotted gardens. There are large indoor and outdoor thermal pools, as well as children's pools. Therapeutic treatments include massages, hot rooms, and Jacuzzis, as well as wine therapies and herbal, Turkish, and mud baths.

Slightly to the south, **Termas de Quinamávida** is a spa with similar facilities and services. Its therapies also include steam treatments in cactus-wood bathtubs. The resort is closer to the mountains and is a modern complex of honey-colored buildings set in century-old eucalyptus and pine forests.

Termas de Quinamávida
Camino Linares-Colbún km 16 8:30am-8pm daily termasdechile.cl

Maule

B7 47 miles (76 km) S of Santa Cruz

Offering a Ruta del Vino that takes in eight of the region's wineries, Maule is one of Chile's top wine-producing regions. The area around the city of Talca is renowned for its reds, but there are also a few refreshing white wines being produced here.

Viña Bouchon, located in a 180-year-old adobe hacienda in the Maule valley, is home to the Casa Bouchon boutique hotel. Cabernet Sauvignon and the more unusual Pais and Carignan grapes are grown in the vineyards here. Tours and tastings need prior booking.

Only 9 miles (15 km) south of Talca, the town of San Javier is home to **Viña Balduzzi**, a family-run winery that welcomes drop-ins. They produce a range of reds and whites, including a superb Sauvignon Blanc, but the truly premium wines are the Cabernet Sauvignon and the Syrah.

To the west of San Javier, on the highway to Constitución, **Viña Gillmore** focuses on reds, with Merlot, Cabernet

↑ Preparing to ride the waves from the beach of Punta Lobos in Pichilemu

Franc, and Cabernet Sauvignon, plus blends of these grapes. It's open for tours and tastings at short notice, but call ahead. It also has its own exclusive spa that specializes in wine-based therapies.

East of San Rafael, **Via Wines** is based on the Fundo Las Chilcas. It is known for its sustainable approach and its terrific Syrah and Sauvignon Blanc. Advance booking is mandatory for the organic winery tour.

HISTORY OF WINE IN CHILE

Chilean winemaking began in the 16th century for use in religious rites. Secular demand followed, and by the 19th century it was fashionable in elite circles for families to plant vineyards at their country estates. High-quality vines were introduced from France and Chile set up its first wineries. In the 1980s, foreign wine-makers and consultants built ultra-modern wineries. Chile rediscovered its signature Carménère grape and the wine-tourism industry emerged.

Reserva Nacional Altos de Lircay, and *(inset)* Chucao tapaculo, a local bird ↑

Viña Bouchon
Camino a Constitución km 30 casabouchon.com

Viña Balduzzi
Avenida Balmaceda 1189, San Javier 9am-6pm Mon-Sat balduzzi.com

Viña Gillmore
Camino a Constitución km 20 9am-6pm Mon-Fri gillmorewines.cl

Via Wines
K-409 viawines.com

29  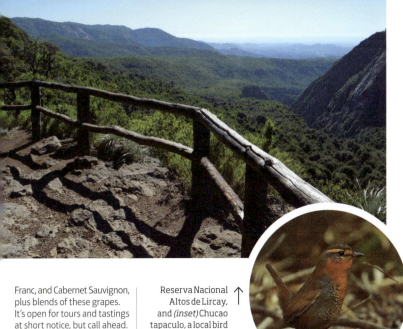 

Reserva Nacional Altos de Lircay

B7 42 miles (67 km) E of Talca; Ruta Internacional Pehuenche, Cruce Vilches Alto 8:30am-5pm daily (book ahead) conaf.cl

Conserving a wilderness area of southern-beech *(Nothofagus)* forest and rugged river-canyon country, Reserva Nacional Altos de Lircay offers activities such as mountain biking, hiking, and horseback riding. Birds can be spotted along nature-watching trails, including Andean condors and, in forests, the loro tricahue (an endangered native parrot), and Magellanic woodpeckers.

The two most popular hiking trails strike out from the park entrance. The Sendero Laguna del Alto is an eight-hour return trek through southern-beech forests to the mountain-ringed Laguna del Alto. The Sendero Enladrillado is a seven-hour return trek, of similar difficulty, that ascends through native woods to the Enladrillado, a soaring platform of hexagonal basalt. A stunning vantage point, it overlooks a deep river canyon and has 360-degree vistas of an area that includes the peaks of three volcanoes – Cerro Azul, Volcán Quizapú, and Descabezado Grande (The Big Headless). The latter can be climbed on a five-day circuit, organized through tour agencies such as Trekking Chile *(trekkingchile.com)*.

30    

Parque Nacional Radal Siete Tazas

B7 78 miles (125 km) SE of Santa Cruz 8:30am-4:30pm Tue-Sun (book ahead) conaf.cl

This national park is named for its most striking natural feature, the Siete Tazas (Seven Cups). Located in the western section of the park, these are seven connected rock pools formed by the erosive waters of the Río Claro that plunges down a narrow gorge here. Nearby are two breathtaking waterfalls: the 131-ft- (40-m-) high Velo de la Novia and the 82-ft- (25-m-) high Salto de la Leona. The trail linking Salto de la Leona with the Siete Tazas passes transition forest that features both Central Valley flora and temperate rainforest common to the Lake District farther south. A short distance from the pools, the Sector Parque Inglés has scenic walking, horseback riding, and mountain-biking trails. The Sendero El Bolsón offers visitors a full day's hike to a refuge; beyond, an unsigned trail continues to Reserva Nacional Altos de Lircay *(p143)*. Nature-watching, swimming, and kayaking are all popular activities here.

31   

Lago Vichuquén

B7 60 miles (96 km) SW of Santa Cruz Manuel Rodríguez 315, Vichuquén

Central Valley's most beautiful lake, Lago Vichuquén is an intensely blue tongue of water ringed by green, pine-swathed hills. The lake and its surrounds attract birdlife, including species of swan, heron, and duck. In colonial times, the rich suggestiveness of this area led to its notoriety as a supposed meeting place of sorcerers and witches. Today, it attracts bikers, anglers, windsurfers, water-skiers, horseback-riding aficionados, and nature-watchers.

Some 4 miles (7 km) east of the lake is the historical settlement of Vichuquén, built by the Spanish in 1585 on the site of an old Inca colony. Today, it preserves warrens of winding colonial streets lined with orange trees and fronted by adobe houses. Both Vichuquén and its lake can be included on wine tour itineraries of the Valle de Curicó *(p141)*.

INSIDER TIP
Surf's Up

Those looking to catch some waves should consider driving just beyond Vichuquén to the seaside town of Llico, popular for its surf. It also hosts surfing competitions in January and February.

Chillán

F1 252 miles (405 km) S of Santiago 18 de Septiembre 510; municipalidadchillan.cl

The birthplace of Chile's founder Bernardo O'Higgins, Chillán is one of the oldest cities in the country. It is centered on a main square fronted by a Modernist cathedral that is supported by 11 giant parabolic arches made from reinforced concrete. Built after the 1939 earthquake, the cathedral has a tunnel-like interior. Above its altar, on a wooden

Water tumbling between the rock pools of the Parque Nacional Radal Siete Tazas

↑ Arches of Chillán Cathedral resembling hands joined in prayer

cross pulled from the quake's rubble, is a figure of Christ sculpted in Italy.

Also of interest in Chillán is the **Escuela México** primary school, whose interior contains two giant murals painted in 1941–2 by Mexican artists David Alfaro Siqueiros and Xavier Guerrero. Siqueiros' allegorical *Muerte al Invasor* (Death to the Invader) combines the bold Cubist and Impressionist styles to symbolize the struggle for independence of the Mexican and Chilean peoples. Guerrero's Realist *De México a Chile* (From Mexico to Chile) depicts, among many scenes, a Mexican woman pulling a Chilean baby from rubble.

Another site worth visiting is Chillán's indoor food market, the **Mercado Chillán**, which is an absolute delight for foodies. The food stalls here serve various regional specialties; don't miss out on the city's wonderful chorizo-esque *longaniza* sausages at Cecinas Villablanca *(villablanca.cl)*.

Escuela México

Avenida O'Higgins 250 (042) 2212 012 8:30am-5pm Mon-Thu, 8:30am-2pm Fri

Mercado Chillán

5 de Abríl, Isabel Riquelme, El Roble Summer: 7am-3pm daily (to 8pm Mon-Fri & to 6pm Sat); winter: 7:30am-3pm daily (to 7pm Mon-Fri & to 6pm Sat)

33   

Nevados de Chillán

F1 51 miles (82 km) E of Chillán Daily nevadosdechillan.com

This year-round resort is known for skiing, but it also features a state-of-the-art thermal spa complex. The winter ski resort sits on the slope of Volcán Chillán and has 28 runs, including the longest one in South America. Expert skiers can enjoy the excellent off-piste skiing here, while the lower part of the mountain also offers great terrain for beginners. The spa complex has thermal pools and outdoor hot springs that rise from natural geothermal fissures. Treatments on offer here include massages, mud baths, aromatherapy, and hydrotherapy. There are several excellent hotels around the region, including the ski area's Hotel Nevados de Chillán and the posher Hotel Termas de Chillán *(termaschillan.cl)*.

EAT

Chil-in

Load up on carbs at this ski cabin-styled restaurant, with local craft beers, decent pizzas, and French-inspired dishes.

F1 Camino a las Termas, Nevados de Chillán chil-in.com

EARTHQUAKE OF 2010

In the early hours of February 27, 2010, an earthquake measuring 8.8 on the Richter scale struck central Chile, destroying homes and buildings, and flattening highways across the region. The quake's epicenter was Concepción, one of Chile's most densely populated cities. Nearby towns were the worst hit, but there was also widespread damage reaching as far as Santiago, 322 miles (518 km) away. Over 500,000 homes were destroyed or severely damaged and an estimated 500 people killed.

Saltos del Laja

F1 298 miles (480 km) SW of Santiago From Chillan & Los Angeles 8am-8pm daily saltosdellaja.com

Natural marvels at the southern end of the Central Valley, the Saltos del Laja are four waterfalls plunging into a rocky canyon ringed by green forest. Vapor-drenched trails lie at the base and top of the falls. Reaching 167 ft (51 m), Salto del Laja is the highest fall in the chain, and forms a curtain of white water. Facilities around the falls include hotels and camps.

Concepción

F1 322 miles (518 km) SW of Santiago Aníbal Pinto 460; concepcion.cl

A vibrant university city, Concepción was founded in 1550 as a frontier settlement on the banks of Río Biobío, and in colonial times acted as the springboard for Spanish attacks on the Mapuche-held Lake District south of the river.

Much of the city's architectural heritage was destroyed in the 19th century by earthquakes and tsunamis, which left behind a rather bland and empty metropolis. The historical highlight is the *Mural Historia de Concepción*, a huge mural in the regional government headquarters, the Edificio Gobierno Regional. Painted in the Socio-Realist style between 1943 and 1946 by Chilean artist Gregorio de la Fuente, this mural is a visual description of this region's turbulent history from pre-Hispanic times onward.

Opposite this building, Plaza España has many lively bars and restaurants, while to its north, Plaza Independencia is the historic square from where Bernardo O'Higgins proclaimed Chile's independence in 1818.

The city suffered severe damage in the 2010 earthquake, but it has since managed to rebuild.

Parque Nacional Laguna del Laja

F1 348 miles (561 km) S of Santiago 9am-6pm daily (book ahead) conaf.cl

This compact park protects Chile's northernmost distribution of araucaria trees and mountain cypress. Its grandest natural feature is the Volcán Antuco, whose summit is reached by an undemanding eight-hour return trek. The trail has views of the glacier-covered Sierra Velluda range, just beyond the park's boundaries. A small ski center operates on the volcano between June and October. The park's namesake lake, the Laguna del Laja, was formed by an eruption in 1752. An easy trail skirts this lake and leads to two gorgeous falls: Salto las Chilcas and Salto el Torbellino. Along the trails, hikers can see plenty of birdlife, as the park is refuge to over 50 bird species, including the Andean condor.

Lota

F1 333 miles (537 km) SW of Santiago Municipalidad, P. Aguirre Cerda 200; lotasorprendente.cl

For 150 years, Lota lay at the heart of the Central Valley's coal-mining industry. Its mines were owned by the Cousiño family, who oversaw their investment from a grand villa in town. An earthquake in 1960 destroyed the villa, but its magnificent gardens are open for visits. At their entrance, the **Museo Histórico de Lota** has historical displays on the Cousiño family. The now-closed mines can be seen on tours: visitors descend into the tunnels in a metal cage elevator, and take a look at *Pueblito Minero*, a re-creation of miners' houses that were used as a prop in the Chilean movie *Underground (Subterra)*.

Museo Histórico de Lota
Avenida El Parque 21, Lota Alto 10:30am-6pm Mon-Fri, 10am-6:30pm Sat & Sun lotasorprendente.cl

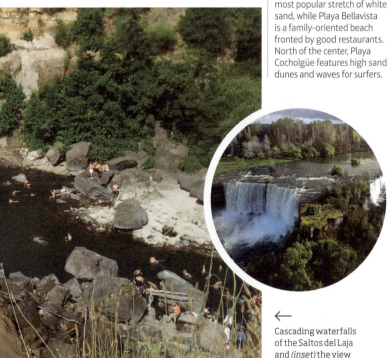

Tomé

F1 293 miles (472 km) SW of Santiago Municipalidad, Mariano Egaña; tome.cl

A seaside town, Tomé was founded in 1875 as a port for shipping wine and maize from the Central Valley; it later became Chile's main textile port. The earthquake in 2010 caused damage but Tomé's sandy beaches still attract visitors. Central El Morro is the most popular stretch of white sand, while Playa Bellavista is a family-oriented beach fronted by good restaurants. North of the center, Playa Cocholgüe features high sand dunes and waves for surfers.

←

Cascading waterfalls of the Saltos del Laja and *(inset)* the view from one side

A DRIVING TOUR
COLCHAGUA VALLEY

Length 47 miles (75 km). The tour needs at least two days.
Starting point San Fernando, 27 miles (43 km) E of Santa Cruz

Chile's premier winemaking region, the Colchagua Valley starts at the Andean foothills and sweeps westward toward the Pacific coast. The valley's fertile floor and rolling hills are home to many wineries that specialize in red wine; nearly all are open for tours and tastings. They feature various architectural styles, ranging from ultra-modern designs to colonial-era estates, plus excellent restaurants and hotels.

Visitors can make and label wines at ***Viña MontGras****. In March the winery hosts the annual grape harvest festival, Fiesta de la Vendimia.*

Owned by the French Rothschild family, ***Viña Los Vascos*** *runs group tours. It is notable for Cabernet Sauvignon and Carménère aged in French oak barrels.*

At the center of Chile's leading winemaking region, ***Santa Cruz*** *is the springboard for Colchagua's wineries. Take an evening visit to the astronomical center for wine tasting under the stars.*

Founded in 1935, ***Viña Viu Manent*** *is housed in a Spanish-style hacienda. It offers vineyard carriage rides, an excellent handicrafts store, and an equestrian club.*

↑ Winding path down to Santa Cruz Vineyards

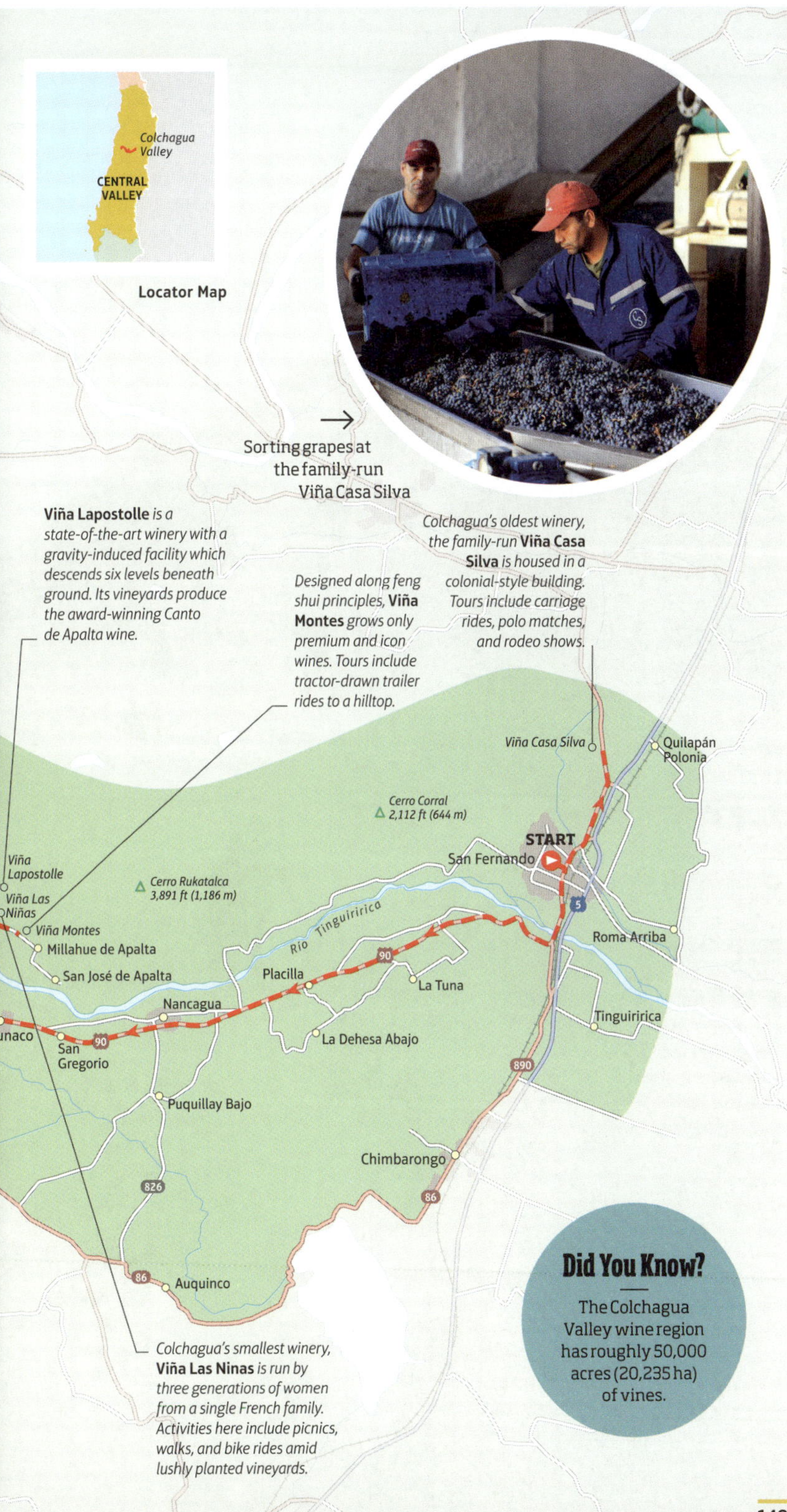
Colchagua Valley
CENTRAL VALLEY
Locator Map
Viña Lapostolle *is a state-of-the-art winery with a gravity-induced facility which descends six levels beneath ground. Its vineyards produce the award-winning Canto de Apalta wine.*
Designed along feng shui principles, **Viña Montes** *grows only premium and icon wines. Tours include tractor-drawn trailer rides to a hilltop.*
Colchagua's oldest winery, the family-run **Viña Casa Silva** *is housed in a colonial-style building. Tours include carriage rides, polo matches, and rodeo shows.*
Viña Casa Silva
Quilapán Polonia
Cerro Corral 2,112 ft (644 m)
START
San Fernando
5
Viña Lapostolle
Cerro Rukatalca 3,891 ft (1,186 m)
Viña Las Niñas
Viña Montes
Río Tinguiririca
Roma Arriba
Millahue de Apalta
90
San José de Apalta
Placilla
La Tuna
Nancagua
Tinguiririca
unaco
90
San Gregorio
La Dehesa Abajo
890
Puquillay Bajo
Chimbarongo
826
86
86
Auquinco
Colchagua's smallest winery, **Viña Las Ninas** *is run by three generations of women from a single French family. Activities here include picnics, walks, and bike rides amid lushly planted vineyards.*
Did You Know?
The Colchagua Valley wine region has roughly 50,000 acres (20,235 ha) of vines.

→ Sorting grapes at the family-run Viña Casa Silva

Hiking along a path in the Atacama desert

NORTE GRANDE AND NORTE CHICO

The north is Chile's desert region: an epic landscape of sand dunes, ocher earth, and white-sand cliffs. The land rises from the coast to the altiplano, where camelids roam, flamingos fly, and volcanoes overlook brilliant blue lagoons. Port cities line the coast, while Indigenous hamlets and oasis villages with adobe churches bring the desert to life.

The ever-changing Atacama Desert blankets much of the arid Norte Grande (Big North) and the semi-arid Norte Chico (Little North). The original inhabitants of this area belonged to the Diaguita, Aymara, and El Molle cultures, important pre-conquest societies ruled in the past by the Tiwanaku (500–1000 CE) and Inca (1450–1540) empires. The latter was supplanted by Spanish conquistadores and colonizers, who coveted the metal and mineral wealth of the desert, particularly gold, a symbol of power among pre-Hispanic peoples. Pirates of this time, most notably Bartholomew Sharp, sacked cities such as La Serena, and burned down historic buildings like churches.

Today, mining in the Atacama is the bedrock of Chile's economy and port cities have prospered from the growth in the industry. Workers have moved to the region, and universities are drawing on local expertise and experience to provide training to aspiring mining engineers.

NORTE GRANDE AND NORTE CHICO

Must Sees

1. Arica
2. San Pedro de Atacama
3. Iquique
4. Parque Nacional Lauca
5. La Serena
6. Valle de Elqui

Experience More

7. Iglesia de San Jerónimo de Poconchile
8. Putre
9. Reserva Nacional Las Vicuñas
10. El Gigante de Atacama
11. Humberstone and Santa Laura
12. Parque Nacional Volcán Isluga
13. Mamiña Hot Springs
14. La Tirana
15. Pica
16. Cerro Pintados
17. Caspana
18. Calama
19. Chiu-Chiu
20. Pukará de Lasana
21. Chuquicamata
22. Termas Baños de Puritama
23. Valle de la Luna
24. Géiseres del Tatio
25. Salar de Tara
26. Salar de Atacama
27. Cerro Paranal Observatory
28. Antofagasta
29. La Portada
30. Copiapó
31. Caldera
32. Parque Nacional Pan de Azúcar
33. Parque Nacional Nevado Tres Cruces
34. Ovalle
35. Laguna Verde
36. Reserva Nacional Pingüino de Humboldt
37. Monumento Natural Pichasca
38. Monumento Nacional Valle del Encanto
39. Termas de Socos
40. Parque Nacional Bosque Fray Jorge

Pacific Ocean

PERU
Tacna
Chacalluta International Airport
Azapa
PUTRE
8
4 PARQUE NACIONAL LAUCA
ARICA 1
7
9 RESERVA NACIONAL LAS VICUÑAS
IGLESIA DE SAN JERÓNIMO DE POCONCHILE
Codpa
Oruro
Challapata
Cuya
Camiña
Enquelga
TARAPACA
12 PARQUE NACIONAL VOLCÁN ISLUGA
Potosi
EL GIGANTE DE ATACAMA
10
HUMBERSTONE AND SANTA LAURA
13 MAMIÑA HOT SPRINGS
IQUIQUE 3
11 LA TIRANA
Diego Aracena International Airport
14
15 PICA
16 CERRO PINTADOS
Salar de Uyuni
Uyuni
Lagunas
Atacama Desert
BOLIVIA
Ollagüe
Quillagua
Volcán San Pedro 20,206 ft (6,158 m)
Tupiza
Tocopilla
PUKARÁ DE LASANA
20
24 GÉISERES DEL TATIO
CHUQUICAMATA 21
19
17 CASPANA
Pumahuasi
El Loa Airport 18
CALAMA
CHIU-CHIU
22 TERMAS BAÑOS DE PURITAMA
2 SAN PEDRO DE ATACAMA
Mejillones
VALLE DE LA LUNA 23
25 SALAR DE TARA
26
SALAR DE ATACAMA
Humahuaca
LA PORTADA 29
Andrés Sabella Gálvez Airport
ANTOFAGASTA 28
Socaire
Cerro Rincón 18,353 ft (5,594 m)
ANTOFAGASTA
Volcán Socompa 19,786 ft (6,030 m)
San Salvador de Jujuy
CERRO PARANAL OBSERVATORY 27
Paposo
Atacama Desert
Salta
Catalina
Taltal
Volcán Azufre 18,635 ft (5,679 m)
La Viña
PARQUE NACIONAL PAN DE AZÚCAR 32
ARGENTINA
El Salvador
Chañaral
El Peñón
Diego de Almagro
35 LAGUNA VERDE
San Miguel de Tucumán
CALDERA 31
Volcán Ojos del Salado 22,609 ft (6,891 m)
33
Desierto de Atacama Airport
30 COPIAPÓ
PARQUE NACIONAL NEVADO TRES CRUCES
Bahía Copiapó
Tierra Amarilla
Punta de Díaz
Belén
Juntas
Carrizal Bajo
ATACAMA
Cerro del Potro 19,127 ft (5,829 m)
Huasco
Catamarca
Vallenar
Alto del Carmen
RESERVA NACIONAL PINGÜINO DE HUMBOLDT 36
Domeyko
Cerro del Toro 20,931 ft (6,379 m)
Chilecito
La Higuera
Guandacol
La Rioja
LA SERENA 5
La Florida Airport
Casa de Piedra
Coquimbo
Vicuña
6 VALLE DE ELQUI
Patquía
OVALLE
37
PARQUE NACIONAL BOSQUE FRAY JORGE 40
34
MONUMENTO NATURAL PICHASCA
Chañar
TERMAS DE SOCOS 39
38
MONUMENTO NACIONAL VALLE DEL ENCANTO
COQUIMBO
Salamanca
San Juan
Los Vilos
0 kilometers 150
0 miles 150
N
CENTRAL VALLEY p114

1 ARICA

B1 1,034 miles (1,664 km) N of Santiago
Aeropuerto Chacalluta Sernatur, San Marcos 101

The coastal city of Arica has palm-lined plazas and a vibrant Indigenous culture. Grand Peruvian-era buildings, including some by France's Gustave Eiffel, are spread across this compact grid of streets and plazas. Indigenous crafts and markets add bursts of color, alongside sweeping beaches, outstanding archaeological highlights, and fantastic restaurants.

1 Morro de Arica

Camino Al Morro, off Colón
10am-8pm Tue-Sun

This 456-ft- (139-m-) high cliff towers above the city center and marks the end of Chile's coastal cordillera. It stands as a symbol of national glory, marking the site where, in 1880, Chilean forces stormed Peruvian fortifications to win possession of Arica in the War of the Pacific. At the summit sits the Museo Histórico y de Armas, which houses objects of war. A monument to the unknown soldiers of Chile and Peru and a 33-ft- (10-m-) high bronze statue of Christ, raised as a symbol of peace between the two countries, also adorn the summit.

Morenada dance group performing during a parade at the Carnaval in Arica

2 Catedral de San Marcos

San Marcos 260
9am-7pm daily

Built by French engineer Gustave Eiffel, Arica's cast-iron,

INSIDER TIP
Beaches

South of Arica center, Playa El Laucho and the pretty Playa La Lisera have calm waters. North of the center, Playa Chinchorro is popular for its big surfer waves, as is the rustic Playa Las Machas farther on.

↑ The Chilean national flag marking the summit of the Morro de Arica

Neo-Gothic cathedral was prefabricated in France and assembled in Arica in 1876. Its latticed facade is a rich chocolate color, and the interior is notable for a delicate tracery that props up the cathedral's columns. The bell near the entrance is from 1729 and belonged to the basilica that stood on this site. Above the altar is a 17th-century sculpture of Christ.

Museo de Sitio Colón 10

Avenida Colón 10 (058) 2205 041 10am-6pm Tue-Sun

In 2004, during excavations for a residential project, construction workers found a host of mummies and skeletons from the pre-Columbian Chinchorro culture. Although many similar finds are already displayed at the museum in Azapa, archaeologists decided to leave them in situ, under glass, on the slope just before the Morro, where they now represent an unmissable sight.

Poblado Artesanal

Hualles 2825 10am-1:30pm & 3-8pm Tue-Sun pobladoartesanal.cl

On the outskirts of Arica, this craftspeople's village is the place to buy Quechua crafts such as weavings of alpaca and llama wools, ceramics, jewelry, and leather-ware. The colony is built in the image of an altiplano village and includes workshops and lodgings that are occupied by local craftspeople. The village has a beautiful church with fascinating murals.

STAY

Hotel Apacheta

The rooms at this modern, beachside hotel offer spectacular views of the ocean. Breakfast is served on the wooden terrace.

Avenida Comandante San Martín 661

hotelapacheta.com

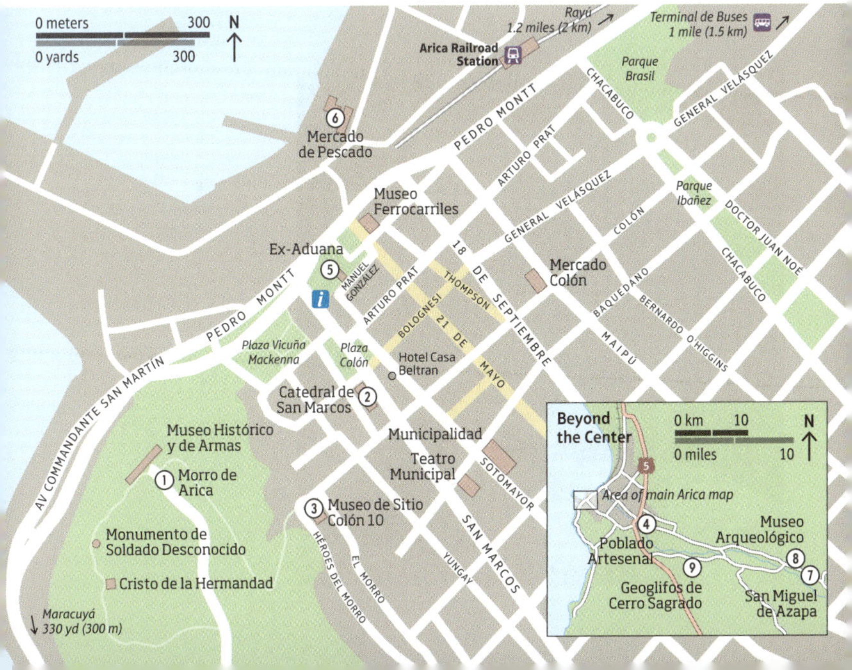

EAT

Rayú
A smart restaurant serving up Peruvian classics such as *ceviche* and *lomo saltado* (a combo of steak strips, onions, tomatoes, fries, and rice). Book ahead on weekends.

2590 Ingeniero, Raúl Pey

Maracuyá
Fish and seafood are the specialties here, with highlights including the grilled *corvina* (fish similar to sea bass) with shrimps. Ask to be seated on the glorious terrace, which overlooks the sea.

321 Avenida Comandante San Martín

Ex-Aduana

Arturo Prat 305 For occasional events

Another building designed by Gustave Eiffel, the city's former customs house (officially called the Casa de la Cultura) was prefabricated in France and erected in Arica in 1874. This squat, brick building has an attractive pink-and-white striped exterior. Its interior, with cast-iron pillars and spiral staircase, houses art exhibitions. Photographs show pre-urban Arica, including shots of Morro de Arica with thousands of penguins.

Mercado de Pescado

Avenida Comandante San Martín 6am-3pm daily

In Arica's port area, Mercado de Pescado (Fish Market) is a smelly but colorful experience. Boisterous water birds and sea lions vie over discarded scraps, while fishermen clean and gut the day's catch at stalls. Frequent boat tours of the bay depart from here.

San Miguel de Azapa

Azapa Valley, 7.5 miles (12 km) E of Arica

A short drive from Arica, tranquil San Miguel de Azapa is a pleasant spot for a morning or late-afternoon stroll. Known for its enticing olive groves and beautiful tropical fruit trees, the village is home to a bright and colorful cemetery, which is situated dramatically in the desert, loomed over by a stark cliff face.

Museo Arqueológico San Miguel de Azapa

Camino Azapa, km 12 10am-6pm Tue-Sun (Jan & Feb: to 7pm) masma.uta.cl

This outstanding museum of archaeology displays objects ranging from up to 10,000 years ago. The highlight here is the Sala Chinchorro, a room containing the remains of the Chinchorro mummies, the world's oldest known mummies. They were buried in mass graves between 4,000 and 8,000 years ago. The site also includes a display of severed heads, part of a "cult of the head" that existed between 500 BCE and 500 CE. Museo Arqueológico San Miguel de Azapa also has an intriguing display, which shows some of the

Sea lions and pelicans watching over the fishing boats at Mercado de Pescado

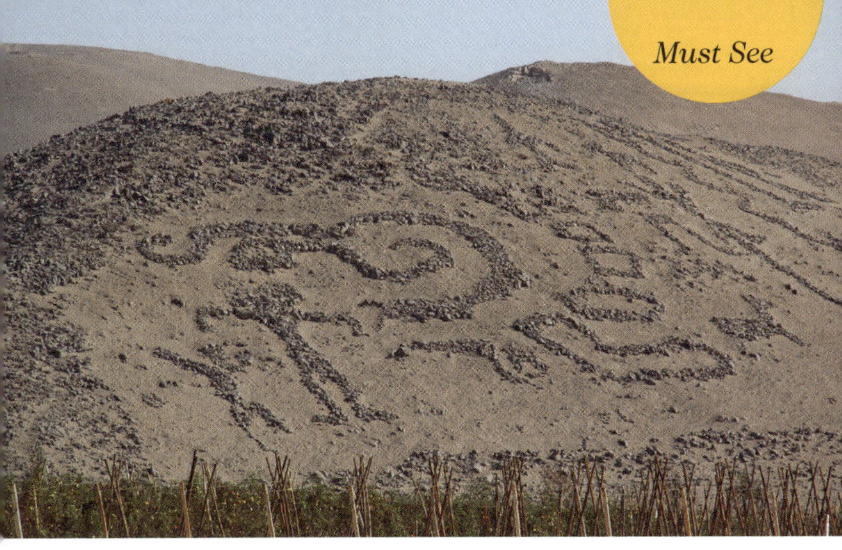

utensils that were carved by the Tiwanaku people (500–1000 CE) to manufacture hallucinogens. Visitors can also explore a series of ancient petroglyphs, which are rock carvings made by chipping away directly at the surface of the rock, usually using a stone chisel, a hammerstone, or another similar tool. All the displays are accompanied with a handy audio guide in English.

9

Geoglifos de Cerro Sagrado

 **Alto Ramírez, Valle Azapa**

The great stone mosaic on the Cerro Sagrado (Sacred Mount) hillside is the most eye-catching of several enormous geoglyphs in the Valle Azapa. A mosaic of anthropomorphic and zoomorphic motifs, it depicts giant human figures – adult and child – as well as mammoth lizards and llamas. The latter are composed in dynamic form, as if scaling up or bounding across this barren hillside. The geoglyphs date from this region's Inca period (1450–1500 CE), when farmers settled this green valley. Close to Cerro Sagrado is the quaint and beautiful village of Pampa Alto Ramíre, which is still home to the remains of 30 dwellings, all of which are made of various lightweight materials. Geoglifos de Cerro Sagrado is also home to small llama corrals, some storehouses, a cemetery, and two fresh water springs that once provided the water needed for crop irrigation and consumption. Visitors can stroll around and explore all of these sites.

↑ Geoglyphs cut into the hillside on the Cerro Sagrado

CHINCHORRO MUMMIES

The Chinchorro populated Norte Grande during 6000-2000 BCE and their mummies, buried in the Atacama Desert, are the oldest in the world. The Chinchorro method of mummification was complex - it entailed the removal of the skin, extraction of the internal organs and extremities, and filling in of cavities with mud, ash, and resinous substances. The mummies were then buried in an extended position in collective tombs, which comprised adults, children, and fetuses.

2

SAN PEDRO DE ATACAMA

C2 304 miles (490 km) SE of Inique Toconao 405 9am-6pm Mon-Fri, 9am-5pm Sat

Picturesque San Pedro de Atacama is northern Chile's traveler hub, the springboard for trips into an other-worldly region of dazzling salt flats, lunar valleys, soaring volcanoes, high-altitude lagoons and hot springs, and the ruins of pre-Inca forts.

Iglesia de San Pedro de Atacama

Caracoles 362 (055) 2851 077 9am-8pm daily

Overlooking the town's pretty plaza, lined with *algarrobo* (carob) and pepper trees, the Iglesia de San Pedro de Atacama is a white adobe structure whose doors and ceiling are made from cactus wood bound together with llama leather. The roof is made of large rafters of *algarrobo* wood overlaid by slices of cactus logs. The church was built after the town's first church was destroyed. The current structure dates from the 1740s, though the rustic bell tower was added in the 1800s and the surrounding white walls were renovated in the 1970s. Further restoration work occurred in 2009. Inside, visitors will find numerous religious icons, most notably one of San Pedro (St. Peter), from whom the town takes its name, and St. Mary and St. Joseph, both softly illuminated by a fluorescent lighting feature. The interior also contains an altarpiece that is delicately carved and painted in bright and vibrant colors, providing a contrast against the white walls.

Did You Know?

San Pedro de Atacama does not allow buildings above two stories to enhance the impression it's an oasis.

Casa Incaica

(057) 2544 734 Hours vary; call ahead

Standing directly opposite the Iglesia de San Pedro de Atacama, the Casa Incaica (Inca House) is the oldest house in the town. Rickety and with a roof that is seemingly on the verge of collapse, the house was reputedly built for the founder of Chile, Pedro de Valdivia, back in 1540. Today, rather more prosaically, it is home to a store selling local

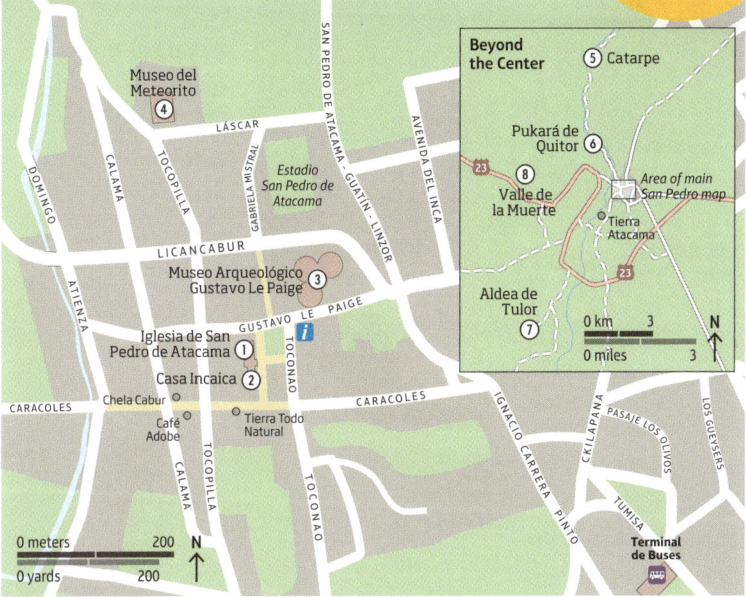

souvenirs, but it is still worth having a quick look inside. The range of souvenirs on offer include alpaca knitware and rica-rica, a common herb found in the region, characterized by its aroma and often praised for its various medicinal and digestive benefits.

③

Museo Arqueológico Gustavo Le Paige

Gustavo Le Paige 380
9am-12:30pm & 2:30-6pm daily **iaa.ucn.cl**

Named after the Jesuit missionary and pioneer in archaeological research who was its founder, the Museo Arqueológico Gustavo Le Paige (Archaeological Museum Gustavo Le Paige) is home to about 380,000 pre-Columbian artifacts and archaeological objects from the Atacameño culture. The vast collection includes stone paraphernalia sculpted with images of animalistic deities, which members of the Tiwanaku (500–1000 CE) culture once used to make hallucinogens. You can also find a valuable collection of clothes, ceramics, and utensils on display.

A traditional street café found in the town center of San Pedro de Atacama

EAT

Tierra Todo Natural

Housed in a building resembling a thatched Nissen hut, this restaurant is renowned for its extensive vegetarian menu.

Caracoles 271, San Pedro de Atacama
(056) 0558 51585

$$$

Café Adobe

This large café serves skillfully presented versions of Chilean specialties. The space itself is an attraction, warmed by an open fireplace, and there is live Andean music.

Caracoles 211
cafeadobe.cl

$$$

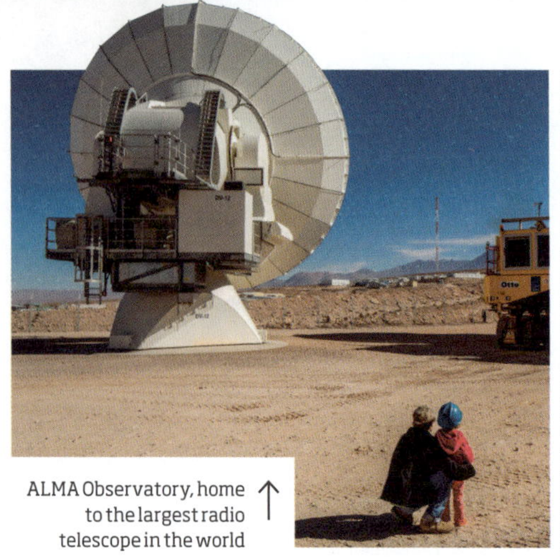

ALMA Observatory, home to the largest radio telescope in the world

4 Museo del Meteorito

Tocopilla 201 5-8pm Tue-Sun museodelmeteorito.cl

This is a little gem of a museum which, although quite small, tends to generate lots of interest from visitors. Based in a series of compact, interlinked geodesic domes just north of the center of San Pedro de Atacama, the Meteorite Museum is a great place to visit before embarking on a stargazing tour or a visit to the incredible ALMA Observatory, the biggest astronomical project on earth, comprising 50 antennae, each 39 ft (12 m) in diameter. As the name suggests, the museum has a collection of 80 different meteorites, most of which have been found in or around the Atacama Desert. Visitors are invited to examine, and in some cases handle, the meteorites. There are useful explanatory and educational panels available, as well as interactive displays, including a great multilingual audio guide which is included in the admission price. The museum can also arrange tours to a nearby meteoric crater where visitors can search for meteorites in the desert.

INSIDER TIP
Keep Active

Beyond the normal 4X4 trips, there are plenty of other interesting activities on offer around San Pedro de Atacama, including hikes and climbs. Agencies like CaminAndes *(caminandesagencia.com)* can take you up Volcán Lascar and other volcanic peaks.

5 Catarpe

5 miles (8 km) N of San Pedro de Atacama

From Pukará de Quitor, determined visitors can continue 3 miles (5 km) north to Catarpe, site of the ruins of a *tambo*, an Inca administrative center. Although the site is far less intact than the *pukará* (defensive hilltop fortress), the journey to it traverses some breathtakingly wild canyon country and stretches through a difficult but nonetheless beautiful old road that leads to a tunnel built in 1930. The road offers visitors some amazing views of the Catarpe Valley and the incredible surrounding rock formations.

6 Pukará de Quitor

2 miles (3 km) N of San Pedro de Atacama 8am-5pm daily monumnetos.gob.cl

Accessible by taxi, mountain bike, or even on horseback from San Pedro de Atacama, the Pukará de Quitor gets its name from the Ayllu de Quitor, once locals whose fields were based at the foot of the site. Pukará de Quitor comprises the ruins of a red-stone pre-Inca fortress, built in the 12th century during a period of warfare. The *pukará* was attacked by the Spanish in the 1520s but remarkably its defenders managed to hold out for some two decades until they were finally defeated by conquistador Francisco de Aguirre and his band of men in 1540. The fortress has since been partially restored and it is easy to see why it was once so impregnable. The ruins sprawl across a steep hillside, which overlooks the stunning San Pedro river canyon, and consist of an outer wall, narrow passageways, some living quarters, grain storehouses, herding pens, and a collection of communal squares. Visitors can take a walking trail and climb to the top of the fortress for fantastic views of the canyon, volcanoes, and the Valle de la Muerte. Pukará de Quitor was designated a national monument in 1982.

7 Aldea de Tulor

6 miles (9 km) SW of San Pedro de Atacama 8am-noon & 1-5pm daily (book ahead) conaf.cl

Excavated in 1982, after being buried under sand for 1,500 years, the Aldea de Tulor comprises the 2,800-year-old red-clay ruins of one of Chile's first sedentary settlements.

The Atacameño abandoned this site in 500 CE owing to the encroaching desert. The remains of the settlement were eventually rediscovered in the late 1950s by an intrepid Belgian priest and amateur archaeologist, Gustavo Le Paige, who also founded the eponymous museum in San Pedro de Atacama *(p159)*. Today the walls of their settlement and its doorways, passageways, and huge honeycomb-like patterns of rooms lie partially or fully exposed to view. Most visitors travel to Tulor independently by car via its sandy tracks, on mountain bike or even horseback, crossing the dusky Atacama Desert in the dark shadows of impressive and towering volcanoes. Buggy safaris and guided archaeological tours take travelers around the sites of the ancient settlement.

8

Valle de la Muerte

C2 6 miles (10 km) W of San Pedro de Atacama; Camino a Calama

An otherworldly spectacle of huge sand dunes and jagged red-rock pinnacles, Valle de la Muerte (Valley of Death) was thrust upward from the earth's crust 23 million years ago during the violent upheaval that created the Andes. Also known as Valle de Mart (Valley of Mars), this region's death tag is no misnomer – though rich in mineral deposits, it is one of the driest, most inhospitable places on the planet and no known life exists here. Guided tours to Valle de la Luna *(p184)* stop briefly en route, often at sunset. Travelers with more time can join horseback excursions, including full-moon rides.

DRINK

Chelacabur

This bar offers a great range of Chilean and imported beers and has a welcoming vibe.

Caracoles 212
(055) 285 1576

STAY

Tierra Atacama

This gorgeous boutique hotel on the edge of town features swish en suites and an excellent restaurant-bar serving innovative twists on Chilean cuisine.

Séquitor s/n
tierrahotels.com

$$$

Excavated in 1982, after being buried under sand for 1,500 years, the Aldea de Tulor comprises the 2,800-year-old red-clay ruins of one of Chile's first sedentary settlements.

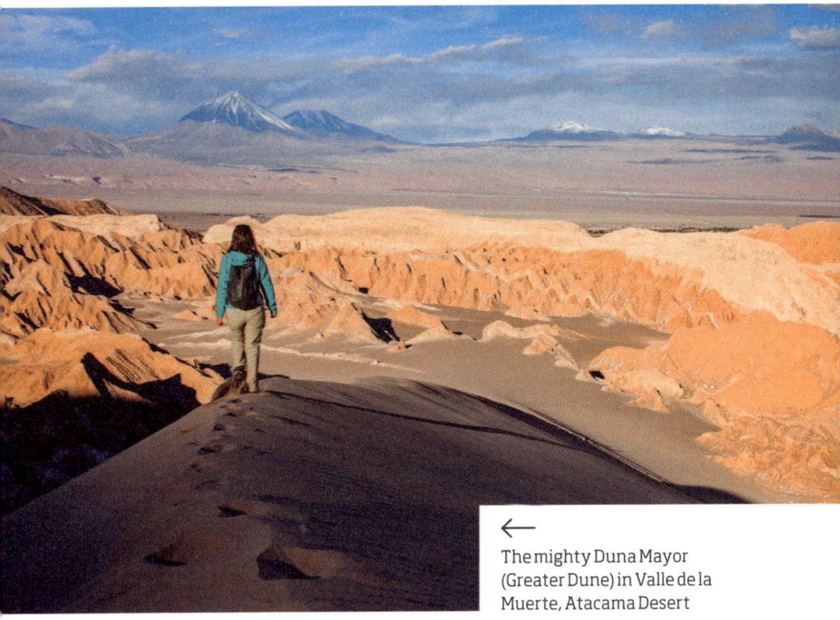

←
The mighty Duna Mayor (Greater Dune) in Valle de la Muerte, Atacama Desert

IQUIQUE

B2 196 miles (316 km) S of Arica Sernatur, Aníbal Pinto 436; 9am-6pm Mon-Fri, 10am-2pm Sat; iquique.cl

Originally part of Peru, Iquique was annexed by Chile during the War of the Pacific (1879–83) and emerged as its nitrate capital. Opulent buildings from the nitrate era are testament to the city's decadent past, when Iquique is said to have consumed greater quantities of champagne per capita than any other city in the world.

Palacio Astoreca

O'Higgins 350 (057) 2526 890 10am-6pm Mon-Fri, 11am-2pm Sat

One of Iquique's extravagant mansions, Palacio Astoreca is a beautiful 27-room house that was designed in British Georgian style for a nitrate magnate in 1903. The building was constructed with Douglas fir that was shipped from the US. The house retains vestiges of a glorious past that include silk wallpaper, a grand staircase, and a stained-glass skylight in its reception hall. Today, this grand building serves as Iquique's cultural center and hosts occasional art exhibitions and workshops.

The permanent exhibitions include re-creations of nitrate-era living quarters with original Art-Nouveau furnishings. On display is a collection of seashells of varying sizes from around the world. The work of local and national artists is featured, including a fine collection of engravings by the Chilean painter Roberto Matta, who was considered one of the great representatives of Surrealism.

Cerro Dragón

Popular with *parapente* (paragliding) enthusiasts, the massive Cerro Dragón sand dune looms high above the city and acts as a launching point for paragliders. After a running start off the dune, soar above the city and get

Did You Know?

Iquique is one of only two free ports in Chile, the other one being Punta Arenas, in the country's far south.

↑ Iquique set below a vast sand dune popular for paragliding

propelled by the currents before landing on the beach. Paragliding here makes for a truly memorable experience. Stretching 2.5 miles (4 km), the coastal dune probably originated some 20,000 years ago.

③

Teatro Municipal

Calle Thompson 269
(057) 2544 734
For restoration until further notice

Built in 1890 at the height of the Chilean nitrate boom, Iquique's Teatro Municipal is housed in a magnificent wooden structure, whose Neo-Classical facade is ornamented with female figures cut in stone, symbolizing various theatrical elements, such as costume and dance. The foyer, which is topped by a cupola, has a ceiling painted with cherubic allegories of music, dance, painting, and theater, as well as various depictions of famed literary and musical masters, including William Shakespeare, Frédéric Chopin, and Wolfgang Amadeus Mozart. A domed ceiling crowns the beautiful auditorium and is painted with more theatrical motifs, including musical instruments and theater masks that symbolize comedy and tragedy.

Adjacent to the stage is a set of stairs that descend to the bowels of this edifice, where century-old wooden pulleys and wheels still serve as stage machinery. Restoration work is yet to begin on the theater and the reopening date for live performances has not been announced. The theater was heavily damaged in the 1906 earthquake and a fire in 1927. It was declared a national monument in 1974.

STAY

Hotel Terrado Suites

This high-rise hotel, based at Playa Cavancha, has various rooms on offer, including ones with balconies and sea views. There is a selection of good restaurants to be found nearby.

Capitán Roberto Pérez 126 **terrado.cl**

The historic Torre Reloj, a symbolic landmark of the city located on Plaza Arturo Prat

EAT

El Tercer Ojito
The menu features various options, including sushi, satay, pad thai, and curry.

Patricio Lynch 1420

El Rincón de Cachuperto
The seafood empanadas served at El Rincón de Cachuperto, Iquique's best empanaderia, are superb. The empanadas tend to run out quickly, so get here before 12:30pm.

Filomena Valenzuela 125

Plaza Arturo Prat

Between Calle Aníbal Pinto & Avenida Baquedano

Iquique's main square, Plaza Arturo Prat, is located in the heart of the city's historic center. Dominating the plaza is the city's emblematic landmark, the flamboyant Torre Reloj. Built from Douglas fir by the English community in 1877, this clock tower is made up of three tapering tiers that are painted white and rise to 82 ft (25 m). The tower's arched base features a bust of Arturo Prat, considered Chile's greatest naval figure. He captained the *Esmeralda* schooner that was sunk by the Peruvian battleship *Huáscar* at the Battle of Iquique during the War of the Pacific. This battle ended with the death of Prat and much of his crew, but proved to be the turning point in a war that secured possession of Iquique for Chile and dominion over this area's lucrative nitrate deposits.

Casino Español

Plaza Prat 584
12:30am-4pm & 8-11pm Mon-Sat, 12:30-4pm Sun
casinoespanoliquique.cl

Constructed by the city's Spanish community in 1904, the Casino Español occupies a Moorish-style wooden edifice with an arched, Arabesque facade. Its domed interior recalls the Moorish palaces of Andalusian Spain with every inch of floor, wall, and ceiling space decorated with glittering Moorish motifs, patterns, and inscriptions. Arabesque archways and columns divide the salons, and kaleidoscopically glazed tiles decorate floors overlooked by Spanish stained glass, mirrors, and statues.

There is also a public restaurant housed in Casino Español, the walls of which

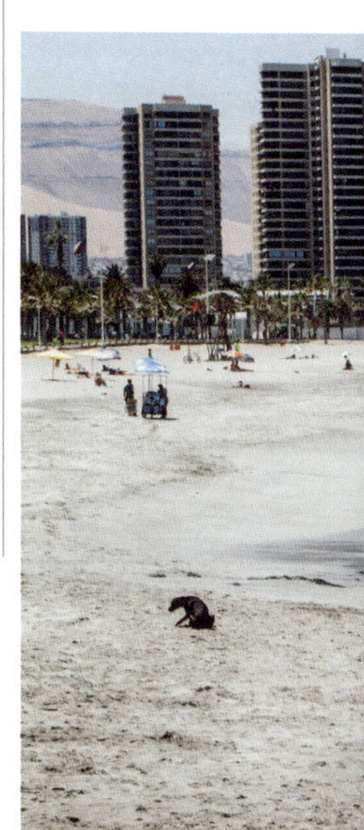

A mix of high-rise buildings and mountains creating the backdrop to Playa Cavancha

are embellished with eight giant oil paintings by well-known Spanish artist Antonio Torrecilla. Completed in 1907, these depict scenes from Miguel de Cervantes' famous novel *Don Quijote de la Mancha* (1605).

Beaches

Along Avenida Arturo Prat

Located within walking distance south of the city center, Playa Cavancha is Iquique's most popular beach for swimming. Further south lies Playa Brava, accessible via shared taxis, a favorite among sunbathers, but with treacherous rip currents. While it is possible to ride some waves toward the northern end of Playa Cavancha, serious surfers make their way farther south to the exhilarating breaks of Playa Huaiquique.

Museo Regional

Baquedano 951 9am-5pm Mon-Thu, 9am-4pm Fri, 10am-1:50pm Sat registromuseoschile.cl

Originally founded in 1960, the Regional Museum has been located at its current site since 1987, in the building that once housed the Courts of Justice. The museum traces the original cultures of the area, the emergence of the old city of Iquique, and its growth as a port city, through a series of photographs, while giving an insight into the nitrate industry.

The museum is divided into three areas. Among the important pieces on display are the Isluga ethnographic collection and an Inca mummy found on the Esmeralda Hill of Iquique, which provides evidence of the connection of the region with the great empire of the Incas.

Constructed by the city's Spanish community in 1904, the Casino Español occupies a Moorish-style wooden edifice with an arched, Arabesque facade.

THE WAR OF THE PACIFIC

Until the outbreak of this conflict (1879-83), Chile's northern border territory extended only as far as Copiapó in the northern region of Atacama, a seven-hour bus ride from Iquique. The nitrate-rich lands of the Atacama belonged to Bolivia and Peru, though many were controlled by Chilean investors. A dispute over export taxes served to provoke a Chilean invasion of Bolivian territory in 1879 and Peru was soon sucked into the conflict on the side of Bolivia. The War of the Pacific ended with an overwhelming victory for Chile, which significantly expanded its territory and natural resources at the expense of both its adversaries; Bolivia, in contrast, was left landlocked.

4

PARQUE NACIONAL LAUCA

C1 102 miles (165 km) E of Arica CONAF, Putre; conaf.cl

This is one of Chile's most popular national parks. Wherever you turn the scenery is spectacular – snowcapped mountains, glistening lakes, and roaming wildlife. Looming over it all is Volcán Parinacota, a dormant volcano, whose sibling Pomerape sits northeast on the Bolivian border.

Northern Chile's most scenic sanctuary, Parque Nacional Lauca protects around 532 sq miles (1,378 sq km) of altiplano wilderness. The park features a tiered ecology that starts at 10,500 ft (3,200 m) in its western zone and rises to over 20,700 ft (6,300 m) in the east. The accessible, high-altitude attractions include brilliantly colored lakes, snowy volcanoes, lava islands, stretches of high tableland, and tiny Aymara villages. There is also an abundance of wildlife. Over 140 bird species find refuge in this area, key among them the ostrich-like ñandú and three species of flamingo, which feed and nest on lakeshores. Wild populations of vicuña and viscacha are also easily spotted.

Exploring the Park

Parque Nacional Lauca can be reached via hired vehicles, organized tours, or the Arica-Bolivia international bus, whose route passes through this area. Within the park, the CH-11 international highway runs east to west, and walking trails link the popular sites of Parinacota, Lago Chungará, and Lagunas Cotacotani. There are CONAF stations at Las Cuevas, Parinacota, and Lago Chungará. The last of these has *refugio* accommodation and Parinacota has a visitors' center.

1 A hiker crosses a bridge in Las Cuevas. This area marks the start of the Altiplano region and is a great place for spotting local wildlife.

2 Llama are commonly sighted in Parque Nacional Lauca, as are its relatives, vicuña.

3 Llareta is a cushion plant found at high altitudes.

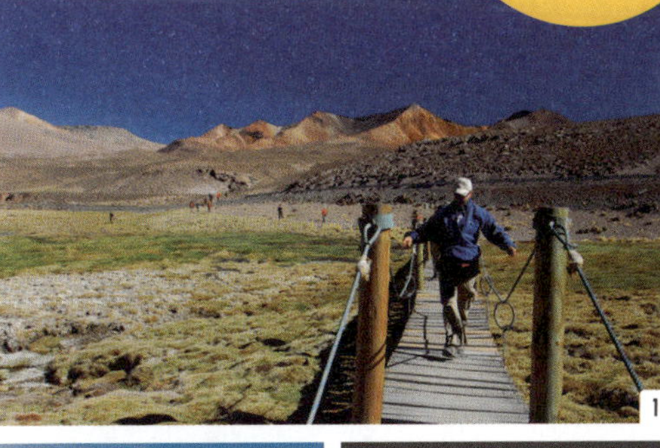

INSIDER TIP

Altitude Sickness

Avoid traveling to high altitudes from sea level. Instead ascend slowly, allowing time to acclimatize. The town of Putre, at 11,500 ft (3,500 m), is a good place to break the journey. Avoid alcohol, drink lots of water, and don't overexert yourself.

STAY

Terrace Lodge

Just outside Putre - the best base for visiting the park - this B&B has cozy rooms.

Circunvalación 25, Putre terracelodge.com

Hotel Kukuli

Clean, basic, and cheap rooms. Be sure to bring layers of warm clothes.

Baquedano 301, Putre hotelkukuli.cl

Parinacota volcano reflected in the waters of Lago Chungará

5

LA SERENA

B5 435 miles (700 km) S of Antofagasta Aeropuerto La Florida Sernatur, Matta 46; 8:30am-1:30pm & 2:30-5:30pm Mon-Thu (to 4:30pm Fri)

Founded in 1544, La Serena is Chile's second-oldest city and one of its biggest coastal resorts. At La Serena's historical heart, the bell towers of colonial-era churches ring out amid contemporary Spanish-style architecture. On the coast are golden beaches, rolling white waves, and modern buildings lining avenues. At the mouth of Río Elqui, La Serena is the gateway to the lush Valle del Elqui.

Plaza de Armas

Museo Histórico Gabriel González Videla: Matta 495 10am-5:50pm Mon-Thu, 10am-4:50pm Fri museohistorico laserena.gob.cl

La Serena's central plaza marks the site of the city's second founding by conquistador Francisco de Aguirre (1507–81). Located here is the beautiful limestone Catedral de La Serena as well as the Neo-colonial Tribunales de la Justicia (Law Courts) and Municipalidad (City Hall). The latter two date from the 1930s and have extravagant red-and-white exteriors. A Modernist fountain by the sculptor Román Rojas adorns the center of this square. On a corner of the plaza is the Museo Histórico Gabriel González Videla, housed in the 19th-century family home of the former Chilean president whose

STAY

Hostal La Sombra del Viento

Run by a welcoming French host, this guesthouse is set in a converted colonial mansion. It is tastefully decorated and has a sunny patio.

Los Carrera 224
(051) 2484 775

name it bears. The first floor displays personal objects which once belonged to the former president, and a regional historical museum occupies the floor upstairs.

②

Catedral de La Serena

Plaza de Armas
(051) 2225 658 10am-1pm & 4-8pm Mon-Sat, 10am-1pm Sun

The Neo-Classical facade and tower of La Serena's cathedral stand over the Plaza de Armas. Built under the direction of French architect Juan Herbage in 1844, this cathedral preserves the tomb of conquistador Francisco de Aguirre. The building stands on the site of a previous cathedral destroyed in 1680 by English pirate Bartholomew Sharp, who sacked the city over three days before razing it to the ground. Beautiful stained-glass windows from France ornament the cathedral's walls. Located in the grounds, the Museo Sala de Arte Religioso displays religious art and objects from the 17th to 19th centuries.

A charming Modernist fountain in Plaza de Armas

DESIERTO FLORIDO

Every four to five years, the rainfall on a section of the Atacama causes seeds to explode into life in a phenomenon called the *Desierto Florido* (Flowering Desert). The event can be seen from La Serena. The desert turns into a carpet of flowers of vibrant blues, reds, purples, and yellows that attract thousands of visitors. It is impossible to predict the year of *Desierto Florido*, but it occurs between September and November.

Iglesia de San Francisco

Balmaceda 640
(051) 2 2474 5185
9:30am-1:30pm Mon-Fri, 10am-12:30pm Sun

Built between 1585 and 1590, the Iglesia de San Francisco is the oldest of La Serena's wonderful stone churches, and the only one of the city's temples to escape destruction at the hands of several pirates, most notably Bartholomew Sharp. Iglesia de San Francisco is crowned by a bell tower and cupola, and its exterior walls are flamboyantly carved with Baroque motifs – a design that is considered *mestizo* for its South American influences. In the early years of the 20th century, part of the convent was sold and demolished to build the Barrio París-Londres. Adjacent to the church, the Museo de Colonial Iglesia San Francisco holds an inter-esting collection of religious art and imagery dating from the arrival of the Franciscan Order to Chile in the 16th century, including a Bible penned in 1538.

INSIDER TIP
Andean gifts

La Recova is a bustling local market, which provides a perfect opportunity to find local gifts for friends and family. Options include rain sticks, artisan jewelry, and a range of Andean wool clothing.

Museo Arqueológico

Cordovez, Cienfuegos
10:30am-5:30pm Tue-Sat **museoarqueologicolaserena.cl**

Entered via an 18th-century Baroque portal, La Serena's archaeological museum displays various pre-Columbian objects stemming from the regions of Norte Chico, Norte Grande, and Easter Island. The focus here is on the Diaguita culture (1000–1536 CE), with English language displays showcasing ceramics – the designs of which were inspired by hallucinogenics. Perhaps the most remark-able exhibit at the Museo Arqueológico is the 1,500- year-old mummy dug up in the dusty Atacama Desert near the village of Chiu-Chiu, which is essential highland viewing for people who are interested in pre-Columbian history. Another must-see is the 10-ft- (3-m-) tall *moai* statue that came from Easter Island.

Coquimbo

7 miles (12 km) S of La Serena **turismoregiondecoquimbo.cl**

At the southern end of Avenida del Mar lies the former mining city of Coquimbo. English and American immigrants flocked here during the 19th century to make their fortunes, building grand homes in what became known as the Barrio Inglés (English Quarter). Casa Novella *(Aldunate 569)* dates back to 1840, with its Oregon pine and American oak structure, expansive wooden balconies, and zinc-lined walls representative of the city's iconic *arquitectura portuaria* (port architecture). Next door, the grander Casa Chesney Cosgrove, built in 1892, is similarly faithful to this style.

↑ Fascinating *moai* statue at the Museo Arqueológico

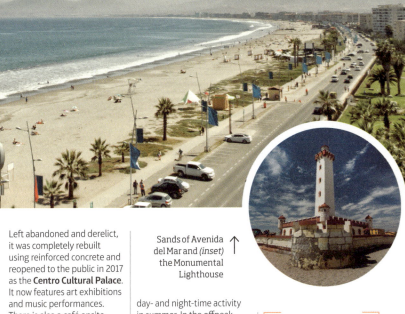

Left abandoned and derelict, it was completely rebuilt using reinforced concrete and reopened to the public in 2017 as the **Centro Cultural Palace**. It now features art exhibitions and music performances. There is also a café onsite.

Centro Cultural Palace
Aldunate 599
(051) 2256 418 9am-7pm Mon-Sat

6

Avenida del Mar

Benavente 980

La Serena's 4-mile- (6-km-) long coastal boulevard is the city's thriving restaurant and bar zone, where visitors can drink interesting cocktails before grabbing something to eat. The avenue, which is lined by sandy beaches and big white waves on one side and by modern hotels, apartment blocks, bars,and restaurants on the other, is a frenzy of day- and night-time activity in summer. In the offpeak season, it offers dramatic sea walks, especially at sunset. A 20-minute walk from the center, west along the city's main Avenida Francisco de Aguirre, leads to El Faro Monumental, a fascinating lighthouse marking the northern end of Avenida del Mar.

The lighthouse, which was built between 1950 and 1951 at the request of President Gabriel González Videla, is one of the most popular tourist attractions in the area. Beaches around this area are rustic, with massive waves that attract surfers from across Chile. Just south of the El Faro Monumental lighthouse are the main bathing beaches, Playa 4 Esquinas and Playa Canto del Agua, which have plenty of bars and restaurants.

Sands of Avenida del Mar and *(inset)* the Monumental Lighthouse ↑

La Serena's 4-mile- (6-km-) long coastal boulevard is the city's thriving restaurant and bar zone, where visitors can drink interesting cocktails before grabbing something to eat.

EAT

Casona del 900
The menu at the traditionally decorated Casona del 900 is extensive. Most people share mixed grills, but there are seafood options too.

Francisco de Aguirre 443 casonadel900.cl

Mar Adentro
Overlooking Playa Los Pescadores, this *picada* (a place to eat cheaply but well) offers an ample seafood selection and occasional live music.

Rengo 4629 Tue maradentro restaurant.cl

$$$

6

VALLE DE ELQUI

B5 From La Serena and Santiago chile.travel/en/where-to-go/destination/elqui-valley

East of La Serena, the tranquil, slow-paced Valle de Elqui (Elqui Valley) feels like another world. A welcome contrast to the largely arid landscapes of the Norte Chico, this lush valley is a famous stargazing destination, home to Chile's finest *pisco* distilleries, and has strong associations with Nobel Prize-winning poet Gabriela Mistral, who was born and raised here.

Vicuña

39 miles (63 km) E of La Serena Gabriela Mistral, San Martín; municipalidadvicuna.cl

Set in the valley of Río Elqui, Vicuña is a small town of adobe houses ringed by rippled mountains. The birthplace of Chile's Nobel Prize-winning poet, Gabriela Mistral *(p38)*, Vicuña is a popular pilgrimage site for writers and artists. The **Museo Gabriela Mistral** displays personal items of the celebrated poet, including books, paintings, and awards. At the center of town, sculptures inspired by Mistral's works and concrete planters, decorated using geometric patterns commonly found in Diaguita pottery, adorn Vicuña's plaza. It becomes the hub of lively folk dancing and traditional music during the Carnaval Elquino, the town's largest festival held from mid-January through mid-February. Overlooking the plaza is the landmark Torre Bauer, an incongruous yet charming red Bavarian tower. It was constructed in 1905 at the behest of Vicuña's former mayor of German descent, Alfonso Bauer. Adjacent to the tower, the *cabildo* (town hall) dates from 1826 and houses a small, historically themed museum as well as an information office for visitors. Also bordering the plaza, the Iglesia de la Inmaculada Concepción was built in 1909 and has a luminous interior with beautiful frescoes on the ceiling. The font here was used to baptize Mistral in 1889.

At the edge of town is **Capel**, Chile's biggest distillery operated by a cooperative of *pisco* producers. Guided tours take visitors to its vineyards, plant facilities, and a *pisco* museum, which displays original distilling machinery. The tour ends with tastings or a cocktail workshop.

GREAT VIEW
View from the Top

It's well worth the climb to the summit of the Cerro de la Virgen, a hill near Vicuña, where you will have panoramic views of the Valle de Elqui and wonderful photo opportunities.

→ A courtyard displaying various sculptures at the Museo Gabriela Mistral

Museo Gabriela Mistral
Gabriela Mistral 759 10am-5pm Tue-Sat mgmistral.gob.cl

Capel
Camino a Peralillo s/n 10am-7:30pm daily centroturisticocapel.gob.cl

Pisco Elqui

65 miles (105 km) SE of La Serena From La Serena & Montegrande piscoelqui.com

Set 4,100 ft (1,250 m) above sea level, Pisco Elqui is one of the prettiest villages of Valle del Elqui. It was originally called La Unión by the Spanish, but was renamed in 1936 as part of a government initiative to boost the area's famous commodity, *pisco*. Among the best-known distilleries here is the **Destileria Pisco Mistral**. This facility has been making *pisco* for over a century. Tours cover its museum and the production, barreling, and bottling salons, and end with tastings.

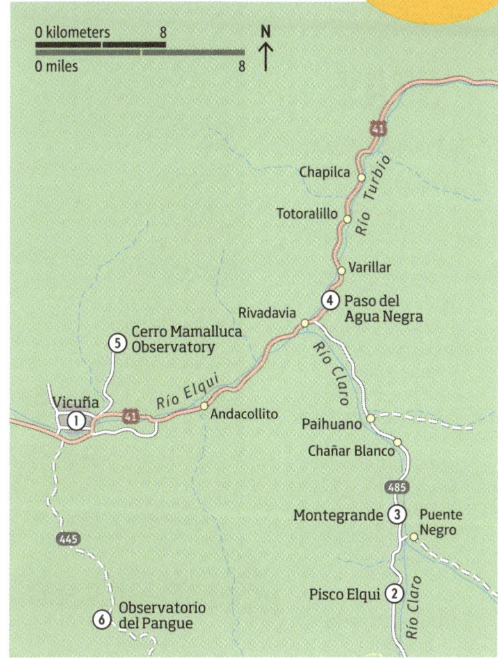

Destileria Pisco Mistral
O'Higgins 746 11am-5:30pm daily (Jan & Feb: to 6:30pm) piscomistral.cl/destileria/destileria.html

Montegrande

63 miles (101 km) E of La Serena From La Serena & Vicuña

The tiny village of Montegrande lies at the eastern end of Valle del Elqui, at 3,600 ft (1,100 m) above sea level. Here, the valley narrows and is surrounded by the steep slopes of the pre-cordillera, behind which the snowcapped peaks of the Andes form a backdrop.

The poet-diplomat Gabriela Mistral spent her childhood in Montegrande, having moved from Vicuña with her mother and stepsister when she was three years old. The house in which Mistral grew up is preserved as the **Museo de Sitio Casa-Escuela Gabriela Mistral**. It doubled as a school when Mistral lived here and has furniture and personal belongings of the poet.

Prior to her death in 1957, Mistral had requested that she be laid to rest in Montegrande; her tomb lies on the crest of a low hill near the village plaza. Facing this tree-lined plaza is a church. Mistral took her first communion in its interior.

Museo de Sitio Casa-Escuela Gabriela Mistral
Calle principal s/n 10am-1pm & 3-6pm Tue-Sun caminoagabrielamistral.cl

> **The birthplace of Chile's Nobel Prize-winning poet, Gabriela Mistral, Vicuña is a popular pilgrimage site for writers and artists.**

STAY

El Tesoro de Elqui
Delightful German-run establishment with modern rooms surrounded by peaceful gardens, plus a swimming pool, hammocks, and a great little café. The property also offers various unique activities, including hot tubs under the starry night skies and therapy with basins.

Arturo Prat s/n, Pisco Elqui
eltesorodeelqui.cl

Refugio Misterios del Elqui
A collection of thatched-roof cabins with stylish fittings and superb views are set in well-kept grounds, which are also home to a wonderful swimming pool and a state-of-the-art telescope.

Arturo Prat s/n, Pisco Elqui
misteriosdelelqui.cl

Cabañas Los Sauzales
This charming establishment is located next to the river, with handy private parking and surrounded by gorgeous fruit trees. The cabins offer visitors a taste of nature and tranquility.

Los Copihues 51, Pisco Elqui, Paiguano
lossauzales.cl

↑ The Paso del Agua Negra snaking around the mountains, (*inset*) partly covered in snow

Paso del Agua Negra

115 miles (185 km) E of Vicuña

The spectacular road, Ruta 41, is on the Chilean side of Paso del Agua Negra. It twists and turns through mountains and skirts the Andean border between Chile and Argentina The road rises to 15,633 ft (4,765 m) above sea level.

The views are made even more spectacular by the presence of *penitentes* (enormous snow pinnacles that are sculpted into unearthly shapes by the fierce wind); so called as they resemble hooded figures of Holy Week. The route also passes the turquoise reservoir known as La Laguna and leads to the hot-springs resort of Termas de Pismanta in Argentina and to the provincial capital San Juan.

Note that Paso del Agua Negra is normally only open in summer – snows often close the route between May and October. If you're planning on crossing early or late in the season, check with the authorities beforehand that the road is still passable.

5   

Cerro Mamalluca Observatory

6 miles (9 km) NE of Vicuña **Tours are mandatory**
observatoriomamalluca.cl

One of the valley's greatest attractions is stargazing. Opened to the public in

November 1998 as the first project of its kind, the fascinating Cerro Mamalluca Observatory provides the perfect spot to do so. It is a large complex of huge telescopes and white domed buildings that sit like giant golf balls on the mountainside.

The facility can only be seen by taking two-hour guided tours that are conducted in English and Spanish by specialized guides. Visitors are invited to participate in a cosmic journey through sounds and images, and to use the lens of a powerful 24-in (60-cm) telescope to view stars and planets. The observatory's spherical roof slides open to reveal the Milky Way, constellations, planets, nebulae, and clusters, as well as blue and red stars. Other highlights include watching the rings on Jupiter and Saturn, and craters on the surface of the moon, all of which appear with a photographic clarity in what is one of the clearest night skies in the world.

HIDDEN GEM

Cochiguaz

On the eastern edge of the valley, the village of Cochiguaz has a strong new age vibe and locals offer an array of therapeutic treatments and classes. It's also, reputedly, a good place to spot UFOs.

6  

Observatorio del Pangue

11 miles (17 km) S of Vicuña observatoriodelpangue.blogspot.com

Run by French and Chilean astronomers, Observatorio del Pangue arranges nightly tours of the stars, which start at different times according to the time of year. The tours have to be booked in advance and have a maximum capacity of ten people. Visitors are shown the wonders of the universe using state-of-the-art telescopes.

The observatory stands atop a hill, in a mountainous landscape, from where the views are stunning. Yet the most noticeable feature here is the quality of the sky, which is the result of a rare combination of an adjusted geology, a favorable local climate, and an absence of light pollution.

PISCO

Developed by Spanish settlers in the 16th century, *pisco* is an aromatic, fruity brandy made from distilled Muscat grape wine. The national drink of Chile (and Peru, which claims its version is superior) is commonly consumed neat, in a *pisco* sour (a refreshing aperitif that features lemon juice and sugar), or as a *piscola* (mixed with cola). The Valle de Elqui is the home of Chile's *pisco* industry and many distilleries offer tours and tastings, including Pisco Capel *(cooperativacapel.cl)*, Pisco ABA *(pisquera-aba.cl)*, Pisco Mistral *(piscomistral.cl)* and Los Nichos *(fundolosnichos.cl)*.

EXPERIENCE MORE

Iglesia de San Jerónimo de Poconchile

B1 22 miles (35 km) E of Arica; Poconchile

Located in the village of Poconchile, Iglesia de San Jerónimo is the oldest of northern Chile's early colonial churches. It was built by Spanish priests in 1580, on a site along the old Camino del Inca (Inca Road), and served to evangelize the Aymara people of this area. The church's dazzlingly white exterior is faithful to the classic Spanish colonial style – a thick adobe perimeter wall marks the boundary of this sacred site and twin bell towers flank its entrance. The restored interior is wooden and painted white. At the back of the church, a desert cemetery contains old graves marked by pebbles and simple wooden crosses.

Did You Know?

Llamas and guanacos are the largest of the Andean camelids.

Putre

C1 90 miles (149 km) NE of Arica

The largest of the high-altitude settlements close to Arica, Putre is an oasis town ringed by the pointed peaks of several snow-swathed volcanoes. At 11,500 ft (3,500 m) above sea level, it is a stopover for travelers seeking acclimatization before continuing onward to higher altitude highlights such as the adjacent Parque Nacional Lauca *(p166)* and the more distant Reserva Nacional Las Vicuñas. Putre's roots lie in pre-Inca Chile, but the present town was founded by the Spanish around 1580 as a resting place for muleteers transporting silver from the mines of Potosí, in modern-day Bolivia, to the Pacific coast. The town's most attractive structure is the heavily restored church fronting the plaza. This edifice dates from 1670 and stands on the site of the original temple that was destroyed by earthquake, and which, according to Spanish chronicles, was completely clad in silver and gold. The rest of Putre is a compact grid of cobbled streets lined with concrete-and-zinc buildings and old Spanish adobe houses. A selection of hotels and restaurants dot this pleasant altiplano town; tour agencies are found on Calle Baquedano.

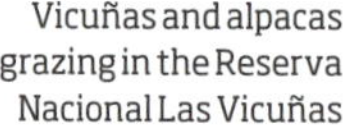

Vicuñas and alpacas grazing in the Reserva Nacional Las Vicuñas

Reserva Nacional Las Vicuñas

C1 143 miles (230 km) E of Arica CONAF, Guallatire; conaf.cl

Spectacular and remote, the Reserva Nacional Las Vicuñas protects a vast wilderness of giant volcanoes, high-altitude tablelands, abandoned Aymara settlements, and diverse indigenous fauna. This reserve has a steppe landscape that rises from 13,120 ft (4,000 m)

Exploring the striking adobe buildings of a hamlet near Putre

above sea level at its lowest elevation, to 18,370 ft (5,600 m) at its highest. It is overlooked by three 20,000-ft (6,000-m) volcanoes: Volcán Acotango, Volcán Capurata, and Volcán Guallatiri. Vicuñas, for whose protection this park was founded in 1983, can be seen bounding across the *puna* (grassland) region; ñandus, ostrich-like birds, sprint over open plains; pink flamingos congregate on the banks and vizcachas (large, chinchilla-like rodents) scurry over rocks.

In the central sector of the reserve, the llama-herding hamlet of Guallatiri has a couple of basic lodging options (closed January–March). There is also the National Forest Corporation (CONAF) ranger post and a 17th-century church. South of this hamlet, the Monumento Natural Salar de Surire is a dazzlingly white salt plain. Three different species of flamingo nest on its shores in the summer. The weather throughout the reserve resembles a desert, so expect drops in temperature at night. It's also possible to see llama, alpaca, and puma in the reserve.

El Gigante de Atacama

C1 50 miles (80 km) NW of Iquique

Located 9 miles (14 km) east of the town of Huara, this 283-ft- (86-m-) tall geoglyph is the world's largest image of a human being. It rests on the west slope of Cerro Unitas hill, along the Huara-Colchane road. Although there is no public transportation to its location, tours of Humberstone *(p178)* from Iquique generally stop here.

PUKARÁS AND THE CAMINO DEL INCA

Northern Chile's pre-Inca fortresses, built between 1000 CE and 1450, are known as *pukarás*. In the 11th century, the reigning Tiwanaku empire collapsed, returning autonomy to the Norte Grande's Aymara and Atacameño peoples. However, the empire's peace was replaced by intermittent warfare as local warlords competed for resources. To protect ancestral trading routes, the warlords built *pukarás* on strategic hillsides. The *pukarás'* role as a powerbase continued until the 1450s, when Inca forces sacked them and incorporated their routes into the Camino del Inca (Inca Road), a 3,720-mile (6,000-km) highway that ran the length of the Inca empire.

An abandoned schoolyard in the ghost town of Humberstone

Humberstone and Santa Laura

C1 30 miles (48 km) E of Iquique; Ruta A16, km 3 9am-6pm daily (summer: to 7pm) museodelsalitre.cl

In the 1930s, British investors built the towns of Santa Laura and Humberstone to provide housing and leisure for the workers and management of the area's nitrate mines. By 1960, the advent of artificial nitrates had closed the mines, leaving the two towns eerily abandoned. Today, these UNESCO-protected nitrate ghost towns have become popular visitor attractions. The more-visited Humberstone is a silent grid of named roads, empty plazas, creaking street signs, and shells of deserted buildings and facilities. These include quarters that once housed 3,700 employees, a hospital and school, an outdoor pool, sports fields, a marketplace, a church, clock tower, and a theater that could seat up to 800 people. Each of these desolate structures is signposted with panels bearing historical information that helps visitors explore the town independently. Adjacent to these buildings stands the rusting machinery of the town's nitrate mine.

About 1 mile (1.5 km) east of Humberstone, the smaller ghost town of Santa Laura feels all the more abandoned for receiving fewer visitors. Its hulking processing facilities – which include giant chimneys and mills – are perfectly preserved.

Parque Nacional Volcán Isluga

C1 155 miles (250 km) NE of Iquique CONAF; conaf.cl

Isolated from northern Chile's beaten path, Parque Nacional Volcán Isluga protects around 674 sq miles (1,741 sq km) of altiplano wilderness that embraces brilliantly hued lagoons, forgotten Aymara villages, and soaring volcanoes, including the 18,209-ft- (5,550-m-) high Volcán Isluga. Home to similar flora and fauna as Parque Nacional Lauca *(p166)* but much less visited, it's an excellent option for those looking to escape the tourist crowds. The park's highlights are clustered in its eastern sector, accessible via the paved A-55 international highway that connects Iquique with neighboring Bolivia. Close to the park entrance, Isluga is an Aymara village with a beautiful 17th-century church as well as the Pukará de Isluga, a ruined fortress dating from pre-Columbian times.

Also located in the eastern sector, the Aymara village of Enquelga is the gateway to the park's hot springs. This sector has two pristine lakes: Laguna Arabilla has a walking trail along its shore, while Laguna Parinacota is popular for sightings of

Did You Know?

Saltpeter Week is celebrated in the Tarapacá region every third week of November.

The vast desert landscape of Parque Nacional Volcán Isluga

wildlife, including pink flamingos, camelids, and the taruca, a mid-sized Andean deer.

13 Mamiña Hot Springs

C1 78 miles (125 km) E of Iquique; Mamiña termasdemamina.cl

Located 8,860 ft (2,700m) above sea level, the Mamiña Hot Springs have historically been used to cure afflictions ranging from eczema to anxiety since the age of the Incas. They comprise a number of springs, such as Baños Ipla with its sodium-rich waters and Baños Barros Chinos, famous for its mud baths. Adjacent to the springs you'll find the village of Mamiña, with stone houses, terraced fields, and Inca ruins. The village's restored Iglesia de San Marcos, dating from 1632, is unique among Andean churches for its twin bell towers.

FESTIVAL DE LA TIRANA

Chile's biggest religious event, the Festival de la Tirana offers a peek at Andean culture. It venerates the Virgen del Carmen via costume and dance. On its first day, dancers enter La Tirana's church and ask the Virgin's permission to dance. They then embark on four days of frenetic dancing that culminate on the Day of the Virgin, when a hoisted image of the saint leads a mass procession through the village.

14 La Tirana

C2 45 miles (72 km) SE of Iquique 

A somnolent oasis village with adobe houses, La Tirana springs to life each July for the Festival de la Tirana. A religious celebration, the festival draws over 200,000 devotees to the village.

The origins of the village can be traced to the 1500s when an Inca princess, notorious for killing Christians, ruled the area. The princess, who was known as La Tirana (The Tyrant), eventually fell in love with a Portuguese prisoner and converted to Christianity, only to have her irate subjects kill them both on their wedding day. In 1540, a Jesuit missionary found the cross marking the princess's grave and ordered the construction of a church on the site. Named the Iglesia de la Virgen del Carmen de la Tirana in honor of Chile's patron saint and the Inca princess, the church became the progenitor of the cult of La Tirana. The **Iglesia de la Tirana** comprises the present-day wooden church; a plaza adorned with effigies of the Virgin and the princess; and the Museo de la Virgen de la Tirana, which displays costumes and masks from the Festival de la Tirana. Inside the church is a polychrome shrine to the Virgin.

Iglesia de la Tirana

9am-1:30pm & 3:30-7pm Tue-Sat, 9am-7pm Sun santuariodelatirana.cl

Pica

C2 71 miles (114 km) E of Iquique Avenida 27 de abril; pica.cl

Known locally as the Flower in the Sand, Pica is an oasis village famed for its orchards. Regional and local varieties of fruit trees thrive in Pica's microclimate, and adobe houses line its streets. Facing the main plaza, the Iglesia de San Andrés was built in 1886, and its polychrome interior holds a life-size representation of the Last Supper carved from wood. East of the plaza, the **Museo Municipal de Pica** displays millennia-old preserved Chinchorro mummies *(p157)*. Southwest of town, the **Valle de los Dinosaurios** has models of the dinosaurs whose fossilized footprints were found nearby.

Museo Municipal de Pica
Balmaceda 178 (057) 2741 665 9am-2pm & 3-5:45pm Mon-Thu, 9am-2:30pm Fri

Valle de los Dinosaurios
Camino a Matilla
24 hours

> **Regional and local varieties of fruit trees thrive in Pica's microclimate, and adobe houses line its streets.**

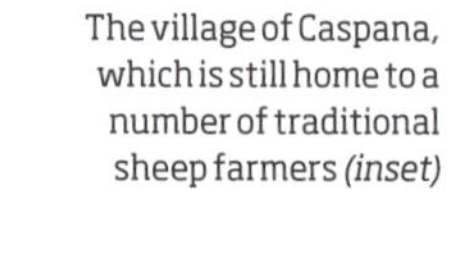

The village of Caspana, which is still home to a number of traditional sheep farmers *(inset)*

Cerro Pintados

C2 59 miles (96 km) SE of Iquique; El Cruce de Geoglifos de Pintados, La Panamericana
(056) 9859 53756
9:30am-5pm Tue-Sun

The barren hillsides of Cerro Pintados are etched with more than 420 gigantic geoglyphs *(p41)*. Dating from 500–1450 CE, when this region was part of a caravan route to the Pacific coast, the geoglyphs comprise huge geometric shapes as well as anthropomorphic and zoomorphic figures, including depictions of fish, llamas, and the ñandu, a native ostrich-like bird. These are accessible via a 3-mile- (5-km-) long path that skirts the base of the hills.

Caspana

C2 52 miles (84 km) E of Calama

One of the oasis villages that dot the high mountain pass between Calama and San Pedro de Atacama, Caspana is spectacularly situated 11,870 ft (3,260 m) above sea level in a steep gorge irrigated by a tributary of the Río Salado. The village is an adobe jewel, with monochrome stone-and-mud houses that were inhabited by the Atacameño people before the arrival of the Incas and Spanish. Today, it subsists on farming, and sinuous rows of green

Interior of the church of San Andrés in Pica, with its beautiful sky-blue ceiling

terraces can be seen along the contours of the lower slopes of the gorge. These are planted with root vegetables, grown to be sold at the market in Calama. At the edge of the village, the adobe and cactus-wood Iglesia San Lucas dates from 1641 and backs on to a small cemetery. The village's **Museo de Caspana** has archaeological and ethnographic exhibits. The tiny village plaza offers vistas of the rocky gorge, pale houses, and verdant terraces.

Museo de Caspana
Los Tres Alamos s/n (056) 9321 64305
10am-1pm & 3-6pm Tue-Fri

Calama

C2 242 miles (390 km) SE of Iquique El Aeródromo El Loa de Calama Avenida O´Higgins s/n sector Parque El Loa; calamacultural.cl

The industrial city of Calama is the base for visits to the great copper mines of Chuquicamata. An oasis city in the driest zone of the planet's driest desert, Calama has its roots in pre-Columbian Chile, and derives its name from the Kunza word *kara ama*, meaning "water haven." Though this name seems rather non-sensical now, until the mid-20th century the town was surrounded by the River Loa.

Did You Know?

Not a single drop of rain fell in Calama between 1570 and 1971.

In the 1920s, Calama boomed as a service town and provider of some of the more debauched diversions to pit workers. It experienced an influx of inhabitants from nearby Chuquicamata, in 2003, after the open-pit copper mine there was closed permanently. Calama's single daytime attraction is the **Parque El Loa**, a riverside tourist park featuring a replica of the church at Chiu-Chiu *(p182)*. The grounds are also the site of the city's Museo Arqueológico y Etnografico Parque El Loa, which houses artifacts belonging to this area's pre-Inca oasis villages.

Parque El Loa
Avenida Bernardo O'Higgins s/n (055) 2845 585
10am-8:30pm daily

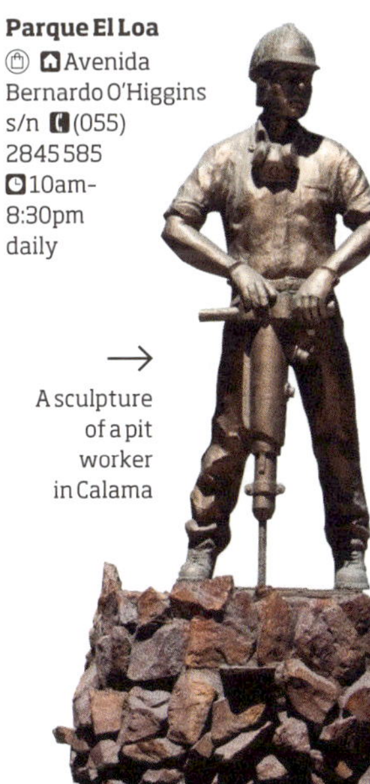

→ A sculpture of a pit worker in Calama

The exterior and interior *(inset)* of the Iglesia San Francisco de Chiu-Chiu

19

Chiu-Chiu

C2 22 miles (36 km) NE of Calama 

Founded by the Spanish around 1610, Chiu-Chiu is an oasis village of whitewashed adobe houses and cactus-wood doors. Visited on tours from Calama *(p181)*, or more usually from San Pedro de Atacama *(p158)*, the village conserves one of Chile's oldest churches, the Iglesia San Francisco de Chiu-Chiu. This whitewashed adobe church was built in 1674 in the Spanish colonial style, with two interesting bell towers, walls over 3 ft (1 m) thick, and a well-preserved interior of mini altars and polychrome statues of saints and virgins. The church's small and quaint grounds, protected by a thick perimeter wall, contain a tiny cemetery that is certainly worth exploring.

One block from the main plaza of Chiu-Chiu is the **Museo Geológico de Chiu-Chiu**, which is worth visiting for some interesting rock and fossil exhibits.

Museo Geológico de Chiu-Chiu
(056) 4122 03029
3-6:30pm Sat & Sun

EAT

Talatur

Family-run restaurant serving homemade Chilean food such as delicious casseroles. Rabbit also features prominently.

Ruta 21 128, Esmeralda 881, Chiu-Chiu
(056) 4255 3561

$$$

20 

Pukará de Lasana

C2 28 miles (45 km) N of Calama; Pueblo Lasana, Valle Lasana 9:30am-5pm daily

The stone ruins of the pre-Inca Pukará de Lasana occupy a natural promontory that overlooks the green Valle Lasana from within a rocky canyon. The people of the Atacameño civilization (400 BCE–1400 CE) erected this fortress from a pre-existing village during a period of war in the 11th century. Today, the well-preserved ruins are a hilly maze of perimeter walls, roofless houses, storehouses, patios, narrow passageways, and fortifications. Inca forces sacked this site in 1447, and converted it into a strategic administrative center for control of the valley. They abandoned it in the 16th century on the arrival of the Spanish to this region.

Chuquicamata

C2 10 miles (16 km) N of Calama; Entrada al Campamento, J.M. Carrera Tours Mon, Fri & Thu (book in advance; passport needed for entry) codelco.com

Visited only by guided tour, Chuquicamata – or "Chuqui," as it is affectionately known to locals – is the world's biggest open-pit mine. This huge copper quarry is about 2 miles (3 km) wide, 3 miles (5 km) long, and an impressive 2,300 ft (1,000 m) deep. The mine is to copper what Saudi Arabia is to oil – the commodity accounts for approximately 11 per cent of global production, and any blip in the production process here strikes panic in world copper markets. Chile's biggest state company, Codelco, oversees the mine. It employs 20,000 workers, operates 24 hours per day, and is the single biggest contributor to Chile's coffers, bankrolling the country's health and education systems. Each year this hole in the Andes mountains is gouged ever deeper, a phenomenon brought into stunning perspective on one-hour coach tours of the site. Tours pass refineries and crushing and smelting plants to a viewpoint that overlooks the open pit. Here, visitors can peer into the depths of Chuquicamata, and glimpse the giant 394-ton (400-tonne) dump trucks, with 10-ft- (3-m-) high wheels, that ascend and descend its terraced walls like worker ants. It is advisable to wear comfortable shoes and choose clothes that cover the arms and legs.

In 2018 the mine performed its last blast at the bottom of the open pit, and its processes are currently transitioning to underground block cave mining. This is a far more efficient and more sustainable method, and is expected to extend the mine for another 50 years. The switch cost an estimated US$5.6 billion, but hit delays and in 2024 the project was extended at a cost of an additional US$720 million.

Did You Know?

A young Che Guevara visited Chuquicamata during his legendary motorcycle trip across South America.

Termas Baños de Puritama

C2 17 miles (28 km) NE of San Pedro de Atacama; Camino al Tatio, km 32 9:30am-1:30pm & 2:30-6pm daily termas depuritama.cl

A half-day excursion from San Pedro, the Termas Baños de Puritama are terraced hot springs that tumble down a canyon. At 82–86°F (28–31°C), you can bathe in these natural volcanic pools. There are changing rooms nearby, and wooden footbridges link the interconnected pools.

A half-day excursion from San Pedro, the Termas Baños de Puritama are terraced hot springs that tumble down a canyon.

→ Bathing in the warm waters of the Termas Baños de Puritama

Valle de la Luna

C3 12 miles (19 km) SW of San Pedro de Atacama; Sector 6, Reserva Nacional Los Flamencos 10:30am-6pm daily (Sep-Mar: to 7:30pm; book ahead) conaf.cl

Valle de la Luna is a stark landscape of otherworldly rock formations, salt caves, natural amphitheaters, and vast sand dunes. Set 7,870 ft (2,400 m) above sea level in the Cordillera de Sal (Salt Mountain Ranges), it is explored via a well-marked circuit. There are a number of caverns en route, so it's best to come prepared with a torch if you'd like to dip into these. The path also includes Las Tres Marías, eroded rock sculptures that resemble three praying women, and the Duna Mayor, the greatest of this valley's massive sand dunes. The valley is well known for its exceptional sunsets, so most tours climb the Duna Mayor at dusk for stupendous views of the Andean peaks and volcanoes washed in indigo, orange, and red tones. The vistas include Volcánes Licancabur and Láscar; the latter being one of Chile's most explosive peaks. It is best to visit during the hotter months, from December through February.

Géiseres del Tatio

C2 74 miles (119 km) E of Calama; Camino a Tatio 6am-4pm daily eltatio.net

A natural spectacle, the Géiseres del Tatio shoot skyward in columns of white vapor at an altitude of 14,200 ft (4,320 m) above sea level. There are some 40 geysers and 70 fumaroles here, each a scar on the surface of a flat geothermic basin that is ringed by rust-colored mountains and pointed volcanoes. Their origin lies in the contact of a cold river with hot, magmatic rock deep underground. This contact causes jets of vapor to stream upward through fissures in the earth's crust and to exit here, in white-vapor streams that rise to a height of 33 ft (10 m) and reach a temperature of 185°F (85°C). It is best to visit the geysers on 4WD excursions that depart from San Pedro de Atacama at 4am, reaching

Exploring the strangely shaped salt caves of the Valle de la Luna

↑ Dusk falling across the Salar de Atacama, creating a gorgeous purple sky

the geysers at around daybreak, when they are at their most impressive. Visitors who make this early trip will be able to view the geyser field at its most elemental; hear it groan, grumble, spit, and ultimately, both audibly and visibly exhale. Half-day trips to the Géiseres del Tatio end with a dip in sulfur-rich hot springs. Full-day excursions continue to the city of Calama, visiting Caspana, Chiu-Chiu, and the Pukará de Lasana, before returning to San Pedro de Atacama.

Salar de Tara

D3 62 miles (100 km) E of San Pedro de Atacama; Reserva Nacional Los Flamencos 9am-6pm daily Control de CONAF; conaf.cl

Adventurous travelers make the arduous yet memorable excursion from San Pedro de Atacama to the Salar de Tara, a salt lake located 14,100 ft (4,300 m) above sea level. Tough roads lead to this breathtaking white spectacle decorated by jewel-like lakes and green vegetation with abundant fauna. Its birdlife includes Chile's three species of flamingo, Andean geese, and horned coots. Herds of vicuña can be seen grazing at the salt pan's edge. Visitors on tours should get the opportunity to see Catedral de Tara, a giant rock wall in the middle of the desert that was once surrounded by an ancient volcanic crater. You can also experience de la Pacana, which are rock formations sculpted by the erosion of the wind.

Salar de Atacama

C3 15 miles (25 km) S of San Pedro de Atacama; RN Los Flamencos Control de CONAF, Sector Soncor; conaf.cl

Occupying 1,160 sq miles (3,000 sq km) of surface area, Salar de Atacama is Chile's largest, and the world's third-largest, salt flat. It lies 7,700 ft (2,350 m) above sea level in a great geological depression between the Domeyko and Andes mountain ranges. The *salar* formed when lakes that originally filled this basin evaporated, leaving a thick coat of silver-gray salt crystals. Not blindingly white like other salt pans in this region, the Salar de Atacama is nevertheless a vision of beauty, with lagoons of intense hues decorating its surface. Laguna Cejar is a brilliantly blue lake whose high salt and lithium content allows bathers to float weightlessly on its surface. Laguna Chaxa has shallow waters, a volcanic backdrop, sure flamingo sightings, and stunning sunsets.

Lying 13,100 ft (4,000 m) above sea level, a short drive east from Salar de Atacama, are the beautiful Laguna Miscanti, Laguna Miñiques, and Laguna Lejía, famous for their birdlife. Also east are Toconao, Peine, and Socaire, oasis villages with early-colonial churches, pre-Inca ruins, and petroglyphs.

Occupying 1,160 sq miles (3,000 sq km) of surface area, Salar de Atacama is Chile's largest, and the world's third-largest, salt flat.

Cerro Paranal Observatory

B3 75 miles (120 km) S of Antofagasta; Cerro Paranal, Ruta B-710 Tours: 10am & 2pm Sat (book in advance) eso.org

One of the world's most advanced astronomical facilities, the Cerro Paranal Observatory is housed in a futuristic complex of brilliant-white buildings, sharp lines, and curved domes. It stands at 8,500 ft (2,600 m) above sea level atop Cerro Paranal and is overseen by the European Southern Observatory (ESO). Its star attraction is the Very Large Telescope (VLT). One of the world's most powerful optical instruments, the VLT comprises four separate telescopes that combine to form one gigantic mirror, measuring 650 ft (200 m) in diameter. This mirror can define objects four billion times fainter than any that are visible to the naked eye – that is the equivalent of distinguishing car headlights from the surface of the moon. Fascinating two-hour guided tours follow a presentation on astronomy with visits to the VLT and its control room. Some scenes from the James Bond movie *Quantum of Solace* (2008) were shot here.

Did You Know?

Norte Grande comprises 25 per cent of Chile's mainland, but is home to just 5 per cent of the population.

Antofagasta

B3 194 miles (313 km) SW of San Pedro de Atacama Aeropuerto Cerro Moreno Avenida Prat 384; municipalidad antofagasta.cl

This historic port city is the sea outlet for the metals and minerals mined in the Atacama Desert. Founded in 1869 as part of Bolivia, Antofagasta was absorbed by Chile in the War of the Pacific (1879–83) and used to ship silver, nitrates, and, from 1915, copper from the great Chuquicamata mine *(p183)*. Chile's most progressive city by the 1930s, it appears today as a slightly grimy place, but some historic charm remains.

Set in the city center, the Neo-Gothic cathedral dates from 1917 and faces the Plaza Colón. The clock tower adorning the plaza was donated in 1910 by the city's English community, and is a tangible reminder of British influence in Antofagasta. Just north of the plaza, the former Customs House, dating from 1869, is home to the **Museo Regional de Antofagasta**. The museum's collection of over 9,000 objects includes fossils from the region, objects salvaged from the old nitrate mines, and period furniture.

At the end of the same road is **Ex-Estación de Ferrocarril de Antofagasta a Bolivia**, the city's former train station. Built in 1873 using British capital, this was the terminus for the Antofagasta-Bolivia railroad.

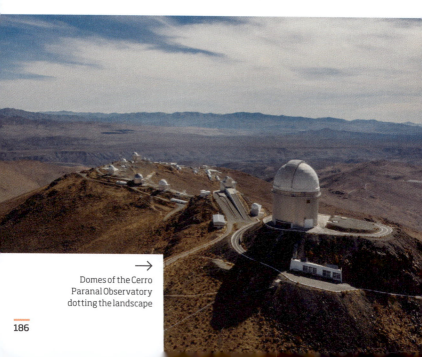

→ Domes of the Cerro Paranal Observatory dotting the landscape

Designated a National Historic Landmark in 1981, it conserves Scottish steam trains, English clocks, and red telephone boxes. Trains carrying copper from the Chuquicamata mine still pass through this station on their way to the port. Also near the port is the Muelle Histórico Salitrero (Nitrates Wharf), which dates from 1872, and the Mercado de Pescado, Antofagasta's fish market.

Facing the Pacific Ocean, some 5 miles (8 km) south of the city center, are the massive stone remnants of a silver refinery dating from 1888–92. Known as the **Ruinas de Huanchaca**, this fascinating and intact site occupies a desert hillside in stepped terraces, and features a steep central staircase, a round tower, narrow passageways, and rows of stone storehouses. The casino opposite the ruins, Enjoy Antofagasta, runs tours (including night tours) for visitors. The casino's glitzy architecture mirrors the ruins with a round tower and terraced facade that lends a quasi-Aztecan symmetry to this site.

A small on-site museum displays geological, archaeological, and anthropological objects, including antique silver-refining machinery.

Museo Regional de Antofagasta
Balmaceda 2786
10am-2pm Mon-Fri
museodeantofagasta.cl

Ex-Estación de Ferrocarril de Antofagasta a Bolivia
Bolívar 255 5-6pm Fri, 10am-1pm & 3-6pm Sat & Sun fcab.cl

Ruinas de Huanchaca
Avenida Angamos 01606 From Antofagasta
10am-6pm Tue-Sun
ruinasdehuanchaca.cl

29  

La Portada

C2 10 miles (16 km) N of Antofagasta; Ruta 5, Lado Norte From Antofagasta Daily conaf.cl

La Portada (The Gateway) is a natural sedimentary arch that faces dramatic coastline. The arch, eroded over seven million years, is visible from a parking area a short distance to its north; however, descending from the unstable headlands to the beach is prohibited. Visitors can explore the small CONAF-run museum on the cliff that overlooks the arch.

↑ Posing by the dramatic natural coastal arch of La Portada

STARGAZING IN THE ATACAMA DESERT

The Atacama Desert has some of the world's clearest night skies and most advanced observatories, such as Cerro Mamalluca *(p174)* and Cerro Paranal. Visitors can travel to the desert as night descends to view the dazzling array of stars. Guided tours are available in the region to provide information on star and planet formations billions of light years away. Work is currently underway on the new ELT telescope in the desert - it will be the world's largest optical telescope when it is operational in 2028.

Outside the attractive Neo-Classical Iglesia de San Francisco in Copiapó

Copiapó

B4 351 miles (566 km) S of Antofagasta Sernatur, Los Carrera 691; copiapo.cl

The capital of Chile's Atacama (III) region, Copiapó is a low-key city whose attractions are linked to its silver-mining heritage. Silver was first found here in 1832 by the muleteer Juan Godoy. His statue stands in a plaza fronting the Iglesia de San Francisco, an 1872 church with ornate paintings. Chile's first (and now defunct) railroad was built in 1851 to take silver from Copiapó to the port at Caldera.

Copiapó is centered around a plaza, which is fronted by a wooden cathedral from 1851. The Neo-Classical design of this edifice features an unusual three-tiered bell tower. Set at the city's western end is its grandest mansion, the Palacio Viña de Cristo, built in 1860 in the Georgian style for a silver baron. The **Museo Mineralógico** and **Museo Regional de Atacama** recount the Atacama region's history and mineral wealth. The latter houses the capsule used to rescue the San José miners. Flash floods in early 2015 damaged some of the lovely wooden buildings on Avenida Manuel Matta that date from the 1800s.

Museo Mineralógico

Colipi 587 (056) 522255626 10am-1pm & 3-5:30pm Mon-Thu, 10am-4:30pm Fri

Museo Regional de Atacama

Avenida Alameda 265 9am-5:45pm Mon-Fri, 10am-12:15pm & 3-5:45pm Sat, 10am-1:15pm Sun museodeatacama.gob.cl

Caldera

B4 50 miles (80 km) W of Copiapó Plaza Carlos Condell; turismo caldera.com

The colorful harbor town of Caldera grew in the late 1800s as a port for shipping silver brought in by the railroad from Copiapó. Today, it has a picturesque waterfront of sparkling ocean and sandy beaches where pelicans congregate.

On the waterfront, the Mercado de Pescado is the fishermen's harbor and market, where small ma-and-pa food stalls serve fresh seafood specialties. Located next to it, the **Museo Paleontológico**, built in 1850, is housed in Caldera's recycled railroad station and displays mammoth marine fossils. Its stand-out exhibit

THE RESCUE OF THE 33 SAN JOSÉ MINERS

On August 5, 2010, 33 miners at the San José gold and copper mine near Copiapó were trapped around 2,300 ft (700 m) underground after a collapse. Their families camped out on the surface, urging the mining company and the authorities to keep searching for their loved ones. Improbably, 17 days later, rescuers found a drillhead with a note attached: "We are fine in the shelter - the 33." The story gained international attention and finally, after 69 days underground, the men were safely brought to the surface on October 13.

is the fossilized skull of a bearded whale that lived 10 million years ago.

Once home to an Italian immigrant family, the red Neo-Classical mansion, **Casa Tornini**, was built in the 1890s. Guided tours in English, German, and Spanish take in the appealing original furniture owned by the family. Occasional art exhibitions are also held here.

Just south of Caldera is northern Chile's most beautiful beach, named **Bahía Inglesa** (English Bay) for the swashbuckling English pirates who dropped anchor here in the 17th century. The long sweep of bleach-white sand is fronted by a turquoise ocean of calm, sheltered waters and blissfully little construction save a smattering of upscale hotels and restaurants.

Museo Paleontológico
Plaza del Cabildo s/n 10am-5pm Tue-Fri, 11am-6pm Sat & Sun museo-paleontologico-chile.es.tl

Casa Tornini
Paseo Gana 210 Daily tours: 11:30am & 8pm (book ahead) casatornini.cl

Bahía Inglesa
4 miles (6 km) S of Caldera Next to Hotel Rocas de Bahía; bahiainglesachile.com

Parque Nacional Pan de Azúcar

B4 120 miles (194 km) NW of Copiapó; Ruta C-120, km 27 de Chañaral 9am-5pm Tue-Sun conaf.cl

Created in 1985 to protect 169 sq miles (438 sq km) of coastal desert, this park has beaches, sheltered coves, and vertiginous sand cliffs. The coastline offers refuge to easily sighted marine fauna. Dolphins, southern sea lions, gulls, Humboldt penguins, cormorants, and pelicans populate the shoreline. Coastal attractions include the offshore Isla Pan de Azúcar, a refuge for penguins and other seabirds that can be reached by boat excursion; and Caleta Pan de Azúcar, a picturesque fishers' hamlet with campgrounds and cabins. Farther inland the flora and fauna includes guanacos, foxes, condors, and over 20 species of cactus. Highlights include the Quebrada del Castillo and Quebrada Pan de Azúcar canyons; and the Mirador and Las Lomitas viewpoints.

EAT

Legado

Popular with journalists during the rescue of 33 miners in 2010 *(p188)*. Today, the ambience is calmer, but food remains sophisticated. Many dishes feature game from across Chile.

B4 Bernard O'Higgins 12, Copiapó legadorestaurant.com

$$$

Scenic coastline and *(inset)* Humboldt penguins in the Parque Nacional Pan de Azúcar

Located high in the Andes, at 13,780 ft (4,200 m) above sea level, Laguna Verde is a breathtaking lake of green and turquoise tones that change hue according to the light and time of day.

Parque Nacional Nevado Tres Cruces

C4 94 miles (151 km) E of Copiapó 9am-6pm daily CONAF, Laguna del Negro Francisco; conaf.cl

This remote but stunning national park conserves some 228 sq miles (591 sq km) of altiplano wilderness typified by colored lakes, snowy volcanoes, and abundant native fauna. Most visits focus on the northern sector, where Laguna Santa Rosa, an intensely blue saltwater lake, fills a depression ringed by the snowy peaks of the Nevado Tres Cruces massif. Next to the lake, the white Salar de Maricunga is Chile's southernmost salt flat.

Accessed via a 4WD route from Laguna Santa Rosa, the park's southern sector is less visited. Its greatest natural feature is Laguna del Negro Francisco, a lake with mirror-like waters which reflect the pointed cone of Volcán Copiapó and the giant wings of flapping flamingos. Chile's three flamingo species are present on the lakeshore here, part of a wildlife bonanza that features some 30 bird species and easily sighted mammals, including vicuñas, guanacos, vizcachas, and Andean foxes. Walking trails circle around Laguna Santa Rosa and Laguna del Negro Francisco, where a 12-bed CONAF *refugio* offers lodging and hot showers.

Ovalle

B5 53 miles (86 km) S of La Serena 38 Vicuña Mackenna; ovalleturismo.cl

The Valle del Limarí is a fertile area of orchards and farms that feeds much of the arid Norte Chico. The valley's largest settlement is Ovalle, a small city ringed by interesting monochrome peaks. Farmers working in and around the valley sell their fresh produce – including goat's cheese and fish – at Feria Modelo de Ovalle, the city's food market.

In the city center, the Iglesia de San Vicente Ferrer faces Ovalle's tree-lined plaza. Built in 1888, it has a tall bell tower and an ornate interior. The city's big draw, however, is the outstanding **Museo del Limarí** which exhibits pre-Hispanic items from the local area and features Chile's most impressive displays of Diaguita ceramics (1000–1536 CE).

Ovalle is a springboard for visits to Valle del Limarí's wineries and villages. West of the city is the oasis village of Barraza, with narrow adobe streets and a church that dates from 1681. The tombs of former priests are encased within its adobe walls. Also in the western sector are the wineries **Viña Ocho Tierras** and **Viña Tabalí**,which open for tours and tastings. The area is best known for its white wine production.

Museo del Limarí

Covarrubias, Antofagasta, Ovalle
10am-6pm Tue-Fri, 10am-1pm & 2-6pm Sat
museolimari.gob.cl

Viña Ocho Tierras
D-505 57, Ovalle
8:30am-5:30pm Mon-Fri
ochotierras.cl

Viña Tabalí
Hacienda Santa Rosa de Tabalí, Ruta Valle del Encanto 9am-2pm & 2:30-5pm Mon-Fri
tabali.com

Laguna Verde

C4 164 miles (265 km) NE of Copiapó Oct-Mar Sernatur, Los Carrera 691, Copiapó; (052) 6006 006066

Located high in the Andes, at 13,780 ft (4,200 m) above sea level, Laguna Verde is a breathtaking lake of green and turquoise tones that change hue according to the light and time of day. On the lake's western shore, rustic hot springs provide blissful relaxation. Mighty volcanoes, including El Muerto, Peña Blanca, Incahuasi, Barrancas Blancas, and Vicuñas, encircle the area. Their snowy peaks and the brown, red, and ocher tones of their flanks complete an artist's palette of sharply contrasting colors. However, most of these peaks are challenging and hard to climb. Wildlife in this area includes flamingos, ducks, foxes, and horned coots, all of which have adapted to live in the extreme temperatures of this desert environment.

Reaching 22,615 ft (6,893m), Volcán Ojos del Salado towers over the southern basin of Laguna Verde. This is the world's highest volcano, as well as Chile's highest peak. The climb to the summit is physically challenging but technically undemanding.

Those seeking to climb Ojos del Salado must acquire permits from Chile's foreign ministry *(difrol.cl)*. The best time to attempt a climb is between December and late March, and the easiest way up is from the Chilean side (the volcano can also be tackled from Argentina). There are shelters at several levels.

Reserva Nacional Pingüino de Humboldt

B5 54 miles (87 km) N of La Serena 8:30am-4pm Wed-Sun (book ahead) CONAF, park entrance; conaf.cl

Named after the Humboldt penguins that breed here, this 2,195-acre (888-ha) reserve consists of three islands off the rocky coast. It is a popular day trip from La Serena. Over 12,000 pairs of this vulnerable penguin species nest in the reserve, particularly on Isla de Choros. There are boat tours that make landings on the more accessible Isla Damas. For conservation reasons, visitors are advised to stick to the established paths and not to disturb the birds. While on the boat, visitors can hear and smell the sea lion colony that also call this area home. Pods of bottle-nosed dolphins and sea otters make the occasional appearance.

SHOP

Feria Modelo de Ovalle

Farmers and producers from across the region come to this market to sell their goods. You can easily spend a few hours wandering around the colorful stalls.

B5 Cnr of Avenida la Feria & Benavente, Ovalle

↑ A road unfurling toward the pristine turquoise waters of Laguna Verde

A replica dinosaur in the Monumento Natural Pichasca

Monumento Natural Pichasca

B5 34 miles (55 km) NE of Ovalle, Valle del Limarí From Ovalle to 3 miles (5 km) before entrance 9am-5pm daily (book ahead) conaf.cl

Rich in paleontological and archaeological finds, the Monumento Natural Pichasca is a site featuring petrified forests of fossilized tree trunks, gigantic dinosaur fossils, and 11,000-year-old rock paintings in ancient lava caves. The area was also a refuge for hunter-gatherers around 8000 BCE.

Tours begin at a visitors' center that has displays on the area's fauna and flora, paleontology, and archaeology. From here, a walking trail explores the site, which passes life-size replicas of the gigantic dinosaurs that once roamed this region.

GREAT VIEW

Heading Higher

For mountain views (and a cooler climate), travel 22 miles (35 km) from Monumento Natural Pichasca to Hurtado, an oasis village around 3,940 ft (1,200 m) above sea level.

38  

Monumento Nacional Valle del Encanto

B5 16 miles (25 km) SW of Ovalle; D45, Valle del Encanto From Ovalle to 3 miles (5 km) from entrance 9am-5:30pm daily

An ancient ceremonial and hunting ground, this site has Chile's finest collection of El Molle petroglyphs, dating from around 700 CE. Viewed from a marked circuit, there are more than 30 petroglyphs, which were etched onto rock faces using sharp stones. Most are line drawings depicting human, zoomorphic, abstract, and geometric shapes. The human portraits are most interesting: entire families are shown in various poses with fingers pointing upward at the sun or downward, at Mother Earth. The shamans and deities in these carvings are crowned with tiaras and headdresses. The petroglyphs are best seen at noon, when the sharp midday light shows them at their most impressive.

Another highlight of the site is the *piedras tacitas* – slabs of flat rock gouged with large patterns of identical, circular, and deep holes that were probably used as mortars for grinding food and for ceremonial purposes, including the preparation of hallucinogens. There are also smaller, earlier depressions known as cupules, the purpose of which was decorative.

Riding down Parque Nacional Bosque Fray Jorge

Termas de Socos

B5 24 miles (38 km) SW of Ovalle; Panamericana Norte, km 370 8:30am-7pm daily (spa) termal.cl/coquimbo/socos

Encircled by rugged and dusty canyons in the Valle del Limarí, Termas de Socos is a family-owned spa retreat open to day and overnight visitors. Its amenities include massage treatments, thermal baths, and an exterior pool that is ringed by various cacti and eucalyptus trees. There is a rustic but refined feel to this place – poolside vistas rise to rocky canyons, wild honey grows in the spa's gardens, and guests are accommodated in cozy, comfortable rooms.

For budget travelers, there is a separate campground with its own thermal baths. Staff run trips to Monumento Nacional Valle del Encanto and Parque Nacional Bosque Fray Jorge. At night, guests can gaze at the clear, bright stars from the canyon-top observatory.

Parque Nacional Bosque Fray Jorge

B5 56 miles (90 km) W of Ovalle; km 26 de la Ruta Patrimonial 9am-3pm daily (book ahead) CONAF, park entrance; conaf.cl

The highlight of this UNESCO biosphere reserve is a relictual Valdivian rainforest – a remnant of the temperate rainforest that once cloaked all Norte Chico prior to the southward advancement of the Atacama Desert, some 30,000 years ago. The densest forest occurs on the western slopes of the coastal mountains that reach as high as 1,837 ft (560 m). It owes its continued existence to the high rainfall that hits the mountain peak each year – around 47 in (120 cm) per year compared with just 4 in (10 cm) on the semi-arid lowlands directly to the mountain's east. Parque Nacional Bosque Fray Jorge is at its most impressive between October and December, when, after heavy rainfall, the forest floor is carpeted with flowers.

A vehicle route and a 6-mile (10-km) walking trail strike west from the park entrance, where a CONAF center has displays on the area's flora. Overlooking the Pacific, a short boardwalk traverses the lush forest. At mid-morning visitors can see the mist-shrouded rainforest.

> **Parque Nacional Bosque Fray Jorge is at its most impressive between October and December, when, after heavy rainfall, the forest floor is carpeted with flowers.**

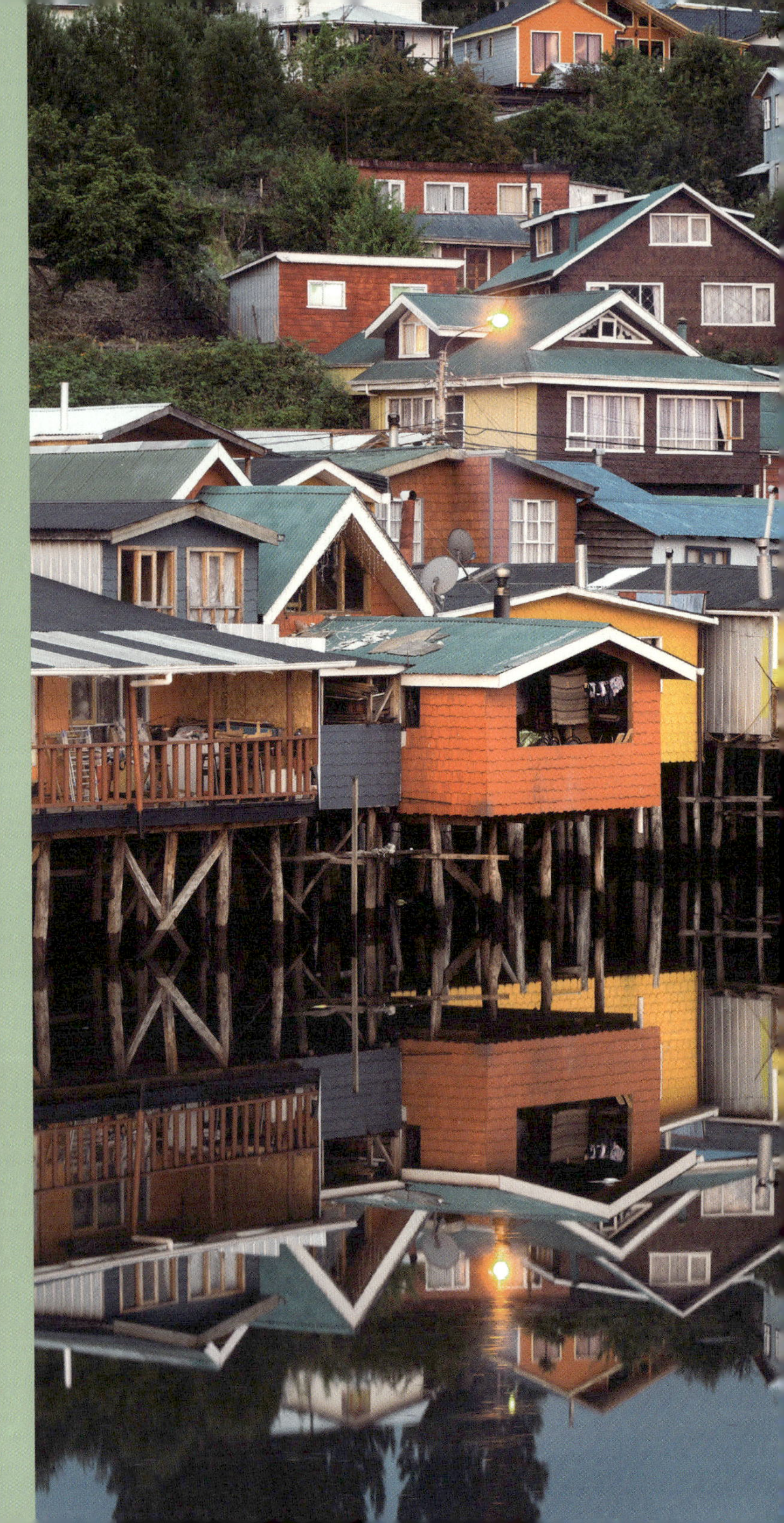

Colorful *palafitos* lining Castro's waterfront

LAKE DISTRICT AND CHILOÉ

Chile's Lake District features emerald forests, smoldering volcanoes, and rivers and waterfalls. South of the district lies Chiloé, a beautiful island archipelago of misty bays, quaint *palafitos*, and historic Jesuit churches. The Lake District is bound to its north by Río Biobío and to its south by the Canal Chacao, the channel that links it to Chiloé.

In pre-Columbian times, the Lake District was populated by Mapuche communities, and Chiloé by the seafaring Chono. Spaniards arrived in 1552 and established what are today the region's largest cities, including Valdivia, Villarrica, and Osorno. Much of the area remained a Mapuche stronghold even after independence, when Chile launched the Araucanian wars to suppress Indigenous resistance. Around 100,000 Mapuche people were massacred or forced off their land, which was offered up to European immigrants, especially German settlers. The Mapuche were forced to settle on small reservations in the region's south, causing irreversible damage to their culture and contributing to the continued tensions between the community and the government today.

By the 19th century, railroad construction had sparked agriculture, forestry, and port industries, with Temuco emerging as the Lake District's main commercial center. In the Chiloé archipelago, fishing has become the bedrock of the economy. More recently, a boom in tourism has brought added prosperity to the Lake District and Chiloé, with visitors attracted by the area's national parks.

LAKE DISTRICT AND CHILOÉ

Must Sees

1. Parque Nacional Conguillío
2. Valdivia
3. Parque Nacional Villarrica
4. Parque Nacional Vicente Pérez Rosales

Experience More

5. Temuco
6. Termas de Malalcahuello
7. Centro de Ski Corralco
8. Parque Nacional Tolhuaca
9. Puerto Montt
10. Nevados de Sollipulli
11. Lago Caburgua
12. Ojos del Caburgua
13. Villarrica
14. Coñaripe
15. Santuario El Cañi
16. Santuario de la Naturaleza Carlos Anwandter
17. Parque Nacional Huerquehue
18. Panguipulli
19. Licán Ray
20. Pucón
21. Reserva Biológica Huilo-Huilo
22. Parque Nacional Puyehue
23. Lago Ranco
24. Termas de Puyehue
25. Osorno
26. Lago Llanquihue
27. Puerto Octay
28. Puerto Varas
29. Frutillar
30. Ancud
31. Monumento Natural Islotes de Puñihuil
32. Dalcahue
33. Parque Nacional Chiloé
34. Castro
35. Curaco de Vélez
36. Achao
37. Chonchi
38. Quellón
39. Parque Tantauco

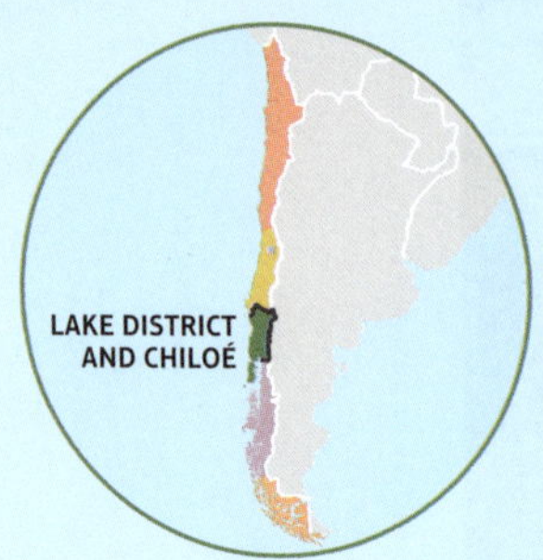

Pacific Ocean

CENTRAL VALLEY
p114
Renaico
Mulchén
Angol
Trintre
Collipulli
Volcán Copahué
9,776 ft (2,979 m)
PARQUE NACIONAL TOLHUACA 8
Volcán Tolhuaca
9,203 ft (2,805 m)
Victoria
Traiguen
7 CENTRO DE SKI CORRALCO
6 TERMAS DE MALALCAHUELLO
Curacautín
ARAUCANIA
Tirúa
PARQUE NACIONAL CONGUILLÍO 1
Lautaro
Volcán Llaima
10,253 ft (3,125 m)
Cherquenco
Carahue
TEMUCO 5
Melipeuco
Puerto Saavedra
La Araucanía International Airport
Cunco
Freire
10 NEVADOS DE SOLLIPULLI
Puerto Domínguez
LAGO CABURGUA 11
17 PARQUE NACIONAL HUERQUEHUE
Gualpín
OJOS DE CABURGUA 12
15 SANTUARIO EL CAÑI
VILLARRICA 13
20 PUCÓN
Curarrehue
LICÁN RAY 19
3 PARQUE NACIONAL VILLARRICA
Mehuín
Lanco
Lago Calafquén
14 COÑARIPE
PANGUIPULLI 18
Pichoy Airport
Máfil
Lago Panguipulli
Neltume
SANTUARIO DE LA NATURALEZA CARLOS ANWANDTER 16
Riñihue
21 RESERVA BIOLÓGICA HUILO-HUILO
VALDIVIA 2
Lago Riñihue
Los Lagos
Corral
Volcán Mocho Choshuenco
7,923 ft (2,414 m)
San Martín de los Andes
Paillaco
Futrono
Lago Ranco
LOS LAGOS
La Unión
23 LAGO RANCO
ARGENTINA
Río Bueno
San Pablo
Volcán Puyehue
7,334 ft (2,236 m)
OSORNO 25
Lago Puyehue
22 PARQUE NACIONAL PUYEHUE
Maicolpué
Cañal Bajo Carlos Hott Siebert Airport
Entre Lagos
24 TERMAS DE PUYEHUE
Volcán Casablanca
6,529 ft (1,990 m)
PUERTO OCTAY 27
Purranque
Bariloche
Volcán Osorno
8,700 ft (2,652 m)
Volcán Tronador
11,351 ft (3,460 m)
Petrohué
FRUTILLAR 29
26 LAGO LLANQUIHUE
4 PARQUE NACIONAL VICENTE PÉREZ ROSALES
Fresia
Llanquihue
PUERTO VARAS 28
Ralún
El Tepual Airport
9 PUERTO MONTT
La Arena
Maullín
Calbuco
Pargua
El Bolsón
ANCUD
Chacao
30
MONUMENTO NATURAL ISLOTES DE PUÑIHUIL 31
Golfo de Ancud
NORTHERN PATAGONIA
p228
Quemchi
Degán
Quicaví
DALCAHUE 32
35 CURACO DE VÉLEZ
CASTRO 34
36 ACHAO
Caleta Gonzalo
PARQUE NACIONAL CHILOÉ 33
Rilán
CHONCHI 37
Esquel
Aituy
Parque Nacional Los Alerces
Queilen
Chaitén
Isla Grande de Chiloé
Futaleufú
Lago Yelcho
PARQUE TANTAUCO
38 QUELLÓN
39
Golfo de Corcovado
Inio
0 kilometers 60
0 miles 60
N

1

PARQUE NACIONAL CONGUILLÍO

F1 74 miles (120 km) E of Temuco From Temuco. Taxi from Melipeuco & Curacautín CONAF, Sector del Lago Conguillío 8:30am-5:30pm Tue-Sun (book ahead) conaf.cl

Home to araucaria trees, deep canyons, alpine lakes, and native forests, Parque Nacional Conguillío is a prime location for visitors throughout the year. The park offers mountain trails for hikers, deep and plentiful snow for skiers, and an abundance of wildlife for nature lovers.

One of the Lake District's great natural attractions, Parque Nacional Conguillío stretches over 235 sq miles (609 sq km) of volcanic wilderness, crowned by the smoking cone of the 10,253-ft- (3,125-m-) high Volcán Llaima. A diverse, spectacular landscape surrounds this colossal peak and features ancient araucaria forests, rolling sierras, crystalline lakes, and deep valleys scarred by jagged lava flows. The park abounds with rich wildlife, including pumas, smaller wildcats, red and gray foxes, woodpeckers, hawks, and condors. Splendid hiking trails, skiing down volcanic slopes, and boat trips across serene lakes draw a large number of visitors to the park throughout the year.

Exploring the Park

Parque Nacional Conguillío comprises two sectors separated from each other by Volcán Llaima. The western sector, Sector Los Paraguas, offers winter skiing, while the bigger eastern sector, Sector del Lago Conguillío, has great hiking trails, including the popular Sendero Sierra Nevada. This sector is served by the gateway towns of Melipeuco in the south and Curacautín in the north. Heavy snowfall usually makes this sector impassable between May and September.

THE WRATH OF VOLCÁN LLAIMA

Smoldering Volcán Llaima is one of Chile's two most explosive volcanoes, the other being Volcán Villarrica *(p202)*. More than 40 eruptions have been recorded since 1640, and Volcán Llaima's lava has shaped Parque Nacional Conguillío's landscape. Eruptions in 2008-9 created 9,800-ft- (3,000-m-) high smoke columns, forced the evacuation of villages, and dumped ash on Argentina. Over the years, lava flows blocked rivers, turning forests into lakes. Today, lava fields scar the earth where lush forests once stood, and dense woods are still visible in the water.

Hiking the Sendero Sierra Nevada ↑

→ Vibrant lizard resting on lava rock

Expansive views of the beautiful Lake Conguillío

Must See

Boats docked alongside the Río Valdivia, near the lively Mercado Fluvial

VALDIVIA

F2 100 miles (162 km) SW of Temuco
Arturo Prat 555

Spread along the banks of three rivers, Valdivia was a prized possession of the Spanish, who guarded it with military forts for over 200 years. In 1960, a massive earthquake devastated Valdivia, but today, it is a vibrant city whose lush riverside is fronted by fine museums and 19th-century Teutonic architecture.

Mercado Fluvial

Avenida Arturo Prat s/n
8am-4pm daily

Set on the banks of the Río Valdivia, Mercado Fluvial, the city's bustling fish market, is a colorful snapshot of coastal Chilean life as well as the prime industry that sustains it. Traders clean the day's catch, while live crabs scuttle about in huge crates and bobbing sea lions bellow for scraps by the water's edge – the scene watched over by hundreds of seabirds. Inexpensive seafood restaurants serving local specialties edge the market.

Centro Cultural El Austral

Yungay 733 10am-6pm Tue-Fri centro-cultural-el-austral.negocio.site

Set in a large, beautifully restored house, Valdivia's Centro Cultural El Austral dates from the period of German settlement in the Lake District. Built in the 1870s for a pioneer family, it was made entirely from local wood in the German chalet style and features a striking Bavarian steeple. The interiors reflect typical living quarters of early German settlers. Dazzlingly furnished, the rooms feature Art-Nouveau chandeliers, extravagant wall mirrors, and stately 19th-century European furniture. Other rooms in the building showcase notable works by contemporary artists.

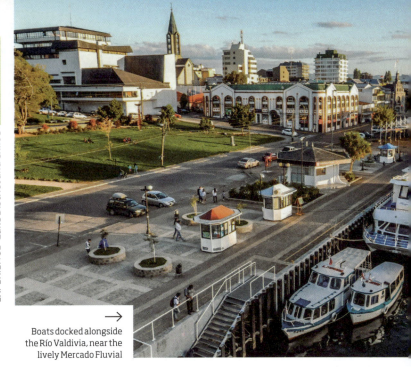

INSIDER TIP
Up All Night

Head to Valdivia on the third Saturday in February to experience Noche de Valdivia, a festival that includes a fleet of beautifully decorated riverboats, fireworks and flares, and a night of dancing.

Museo de Arte Contemporáneo

Los Laureles s/n, Isla Teja
Hours vary, check website macvaldivia.cl

On the banks of the river, a recycled brewery building with a strikingly modern glass facade is the post-Industrial setting for the city's Museo de Arte Contemporáneo, often referred to as MAC. The exhibitions here feature video and installation art, paintings, photographs, and sculptures by emerging and established artists, international and Chilean.

The collection is spread over two floors of abandoned industrial workspace, which is characterized by bare cement flooring and cast-iron columns. These still bear the scars of the devastating earthquake that hit this area in 1960.

The museum building was closed in 2019 for a major restoration program that lasted a few years.

④

Museo Histórico y Antropológico Maurici Van de Maele

Los Laureles s/n, Isla Teja
10am-1pm & 3-6pm Tue-Sun museosaustral.cl

Adjacent to the Museo de Arte Contemporáneo is the 19th-century mansion and former home of the founder of Chile's first brewery, Karl Anwandter (1801–89). Today, the edifice houses the Museo Histórico y Antropológico Mauricio Van de Maele, whose collection is displayed in a series of themed salons, each depicting different periods in local history, from pre-Columbian times to the 20th century. Each salon has a multilingual information panel that shows historical details about the period that it represents.

Sala de Platería Mapuche has various exhibits showing Mapuche tools and textiles. The stunning jewelry display portrays the Indigenous Mapuche's belief in silverware as a symbol of power and prestige. Dedicated to Thomas Cochrane (1775–1860), the Sala Lord Cochrane displays some of his personal belongings. This buccaneering British naval officer led Chile's naval forces during the 1820 attack on Valdivia that ended Royalist resistance in the area. The museum also re-creates a colonial-period lounge embellished with ornate wall hangings, damask tapestry, and a Venetian mirror.

DRINK

El Growler

Hailed as Valdivia's best beer place, this spot offers 15 taps with IPAs, red ales, and stouts. It also has great bar food and interesting vegetarian and vegan options.

Saelzer 41
elgrowler.cl

3 

PARQUE NACIONAL VILLARRICA

F2 5 miles (8 km) SE of Pucón Taxi from Pucón 8:30am-5:30pm Tue-Sun
CONAF, Al Volcan 68-166, Pucón; conaf.cl

The soaring, volcanic peaks of Villarrica, Lanín, and Quetrupillán rise high over Parque Nacional Villarrica, one of Chile's most popular national parks. Alongside this fiery triumvirate, the park is home to tranquil lakes and rushing rivers, snowy mountains and lush forests.

Conserving 243 sq miles (629 sq km) of wilderness, Parque Nacional Villarrica extends from south of Pucón to the frontier with Argentina. The 9,341-ft- (2,847-m-) high snow-swathed cone of Volcán Villarrica forms the park's centerpiece, crowning a landscape that embraces two other volcanoes, several small lakes, and forests of southern beech and araucaria. The park provides shelter to a rich array of wildlife, including the rare Chilean shrew opossum. Eruptions in February and March 2015 closed the park until late 2016. Current volcanic activity remains at a low level but is carefully monitored by volcanologists.

Discovering the Park

Parque Nacional Villarrica has three sectors, each with hiking trails and a ranger station. The westernmost sector, accessible from the gateway town of Pucón, features the park's major highlights, including the magnificent Volcán Villarrica. The two sectors to the east are remote, yet beautiful; the park's wildest sector is in the area bordering Argentina.

2015

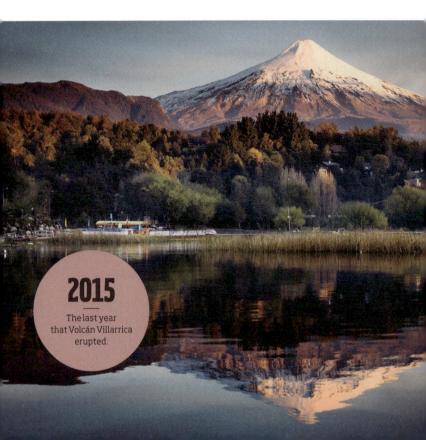

The last year that Volcán Villarrica erupted.

HOUSE OF THE DEVIL

The Mapuche of the area refer to Volcán Villarrica as Rucapillán, or House of the Devil - an apt description for one of Chile's most explosive peaks. It erupted 18 times in the 20th century alone. An explosion in 1971 almost destroyed the nearby village of Coñaripe *(p212)*. It last erupted in 2015, and remains constantly active. Its crater smokes, hisses, and belches, and is one of only a few craters on the globe that has an active lava lake.

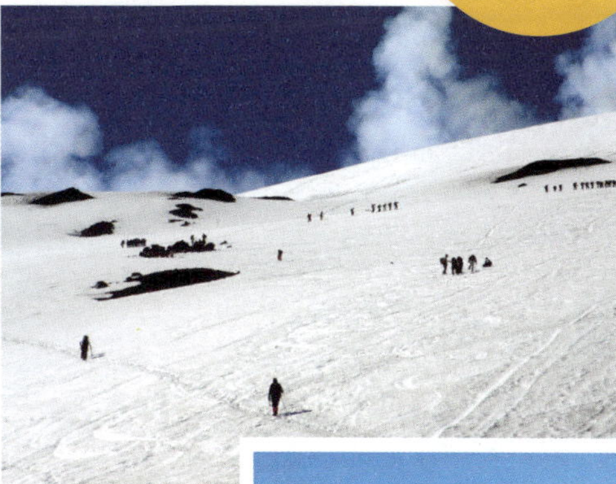

↑ Climbing up a snow-covered Volcán Villarrica

→ Hikers exploring the stark terrain of Volcán Villarrica

Volcanoes

Volcán Villarrica

▶ The trek to Volcán Villarrica's steaming crater features a physically challenging but technically undemanding hike through blue-tinged, icy glaciers and a slide down the slopes via glistening snow tunnels. The route has reopened for trekkers after the 2015 volcanic activity.

Volcán Lanín

◀ Located on the border between Chile and Argentina, the snow-topped, cone-shaped Volcán Lanín is the biggest volcano in southern Chile. The spectacular hike from Laguna Abutardes to Lago Quilleihue offers some of the most fabulous vistas of this truly awe-inspiring volcano.

Volcán Quetrupillán

▶ This dormant, snowcapped volcano lies on the border between the Los Rios Region and the La Araucanía Region, neighboring Volcán Villarrica. The volcano's name, Quetrupillán, means "mute devil" in the language of the Mapuche people.

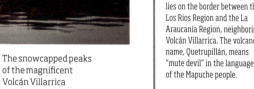

↑ The snowcapped peaks of the magnificent Volcán Villarrica

Did You Know?

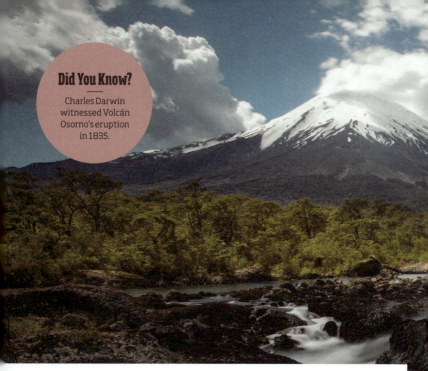

Charles Darwin witnessed Volcán Osorno's eruption in 1835.

PARQUE NACIONAL VICENTE PÉREZ ROSALES

F2 NE of Puerto Varas From Puerto Montt & Puerto Varas, via Ensenada & Petrohué 9am-6pm daily (book ahead) CONAF, Petrohué; conaf.cl

The oldest national park in Chile, Parque Nacional Vicente Pérez Rosales is one of the principal destinations in Los Lagos. The celestial lakes and abundant forests attract horseback riders and swimmers, hikers and nature enthusiasts, while the soaring volcanoes offer outstanding panoramic views and bring skiers to the slopes over the winter period.

Created in 1926, Parque Nacional Vicente Pérez Rosales is one of Chile's most breathtaking parks. Its landscape of lost-world beauty encompasses volcanoes, crystalline lakes and lagoons, gushing waterfalls, and evergreen forests. Its crowning glory is the perfect cone of the active Volcán Osorno. Two more great volcanoes – Tronador and Puntiagudo – pierce the skyline here. They, along with Lago Todos los Santos and Saltos de Petrohué, protect an abundant bird and mammal life, and offer activities such as boat rides, horseback riding through forests, lava treks, and volcano skiing.

Exploring the Park

Parque Nacional Vicente Pérez Rosales' star sights are concentrated in its western sector, which is served by road and local bus, and is linked to the gateway city Puerto Varas *(p218)*. Located in the western sector are the villages of Ensenada and Petrohué, which offer hotel and campground accommodation. From Petrohué, catamarans make the daily two-hour trip over the teal-colored waters of the Lago Todos los Santos to the park's eastern sector, called Peulla, which has numerous trails leading to scenic waterfalls.

↑ Magical Saltos de Petrohué and Volcán Osorno

INSIDER TIP

Cruce de los Lagos

This spectacular crossing over the Andes, between the lake districts of Chile and Argentina, traverses two national parks and four lakes. The full-day journey, beginning at Petrohué, over both land and lakes, ends at Bariloche, Argentina. En route, there are four volcanoes, many great waterfalls, and abundant wildlife.

← Volcán Tronador, seen from the Andean crossing

↓ Wild horses grazing near Volcán Tronador

EXPERIENCE MORE

Temuco

F2 385 miles (620 km) S of Santiago Bulnes 590; destino temuco.cl

Set in the former Mapuche heartland, Temuco traces its origins to a fortress settlement established during the 19th century – the city itself was officially founded in 1881. The construction of the railroad and European immigration in the 20th century brought about rapid growth. Today, Temuco is a commercial hub with busy plazas and museums. The city is famous for the Wallmapu festival of Indigenous films held between October and November every year. It is also an ideal base for exploring the natural beauty of the surrounding countryside.

The **Museo Regional de la Araucanía** makes a good place to start wandering the city. Housed in a 1924 mansion, this museum records the often bloody history of Chile's Araucanía region through a collection of some 3,000 archaeological, ethnographic, and historical objects. Among them is one of the country's most impressive collections of Mapuche objects, including stunning 19th-century weavings and an array of silver jewelry, heavy necklaces, and belts. Also on display is a life-size reconstruction of a *ruca* (communal thatched house).

A protected hillside, the **Monumento Natural Cerro Ñielol** is also of interest. It harbors a species-rich temperate rainforest that once covered the Araucanía region. Walking trails explore native evergreen woods of coigüe and arrayan, and lagoons that provide refuge for an abundant birdlife. One of the trails leads to La Patagua del Armisticio, a site commemorating the signing of an armistice in 1881 between the Mapuche and the Chilean government, by which the Mapuche ceded territory for the founding of Temuco. The hill's crest offers extraordinary panoramic city vistas.

Shaded by lime, oak, and palm trees, **Plaza Teodoro Schmidt** is best known as the site of the city's Feria Arte. This important weekly crafts fair, held each year in February, features woodcarvings, ceramics, and weavings made by artisans from across the country.

Examining an old engine at the Museo Nacional Ferroviario Pablo Neruda

EAT

El Corralero

This is arguably central Temuco's finest restaurant. A classy steakhouse, it also serves a handful of fish dishes. The decor is bright and cheery and the service is excellent.

F2 Vicuña Mackenna 811, Temuco (045) 2401 355

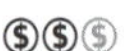

Plaza Aníbal Pinto, the city's main square, is planted with native trees and foreign palms, and centered on the Monumento a la Araucanía, a bronze-and-stone sculpture that pays homage to this area's principal colonizers. The figure of a robed *machi* (female Mapuche shaman) crowns the monument and is flanked by four other figures – a Mapuche hunter with a spear; a Spanish conquistador with a Christian cross; a 19th-century soldier; and a settler farmer. A stylized rock face symbolizing the Andes forms the base of the monument.

The **Feria Libre Aníbal Pinto**, Temuco's rustic open-air market, is a high-energy nexus of feverish trading and stimulating smells. Traders here sell pungent cheese, herbs, spices, vegetables, and fruit, including *piñones* (araucaria nuts), *cochayuyo* (dried seaweed), and *merquen* (smoky, spicy chili powder), a staple part of the Mapuche diet. Mapuche women travel from outlying districts to sit in groups selling flour, eggs, and *mote* (husked wheat). Small restaurants in the center of the market serve

↑ Wandering through the pleasant and leafy Plaza Aníbal Pinto

local specialties such as *pastel de choclo* (beef pie with a corn crust) and seafood dishes. More stalls stocking traditional *huaso* hats, stirrups, and spurs ring this market's outer limits.

The **Museo Nacional Ferroviario Pablo Neruda** is Chile's national railroad museum and occupies the old headquarters of the country's national railroad, a UNESCO World Heritage Site. Its great attraction is the old Casa de Máquinas (Locomotive Hall), a cavernous oval construction built 1929–43 for the maintenance of locomotives. Today, the hall preserves rows of old trains, like the Presidential Train, built in Germany in 1920 and used by all Chilean presidents between 1924 and 2004, barring General Pinochet. Tours of the train's opulent interior include the presidential quarters, linked to the First Lady's bedroom via a hidden door. The old Administrative Hall features photographic displays.

The museum is named for Temuco's most celebrated son, Pablo Neruda *(p105)*, whose father was a lifelong employee of the railways. Neruda's odes to Chile's railroad adorn plaques throughout this large and beautifully curated museum.

Museo Regional de la Araucanía
Avenida Alemania 84
9:30am-5:30pm Tue-Fri
museoregionalaraucania.gob.cl

Monumento Natural Cerro Ñielol
Avenida Arturo Prat s/n
8:30am-5:30pm Tue-Sun (book ahead)
conaf.cl

Plaza Teodoro Schmidt
Avenida Arturo Prat

Plaza Aníbal Pinto
Avenida Arturo Prat, Claro Solar

Feria Libre Aníbal Pinto
Avenida Aníbal Pinto, Balmaceda
9am-5pm Mon-Sat

Museo Nacional Ferroviario Pablo Neruda
Avenida Barros Arana 565
Hours vary, check website
museoferroviariopabloneruda.cl

MAPUCHE CULTURE

The Mapuche are the largest Indigenous group in Chile, with around 1.5 million people (ten per cent of the population) having Mapuche heritage. The biggest communities are in the Lake District, Patagonia, and Santiago. They fiercely resisted the Spanish colonialists and - in the face of entrenched racism, prejudice, and marginalization - continue to struggle against the Chilean state for their rights. Get an insight into Mapuche history and culture and admire examples of Mapuche craftsmanship at the Museo de Volcanes near the Salto del Huilo-Huilo *(p215)*.

↑ Ski climbers scaling a snowcapped volcano in the Centro de Ski Corralco

6  

Termas de Malalcahuello

F1 Ruta Bioceánica 181-CH, km 86, Región de la Araucanía, Malalcahuello 10am–6pm daily malalcahuello.cl

The serene location for the modern spa complex of Termas de Malalcahuello is a lushly forested valley at the foot of the 9,400-ft- (2,865-m-) high Volcán Lonquimay. Both day and overnight visitors are welcome here. On offer are three indoor thermal pools, each filled with mineral-rich water that bubbles up from deep beneath the earth's crust – the temperature of the water ranges from 99°F (37°C) to 109°F (43°C). Floor-to-ceiling windows surround the pools and offer bathers dreamy views of the fertile Lonquimay Valley and the snow-covered peak of its volcano. There is also a sun terrace overlooking the valley.

A range of therapeutic treatments are on offer at the resort, while accommodation options include a mountain lodge-style hotel, log cabins, and family-sized bungalows. Local bus services and private transfers connect the Termas de Malalcahuello to the nearby Centro de Ski Corralco.

EAT

Cotelé

A short drive from Puerto Montt's city center, Cotelé is a top-notch steakhouse, serving perfectly cooked prime cuts along with wines.

F2 Manfredini 1661, Puerto Montt cotelerestaurante.com

$$$

7   

Centro de Ski Corralco

F1 Volcán Lonquimay, Camino a RN Malalcahuello 9am–4pm daily corralco.com

The scenic Centro de Ski Corralco is one of Chile's newest resorts. Skiers can descend Volcán Lonquimay on seven pistes that have a maximum drop of 3,018 ft (920 m). The off-piste opportunities are best suited to experts. There are snow-boarding runs as well, and Nordic skiing circuits. In summer, activities include trekking, horseback riding, and mountain biking.

8  

Parque Nacional Tolhuaca

F1 81 miles (130 km) NE of Temuco; Acceso 1, road via village of Inspector Fernández 8:30am–5:30pm Tue–Sun CONAF office near southeastern entrance to park; conaf.cl

Set in the far north of the Lake District and distant from the region's more traveled routes, the Parque Nacional Tolhuaca conserves a highly scenic area of the Andean foothills across varying altitudes. The park encompasses wild temperate rainforest famous for the prehistoric araucaria *(Araucaria araucana)*, also called the monkey-puzzle tree. Attractive trails through the pristine forests offer great bird-watching; among the more easily observed species

Moody skies looming over Puerto Montt's waterfront

are the Chilean parakeet, several types of duck, and the Andean condor. Swimming, fishing, and hiking are also popular activities in this park. Tolhuaca's most hiked trail, the Sendero Salto Malleco, skirts the northern shore of Lago Malleco, the park's dominant feature, before crossing native forest to the stunning 164-ft (50-m) Salto Malleco waterfalls.

Another picturesque hike edges along the Laguna Verde, which lies 4,264 ft (1,300 m) above sea level and is ringed by small waterfalls and spindly araucaria woods. Other treks in the area include the Sendero Lagunillas and the Sendero Mesacura. The first is an undemanding climb to a set of mountain lagoons, and the second passes through dense forest. Both are full-day hikes and require advance planning.

Just south of the park lie the thermal pools of Termas Malleco *(termasmalleco.cl)*. Located in a canyon, the natural sauna created by the rocks and sulfurous steam provides the ideal spot to relax after a long hike. Formerly known as Termas de Tolhuaca, Malleco has refurbished the facilities of what was once a worn-down hot-springs resort, and is now open for both day use and overnighters.

Puerto Montt

F2 130 miles (210 km) S of Valdivia
Sernatur, Antonio Varas 415; puertomontt.cl

The port city of Puerto Montt is where the Lake District meets the Pacific Ocean. Founded in 1853 on a hillside overlooking the Seno de Reloncaví, the city grew rapidly around its port, which was used to ship grains and alerce timber. Puerto Montt was badly hit by the 1960 earthquake and much of it was rebuilt thereafter. The city is now used strictly as a transit point by most travelers. It is the departure point for south-bound ferries and cruise ships sailing through Chile's fjords.

Built on the site of the city's foundation, Puerto Montt's main plaza is overlooked by the Neo-Classical Iglesia Catedral. Erected in 1856–96, the cathedral is modeled on Greece's iconic Parthenon, with Doric pillars of Patagonian cypress (alerce) adorning the facade. One of these columns conceals the city's founding stone.

Located on the waterfront, the raucous **Angelmó Fish Market** is the city's biggest attraction. A whirl of vibrant colors and aromas, the market is a maze of narrow, guttered passageways along which traders sell fish, spices, and local delicacies. Wooden stairs climb to numerous small restaurants that serve some of the best seafood platters in the city. On streets bordering the market, craftspeople sell woolen items and woodcarvings made from local Patagonian cypress.

Angelmó Fish Market
Avenida Angelmó s/n
6am-8pm daily

HIDDEN GEM
Río Puelo

This valley, 55 miles (90 km) southeast of Puerto Montt, is a wonderful place to hike, horseback-ride, fish, or simply while away a few days amid tranquil lakes, rivers, and rainforests.

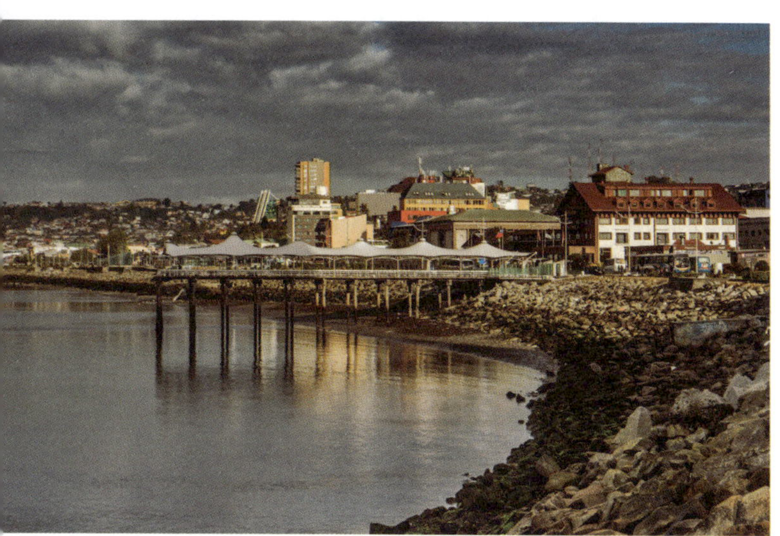

STAY

Cabañas Quilamalen

Located 2.5 miles (4 km) north of Villarrica, these eco-friendly adobe cabins, set within expansive lawns, have heat-preserving grass roofs, large kitchens, and cozy, rustic interiors. The refreshing swimming pool is perfect for hot days.

F2 Km 3, Camino Villarrica-Freire, Villarica quilamalen.cl

10

Nevados de Sollipulli

F2 Nevados de Sollipulli Dome Camp, Camino hacía Carén Alto sollipulli.cl

There are few places in Chile where travelers can witness nature's powerful geological forces more clearly than at Volcán Sollipulli, part of the Nevados de Sollipulli range, which lies close to Chile's border with Argentina. This volcano's ancient crater, and the 5-sq-mile (12-sq-km) glacier that fills it, are two of the primal elements that are responsible for the formation of the massive Andes mountain range.

Visitors can climb to the crater on a day-long hike that passes through dense forests of araucaria, offering sweeping vistas along the way of the Andean peaks, crystalline rivers, and countless parasitic craters. For those looking to push themselves further, there is also a two-day trekking circuit, which includes ice-hikes on the glacier. All hikes start at the Nevados de Sollipulli Dome Camp. Situated next to a forested lake on the volcano's northeastern face, this camp comprises six superbly equipped, centrally heated domes. Among the many luxuries found here are hot tubs in the open air.

Navigating a gaping chasm in Nevados de Sollipulli's glacier

11

Lago Caburgua

F2 76 miles (122 km) SE of Temuco via Pucón

Ringed by forested mountains, Lago Caburgua is a beautiful crystalline lake that is edged by this region's only white-sand beaches. Thermal activity in the depths of the lake make its waters warmer than those of the district's other lakes. There are a number of popular beaches here, including Playa Negra, a black-sand beach, and Playa Blanca, with its stretch of white, crystallized sand. Boat tours of the lake depart regularly from Playa Negra, from where paddleboats are also available for renting. A scenic lakeside walk links these two beaches.

A canoeist on Lago Villarrica, overlooked by Volcán Villarrica ↑

12

Ojos del Caburgua

F2 73 miles (117 km) SE of Temuco via Pucón Camino Internacional 7, km 17 or km 20 9am-7:30pm daily

The waters of Lago Caburgua flow southward and underground for 3 miles (5 km) before gushing out to form the Ojos del Caburgua (Eyes of Caburgua). This necklace of aquamarine rock pools lies at the base of cascading waterfalls and is shrouded in pristine forest. Travelers to the site are able to access the pools at a signposted entrance on the main road from Pucón. There is also a second entrance, which lies 2 miles (3 km) north on the same road and offers a more intimate view of the pools, falls, and forest. Keep your eyes peeled; this approach is marked solely by a wooden roadside statue of Christ on the cross.

Villarrica

F2 54 miles (87 km) SE of Temuco General Urrutia s/n, Plaza de Licán Ray; visitvillarrica.cl

Originally founded in 1552 by the Spanish, Villarrica (Rich Town) was named for the abundant gold and silver deposits discovered here. In 1598, the town was razed in a Mapuche uprising and only resettled in 1883. Today, it is a laid-back, family-oriented destination on the western shore of a sapphire lake of the same name and at the foot of the majestic 9,341-ft- (2,847-m-) high Volcán Villarrica. Lago Villarrica, a big attraction in its own right, features a charming *costanera* (front promenade), and an attractive black-sand beach, Playa Pucará.

Villarrica's wonderful Mapuche heritage finds expression at the excellent **Museo Leandro Penchulef**, home to coigüe wood canoes and other examples of Mapuche craftmanship. On the east of town, the Centro Cultural Mapuche features a Mapuche crafts market in the summer months. At the edge of town is the Mirador Canela, a lookout point with great views of the lake and volcano.

Museo Leandro Penchulef

Bernardo O´Higgins 501, on the Pontificia Universidad Católica campus 9am-12:30pm & 2:30-5:30pm Mon-Fri uc.cl/temas/museo-leandro-penchulef

VOLCÁN LONQUIMAY

North of Villarrica is Volcán Lonquimay, which last erupted on December 25, 1988 (earning it the nickname Navidad). It's great for snowboarding, skiing, and hot springs, but it is also a great place to hike, with three- and five-day circuits around the base of the volcano. More adventurous travelers can climb to the summit - experienced mountaineers could even attempt this during winter (with crampons, ice axes, and a guide).

Coñaripe

F2 83 miles (134 km) SE of Temuco

On the eastern shore of Lago Calafquén, and away from the region's more traveled routes, Coñaripe is a tiny village with a soporific air and a couple of black-sand beaches. The area around the village offers ample opportunities for adventure sports, including white water rafting on the Río San Pedro, and horseback, mountain-bike, and trekking trips. Coñaripe has many accommodation options for overnight guests; budget travelers in particular will enjoy the well-equipped camp-grounds by the beaches.

The hills around Coñaripe are dotted with more than a dozen thermal springs which are scenic, relaxing, and well worth visiting. They range from very basic, rustic pools to modern hotel-and-spa complexes. One of the best among these is the **Termas Geómetricas**. Nestled within a forested ravine, this stylish spa comprises 60 thermal fountains that gush into bubbling bathing pools through a network of wooden water channels. Visitors simply walk across the ravine on a 1,476-ft- (450-m-) long catwalk, and descend via wooden stairs to the pool of their choice.

In terms of the overnight accommodation on offer, the **Termas Coñaripe** is an excellent choice. This modern hotel and spa made of glass and wood offers indoor and semi-covered pools, along with outdoor thermal pools. A number of other appealing amenities are available; guests can slather around in mud baths and enjoy walks and horseback rides to nearby waterfalls and lagoons.

From the Termas Coñaripe, a rough road leads to the Parque Nacional Villarrica *(p202)*, some 11 miles (18 km) to the north.

Termas Geómetricas
10 miles (16 km) NE of Coñaripe 10am-7pm daily (book ahead)
termasgeometricas.cl

Termas Coñaripe
9 miles (15 km) SE of Coñaripe; Camino Coñaripe-Liquiñe, km 15
termasconaripe.cl

15 Santuario El Cañi

F2 83 miles (134 km) SE of Temuco via Pucón; Camino Termas de Huife, km 21, Pichares 8:30am-6pm daily (Jan & Feb: to 8pm) santuariocani.cl

Enclosing a lush swath of temperate Valdivian rain-forest, Santuario El Cañi is home to some of Chile's oldest stands of araucaria. A single trail climbs through forests of southern beech (*Nothofagus*) to reveal hidden mountain tarns and, at higher elevations, pure forests of araucaria. Together, these habitats harbor a rich variety of birdlife and many shy mammals that are usually difficult to spot, including the

11

The number of lagoons in Santuario El Cañi.

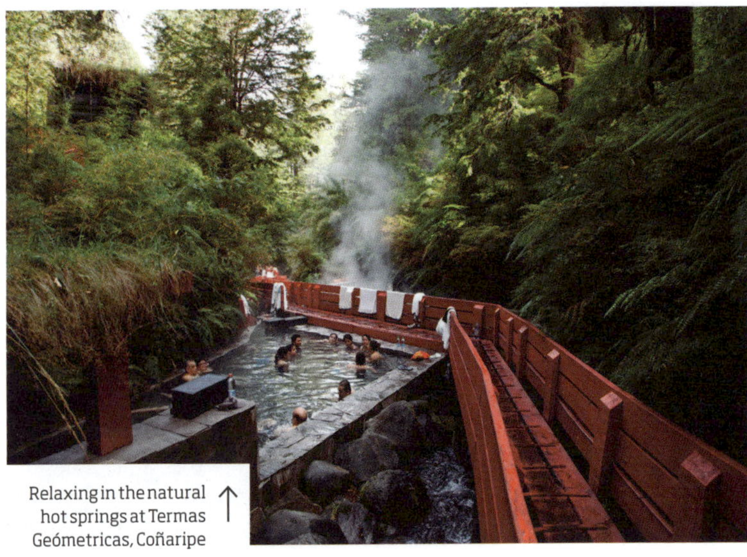

Relaxing in the natural hot springs at Termas Geómetricas, Coñaripe

Walking through the trees in the Parque Nacional Huerquehue

puma and pudú. The steep 6-mile (9-km) trail ends at a lookout point about 5,084 ft (1,550 m) above sea level. This has 360-degree views of the area's four volcanoes – Lanín, Villarrica, Quetrupillán, and Llaima – as well as its three biggest lakes – Caburgua, Villarrica, and Calafquén. Travelers on overnight treks can stay at rustic La Loma campgrounds.

Santuario de la Naturaleza Carlos Anwandter

F2 13 miles (21 km) N of Valdivia 8:30am-5:30pm daily CONAF Valdivia; conaf.cl

Over 23 sq miles (60 sq km) of wildlife-rich wetlands are protected by the Santuario de la Naturaleza Carlos Anwandter. The origin of these wetlands lies in the aftermath of the 1960 earthquake, when a tsunami submerged the area's forests and cattle pastures. The ecosystem attracted a variety of birdlife and was recognized as a nature sanctuary in 1981. Over 100 species of birds, such as pelicans and black-necked swans, can be seen here. It is also possible to spot river otters and coipús.

Parque Nacional Huerquehue

F2 94 miles (152 km) SE of Temuco via Pucón; Camino a Caburgua 8:30am-5:30pm daily (book ahead) CONAF Pucón, Cam. Al Volcan 68-166; conaf.cl

Created in 1967, the compact Parque Nacional Huerquehue protects around 48 sq miles (124 sq km) of native forest that includes 2,000-year-old araucaria woods. The park has some of the Lake District's best short treks and offers spectacular views of Volcán Villarrica and its surroundings. A must-do trail is the 4-mile (7-km) Sendero Los Lagos, which traverses forests of Chilean yew and beech, skirts five different lakes, and two waterfalls. Along the way there are vistas of the volcano and of Lago Tinquilco, the park's largest body of water. The trail ends at Lago Chico, a small alpine lake surrounded by cliffs. Another spectacular hike is the 10-mile (16-km) round trek to Cerro San Sebastián. From here, you can spot up to eight volcanoes from the height of 6,562 ft (2,000 m) on a clear day.

Between hikes, visitors can enjoy lake swimming and nature-watching. Many species of eagle can be seen, and among the mammals here are the puma; the pudú, the world's smallest deer; and the mouse opossum *(Dromiciops gliroides)*, one of the southern Andes' few surviving marsupials.

EAT

Puerto Pucón

This popular traditional Spanish restaurant serves up tasty classics like *pulpo al pil-pil*, *chipirones*, and tortilla to wash down with sangria.

F2 Fresia 246, Pucón (056) 9687 11335

La Maga

An Uruguayan-run joint, La Maga takes its decor cues from gaucho style, though the menu also features Chilean food. Steaks are the main focus here.

F2 Gerónimo de Alderete 276, Pucón lamaga.cl

THE SIETE LAGOS REGION

South of Pucón, the Siete Lagos (Seven Lakes) is a beautiful region that receives fewer tourists than it should. It is made up of interlinked lakes - six of them in Chile, with another over the border in Argentina - that are surrounded by villages and soaring mountains. The area is perfect for scenic drives and nature-based activities.

Panguipulli

F2 90 miles (145 km) SE of Temuco Roberto Bravo 602; sietelagos.cl

Panguipulli is a popular stop for visitors continuing on to the Reserva Biológica Huilo-Huilo. A pleasant lakeshore destination of brightly painted clapboard houses on hillside streets, the town's biggest attraction is the landmark Iglesia Capuchina. The church was built by German Capuchin missionaries in 1947 and stands on the site of a German mission from the 1890s, and the building is fronted by a latticed facade that is painted red, yellow, and black – the colors of Germany's flag.

Panguipulli and its namesake lake lie at the heart of Chile's Seven Lakes region. These lakes – Calafquén, Pellaifa, Pullinque, Riñihue, Neltume, Panguipulli, and Pirihueico – are linked to each other by rivers, which together comprise a single hydrological system. A chain of beautiful and generally uncrowded villages face the shores of these lakes. Although it's possible to spend the night in Panguipulli, Pucón is the main springboard for day trips into the Siete Lagos area.

↑ The town of Pucón, overlooked by the snowcapped Villarrica volcano

Licán Ray

F2 70 miles (113 km) SE of Temuco General Urrutia, Cacique Marichanquin; (045) 2431 516

Licán Ray is the main resort on the hauntingly beautiful Lago Calafquén. The village is a quiet oasis, except in February when hordes of people from Santiago arrive to holiday by Lago Calafquén's mist-shrouded warm waters.

There are two beaches at this miniature retreat – Playa Grande and the more picturesque Playa Chica, which is ringed by rolling forested peaks that sweep down to a shore of black volcanic sand. A wooded peninsula divides these two beaches and is crossed by walking paths that ascend to lookout points with great vistas. Catamaran tours of the lake depart from Playa Chica. At the village center, the main plaza is edged by sandy sidewalks and artisans' fairs.

Pucón

F2 69 miles (112 km) SE of Temuco O'Higgins 483; puconchile.travel

On the eastern shore of Lago Villarrica, Pucón is the Lake District's adventure-tourism capital. It was founded in 1883 as a fort settlement at the foot of Volcán Villarrica; today its compact grid of smoothly paved streets caters mostly to the tourism industry. Nestled in an area of natural beauty, Pucón is a base for trips to nearby hot springs and

INSIDER TIP
High Hiking

For a physical challenge and a memorable experience, try your hand at one of the rock- or volcano-climbing trips with the Panguipulli-based agency Aldea Expediciones *(aldea.cl)*.

national parks, and visitors heading to these areas will find the CONAF offices at Huerquehue National Park and Villarrica helpful. Pucón is also the starting point for many adrenaline-charged activities in the region. It has two black-sand beaches where swimming and water sports are possible: Playa Grande and the smaller La Poza beach which faces a protected inlet. In summer, boat rides from La Poza are a popular way of touring Lago Villarrica.

Reserva Biológica Huilo-Huilo

F2 130 miles (210 km) SE of Temuco; El Portal, Camino Internacional Panguipulli-Puerto Fuy, km 56 huilohuilo.com

Run by a private foundation dedicated to sustainable tourism, Reserva Biológica Huilo-Huilo preserves 232 sq miles (600 sq km) of temperate rainforest that was once the target of large-scale logging. It offers some truly compelling scenery; the most impressive is the Volcán Mocho-Choshuenco, which is, in fact, two volcanoes bridged by a large glacier. The surrounding landscape comprises glacial lakes and Andean prairies.

There is a range of lodging options, from an upscale mountain lodge in the woods, to more inexpensive accommodation in the small towns of Neltume and Puerto Fuy. These were built in the 1930s to house employees of the logging companies. Puerto Fuy is situated near the lovely Lago Pirihueico and is the starting point for fly-fishing, kayaking, and boating trips.

The reserve's lodge, Montaña Mágica (Magic Mountain), is worth a visit even for non-guests. It rises above the forest like a castle from a fairy tale, and its interior is constructed almost entirely from native woods. Next door is the whimsical Nothofagus Hotel, which looks like a giant treehouse. Activities here are mostly guided and arranged at La Montaña Mágica or at the administration center. These include horseback rides and wildlife observation of reintroduced fauna that once roamed freely here. Travelers looking for more rugged activities will also find zip-lining, mountain biking, trekking excursions, and an impressive range of hiking trails. The premises also house the stunning Museo de los Volcanes, which displays Chile's most extensive collection of silver Mapuche items within a pyramid-like interior.

STAY

Montaña Mágica Lodge

Located in the middle of a rainforest, the luxury Montaña Mágica Lodge is designed to resemble a mountain. Enjoy a traditional Chilean meal at the restaurant before relaxing in a hot tub carved from a tree trunk.

F2 Carretera Internacional CH-203, km 55 s/n, Reserva Biológica Huilo-Huilo huilohuilo.com

$$$

A cascading waterfall within the Reserva Biológica Huilo-Huilo

Parque Nacional Puyehue

F2 116 miles (187 km) SE of Valdivia; Aguas Calientes 9am-5:30pm daily Centro de Informacion Ambiental, Aguas Calientes; conaf.cl

Famed for its hot springs, Parque Nacional Puyehue is one of Chile's most popular and remote national parks. It covers 412 sq miles (1,067 sq km) of wilderness that encompasses two volcanoes, around 200 craters, and large swaths of evergreen Valdivian rainforest. Close to the park's entrance, in its Aguas Calientes sector, the **Termas Aguas Calientes** is a rustic hot-springs resort featuring sulfur-rich outdoor rock pools edged by forest and tumbling rivers. In the park's Antillanca sector, Volcán Casablanca, rising to a height of 6,529 ft (1,990 m), has one of the Lake District's least demanding ascents. The base is the starting point for several trails, both easy and challenging, that wind through native forests of lenga, ulmo, and coigüe trees. The park is home to a rich and varied birdlife, including hummingbirds, condors, and kingfishers. Hikers can also hear the distinctive chirp of the endemic, onomatopoeically named chucao (*Scelorchilus rubecula*). Among the park's mammals are pumas, foxes, the native and endangered huemul deer, as well as the tiny, tree-dwelling mouse opossum.

Volcán Casablanca is also the location for the highly rated and popular **Centro de Ski Antillanca**, which operates on the volcano's western wall. Offering excellent off-piste skiing, it features 17 slopes for all levels, snowboard runs, and a maximum drop of 1,640 ft (500 m). The slopes afford panoramic views of the blue skyline pierced by the snowcapped cones of surrounding volcanoes. Services include an equipment rental shop, a ski-school, and a snow park for children. In summer, activities feature mountain biking, horseback riding, caving, and trekking on the volcano, as well as kayaking and fishing excursions. Snowmobile rides through virgin forest are an added draw during the winter months.

In the northern, less trodden sector of the national park, the 7,334-ft (2,236-m) Volcán Puyehue offers a difficult two-day ascent, and is for experienced hikers only. The stunning trails here pass geysers, steaming fumaroles, and gurgling hot springs.

INSIDER TIP

Go Camping

Unlike in many other protected areas found in Chile, camping is allowed inside Parque Nacional Puyehue in designated areas. It is advisable to book in advance, especially during peak season.

←

Hiking in the Parque Nacional Puyehue, and *(inset)* a resident ringed kingfisher

Termas Aguas Calientes
Km 4 Camino Antillanca
termasaguascalientes.cl

Centro de Ski Antillanca
Volcán Casablanca 8am-5:30pm daily antillanca.cl

Lago Ranco

F2 77 miles (124 km) SE of Valdivia Viña del Mar 355; municipalidad lagoranco.cl

Located on the southern shore of the eponymous silver-gray lake, Lago Ranco is a small and quiet village of gravel streets and weather-board houses. These old, weather-beaten structures encircle the forested shoreline of what is possibly the Lake District's most beautiful body of water. Ringed by craggy Andean peaks, the lake's crystalline, warm waters are perfect for a swim. The village's cultural attraction, **Museo Tringlo Lago Ranco**, displays archaeological and anthropological exhibits, including ancient ceramics.

Museo Tringlo Lago Ranco
Ancud s/n Mid-Dec-Feb: 10am-1pm & 3-5pm daily (063) 2491 348

Termas de Puyehue

F2 114 miles (183 km) SE of Valdivia; Ruta 215, km 76, Puyehue 7:30-10pm daily puyehue.cl

The five-star spa resort of Termas de Puyehue is the ideal place to soothe aching limbs after long treks in the nearby Parque Nacional Puyehue. Hidden within forests at the edge of the park, this luxurious yet accessible mountain lodge and spa receives both day and overnight guests. It is possible to relax in the therapeutic waters of three large thermal pools – covered, semi-covered, and outdoor – whose temperatures range from a comfortable 72°F (22°C) to a warm 106°F (41°C). There are hot rooms and hydrotherapy pools, and a tempting variety of indulgent treatments that include honey, algae, and herbal massages, as well as sulfur-rich mud baths. The spa has a daily program of children's activities and a well-equipped playroom. Other facilities include two gourmet restaurants, a small art gallery, and outdoor tennis courts. Visitors can enjoy exhilarating horseback rides to the forested shore of the nearby Lago Puyehue, where the spa arranges several water sports for its guests.

Osorno

F2 66 miles (107 km) S of Valdivia O'Higgins 667; (064) 2234 104

Founded in 1558 by García Hurtado de Mendoza, then governor of Chile, the city of Osorno is located at the center of Chile's cattle heartland. The country's biggest cattle market, the Feria Ganadera de Osorno, is held here on Mondays and Fridays.

La Parrilla de Pepe
Situated at the end of a row of houses built by German pioneers, this spot is an architectural landmark and a reliable grill restaurant.

F2 Mackenna 1095, Osorno (064) 2249 653

$$$

↑ The striking Catedral San Mateo Apóstol in Osorno

Although primarily an agricultural city, Osorno offers many attractions. Most striking of these is the Neo-Gothic Catedral San Mateo Apóstol with its massive facade of reinforced concrete and ogival filigree. Built in 1960, it towers over the city's central plaza.

South of the cathedral is the Calle Juan Mackenna, lined with a row of Teutonic-style wooden houses dating from the 19th century, when German settlers arrived at Osorno. A number have been designated national monuments.

A block west of the houses, an elegant 1929 Neo-Classical building is the setting for the **Museo Histórico Municipal**. Its displays trace the city's history chronologically; exhibits include Mapuche pottery and colonial-era weapons.

Osorno is a convenient base for visits to the nearby Parque Nacional Puyehue; travelers are advised to first visit Osorno's CONAF office for information on the park.

Museo Histórico Municipal
M A Matta 809 (064) 2238 615 9:30am-1pm & 2:30-6pm Mon-Fri, 2-6pm Sat

The peaceful waters of Lago Llanquihue at sunset, with Volcán Osorno in the distance

26   

Lago Llanquihue

F2 99 miles (160 km) SE of Valdivia

Resembling a small sea in size, the breathtakingly beautiful Lago Llanquihue is South America's third-largest natural lake. It covers a surface area of 338 sq miles (875 sq km), plunges to a depth of 1,148 ft (350 m), and its crystal blue waters are bound by Volcán Osorno and Volcán Calbuco. The Mapuche believed this lake and its dominions to be a realm of monsters and evil spirits. The Spanish first came here in 1552, but it was not until the arrival of German immigrants in the 19th century that Europeans colonized the lake's shores. Since then, Llanquihue has been the German heartland of the Lake District and is today fronted by steepled Bavarian towns.

GERMANIC DISTRICT

In 1845, the Chilean government passed the Badlands Law, which aimed to undermine Mapuche control of the Lake District. Some 150 German Catholic families accepted Chile's invitation to colonize the area; more followed, fleeing persecution in their home country. German settlers founded three towns - Puerto Octay, Frutillar, and Puerto Varas. These became a German heartland.

27

Puerto Octay

F2 99 miles (160 km) SE of Valdivia
German Wulf s/n

Set on the northern shore of Lago Llanquihue, Puerto Octay was founded in 1852 by German immigrants and grew into an important lake port. Today, it is a holiday destination with streets of well-conserved Germanic architecture. Occupying an old settler's house, the excellent **Museo El Colono** exhibits period objects. Another noteworthy building is the 1907-built Iglesia Parroquial, constructed in a simple Gothic style.

Puerto Octay faces the peaks of three volcanoes – Calbuco, Puntiagudo, and Osorno. Each is visible from the town's main beach, Playa La Baja, a stretch of volcanic black sand fringed by pine and eucalyptus forests.

Museo El Colono

 Camino Centinela S/N (958) 268 431 Jan & Feb: 10am-1pm & 2-6:30pm Sat & Sun (Mar-Dec: by appointment)

28

Puerto Varas

F2 118 miles (190 km) S of Valdivia
puertovaras.org

Puerto Varas is the biggest town on Lago Llanquihue. It was founded in 1854 by German immigrants, and pioneer-era homes can still be seen on the streets. The town's most remarkable Teutonic building, the **Iglesia Sagrado Corazón de Jesús**, was built in 1915–18 as a to-scale replica of a church in Germany's Black Forest. Made entirely from wood, its Baroque interior has two cupolas, built to the maximum height possible without metal supports.

The town is popular for various adventure sports, and visitors can also trek to Volcán Osorno and hike in Parque Vicente Perez-Rosales *(p204)*.

During winter, the locals celebrate the seasonal rains with the traditional Rain Festival. The most popular of the town's black-sand beaches is Playa de Puerto Chico, with views of Volcán Osorno.

Iglesia Sagrado Corazón de Jesús
Verbo Divino 499, San Francisco Hours vary

Frutillar

F2 105 miles (170 km) SE of Valdivia Avenida Philippi 75; munifrutillar.cl

The lovely town of Frutillar was founded in 1856 by German colonists on the western shore of Lago Llanquihue. The town's Frutillar Bajo (Lower Frutillar) district has stunning views of Volcán Osorno, and its shores are lined by a mix of hotels, craft markets, restaurants, and old Germanic architecture. The **Museo Colonial Alemán** stands in landscaped gardens and re-creates the pioneer era with life-size buildings furnished with period objects.

On the waterfront, the Teatro del Lago Sur is a contemporary theater venue and site of the Semanas Musicales de Frutillar, a music festival held in November and December. At the town's northern edge, the **Reserva Forestal Edmundo Winkler** preserves Valdivian rainforest. A path here climbs to a lookout point with lake and volcano views.

Museo Colonial Alemán
Avenida Vicente Pérez Rosales, Arturo Prat, Frutillar Bajo 10am-2pm & 3-6pm Tue-Sun
museosaustral.cl

Reserva Forestal Edmundo Winkler
Calle Caupolicán s/n, Frutillar Bajo 10am-8pm Mon-Fri (winter: to 5pm)

STAY

Hotel Ayacara
A classic Mitteleuropa-style house overlooking the lake.

F2 Avenida Philippi 1215, Frutillar
casaayacara.cl

$

AWA
Splurge on this luxurious lakeside hotel.

F2 Km 27, Ruta 225CH, Puerto Varas
hotelawa.cl

$$$

Compass del Sur
A friendly hostel with dorms, private rooms, and camping.

F2 Klenner 467, Puerto Varas
compassdelsur.cl

$

A Germanic wooden house located at Museo Colonial Alemán, Frutillar

Ancud

F3 54 miles (87 km) S of Puerto Montt; Isla Grande Blanco Encalada 660; ancud.cl

A picturesque fishing town, Ancud is the first stop for most visitors crossing the Canal de Chacao, from the Lake District to Chiloé. The town was set up by the Spanish in 1768 as a fort settlement on the Bahía de Ancud, a tongue of water dotted with fishing boats, edged by algae-strewn beaches and colorful houses, and ringed by emerald hills. This compact town is easily explored on foot. Its coastal Avenida Salvador Allende runs parallel to the bay, which is overlooked by the ruins of **Fuerte San Antonio**. This Spanish fort marks the site where Royalist forces made their last stand in Chile's War of Independence in 1826. An obelisk at the fort commemorates the Spanish Crown's final defeat. Beneath rocky cliffs nearby is Playa Arena Gruesa, a horseshoe-shaped beach and bathing spot.

In the town itself, **Museo Regional de Ancud** in the central plaza displays archaeological and ethnographic exhibits. It includes an ornate collection of 17th- and 18th-century Jesuit artifacts; carved figures from Chilote mythology; and a life-size replica of *Goleta Ancud*, the Ancud-built schooner that carried the first Chilean settlers to the Strait of Magellan in 1843. Adjacent to the museum is the town's cathedral, whose shingled exterior resembles the facade of a typical Chilote home. Visitors can also explore the scale models of Chiloé's 16 unique churches at Centro de Visitantes Inmaculada. To find out more about the archipelago's churches, visit the Centro de Visitantes de las Iglesias de Chiloé, a visitor center with a number of exhibits that provide information on the area's history and architecture.

MYTHS AND FOLKLORE OF CHILOÉ

Folktales and myths have long enriched Chilote life, with stories handed across generations through oral tradition. Goddesses who protect the land, a lascivious forest dweller who tricks adolescent girls into surrendering their virginity, and a serpent that sucks the lifeblood from a household; these are just a few of the benevolent and evil beings believed by the islanders to roam Chiloé. The origin of these tales lies in Mapuche legend and its later blurring with Spanish superstition and Roman Catholic beliefs. The archipelago's landscape forms an ideal background; mist-shrouded bays, silent forests, and frequent bad weather are all evocative of fantastical worlds.

Fuerte San Antonio
Cochrane San Antonio
9am-8pm daily

Museo Regional de Ancud
Libertad 370
10am-5pm Tue-Fri, 10am-4:30pm Sat & Sun
museoancud.gob.cl

Monumento Natural Islotes de Puñihuil

E3 17 miles (27 km) W of Ancud 9am-6pm daily (book ahead) pinguineraschiloe.cl

Three rocky islets of volcanic origin, the Monumento Natural Islotes de Puñihuil are refuge to colonies of Humboldt and Magellanic

penguins that nest here each year. These islets are among the world's few places where the vulnerable Humboldt shares the same habitat as its close Magellanic relative. Small-boat excursions depart from Bahía Puñihuil on Isla Grande's northwestern coast to observe the penguins and other fauna. This includes marine otters, which scramble across the black rock at the water's edge; red-legged cormorants, agile flyers that can be seen dive-bombing the water for crustaceans; flightless steamer ducks; and two species of oystercatchers.

Dalcahue

F3 17 miles (28 km) NE of Castro

Located on the eastern coast of Isla Grande, the town of Dalcahue faces the smaller islands of the Chiloé archipelago. Dalcahue was not founded on any particular date; it evolved from the 1700s onward as a stop on the Jesuits' Circular Mission – annual trips made by the Jesuits across Chiloé. The town's chief draw is the UNESCO-protected Iglesia Dalcahue, a Neo-Gothic structure built in 1903 on the site of the Jesuits' original mission. Close to it, the Mercado Dalcahue is a wooden dining hall on the waterfront that features the best of Chilote food, including *milcao* (deep-fried potato pancakes).

Dalcahue is also a sales hub for craftspeople from the nearby islands, who arrive daily by boat to offer their wares at the artisans' market.

The picturesque cliffside of the fishing town Ancud

↑ Walking along a boardwalk trail through the Parque Nacional Chiloé

Parque Nacional Chiloé

E3 32 miles (52 km) W of Castro; Sector Chanquín, Cucao 9am-6pm daily CONAF, Gamboa 424, Castro; conaf.cl

The scenic Parque Nacional Chiloé is fringed by the Pacific Ocean on its west and by Chile's coastal mountain range on its east. In between, it protects over 164 sq miles (426 sq km) of indigenous forest, including Chile's southernmost forests of alerce. Parque Nacional Chiloé has abundant wildlife and its coastal sections harbor colonies of southern sea lions, Magellanic and Humboldt penguins, and seabirds.

Most visits to the park focus on the southern sector, where the Cucao village offers rustic accommodation close by the park entrance. The village is the trailhead for the Chanquín–Cole Cole Trail, which skirts past a stretch of the Pacific coastline, marked by white beaches, big surf, and sand dunes edged by native forest. At the end of the trail, members of a Huilliche community organize horseback rides through the verdant woods.

The park's northern sector, although less visited, has forests of greater size and density. Here, the outstanding Castro–Abtao Trek crosses through thick alerce forest and ends at the Pacific Ocean.

Parque Nacional Chiloé has abundant wildlife and its coastal sections harbor colonies of southern sea lions, Magellanic and Humboldt penguins, and seabirds.

CASTRO

F3 48 miles (77 km) S of Ancud Plaza de Armas; municastro.cl

An island gem, Castro is an inevitable stop on any visit to the archipelago. It was founded by the Spanish in 1567 on a hill overlooking the mist-swathed Fiordo Castro. Today, it is a picturesque destination of hilly lanes, gorgeous sea views, and historic *palafitos*.

Museo Regional de Castro

Esmeralda 255 Jan & Feb: 9:30am-7pm Mon-Fri, 9:30am-6:30pm Sat, 10:30am-1pm Sun; Mar-Dec: 9:30am-1:30pm & 3-6:30pm Mon-Fri, 9:30am-1pm Sat museodecastro.com

This small museum traces Chiloé's history from the arrival of hunter-gatherer groups at the archipelago – around 6,000 years ago – to modern times. Historical objects and information panels record the islands' colonization by the Chono and Huilliche communities; the subsequent Spanish conquest during the 16th century; and the primary role played by Chiloé as a Royalist stronghold during Chile's War of Independence (1810–18). The exhibits on modern history feature photographs of the destruction caused by the 1960 earthquake and tsunami, which affected coastal villages throughout the archipelago.

Iglesia San Francisco

Plaza de Armas 9:30am-12:30pm & 3:30-8pm daily

Without a doubt Chiloé's most iconic landmark, the beautiful, sunshine-colored Iglesia San Francisco is an extraordinary work of local craftsmanship. A UNESCO-protected building, it was designed by Italian architect Eduardo Provasoli in 1910 to replace an older church that burned down. Constructed entirely from native woods such as cypress, alerce, and coigüe, the church is finished in flamboyant polychrome fashion. The edifice's striking Neo-Gothic facade is clad with sheets of corrugated tin, painted gold and purple, and features two 130-ft- (40-m)- high bell towers. For decades, these towers were used to guide ships arriving at the port and today their status as Castro's tallest structures is protected by law. The church's vaulted interior is ornamented with opulent religious imagery and the altar, pulpit, and confessional boxes are exquisitely hand-carved from native woods by local artisans. It also has colorful stained-glass windows.

INSIDER TIP
Feria Yumbel Market

A craft and food market northwest of Castro city center, Feria Yumbel is an excellent place to buy traditional Chilote woolen jumpers, hats, socks, and other items of clothing.

↑ Brightly painted wooden *palafitos* along the shores of Fiordo Castro

③

Palafitos

⌂ Shore of Fiordo Castro

Castro's pastel-hued *palafitos*, the city's favorite postcard image, are traditional wooden houses built on stilts along the edge of the Fiordo Castro. These wonderfully picturesque homes are constructed from local woods and painted in vibrant colors. Each *palafito* has two facades: one facing the street and the other overlooking the water. Exquisite examples of vernacular architecture, the *palafitos* were originally built in the 19th century for local fishers, who would moor their boats in the water before climbing a wooden ladder to their family home.

Prior to the 1960 earthquake, the *palafitos* lined most of Isla Grande's eastern shore. However, following the earthquake their numbers have greatly reduced and they are now concentrated on Castro's coastal Avenida Pedro Montt and Calle Ernesto Riquelme, with particularly splendid examples on the northern approach to Castro. Experience Castro by staying in one of the *palafitos* which have been restored and converted into luxurious guesthouses and boutique hotels.

Museo de Arte Moderno Chiloé

⌂ Galvarino Riveros s/n, Parque Municipal ◷ Only during exhibitions; check website for details W mamchiloe.cl

Housed in a former grain warehouse, this excellent contemporary art museum sits atop a windswept hillside that offers spectacular views of the city. It showcases a wide range of styles such as installation, graffiti, and digital art. The permanent collection also includes works by well-known Chilean artists Arturo Duclos and Ricardo Yrrázaval.

Many of the museum's displays make use of indigenous materials such as sheep's wool. It also explores local themes that emphasize Chiloé's identity as distinct from that of mainland Chile.

EAT

Travesía

Come here for traditional Chilote food with a modern, global twist. If you enjoy the food in a homely atmosphere, pick up a copy of the chef's cookbook.

⌂ Eusebio Lillo 188
(065) 2630 137

$$$

La Brüjula del Cuerpo

On Plaza de Armas, this lively, low-cost café serves simple, tasty meals, including sandwiches, soups, burgers, ice cream, and set lunches.

⌂ O'Higgins 308
(065) 2633 229

$$$

JESUIT CHURCHES IN CHILOÉ

In 1608, Jesuit priests arrived at Chiloé to evangelize the Indigenous Huilliche. They established the Circular Mission and built wooden churches. The construction represented a new form of religious architecture – the Chilote School – whose roots lay in the Jesuit architecture of 17th-century central Europe. Over 60 churches survive; some were rebuilt in the 18th and 19th centuries after fires or earthquakes. Sixteen of them constitute a UNESCO World Heritage Site.

CHURCH ARCHITECTURE

Chiloté churches have key characteristics, all of which can be seen in Achao's Iglesia Santa María de Loreto *(p226)*, also known as the Iglesia de Achao. One of the distinctive aspects of the architecture of the churches, as seen with the Iglesia de San Francisco, are the unmistakable bell towers and symmetrical facades. The bell tower of Santa María is typical, soaring above the center of the facade, lending the building its symmetrical design. Rising up from a rectangular base, the octagonal tower is crowned by a cross, which acts as a beacon for fishers and sailors. Windows sit along the church's portico and side walls, providing light to the interior.

↑ The bright yellow and purple facade of Iglesia de San Francisco

The symmetrical wooden interior of Iglesia Santa María de Loreto ↑

ENTRANCE DESIGN

The entrances of Chiloté churches may have a columned and arched arcade in the Neo-Gothic or Neo-Classical style, as seen in Iglesia de Dalcahue. The Jesuits laid out squares in front of entrances for religious processions.

CHURCH INTERIORS

The interior of Chiloté churches can be simple and austere or highly decorative. A vaulted ceiling covers the central nave, as in Iglesia de San Francisco. This elegant feature might be brightly painted or left bare. At the heart of the church is the long nave. Wooden columns, set in stone and carved from trunks. of native trees, separate this part from two lateral naves. Only the central nave reaches the back of the church and the altar. The altar table, crafted from native alerce, cypress, and mañio trunks and richly decorated with Catholic imagery, stands at the church's northern end.

THE JESUITS' CIRCULAR MISSION

Jesuit priests faced one major obstacle to the evangelization of Chiloé: the exceptional isolation of its islands and of its Huilliche populations. In an effort to overcome this, the Jesuits made annual round trips of the archipelago by sea. On this Circular Mission, priests disembarked at each Indigenous settlement, converted its people, deposited a layman for continued spiritual assistance, and returned the following year. The Jesuits built a church at each new mission – there were 200 constructed overall – around which villages grew. After the Jesuits were removed and expelled from the Spanish colonies in 1767, Franciscans continued the Circular Mission.

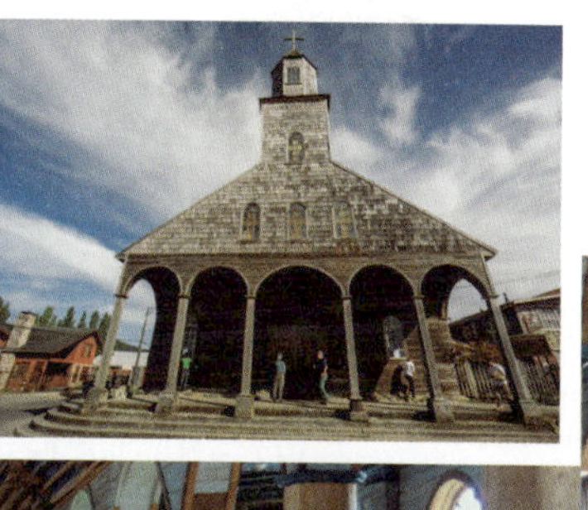

The distinctive exterior of Iglesia Santa María de Loreto

The painted facade and *(inset)* wooden interior of Iglesia San Judas in Curaco de Vélez

Curaco de Vélez

F3 23 miles (37 km) E of Castro
curacodevelez.cl

From Dalcahue *(p221)*, boats cross the Canal Dalcahue – part of the Mar Interior (Inner Sea) that separates Chiloé from mainland Chile – to reach Isla de Quinchao, an island dotted with tiny coastal villages. Facing the canal on this island is the pretty village of Curaco de Vélez, the smallest settlement in the Chiloé archipelago. Its origins can be traced to the 1600s, when Jesuit priests first dropped anchor here on their missionary route. Although the town's original Jesuit church was destroyed in a fire in 1971, a wealth of century-old vernacular architecture can still be seen. Calle Errázuriz is lined with gray wooden houses clad with alerce tiles in the typical Chilote style. These stand as a testament to Curaco de Vélez's prosperous past, when forestry brought wealth and fine craftsmanship. Today, life revolves around a small plaza and church, the Iglesia San Judas. The plaza backs onto a dramatic sweep of shell-strewn beach facing the narrow stretch of sea. Colonies of black-necked swans dot the water's surface in summer. Isla de Quinchao is also visited for its old Jesuit churches, historic wooden houses, seafood restaurants, and crafts markets.

STAY

Tierra Chiloé

This stunning hotel has spacious en suites with sweeping ocean views, a well-equipped spa, an impressive restaurant, and welcoming staff. Rates include full board, excursions, and transfers.

F3 San José Playa s/n, between Castro & Dalcahue
tierrahotels.com

$$$

Achao

F3 28 miles (45 km) E of Castro Amunátegui s/n, Plaza de Armas

On Isla de Quinchao's eastern coast, the small town of Achao makes for a half-day visit. Iglesia Santa María de Loreto, the archipelago's oldest church, is the single surviving structure from the Jesuits' original mission. Built in 1754, it fronts the town's main plaza and is a wooden structure, down to the pegs and nails used in its construction. The vaulted interior features Baroque columns and a beautifully carved altar and pulpit. The church's Neo-Classical facade is clad in alerce tiles in the traditional Chilote style. Also facing the plaza, the **Museo de Achao** has exhibits on the Chono, the nomadic people who lived in Chiloé in the pre-Columbian era, and bright displays of Chilote weavings.

Museo de Achao
Amunátegui 014 (065) 2661 471 10am-1pm & 3-5pm daily

Chonchi

F3 14 miles (23 km) S of Castro Pedro Montt 254; municipali dadchonchi.cl

Referred to as the City of Three Floors for its abrupt topography, Chonchi is actually a hillside village overlooking a scenic bay on Isla Grande. The town, seen by Jesuit priests as a beach-head from where they could evangelize the archipelago's southern zones, evolved around the Jesuits' Circular Mission in the 17th century.

In the late 19th century, Chonchi reached its commercial peak as a major timber port and wooden buildings still line its gravel streets. Dating from 1883, the Iglesia de Chonchi is one of 16 UNESCO-protected churches on the archipelago. Also of interest, the **Museo de las Tradiciones Chonchinas** is housed in a large family mansion that was built for a rich logging baron in 1910. Inside, the museum re-creates the rooms of a typical pioneer-era Chilote home.

Museo de las Tradiciones Chonchinas
Centenario 116 (065) 2672 802 Jan & Feb: 10am-2pm & 3-6pm Mon, 10am-7pm Tue-Sun; Mar-Dec: 10am-2pm & 3-6pm Tue-Sat

Quellón

F3 62 miles (99 km) S of Castro 22 de Mayo 351; muniquellon.cl

A commercial fishing port, Quellón is a departure hub for ferries bound for destinations along the Carretera Austral (Southern Highway). It is also the official end point of the great Pan-American highway. Visitors can use Quellón as a jumping-off point to visit the southern sector of Parque Tantauco, though this requires booking in advance.

Many blue and sei whales migrate through the Golfo de Corcovado, just off Quellón's coast, from December through April. Local operator Quilun *(quilun.cl)* offers tours into the gulf, where you may also spot black-browed abatrosses, and Peale's and Chilean dolphins.

FESTIVAL COSTUMBRISTA CHILOTE

A vibrant celebration of Chilote culture, this festival is Chiloé's biggest annual event, and is held in towns and villages across the archipelago during January and February. Festivities feature folk music and dance, food and drink, craft fairs, and demonstrations of traditional island activities. Ask at a tourist information office for details on what's happening when.

Parque Tantauco

E3 45 miles (73 km) SW of Castro Pasaje las delicias 270, Castro; parquetantauco.cl

Created by business tycoon and former president of Chile Sebastián Piñera, this 456-sq-mile (1180-sq-km) private nature reserve sits in the southwest corner of Chiloé. It is among the world's 35 biodiversity hotspots and is home to a variety of flora and fauna, including Darwin foxes and pudú deer. The park has an excellent infrastructure with its well-kept trails, camping huts, and designated campgrounds. Only a limited number of visitors are allowed in the park at any one time.

Tantauco is divided into two halves; the northern section can be reached via twice weekly buses from Quellón in summer, while the southern section is accessed via a small plane from Castro, or by boat from Quellón to Caleta Inio.

Visitors can choose from a two-day loop trek around the Caleta Inio Peninsula or from a three- to eight-day trek within the park. Several tour companies in Castro organize flights and treks into the park.

↑ Fishing boats crowding the commercial port of Quellón

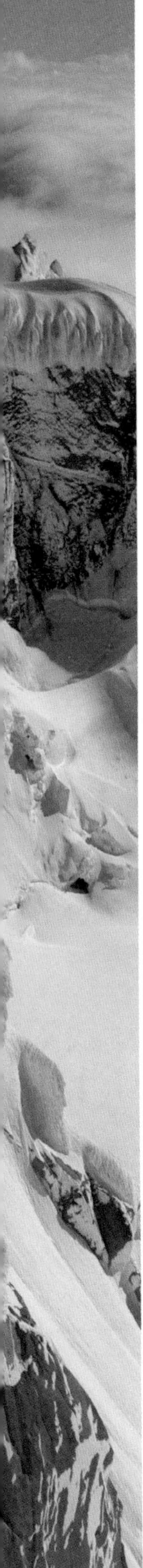

The snowcapped peaks of the Andes in Northern Patagonia

NORTHERN PATAGONIA

Thinly populated Northern Patagonia is home to some of the continent's wildest country, including Chile's most scenic highway, the Carretera Austral. The region embraces glaciers and icebergs, rugged Andean pinnacles, and large forest reserves.

The fjords, forests, and steppes of Northern Patagonia were originally inhabited by a handful of Tehuelche hunter-gatherers and Kawéskar fish-erfolk. During the 16th and 17th centuries, few Europeans penetrated the area, apart from Jesuit missionaries based in Chiloé, and some British seafarers and scientists such as John Byron (1723–86) and Charles Darwin (1809–82). Following independence, Chile was slow to colonize Northern Patagonia, and it was not until 1903 that a huge land grant for sheep ranching and forestry provided the impetus for economic growth in the region. The grant was made by the Chilean government to private agricultural companies in and around the regional capital of Coyhaique. The resulting change in land use led initially to large-scale fires, deforestation, and erosion that closed up Puerto Aisén, the area's main port, at a time when nearly all transportation was seaborne. Road access began to be established in the 1970s with the construction of the Carretera Austral.

Northern Patagonia's many national parks conserve old native forests, wild rivers, rugged peaks, and waterfalls. Explored via ferry routes and road trips, these are ideal for activities, from white water rafting to fly-fishing and trekking.

NORTHERN PATAGONIA

Must Sees

1. Parque Nacional Pumalín Douglas Tompkins
2. Futaleufú
3. Parque Nacional Queulat
4. Parque Nacional Laguna San Rafael

Experience More

5. Chaitén
6. Palena
7. Melinka
8. Hornopirén
9. Puyuhuapi
10. Puyuhuapi Lodge & Spa
11. Puerto Cisnes
12. Puerto Chacabuco
13. Puerto Edén
14. Cochrane
15. Coyhaique
16. Parque Nacional Patagonia
17. Puerto Río Tranquilo
18. Parque Nacional Cerro Castillo
19. Chile Chico
20. Caleta Tortel
21. Río Baker
22. Villa O'Higgins

Pacific
Ocean

0 kilometers 100
0 miles 100
N

LAKE DISTRICT AND CHILOÉ
p194
El Tepual Airport
Puerto Montt
Parque Nacional Hornopirén
8 HORNOPIRÉN
Ancud
Isla Llancahué
LOS LAGOS
Isla Grande de Chiloé
Caleta Gonzálo
Volcán Chaitén 3,681 ft (1,121 m)
Chonchi
Santa Barbara
5 CHAITÉN
1 PARQUE NACIONAL PUMALÍN DOUGLAS TOMPKINS
2 FUTALEUFÚ
Lago Yelcho
Puerto Ramírez
Villa Santa Lucia
Inio
Golfo de Corcovado
6 PALENA
Alto Palena Airport
El Maitén
Cushamen
Paso del Sapo
Esquel
Esquel Airport
Colan Conhué
Tecka
Gobernador Costa
Lago Palena
Melinka Airport
7 MELINKA
La Junta
Lago Rosselot
Lago Verde
9 PUYUHUAPI
10 PUYUHUAPI LODGE & SPA
3 PARQUE NACIONAL QUEULAT
La Tapera
Parque Nacional Isla Magdalena
11 PUERTO CISNES
Villa Amengual
Archipiélago de los Chonos
Los Tamariscos
Alto Río Senguer
Facundo
Puerto Aisén
12 PUERTO CHACABUCO
15 COYHAIQUE
Balmaceda Airport
Balmaceda
Volcán Hudson 6,250 ft (1,905 m)
18 PARQUE NACIONAL CERRO CASTILLO
Reserva Nacional las Guaitecas
AISÉN
Villa Cerro Castillo
Puerto Ingeniero Ibáñez
El Puma
Río Exploradores
Puerto Murta
19 CHILE CHICO
Chile Chico Airport
Lago General Carrera
17 PUERTO RÍO TRANQUILO
Puerto Guadal
4 PARQUE NACIONAL LAGUNA SAN RAFAEL
Lago Bertrand
Puerto Bertrand
16 PARQUE NACIONAL PATAGONIA
Campo de Hielo Norte
14 COCHRANE
Cochrane Airport
Golfo de Penas
21 RÍO BAKER
Bajo Caracoles
Cerro San Lorenzo 12,158 ft (3,705 m)
20 CALETA TORTEL
Puerto Yungay
Las Horquetas
Reserva Nacional Katalalixar
22 VILLA O'HIGGINS
Lago Strobel
Río Chico
Lago O'Higgins
Parque Nacional Bernardo O'Higgins
Campo de Hielo Sur
Gobernador Gregores
Lago Cardiel
ARGENTINA
13 PUERTO EDÉN
MAGALLANES
Tres Lagos
Isla Wellington
SOUTHERN PATAGONIA AND TIERRA DEL FUEGO
p248

1

PARQUE NACIONAL PUMALÍN DOUGLAS TOMPKINS

F3 82 miles (132 km) S of Puerto Montt; Caleta Gonzalo From Hornopirén Klenner 299, Puerto Varas; conaf.cl

Spanning almost 1,550 sq miles (4,020 sq km) of temperate rainforests, deep fjords, and rugged mountains, this park is an exhilarating place to hike.

Founded in 1991 by the late US environmentalist Doug Tompkins and his wife, Kris, Pumalín was the world's largest privately owned reserve until it became a national park in 2018. Several hiking trails start from the main road in the southern sector of the park and snake through its pristine landscapes. There are also trails in the less-visited northern and Amarillo sectors; most of them are relatively short but some are challenging. Hot springs make ideal places for relaxing after a tough day's trekking.

TOMPKINS CONSERVATION

Doug Tompkins (1943–2015), co-founder of North Face, and his wife Kris, former CEO of outdoor clothing company Patagonia, spent more than 25 years conserving huge sections of Chile and Argentina. Their work in Chile started in 1991 with the purchase of a large tract of land that became Parque Pumalín. They first faced resistance from locals but opening the park up to the public, and their commitment to conservation, helped shift opinions. Doug tragically died in 2015, but Kris continues their work. In 2018, their NGO, Tompkins Conservation, made the largest donation of land by a private owner to a state in South American history.

1 Pumalín is home to a number of waterfalls. These can be enjoyed along walking trails.

2 There is a campground by Lago Blanco, which offers spectacular views of the lake.

3 A guide talking to a group of walkers on the Alerce trail, just one of the park's many walking routes.

↑ Michinmahuida volcano viewed through the trees, Parque Nacional Pumalín

TOP 3 PUMALÍN HIKES

Sendero Cascadas Escondidas
1 mile (1.5 km); easy. A short and straight-forward walk that features a trio of beautiful waterfalls.

Sendero Volcán Chaitén
2.7 miles (4.5 km); challenging. A hike up the charred slopes of Volcán Chaitén rewards you with spectacular views of the smoking crater.

Sendero Ventisquero El Amarillo
12 miles (20 km); fairly challenging. This largely flat hike takes you to the foot of the incredible Michinmahuida glacier.

2

FUTALEUFÚ

F3 96 miles (154 km) SE of Chaitén Casa de La Cultura, Costanera Laguna Espejo; futaleufu.cl

Nestled in a secluded and picturesque valley, close to the Argentine border, is the town of Futaleufú. Though charming, it's mainly known for its eponymous river, which is one of the best in the world for white water rafting and kayaking.

The pretty town of Futaleufú, home to pastel-colored houses, is part of the 19-sq-mile (49-sq-km) Reserva Nacional Futaleufú. This region is thick with verdant forests and numerous species of animals, including the endangered huemul deer. There are plenty of opportunities for hiking, horseback riding, mountain biking, and fishing around the town.

The town is a popular base for adventure-sport lovers, thanks to the Río Futaleufú and its impressive Class IV and V rapids. The calmer sections of the river are suitable for novice rafters and kayakers, who can also try the less demanding Río Azul and Río Espolón nearby. Meanwhile, sea kayaking and canyoning are possible on and around Lago Yelcho.

BIG RIVER

The name Futaleufú means "Big River" in Indigenous Mapuche, and locals refer to the valley as "*un paisaje pintado por Dios*" – a landscape painted by God. Its natural beauty aside, the Río Futaleufú has developed an international reputation for white water rafting and kayaking. Several well-regarded operators in the town offer half-, full-, and multi-day trips, including Bochinche Expediciones *(bochinchex.com)*, Expediciones Chile *(exchile.com)*, and Condorfu *(condorfu.cl)*. They are experienced at taking beginners out on the river, though you need to have a good level of fitness and be a confident swimmer.

Kayaking on the choppy waters of Río Futaleufú

A huemul deer, also known as a South Andean deer

INSIDER TIP
Cross into Argentina

If you want to cross the border into Argentina, there are several weekly buses from Futaleufú to the city of Esquel and the town of Trevelín.

↑ Photographing Patagonia's majestic Río Futaleufú

Did You Know?

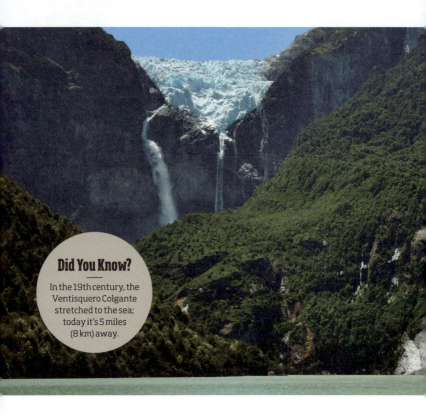

In the 19th century, the Ventisquero Colgante stretched to the sea; today it's 5 miles (8 km) away.

PARQUE NACIONAL QUEULAT

F4 269 miles (434 km) SE of Puerto Montt 9am–2:30pm daily (book ahead)
CONAF, Sector Ventisquero Colgante, Carretera Austral; conaf.cl

This far-flung national park is magnificent, thanks to its sinuous fjords, forested cliffsides, dramatic waterfalls, and epic glaciers – most spectacularly the hanging Ventisquero Colgante glacier. Head to Queulat to experience the great outdoors via various hiking trails.

Covering some of Northern Patagonia's most rugged terrain, Parque Nacional Queulat's dense rainforests, limpid lakes, clear trout streams, and steep mountains span more than 5,800 sq miles (15,000 sq km). Altitudes in the park vary significantly – from sea level up to 7,300 ft (2,255 m), where precipitation falls as snow.

Walking across the Sendero Río Guillermo suspension bridge

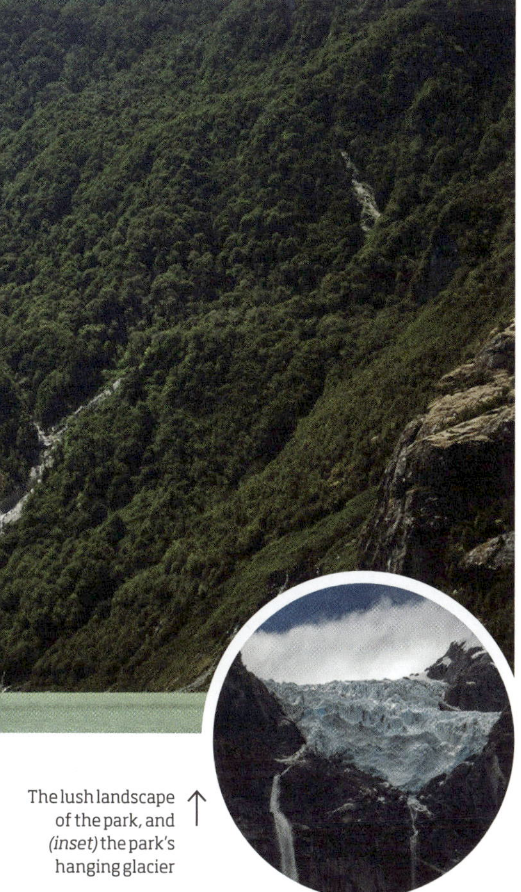

The lush landscape of the park, and *(inset)* the park's hanging glacier

TOP 4 QUEULAT TRAILS

Sendero Ventisquero Colgante
2 miles (3 km); easy. One of the most popular short hikes in the park, offering awesome views of the glacier and the icy lake below.

Sendero Laguna Los Pumas
6 miles (10 km); fairly easy. This Angostura sector trail climbs through lush forests to the vast Los Pumas lagoon.

Sendero Aluvión
Half a mile (1 km); easy. A pleasant stroll through a forested area of the Ventisquero Colgante sector that is rich in birdlife.

Sendero Salto Padre García
0.2 miles (0.3 km); easy. This short walk descends 500 ft (150 m) to a lovely waterfall.

Although Parque Nacional Queulat fronts the Carretera Austral (Southern Highway), its trackless back country is generally left unexplored.

Exploring the Park

The central Ventisquero Colgante sector is the most popular part of the park, with good hiking routes. From the visitor center, a couple of trails offer breathtaking views of the Ventisquero Colgante hanging glacier. From this mass of solid ice, waterfalls plunge into the jade-colored Laguna Témpanos (Iceberg Lake; in spite of the name, there are no icebergs). The lake can be reached via the Sendero Río Guillermo, a 1,969-ft- (600-m-) long route that crosses a suspension bridge over the river from which it takes its name. In the northern Angostura sector of the park, Lago Risopatrón is a popular point for fly-fishing. The southern sector is known as Portezuelo Queulat and, though less visited, it is well worth exploring.

A Magellanic woodpecker residing in Parque Nacional Queulat

PARQUE NACIONAL LAGUNA SAN RAFAEL

F4 118 miles (190 km) SW of Coyhaique 9am-1pm (book ahead) conaf.cl

This is one of Chile's largest protected areas, sprawling across 6,730 sq miles (17,420 sq km), and a UNESCO World Biosphere Reserve. Almost half of the park is covered by the spectacular Campo de Hielo Norte, the second-largest ice sheet in the Southern Hemisphere, outside of Antarctica.

The Campo de Hielo Norte (Northern Patagonian Ice Field) embraces the towering Monte San Valentín, which at 13,314 ft (4,058 m) is the highest summit in Patagonia. This ice field feeds more than 18 glaciers, including the 200-ft- (60-m-) high Ventisquero San Rafael. From the face of this receding glacier, massive chunks of blue ice spill into the Laguna San Rafael below. Tour operators arrange sailing excursions to the glacier through a maze of fjords and channels. While the larger tour boats usually keep a safe distance from the glacier, passengers can often jump in an inflatable dinghy for a closer look. You can also take a plane ride over the park for breathtaking panoramas of the ice field.

A boat sitting in front of the Northern Patagonian Ice Field, and *(inset)* a resident leopard seal ↓

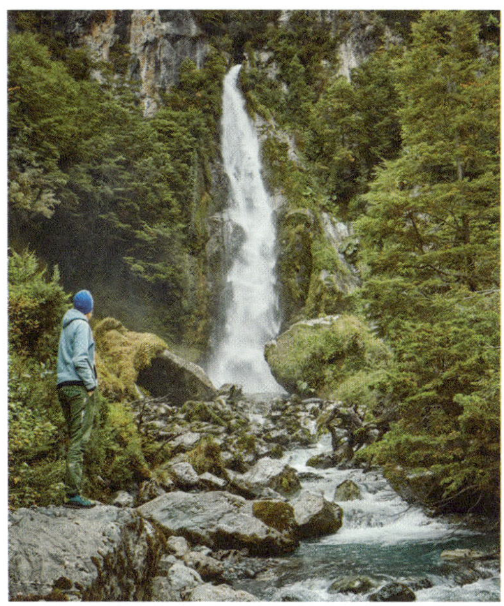

↑ Watching the tumbling Las Cascadas in Parque Nacional Laguna San Rafael

KAYAKING AND TREKKING

While boat trips might be the classic way to explore the Parque Nacional Laguna San Rafael region, there are also other more adventurous activities on offer. AguaHielo Expediciones *(aguahielo.cl)* runs challenging but exhilarating multi-day sea kayaking trips that take in the San Rafael glacier. Out of the water, Patagonia Adventure Expeditions *(patagoniaadventure expeditions.com)* runs adventurous ice trekking tours on and around the Campo de Hielo Norte, which last from five to ten days. While not often technically demanding, all tours do require excellent fitness levels.

Did You Know?

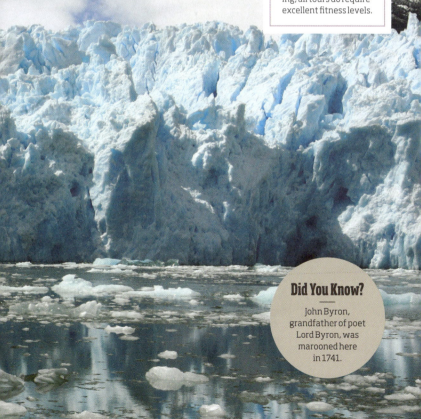

John Byron, grandfather of poet Lord Byron, was marooned here in 1741.

EXPERIENCE MORE

Chaitén

F3 100 miles (160 km) S of Puerto Montt

Located along Chile's Ruta 7, better known as the Carretera Austral *(p245)*, the Patagonian town of Chaitén was popular for its scenic blend of seaside and sierra until the Volcán Chaitén, barely 6 miles (10 km) away, erupted on May 2, 2008. This catastrophe was followed by massive flooding, which swept many houses off their foundations and buried several other houses in soggy ash.

A government attempt to relocate the dishomed residents proved unpopular, however, and many of them returned to the town. In spite of the volcano's presence, the area continues to attract many visitors with its hiking options and the nearby El Amarillo hot springs.

Ferries from Puerto Montt and the Chiloé archipelago arrive at Chaitén's port.

Palena

F3 160 miles (257 km) SE of Puerto Montt
O'Higgins 740; municipalidadpalena.cl

The village of Palena, close to the Argentine border, is named for the river that flows past it. It is notable for the Rodeo de Palena, which showcases Chile's *huaso* heritage. The main event at this rodeo involves costumed *huasos* on horseback, trying to pin a calf to a padded ring.

The Sendero de Chile, a network of trails across Chile, passes through Palena en route to the little-known Reserva Nacional Lago Palena, from where the road continues to the Argentine border.

Did You Know?

Chilean pirate Pedro Ñancúpel was finally captured in Melinka in 1886.

Melinka

F3 171 miles (276 km) SW of Puerto Montt

Off the mainland west of Palena, the Guaitecas archipelago comprises several tiny islands. Of these, Isla Ascensión is home to the fishing village of Melinka, the archipelago's main settlement. The village overlooks Golfo de Corcovado, known for its sizable blue whale population; these are often visible from shore. Melinka has some simple but comfortable lodgings and a few small restaurants.

Hornopirén

F3 73 miles (117 km) S of Puerto Montt

Scenically set on the edge of a serene fjord, Hornopirén is named for the towering,

→ A boat moored in the shallows of the glassy fjord bordering Hornopirén

↑ The Puyuhuapi fjord in the Ventisquero Sound, Patagonia, Aysen

5,150-ft- (1,570-m-) high Volcán Hornopirén that looms over the town. Hornopirén has been prosperous since the 19th century, despite being hard hit by the Volcán Chaitén eruption in 2008. Today, it is the gateway to Parque Nacional Hornopirén, 7 miles (12 km) to the northwest, which offers good wildlife-watching and hiking. Local launches docked at the ferry port take visitors to hot-spring pools nearby, and harborside vendors sell fresh fish.

Puyuhuapi

F3 269 miles (434 km) SE of Puerto Montt Otto Übel s/n; (067) 2325 244

Sitting on the edge of a scenic fjord, Puyuhuapi, unlike the newer settlements along the Carretera Austral, was founded by German immigrants from the Sudetenland (later, part of Czechoslovakia) in the 1930s. As a result, many houses in this area are distinctly Teutonic in style and the traditions of early settlers are still kept alive by the residents. Along with the building of wooden boats, artisanal fishery constitutes the main economic activity of the village.

Puyuhuapi also serves as an ideal base for those who want to explore nearby destinations such as the Parque Nacional Queulat *(p236)* and the adjacent Reserva Nacional Lago Rosselot. Also in the vicinity are the hot springs of the luxurious Puyuhuapi Lodge & Spa *(p242)*. The place also offers activities such as trekking, horseback riding, and boat rides.

Located 4 miles (6 km) south of Puyuhuapi, the **Termas Ventisquero de Puyuhuapi** has four thermal pools overlooking the sound, basic changing rooms, as well as a café.

EAT

Natour

Serving up hearty breakfasts, tasty sandwiches, and the best coffee in northern Patagonia, this food truck in a repurposed lime-green bus makes for a welcome stop on the road to Chaitén.

Playa Santa Bárbara, Chaitén (9) 4234 2799

Chocolateria Y Heladeria Artesanal Hornopirén

This family-run ice cream shop serves traditional Patagonian flavors, including sour cherry, Chilean guava, and red currant.

F3 Los Canelos, camino a Chaqueihua, Hornopirén 56 9 9810 4319

Termas Ventisquero de Puyuhuapi

Carretera Austral Sur km 6 10am-1pm & 2-5pm daily termasventisqueros puyuhuapi.cl

SAILING THE FJORDS OF NORTHERN PATAGONIA

The three-day voyage from Puerto Montt *(p209)* south to Puerto Natales *(p258)* aboard the Navimag ferry *(navimag.com)* is one of Northern Patagonia's top attractions. The journey passes through innumerable fjords, channels, and thousands of uninhabited islands; from the deck, passengers can admire an electrifying landscape - dense rainforests, serene lakes, massive glaciers, and snow-capped mountains. It is also possible to spot some wildlife, including the odd colony of sea lions and pods of dolphins. Entertainment on board includes talks on natural history and screenings of Chilean documentaries. The ferry passes the fishing village of Melinka and the fjord town of Puerto Eden, home to a few remaining Indigenous Yamana people.

Tranquil setting of Puyuhuapi Lodge & Spa, perched by the water's edge

Puyuhuapi Lodge & Spa

F4 277 miles (447 km) SE of Puerto Montt; Bahía Dorita s/n puyuhuapilodge.com

In a country that is well known for its hot-springs resorts, Puyuhuapi Lodge & Spa is one of the top choices. Located in a secluded and exceptional spot on the western side of the gorgeous Seno Ventisquero inlet – a place where the water from the sea, waterfalls, and thermal springs converges – the lodge blends smoothly into the fern- and flower-filled rainforest.

Puyuhuapi Lodge & Spa welcomes overnight guests and day guests. The complex is made up of charming units, the facades of which recall the shingled houses often seen on the islands of Chiloé. Rooms at the lodge feature polished wooden interiors and face the Bahía Dorita. Day visitors have access to three outdoor thermal pools and a café, while hotel guests can also use the heated indoor pool and enjoy a wide range of therapies and treatments. The onsite restaurant also features an exquisite menu, accompanied with a fine selection of Chilean wines.

An interesting variety of package options are available for overnight guests. These include a number of outdoor activities such as hiking through the Parque Nacional Queulat *(p236)*, fly-fishing on the nearby rivers, and a visit to the village of pretty fjordside Puyuhuapi *(p241)*. Most stays conclude with a day trip south to Parque Nacional Laguna San Rafael *(p238)*, sailing on the high-speed catamaran *Patagonia Express*, which passes through serene fjords and canals. The boat then returns north to Puerto Chacabuco, from where the lodge's guests are transferred to Coyhaique *(p244)* and its airport at Balmaceda.

HIDDEN GEM

Puerto Raúl Marín Balmaceda

North of Puyuhuapi Lodge & Spa is this gorgeous river island. Accessed by car ferry, the little-visited fishing village is one of the region's prettiest and well worth the detour.

Puerto Cisnes

F4 320 miles (520 km) SE of Puerto Montt Calle Sotomayor 191; municipalidadcisnes.cl

Sitting at the mouth of the eponymous river, Puerto Cisnes was founded in 1929 as a humble lumber factory. Today it is a pretty fishing village, with colorful boats lining its waterfront. The wooden Neo-Classical Biblioteca Pública Genaro Godoy, the village library, is a notable landmark. Its facade is adorned with figurines from Greek mythology. Puerto Cisnes is also the access point to the Parque Nacional Isla Magdalena, and local fishers shuttle visitors to this lushly forested park.

On the Carretera Austral, immediately east of the turnoff to Puerto Cisnes, is the Viaducto Piedra El Gato, a remarkable engineering achievement. Here the highway runs parallel to the river along the face of a nearly vertical granite pitch. There are several viewpoints on each approach to the viaduct which allow motorists to admire the structure and the landscape.

Puerto Chacabuco

F4 37 miles (60 km) W of Coyhaique

Located on the shores of an attractive natural harbor, Puerto Chacabuco is a small but lively port town, and the center of a thriving fishing industry. It superseded nearby Puerto Aisén as the Aisén region's main port in the 1940s; by this time, deforestation of Patagonia's forests had filled Río Aisén's outlet with sediments that made it impossible to anchor at Puerto Aisén.

Today, Puerto Chacabuco serves as the gateway to appealing nearby sights such as Parque Aikén del Sur and Parque Nacional Laguna San Rafael *(p238)*.

Puerto Edén

F5 272 miles (438 km) SW of Coyhaique

On Isla Wellington, in one of the rainiest sectors of the Pacific fjords, the town of Puerto Edén owes its origin to an air force initiative that contemplated a stop for seaplanes between Puerto Montt *(p209)* and Punta Arenas *(p256)*. However, the site soon became the last outpost of Kawéskar hunter-gatherers, who settled here after the air force abandoned it. Today, Puerto Edén is home to the few surviving members of the Kawéskar community, whose homes are connected by wooden walkways rather than roads. It is possible to purchase a sample of their crafts here. Weather permitting, the town is a stop for Transbordadora Austral Broom ferries that sail out of Puerto Natales *(p258)* to Caleta Yungay.

↑ Guanacos roaming in the Reserva Nacional Lago Tamango

Cochrane

F4 119 miles (192 km) S of Coyhaique
Dr. Steffens S/N; muni cochrane.cl/turismo

Situated at the western edge of the eponymous lake, the tidy town of Cochrane is the last service center on the Carretera Austral (also known as the Southern Highway). Visitors, notably motorists, will find the highway's last gasoline station here. Cochrane is also the gateway to **Sector Tamango** of **Parque Nacional Patagonia** *(p244)*, the southernmost part of the national park, situated 4 miles (6 km) northeast of town. This stunning protected area, which covers nearly 7 acres (3 ha), is a major sanctuary for the endangered huemul deer. From the entrance, hiking trails run to jade-hued Lago Cochrane and up Cerro Tamango.

Sector Tamango, Parque Nacional Patagonia
4 miles (6 km) E of Cochrane; CONAF, Río Neff 417 9am-6pm daily (book ahead)
conaf.cl

STAY

Lafquen Antu
Hostel-restaurant with stunning views of Isla Magdalena, home to Magellanic penguins. If you're lucky, you can spot dolphins.
F4 Avenida Arturo Prat s/n, Puerto Cisnes
56 67 234 6382
$$$

El Pangue
Stay in one of the informal hotels or cabañas here.
F3 Carretera Austral, km 240, Puerto Puyuhuapi
elpangue.cl
$$$

Nómades Hotel Boutique
This bijou option overlooks the river and has gorgeous, Patagonia-inspired interiors.
F4 Avenida Baquedano 84, Coyhaique
hotelnomades.cl
$$$

Patagon Backpackers
This hostel has budget dorms and double rooms.
F4 Pdte. Errázuriz 545, Coyhaique
patagonbackpackers.com
$$$

Rumbo Sur Hotel
An ideal base for those exploring the Southern Patagonia Ice Field.
F5 Carretera Austral, km 1240, Villa O'Higgins
rumbosurhotel.com
$$$

EAT

Mamma Gaucha

This pizzeria dishes up thin-crust offerings with creative toppings. It also has a selection of craft beers, and artwork that pays tribute to the region's gaucho heritage.

F4 Paseo Horn 47, Coyhaique Sun mammagaucha.cl

Casa Vieja

Housed in a converted residence, this cozy restaurant serves tasty Chilean food, with standout seafood dishes.

F4 Almte. Barroso 742, Coyhaique (067) 2212 010

15

Coyhaique

F4 286 miles (461 km) SE of Puerto Montt Bulnes 35; coyhaique.cl

Capital of Chile's Aisén region, and Northern Patagonia's only sizable city, Coyhaique is a labyrinth of concentric roads that encircle the pentagonal Plaza de Armas and change names on every other block. Despite this bewildering orientation, Coyhaique offers the region's best tourist infrastructure and easy access to destinations such as Lago Elizalde and the Reserva Nacional Río Simpson.

Though Coyhaique has no major attractions, it is the only town on the Carretera Austral that has a vibrant dining scene. Those who wish to explore the Carretera Austral can find rental cars in town. Visitors who are headed north or south should take the opportunity to withdraw money from ATMs while in the city.

Just beyond the city limits, the **Reserva Nacional Coyhaique** is a 10-sq-mile (27-sq-km) park with hiking trails through forests of coigüe and lenga. It has a campground and offers great panoramas of the city and its environs.

Reserva Nacional Coyhaique

Ruta 7 Norte 9am-4:30pm Tue-Sun (book ahead) conaf.cl

16

Parque Nacional Patagonia

F4 9am-6pm daily (book ahead) conaf.cl

The second groundbreaking donation of Doug and Kris Tompkins's private land to the Chilean state *(p232)*, Parque Nacional Patagonia has been rewilded from a cattle ranch to its present-day expanse of biodiversity. It features snowcapped

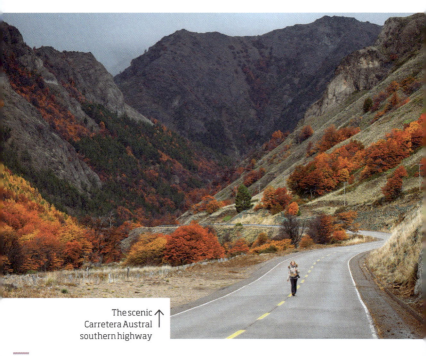

The scenic Carretera Austral southern highway

→ Marble Caves over Lago General Carrera, near Puerto Río Tranquilo

mountains dotted with forests of native lenga and ñirre beech trees, which slide into deep river valleys. The park is home to tracts of wild Patagonian steppe and vast glistening lakes.

The enormous 926-sq-mile (2,400-sq-km) park is divided into three sectors: Sector Tamango (accessed from Cochrane, *p243*), **Sector Jeinimeni** (accessed from Chile Chico, *p246*), and **Sector del Valle Chacabuco**. Hugging the Argentine border, the park is an important wildlife corridor, with guanaco, ñandú, puma, flamingoes, and the endangered huemul deer. Many species have been reintroduced as part of conservation work.

Sector del Valle Chacabuco offers a range of day hikes, including the moderate 14-mile (23-km) Lagunas Altas trail that goes up to Cerro Tamanguito and affords glorious valley views. There's also the Patagonia Park Museum and Visitor Center, which details the landscape and cultural history of the Chacabuco Valley through interactive exhibits. Multiday hikes that traverse the splendid mountain scenery connect this part of the park with Tamango and Jeinimeni.

Hugging the Argentine border, Parque Nacional Patagonia is an important wildlife corridor, with guanaco, ñandú, puma, flamingoes, and the endangered huemul deer.

Sector Jeinimeni

89 miles (143 km) SE of Coyhaique; Blest Gana 121, Chile Chico W conaf.cl

Sector del Valle Chacabuco

108 miles (173 km) S of Coyhaique; Avenida Ogana 1060, Coyhaique W conaf.cl

17 

Puerto Río Tranquilo

F4 78 miles (126 km) SW of Coyhaique

Lying on the western shores of the dazzlingly turquoise Lago General Carrera – Chile's largest lake and one that straddles the Argentine border – Puerto Río Tranquilo would be unremarkable if not for the village's access to the rainbow-colored Capillas de Mármol (Marble Caves). Rising out of the lake as otherworldly grottos, these remarkable caves have been eroded by the elements for over 6,000 years. It's possible to visit the caves and pass through passageways connecting them aboard a speedboat or kayak.

DRIVING THE CARRETERA AUSTRAL

Chile's Route 7 was constructed under the dictatorship to connect remote communities. It passed through Patagonia, running from Puerto Montt *(p209)* to Villa O'Higgins *(p247)*. A regular car is fine for most of the Carretera Austral, though a 4WD is useful for side trips around Patagonia. Most towns along the road have gasoline stations, but it's worth filling up regularly, just in case. Bring a spare tire and all the gear you need to attach it, as well as water, food, a sleeping bag, and a first aid kit, plus a supply of cash, as ATMs are rare in this region.

↑ Trekking across the Parque Nacional Cerro Castillo's craggy landscape

Parque Nacional Cerro Castillo

F4 28 miles (45 km) S of Coyhaique 9am-6pm daily (book ahead) conaf.cl

Covering over 517 sq miles (1,340 sq km) of rugged Andean landscape, Parque Nacional Cerro Castillo is named for the impressive 8,465-ft- (2,581-m-) high Cerro Castillo, which crowns this reserve. A popular destination for hikers, the reserve offers several hiking trails that snake through forests of lenga and around cascading waterfalls and icy glaciers. Wildlife spotted on these hikes includes huemul deer, puma, and fox.

The park's big attraction is the four-day Cerro Castillo Traverse, which takes in panoramic views of glacial-slung mountains and electric-blue lakes, with CONAF-operated campgrounds en route. Day hikers can reach the park's namesake pronged peak and lake below from a trail west of the tiny hamlet of Villa Cerro Castillo, which has basic restaurants and simple lodgings. Just south from this village is **Paredón de las Manos**, a natural rock shelter that is home to spectacular pre-Columbian paintings that date from 3,000 years ago.

Situated along the northern border of Parque Nacional Cerro Castillo, Lago Elizalde is a narrow lake that stretches for 15 miles (25 km), but is less than a mile (2 km) wide at any point. It is a popular spot for fishing, sailing, and kayaking.

Paredón de las Manos

 3 miles (5 km) S of Villa Cerro Castillo 10am-8pm daily

19 Chile Chico

F4 68 miles (110 km) SE of Coyhaique O'Higgins 333; (067) 2411 268

Close to the Argentine border, Chile Chico is part of a fruit-growing belt near Lago General Carrera. The town can either be approached by a scenic and precipitous road from the Carreta Austral, or via an equally exciting ferry ride across the vast, electric-blue lake.

Chile Chico dates from 1909, when Argentines crossed over to settle in this area. It became briefly famous in 1917, when the colonizers faced the ranchers in the War of Chile Chico. In 1991, the eruption of Volcán Hudson nearly smothered the area's apple and pear orchards. This past and a comprehensive overview of the area's natural history are well documented in the **Museo de la Casa de Cultura**, part of which occupies the grounded *Los Andes* steamer, which once toured the lake.

Museo de la Casa de Cultura

O'Higgins 496 (067) 2412 042 8am-1pm & 2-5pm Mon-Fri

Caleta Tortel

F5 172 km (277 miles) SW of Coyhaique

Located on an inlet off the Río Baker's Fiordo Mitchell, Caleta Tortel is arguably Patagonia's most picturesque village. The settlement was unreachable by road until 2003. It still has no streets as such, but rather boardwalks and staircases that link its bayside *palafitos* (overwater bungalows). These homesteads show the influence of the folk architecture of the Chiloé archipelago. Most of the buildings are made of

guaitecas cypress, the world's southernmost conifer species. The tourism industry here has grown, with more basic guesthouses and motorized boat trips to Glaciar Steffens and Glaciar Montt, which is part of Parque Nacional Bernardo O'Higgins *(p259)*. Hiking and horseback riding can also be arranged. The village is also an ideal base for visiting the nearby Reserva Nacional Katalalixar, which can also be reached by basic motor launches.

Río Baker

F5 146 miles (235 km) S of Coyhaique

Flowing between Caleta Tortel and Lago Bertrand, the 116-mile- (170-km-) long Río Baker is Chile's largest river in terms of volume. Owing to its flow, and the mountainous terrain through which it runs, this wild and scenic river has long been a candidate for a massive hydroelectric project; however, the river has not been dammed due to environmental concerns. The area just south of Puerto Bertrand, especially at the stunning confluence of the Baker and the Río Nef, is a paradise for campers, hikers, rafters, fly-fishers, and other recreationists. Rafting trips can be arranged in tiny Puerto Bertrand, north of Cochrane *(p243)*.

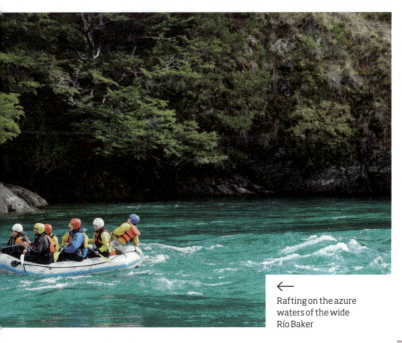

Villa O'Higgins

F5 204 miles (328 km) S of Coyhaique
Plaza de Armas; villaohiggins.com

Beyond Cochrane, services are nearly non-existent on the last 120 miles (200 km) of the Carretera Austral. A free ferry shuttle from Puerto Yungay – near the Río Bravo – takes visitors to the last stretch of the highway, which terminates at Villa O'Higgins.

This village dates from 1966 and is named for the Chilean Bernardo O'Higgins *(p259)*. The village has grown thanks to the arrival of the Carretera Austral *(p245)* in 1999 and the tourism this has brought with it. Surrounded by wild mountain scenery, and within sight of the Campo del Hielo Sur (Southern Patagonian Ice Field), Villa O'Higgins offers ample hiking trails, plus day trips out to the frequently calving Glaciar O'Higgins, part of the Southern Patagonian Ice Field. It is a popular destination for cyclists and trekkers who wish to cross over to Argentina's El Chaltén. There are companies that navigate Lake O'Higgins and connect to El Chaltén. All voyages are subject to weather conditions and require prior planning and confirmation.

Did You Know?

The area around Villa O'Higgins was the site of a short-lived English settlement from 1914 to 1916.

←

Rafting on the azure waters of the wide Río Baker

Torres del Paine touching the clouds

SOUTHERN PATAGONIA AND TIERRA DEL FUEGO

An archipelagic labyrinth, Southern Patagonia is a dramatic wilderness of emerald fjords, rugged peaks, and windswept prairies. Separated from the mainland by the Strait of Magellan, Tierra del Fuego stretches across largely unpopulated territory to Cape Horn, the tip of South America. The original inhabitants of Southern Patagonia and Tierra del Fuego were the Ona Selk'nam, Yaghan, Tehuelche, and Kawésqar communities, who are now greatly reduced in number.

In 1520, Portuguese navigator Ferdinand Magellan became the first European to discover the area. However, permanent settlements were not established until the 19th century, when missionaries, adventurers, and merchants arrived from Spain, Britain, Croatia, and northern Chile.

The late 19th century witnessed a rise in prosperity as a result of sheep ranching. A thriving shipping industry also developed, benefiting from the navigable Strait of Magellan, which served as a passage between the Pacific and Atlantic until the opening of the Panama Canal in 1914. Today, sheep farming, along with oil extraction and tourism, are the mainstays of the economy.

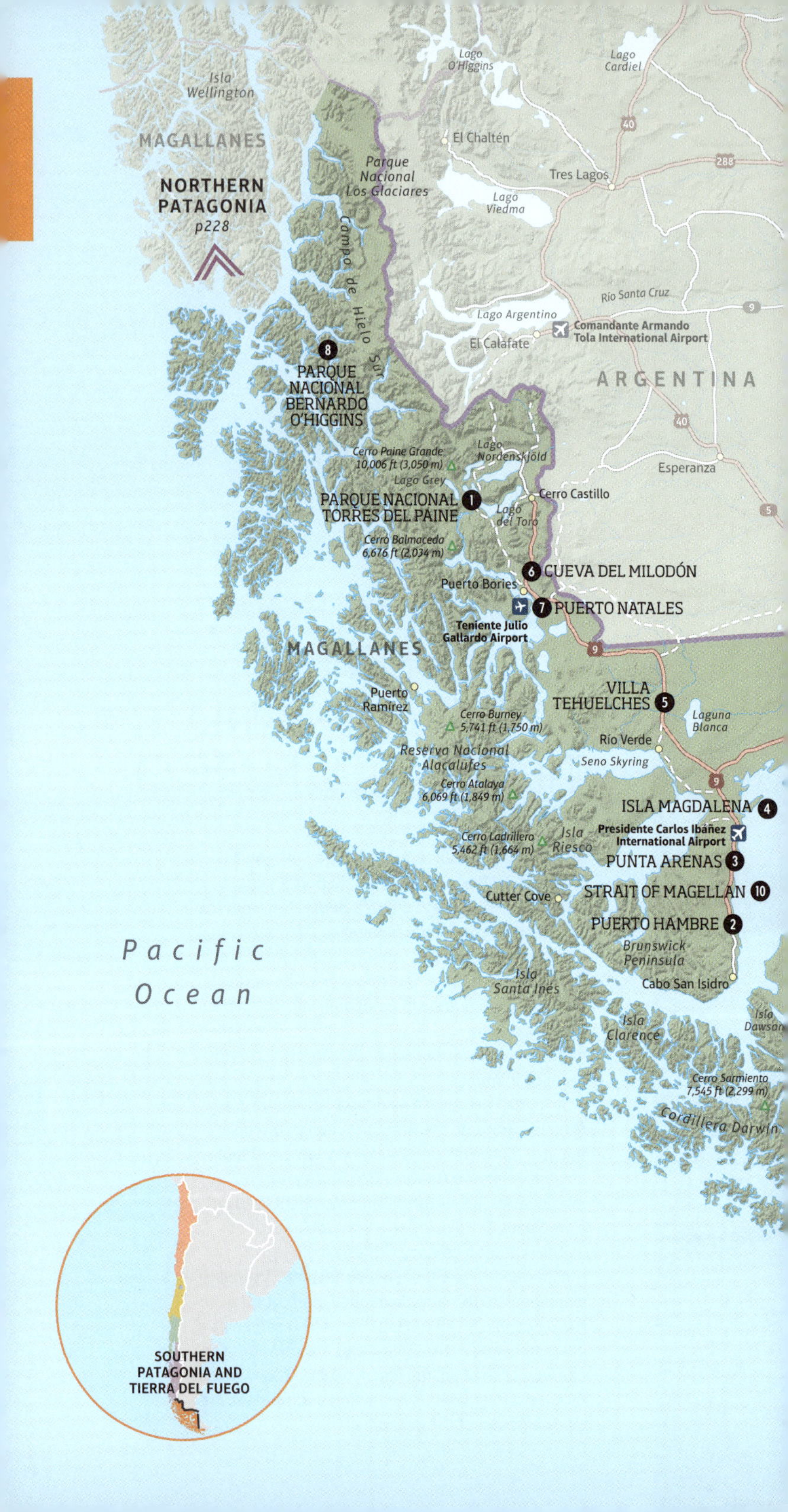

Isla Wellington
MAGALLANES
NORTHERN PATAGONIA
p228
Lago O'Higgins
Lago Cardiel
40
El Chaltén
288
Parque Nacional Los Glaciares
Tres Lagos
Lago Viedma
Campo de Hielo Sur
Río Santa Cruz
9
Lago Argentino
Comandante Armando Tola International Airport
El Calafate
8
PARQUE NACIONAL BERNARDO O'HIGGINS
ARGENTINA
40
Lago Nordenskjöld
Cerro Paine Grande 10,006 ft (3,050 m)
Lago Grey
Esperanza
1
PARQUE NACIONAL TORRES DEL PAINE
Cerro Castillo
Lago del Toro
5
Cerro Balmaceda 6,676 ft (2,034 m)
6
CUEVA DEL MILODÓN
Puerto Bories
7
PUERTO NATALES
Teniente Julio Gallardo Airport
9
MAGALLANES
Puerto Ramírez
VILLA TEHUELCHES
5
Laguna Blanca
Cerro Burney 5,741 ft (1,750 m)
Río Verde
Reserva Nacional Alacalufes
Seno Skyring
9
Cerro Atalaya 6,069 ft (1,849 m)
ISLA MAGDALENA
4
Cerro Ladrillero 5,462 ft (1,664 m)
Isla Riesco
Presidente Carlos Ibáñez International Airport
PUNTA ARENAS
3
Cutter Cove
STRAIT OF MAGELLAN
10
PUERTO HAMBRE
2
Brunswick Peninsula
Pacific Ocean
Isla Santa Inés
Cabo San Isidro
Isla Dawson
Isla Clarence
Cerro Sarmiento 7,545 ft (2,299 m)
Cordillera Darwin

SOUTHERN PATAGONIA AND TIERRA DEL FUEGO
Must See
1 Parque Nacional Torres del Paine
Experience More
2 Puerto Hambre
3 Punta Arenas
4 Isla Magdalena
5 Villa Tehuelches
6 Cueva del Milodón
7 Puerto Natales
8 Parque Nacional Bernardo O'Higgins
9 Cape Horn
10 Strait of Magellan
11 Puerto Williams
12 Porvenir
Río Chico
Puerto San Julián
Río Chico
Comandante Luis Piedrabuena
Parque Nacional Monte León
Coy Aike
Río Gallegos
Piloto Civil Norberto Fernández International Airport
Monte Aymond
Punta Delgada
Puerto Espora
Cerro Sombrero
Cullén
Capitán Fuentes Martínez Airport
12 PORVENIR
Bahía Inútil
Camerón
Tierra del Fuego
Puerto Yartau
Puerto Arturo
Lago Ofhidro
Lago Blanco
Bahía San Sebastián
San Sebastián
Estancia Sara
Río Grande
ARGENTINA
Tolhuin
Atlantic Ocean
Cerro Darwin 8,162 ft (2,487 m)
Cerro de Saboya 6,889 ft (2,099 m)
Ushuaia International Airport
Cerro Castor
Ushuaia
Sierra Lucio López
Bahía Aguirre
Beagle Channel
11 PUERTO WILLIAMS
Guardia Marina Zañartu Airport
Isla Gordon
Bahía Cook
Isla Hoste
Isla Navarino
Península Hardy
Isla Nueva
Isla Lennox
Islas Wollaston
Isla Hornos
9 CAPE HORN
0 kilometers 75
0 miles 75
N

PARQUE NACIONAL TORRES DEL PAINE

F6 43 miles (70 km) NW of Puerto Natales From Punta Arenas From Punta Arenas or Puerto Natales 7am-9pm daily (book ahead) CONAF Administration Headquarters: Laguna Amarga gate; parquetorresdelpaine.cl

Encompassing sweeping mountains, almost vertical soaring granite pillars, dazzling glaciers, glistening azure lakes, and sprawling emerald forests, Parque Nacional Torres del Paine is undoubtably one of South America's most beautiful national parks.

Torres del Paine (Towers of Blue) is a UNESCO World Biosphere Reserve. It is named for the Paine massif, a cluster of metamorphic ridges and needles between the Southern Patagonian Ice Field and the Patagonian steppe. The name itself is a mix of Spanish and Indigenous Patagonian words: *paine* being the Tehuelche term for "blue," a color frequently seen throughout the area in the form of turquoise glaciers, icebergs, rivers, and lakes. The park is Chile's trekking mecca, with numerous day hikes as well as three- to ten-day backpacking routes. The national park is dominated by the Paine massif, which includes the Cuernos formation of mountains, the Torres del Paine peaks, and the park's highest summit – the 10,006-ft- (3,050-m-) high Cerro Paine Grande.

INSIDER TIP

When to Visit

The park is busiest during the Jan & Feb summer months, while temperatures can plummet well below zero during the winter (Jun–Sep), so the best times to visit are Oct–Dec, Mar, and Apr.

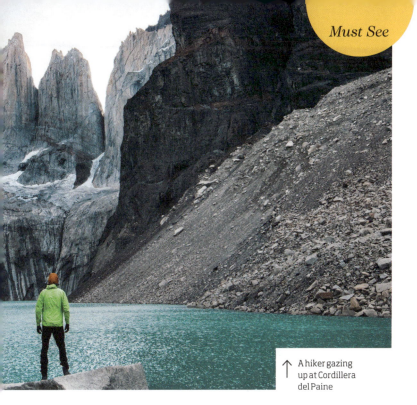

A hiker gazing up at Cordillera del Paine

Guanacos can be spotted on Torres del Paine's grassy tundra

Apart from rugged peaks, there are many other microclimates and geological features throughout the park. These include glaciers, granite spires, beech forests, lakes, and steppe, which can be explored on foot, by vehicle, aboard a catamaran, or on horseback. The park offers a series of campgrounds and *refugios*, in addition to several hotels.

The southern road from Puerto Natales is the most beautiful route into the park, and leads to the CONAF Administration Headquarters. This center gives a compulsory talk on park safety and provides general information about the park as well. It also has educational displays on the flora, fauna, and geological features of the sanctuary. A small kiosk sells maps, books, and sundry items.

WILDLIFE WATCH

Although best known for its spectacular scenery and dazzling landscapes, Parque Nacional Torres del Paine is also incredibly biodiverse, as shown by the classification as a UNESCO World Biosphere Reserve. There are 25 species of mammals, most notably gray and red foxes, guanacos, hard-to-spot huemuls (an endangered deer), and pumas. The park is even richer in birdlife, with around 120 species, including Andean condors, Chilean flamingos, Magellanic woodpeckers, black-chested buzzard-eagles, and Darwin's rheas (large flightless birds that are similar to ostriches and emus).

EXPLORING PARQUE NACIONAL TORRES DEL PAINE

Access to the park is by road from Puerto Natales, or by boat along the Río Serrano. There are three entrances, all manned by CONAF ranger stations. Within its boundaries, 155 miles (250 km) of the sanctuary is covered by marked trails. The longest is the Circuito Grande, a hike that requires eight to ten days and takes visitors to the Paine massif, passing by the lakes of Paine, Dickson, and Grey. It joins up on day five with the park's most popular trail, the W, which continues on to the Valle del Francés and the Torres peaks.

The W

A medium-difficult trail, The W is the most popular multiday trek. Most trekkers begin at the Las Torres, a ranch-style complex with campgrounds, hostels, and a hotel, the Hotel Las Torres. The seven- to eight-hour round trip hike to the iconic Torres del Paine is strenuous, first traversing the beech forests of the Valle Ascencio and ending with a steep, 45-minute hike up a boulder field to the Torres, three stunning granite towers that rise in front of a glacial tarn. The W continues from Hotel Las Torres along the shores of the turquoise Lago Nordenskjold and skirts the flank of the park's famous two-toned Cuernos. About 7 miles (11 km) along this route are the hostel and campgrounds of Refugio Los Cuernos. Trekkers may spend the night here or, if camping, continue onward 4 miles (6 km) to the Valle del Francés and its Campamento Italiano. The trail up and into the Valle del Francés is about 5 miles (8 km), climbing high into the valley ringed with granite peaks and sweeping views of the Patagonian steppe. From the base of the Valle del Francés, it is some 5 miles (8 km) to the Refugio Paine Grande and campground and to the docking area for a catamaran that crosses Lago Pehoé to the Pudeto sector. The trail then heads north for the final leg of The W, 7 miles (11 km) to Refugio Grey. Visitors can arrange trekking excursions to Glaciar Grey. Most trekkers return to Lago Pehoé and take the catamaran to Pudeto, from where transportation is available to Puerto Natales.

Circuito Grande

For a thorough exploration of the park, hikers should consider the Circuito

SHORTER HIKES

Mirador las Torres
11 miles (17 km): This popular trail ends with superb views of the park's famous granite *torres* (towers).

Sendero Mirador Cuernos
4 miles (6 km): An easy hike from the Pudeto catamaran dock to reach a viewpoint of the dramatic Los Cuernos peaks.

Mirador Ferrier
1.2 miles (2 km): A steep trail leads up to Mirador Ferrier, where there are views of glaciers, lakes, and mountains.

↑ Hikers tackling the beautiful John Gardner Pass

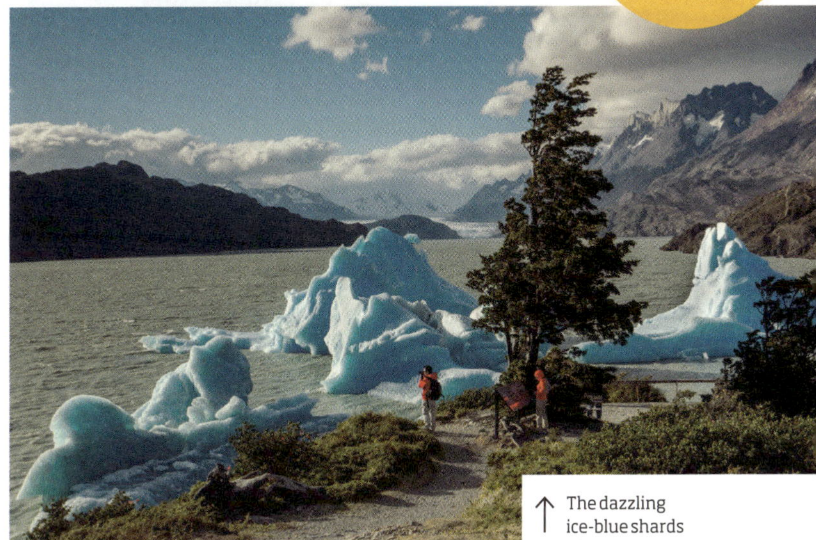

↑ The dazzling ice-blue shards of Glaciar Grey

Grande (Big Circuit Trail), which circles the Paine massif and takes roughly eight to ten days. The trail is often undertaken counterclockwise, starting at Hotel Las Torres or the Laguna Amarga ranger station. The Hotel Las Torres trail begins with a four-hour hike through the Valle Ascencio to Campamento Serón. It continues for 12 miles (19 km) to Refugio Dickson, which offers views of Glaciar Dickson. The trail grows increasingly strenuous. About 6 miles (9 km) through forest and swampy terrain from Refugio Dickson lies the campground Los Perros. The 7-mile (12-km) climb to John Gardner Pass can be difficult during bad weather. It's advisable to wait a few days when crossing, particularly if there are dangerous winds. Views of Glaciar Grey and the Southern Patagonian Ice Field from the pass are the highlights. Hikers can stay at the wonderful Campamento Paso, as the next 6 miles (10 km) to Refugio Grey are quite difficult. Hikers then join the W trek heading in a counterclockwise direction for the final few days of the hike.

Sendero Pingo-Zapata

This infrequently visited trail is good for bird-watching, and has an easy-medium difficulty level. The trail begins at the Lago Grey CONAF station and follows the Río Pingo past views of the granite walls of the Paine massif. After about five hours, visitors arrive at a lookout point to view Glaciar Zapata and its rows of glacial moraine. A guide is required for this hike.

Glaciar Grey

Although its receding rate has increased, Glaciar Grey is still one of the largest and most easily accessed glaciers in Patagonia. The icebergs that break off from the glacier float to the end of Lago Grey. These can be seen along a short walk on flat beach from the Grey sector's ranger station, near Hotel Lago Grey. At the end of the beach, reached by a half-hour walk, a peninsula offers vistas of Glaciar Grey in the distance. A popular journey here is aboard the catamaran *Grey III*, which leaves Hotel Lago Grey four times daily and sails to the face of the glacier.

STAY

EcoCamp Patagonia
Camping in distinctive geodesic domes.

Sector Las Torres, Parque Nacional Torres del Paine ecocamp.travel

$$$

Tierra Patagonia
Blends into its surroundings and offers views of the Torres del Paine massif.

Lake Sarmiento, on the edge of Parque Nacional Torres del Paine tierrahotels.com

$$$

Explora Patagonia
Defines the concept of "rooms with a view," thanks to the vistas.

Sector Lago Pehoé, Parque Nacional Torres del Paine explora.com

$$$

Admiring the view from an outcrop on the edge of Punta Arenas

EXPERIENCE MORE

2  

Puerto Hambre

G7 31 miles (50 km) S of Punta Arenas 10am-7pm daily parquedelestrecho.cl

The first attempt to establish a settlement on the Strait of Magellan took place in 1584 when a Spanish captain left several hundred colonists about 20 miles (50 km) south of Punta Arenas. He called the settlement Rey Felipe, but it was changed to Puerto Hambre (Port Hunger) in 1587 by British captain Thomas Cavendish, who landed here to find just one survivor – the rest had starved or succumbed to the elements. The traces of these ruins are now considered a national monument.

About 2 miles (3 km) to the south is the national monument Fuerte Bulnes, set up in 1843 by colonists from Chiloé who were later transplanted to present-day Punta Arenas in 1848. This became the second, and first successful, colonization of the strait, and the site offers an interesting look into the colonists' lives.

3

Punta Arenas

G7 153 miles (247 km) S of Puerto Natales  **José Fagnano 643; patagonia-chile.com**

The capital of the Magallanes region, Punta Arenas was initially a penal colony and a disciplinary center for military personnel. In the late 19th and early 20th centuries, it drew thousands of Europeans escaping World War I and seeking fortunes in sheep ranching, gold and coal mining, and the shipping industry. Today, the best place to begin exploring the town is at the Plaza Benjamín Muñoz Gamero, the main square, with the Magellan Monument at its center. The ritual is for visitors to kiss the toe of the Tehuelche statue on the monument, for good luck or, as legend goes, to ensure they return to Punta Arenas.

Travelers can appreciate the staggering wealth of the Braun-Menéndez family – owners of mammoth ranching operations in the early 20th century – at the **Museo Regional de Magallanes**. Dating from 1903, the edifice is preserved with its original furniture and finery, which was imported from Europe. The museum also features a room dedicated to the ethnographic history of the region. Another mansion of the Braun-Menéndez family, the Palacio Sara Braun, can be seen on Plaza Benjamín Muñoz Gamero, and is home to a hotel.

Also of interest is the **Museo Regional Salesiano Maggiorino Borgatello**, which was founded in 1893 and charts the history, ecology, and anthropology of the Magallanes region. Displays include stuffed local fauna, pickled marine life, and geological samples collected by Salesian missionaries of the early 20th century, as well as ethnographic exhibits relating to the Kawéskar and Selk'nam peoples, and a floor devoted to the industrial history of Punta Arenas.

The **Cementerio Municipal Sara Braun** is the site of many tombs belonging to Punta Arenas' powerful families, along with the graves of immigrants from Scotland and Croatia.

On the northwest side of the cemetery, the *Indiecito* (Little Indian) statue represents deceased Indigenous groups and is intended to be a totem for good luck.

Located on the banks of Magellan Strait, **Nao Victoria Museum** features replica ships of the great explorers of this region. Visitors can climb aboard Darwin's HMS *Beagle*, and Magellan's *Nao Victoria*, but most impressive is the replica of the lifeboat used by Anglo-Irish Antarctic explorer Ernest Shackleton and his men while navigating the Antarctic Ocean.

The fascinating **Museo de Historia Natural Río Seco** lies 3 miles (5 km) north along the Strait of Magellan. Operated by a team of biologists and artists with the aim to promote conservation, this tiny museum is packed with the skeletons of close to 100 marine and land-based species native to Chile, including the huge condor, Chile's national bird.

Museo Regional de Magallanes
H. de Magallanes 949 For restoration museodemagallanes.gob.cl

Museo Regional Salesiano Maggiorino Borgatello
Avenida M. Bulnes 336 10am-12:30pm & 3-5:30pm Tue-Sat museomaggiorinoborgatello.cl

Cementerio Municipal Sara Braun
Avenida M. Bulnes 29 8am-7pm daily turismo.cementeriosarabraun.cl

Nao Victoria Museum
Off Ruta 9 (09) 9640 0772 8:30am-8pm daily

Museo de Historia Natural Río Seco
Juan Williams 012812, Río Seco 9:30am-12:30pm Fri mhnrioseco.com

Isla Magdalena

G6 22 miles (35 km) NE of Punta Arenas 9am-6pm daily (book ahead) conaf.cl

The 2-hour boat trip to Isla Magdalena is worth the effort with the island hosting up to 60,000 breeding pairs of Magellanic penguins. Each pair produces two chicks November–March, bringing the population to some 240,000 penguins. A roped walkway runs across the area, and an old lighthouse acts as a ranger and research station. Adult penguins take turns guarding the nest and fishing.

Magellanic penguins posing on the shore of Isla Magdalena

EAT

Damiana Elena
In a Magellanic house, this spot has a great wine list and menu.
G7 Magallanes 341, Punta Arenas (061) 2222 818 Sun, Mon
$$

Cangrejo Rojo
A must-visit for seafood lovers. Try the *chupe de centolla* (king crab stew).
F6 Santiago Bueras 782, Puerto Natales (061) 2412 436
$$$

The Singular
Sweeping fjordside views, great wines, and gourmet Patagonian dishes delight here.
F6 Puerto Bories s/n, Puerto Natales thesingular.com
$$$

DRINK

Taberna Club de la Unión
A characterful bar in the basement of the Palacio Sara Braun.
G7 Plaza Benjamín Muñoz Gamero 716, Punta Arenas (061) 2222 777 Sun

5

Villa Tehuelches

G6 96 miles (154 km) SE of Puerto Natales

The pocket-sized outpost of Villa Tehuelches was founded in 1967 as a service center for the regional population. This village is famous for the annual Festival de la Esquila, or Shearing Festival, which draws hundreds of people from across Patagonia and features rodeos, sheep-shearing competitions, and lamb barbecues.

Cueva del Milodón

F6 15 miles (24 km) NW of Puerto Natales 8am-6pm daily cuevadelmilodon.cl

Arguably the most important paleontological and archaeological site in Southern Patagonia, the Cueva del Milodón is named for the now-extinct ground sloth, or milodón *(Mylodon darwinii)*, whose partial remains were discovered here by Hermann Eberhard in 1895.

Did You Know?

A scrap of milodón skin provided the inspiration for Bruce Chatwin's epic travelog *In Patagonia*.

The milodón, measuring up to 10 ft (3 m) in height and weighing around 400 pounds (181 kg), roamed Patagonia until the Pleistocene period, about 10,000 years ago. Today, a replica of this sloth dominates the cave entrance, and its fossil remains are displayed in a visitors' center.

Puerto Natales

F6 1,268 miles (2,040 km) S of Santiago Pedro Montt 19; patagonia-chile.com

Puerto Natales is a windswept town backed by the Sierra Dorotea range. The town overlooks the Seno Última Esperanza (Last Hope Sound) – so called because this was the site that Spanish explorer Juan Ladrilleros considered his last hope while attempting to locate the Strait of Magellan in 1557. The region was originally inhabited by the Indigenous Tehuelche and Kawéskar tribes; the present town was only founded in 1911 when a sheep-ranching boom led to an influx of European immigrants, as well as of people from the Chiloé archipelago. Today, the economy of Puerto Natales is primarily based on its flourishing tourism industry.

The town's **Museo Histórico Municipal** features displays of antique tools and household items, as well as photographs of the vanished Kawéskar and Aónikenk Indigenous communities. The main road, Avenida Pedro Montt, affords splendid views of glacier-topped peaks and the aqua sound, which is dotted with cormorants, black-necked swans, and other birds.

Puerto Natales serves as the main gateway to Southern Patagonia's famous Parque Nacional Torres del Paine *(p252)*, and caters to numerous travelers who stop here en route to the park. Several tour

The overhanging lip of paleontological site Cueva del Milodón ↑

↑ Epic Glaciar Balmaceda, Parque Nacional Bernardo O'Higgins

operators offer activities such as ice trekking, cruises to a glacier, and horseback riding.

Situated 6 miles (10 km) from Puerto Natales, Mirador Dorotea is a moderate trek of 2,625 ft (800 m). After crossing the forest, visitors can enjoy breathtaking views from the summit of Puerto Natales, surrounding mountains, and the glacial valley. The excursion can also be done on horseback.

Just north of Puerto Natales is Puerto Bories, site of the Frígorifico Bories, an old cold-storage plant that was part of the Sociedad Explotadora de Tierra del Fuego, once Patagonia's largest sheep-ranching operation. Today, the Frígorifico Bories is a national monument and has been converted into the luxurious The Singular hotel. In the transit areas of the museum-hotel, antique machinery is still intact and visible.

A short distance northwest of Puerto Prat, Estancia Puerto Consuelo was founded by German immigrant Hermann Eberhard. One of the earliest ranches in Chilean Patagonia, the *estancia* offers stunning views of Parque Nacional Torres del Paine and is typically visited on tours to nearby glaciers.

Museo Histórico Municipal

Manuel Bulnes 285 · 9am-6pm Tue-Fri, 3-7pm Sat · registromuseoschile.cl

---

Parque Nacional Bernardo O'Higgins

F6 · 90 miles (145 km) NW of Puerto Natales · 9am-6pm (book ahead) · CONAF, Manuel Baquedano 847, Puerto Natales; conaf.cl

Created in 1969, Parque Nacional Bernardo O' Higgins is bordered on the east by the mammoth ice field Campo de Hielo Sur and comprises a maze of small islands, fjords, and channels. It is Chile's largest national park, but the lack of land access also makes it one of the least visited. The park is reached after a full-day catamaran cruise from Puerto Natales. Retracing the 16th-century voyage of Juan Ladrilleros through the Seno Última Esperanza, the trip offers spectacular views and includes a visit to the hanging Glaciar Balmaceda and a short trek to the iceberg-laden lagoon of Glaciar Serrano. From the lagoon, kayaks and dinghies navigate up the Río Serrano through a little-known route marked by untrammeled scenery of glaciers, peaks, and dense forest, and ends at Parque Nacional Torres del Paine administration center. This trip can also be made in the opposite direction from Torres del Paine.

BERNARDO O'HIGGINS

Born in Chillán, Bernardo O'Higgins (1778-1842) was the illegitimate son of an Irish officer in the Spanish army and a local woman. His father rose to be Viceroy of Peru, and Bernardo was educated in Europe, where he met revolutionaries intent on Spain's overthrow in Latin America. By 1814, O'Higgins was heading Chile's independence struggle, and eventually became the post-Independence leader.

STAY

The Singular Patagonia

Transformed from a crumbling slaughter-house, this top-end hotel has glorious views of Last Hope Sound.

F6 Puerto Bories s/n, Puerto Natales thesingular.com

$$$

Bories House

This Anglo-Chilean enterprise has turned a traditional *estancia* into a modern hotel, with a welcoming fire blazing in the dining room.

F6 Puerto Bories 13-B, Puerto Natales puertobories house.com

Lakutaia Lodge

A luxury lodge on the Beagle Channel, this is a great base for outdoor activities in the area.

H7 Seno Lauta s/n, Puerto Williams lakutaia.com

$$$

Cape Horn

H7 437 miles (703 km) SE of Punta Arenas

The southernmost "point" of the Americas, Cape Horn, or the Horn as it is often called, actually comprises a group of islands that form the Parque Nacional Cabo de Hornos. Cape Horn was discovered by Europeans during a Dutch sailing expedition in 1616 and named for the town of Hoorn in the Netherlands. From the 18th century until the opening of the Panama Canal in 1914, it served as an important trade route for cargo ships.

The waters around the Cape Horn islands are among the most treacherous in the world, due in particular to the williwaws, blasts of wind that appear out of nowhere. Inhospitable sailing conditions make it difficult to reach the very tip, and Isla Hornos, to its northwest, is usually as far as people can go. Moss-covered Isla Hornos is home to the albatross monument, which honors sailors who died while sailing around the Horn. The island has a rich birdlife, and dolphins and whales can be seen offshore.

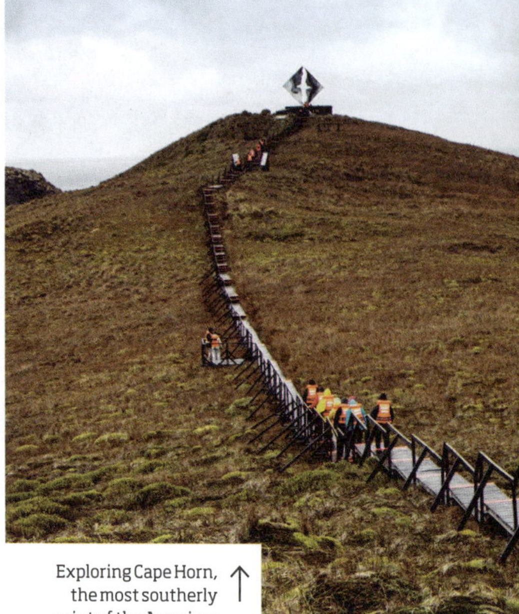

Exploring Cape Horn, the most southerly point of the Americas

Strait of Magellan

G7 62 miles (100 km) S of Punta Arenas

A sea route linking the Atlantic with the Pacific Ocean, this strait is named for Ferdinand Magellan, the first European to discover the passage in 1520. It separates Tierra del Fuego from the Chilean mainland, and offers a safer route for ships rounding the South American continent than the Drake Passage farther south. Until the opening of the Panama Canal, the Strait of Magellan served as the principal route for steamships traveling between Europe and the Americas.

The strait is a breeding and feeding ground for humpback whales, sea lions, and other marine fauna during summer months. Breeding colonies are easily spotted at Isla Carlos III, near the strait's western entrance. The waters surrounding the island comprise the 259-sq-mile (670-sq-km) Parque Marino Francisco Coloane, Chile's first marine reserve. Whale-watching boat trips to Isla Carlos III include a stop at the Cabo San Isidro, which has a lighthouse dating from 1904. Once used to guide ships through the Strait, the lighthouse has now been converted into a lodge with a small museum that charts the history of the region's Indigenous groups such as the Selk'nam and Yaghan communities.

11

Puerto Williams

H7 182 miles (293 km) SE of Punta Arenas O'Higgins 189; imcabodehornos.cl

The solitary town on Isla Navarino, Puerto Williams is the capital of the Magallanes and Chilean Antarctic region, and the southernmost town in the world. Founded in 1953 as a Chilean naval base, it was later named Puerto Williams in honor of English-born officer Juan Williams, who captured the Strait of Magellan for Chile in 1843. The town is backed by the granite peaks of Dientes de Navarino, a rugged area that offers some of south Chile's most challenging trekking. The town's main attraction, the Museo Martín Gusinde, is dedicated to an Austrian anthropologist and clergyman (1886–1969) who did research on the region's Yaghan and Selk'nam communities.

Just east of Puerto Williams, Villa Ukika is home to the few surviving members of the Yaghan community.

12

Porvenir

G7 25 miles (40 km) SE of Punta Arenas muniporvenir.cl

Windswept Porvenir first grew as an outpost for miners working in the Baquedano mountain range during a local gold rush in the mid-19th century. During the 20th century boom in wool production, the town acted as a service center for the region's sheep *estancias* (ranches). Today, Porvenir is the capital of the Tierra del Fuego province, and its main highlight is the **Museo Municipal Fernando Cordero Rusque**. The museum has archaeological and anthropological exhibits on the Indigenous cultures that once inhabited the region. North of the museum, the Cementerio Municipal features antique mausoleums in the shade of cypress trees pruned into cylindrical shapes. On Avenida Manuel Señoret, Parque del Recuerdo displays antique machinery and vehicles from the 19th century, while the Plaza de las Américas features a monument constructed to commemorate the Selk'nam people, the original inhabitants of the region.

Museo Municipal Fernando Cordero Rusque

Padre Mario Zavattaro 402 (061) 2581 800 8:30am-5pm Mon-Sat, 11am-4pm Sun

→

A monument honoring the Selk'nam people in Porvenir

SOUTHERNMOST PRISON

Following the military coup of 1973 *(p48)*, the Pinochet regime sent deposed government leaders to the tiny Isla Dawson in the Strait of Magellan. Its remote location made escaping nearly impossible, and prisoners were subjected to Antarctic weather and truly awful living conditions. Their experience was documented in the 2009 movie *Dawson: Isla 10*. Many of those who survived played a major role in the restoration of democracy in Chile.

VISITING ARGENTINA

In a few hours, travelers to Chile's Parque Nacional Torres del Paine can visit the Argentine town El Calafate, a tourism-oriented spot that forms the base for visits to the Glaciar Perito Moreno and Los Glaciares National Park. Cruise ship passengers can stop over in the Argentine port city of Ushuaia, a phenomenally beautiful town backed by jagged peaks.

Parque Nacional Los Glaciares

227 miles (336 km) NW of Puerto Natales; 50 miles (80 km) W of El Calafate El Calafate El Calafate Bajada de Palma 44, El Calafate; losglaciares.com

Created in 1937, Parque Nacional Los Glaciares is an add-on destination favored by many of the travelers to Parque Nacional Torres del Paine, as there are two border crossings in close proximity. Named after the mesmerizing glaciers that cascade down from the Southern Patagonian Ice Field, this reserve is Argentina's second-largest national park and a trekking and climbing mecca.

The park, which is for the most part inaccessible, covers 1.6 million acres (650,000 ha) of rugged mountains, turquoise lakes, glaciers, and thundering rivers. Dominating the whole park is the Fitz Roy massif, a towering cluster of granite needles. Trekkers to this area can take part in camping-based trips over days, or they can opt to go on shorter day hikes that last between two and six hours. Trips begin at the mountain village of El Chaltén, which is a collection of hotels and restaurants that sprang up in the 1990s along the Río Las Vueltas.

The major crowd-puller at Parque Nacional Los Glaciares is the Glaciar Perito Moreno, which flows roughly 18 miles (29 km) before making contact with a peninsula that provides visitors with ideal lookout points from which to view the glacial marvel. The glacier is one of the few in Patagonia that is not receding, although it cannot grow far either as its terminus is obstructed by land. Every several years, pressure that has built up from the ice's contact with land causes the glacier to calve in a crashing fury, a sight travelers aspire to see when visiting this park. Several agencies offer trekking tours, which take visitors on the glacier with crampons and sturdy ropes. There are also walks and boat rides to some of the other neighboring glaciers of Upsala and Spegazzini and around floating icebergs.

Los Glaciares is accessed from El Calafate, which is a tourism-based town on the shore of Lago Argentino, a five-hour drive from Puerto Natales, Chile. Old *estancias* here have been converted into hotels and restaurants and give visitors a little taste of Patagonian gaucho life and gaucho culture.

INSIDER TIP
Road trip

There are various companies which rent out 4WD and other off-road vehicles. Take a road trip southbound between Chile and Argentina, to see more of the beautiful landscape.

↓ Capturing the ice-blue shards of Glaciar Perito Moreno

Sea lions relaxing on the Beagle Channel, near Ushuaia

Ushuaia

351 miles (564 km) SE of El Calafate Prefectura Naval Argentina 470; turismoushuaia.com

Argentina's southernmost city, Ushuaia is the jumping off point for Antarctica trips and a wildlife-watching destination. Boat companies offer penguin and sea-lion spotting tours on the Beagle Channel.

The city is named in the language of the region's first Indigenous inhabitants, the Yaghan; Ushuaia translates as deep bay. It was established as the capital of Tierra del Fuego in 1904. British missionaries settled the area in the mid-1800s. In 1896, President Julio Argentino Roca founded a penal colony here for criminals and political prisoners from the north and Buenos Aires. The colony not only served as a means of hiding away society's most dangerous criminals, it also established a strong Argentine presence in the region of Tierra del Fuego. The prison was shut down in 1947 and now houses the Museo Marítimo y del Presidio, which has a vast collection of historical, nautical, scientific, and cultural exhibits from around the area.

3   

Parque Nacional Tierra del Fuego

8 miles (11 km) N of Ushuaia From Ushuaia Ruta Nacional 3, km 3067; parquesnacionales.gob.ar

Parque Nacional Tierra del Fuego was Argentina's first coastal national park. It is still popular with Ushuaia locals as an area offering trails, birdwatching, and trout fishing. Pedestrian paths and longer hikes pass through thick forest and past dark-water *turbales* (peat bogs). Visitors may see guanacos and red foxes, or the island's scourge, the Canadian beaver, which was introduced in the 1940s for pelt harvesting.

4   

Cerro Castor

16 miles (26 km) NE of Ushuaia; Ruta Nacional 3, km 26 (029)0149 9301 From Ushuaia Mid-Jun-mid-Oct cerrocastor.com

The base of Argentina's southernmost ski resort is just 640 ft (195 m) above sea level, with the highest elevation at 3,468 ft (1,057 m), yet Cerro Castor receives prodigious snowfall. The retreat consists of the Castor Ski Lodge, with 15 rustic-chic cabins, four restaurants, and four mountain cafés. It has nearly 1,500 acres (607 ha) of skiable terrain, 2,630 ft (800 m) of vertical drop, a snowpark, and seven lifts. Numerous activities are on offer, including ski and culinary events that extend throughout the season.

Palm trees on the incredible Anakena Beach

EASTER ISLAND AND ROBINSON CRUSOE ISLAND

Chile's borders extend over two of the planet's most isolated, remote, and beautiful islands. Easter Island, known as Rapa Nui to its inhabitants, is visited for its *moai* statues, world-renowned icons of archaeology and remnants of a vanished society. Closer to the mainland, Robinson Crusoe Island is the site of one of the greatest adventure sagas.

Five hours from the mainland by plane, Easter Island is a volcanic triangle whose culture, despite its political link to Chile, is more Polynesian than Latin American. The original settlers island-hopped their way across the Western Pacific and arrived at Rapa Nui around 1000 CE. What they lacked in numbers they made up for in ingenuity and creativity, carving monuments that have since made the island famous. Restored to their original platforms, the *moai* attract thousands of visitors each year.

Robinson Crusoe Island is part of the Juan Fernández archipelago. The island takes its name from the Daniel Defoe novel *Robinson Crusoe*, which was inspired by the story of 18th-century Scotsman Alexander Selkirk.

EASTER ISLAND AND ROBINSON CRUSOE ISLAND

Must Sees

1. Rano Raraku
2. Ahu Tongariki

Experience More

3. Hanga Roa
4. Rano Kau and Orongo
5. Ahu Vinapu
6. Ahu Akivi
7. Ana Te Pahu
8. Playa Anakena
9. Península Poike
10. San Juan Bautista
11. Sendero Salsipuedes
12. Cueva Robinson
13. Mirador de Selkirk
14. Plazoleta El Yunque

Pacific Ocean

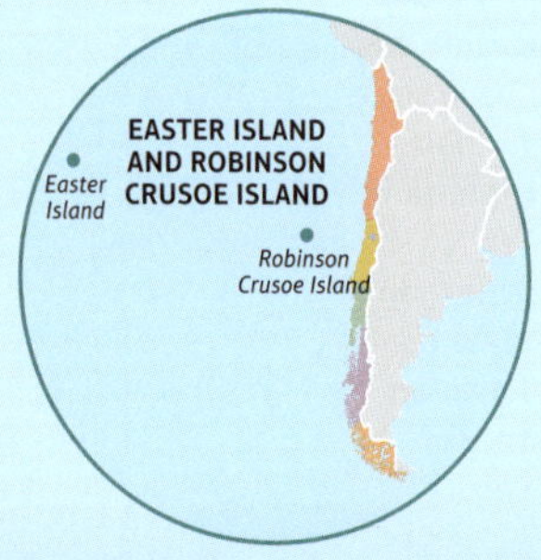

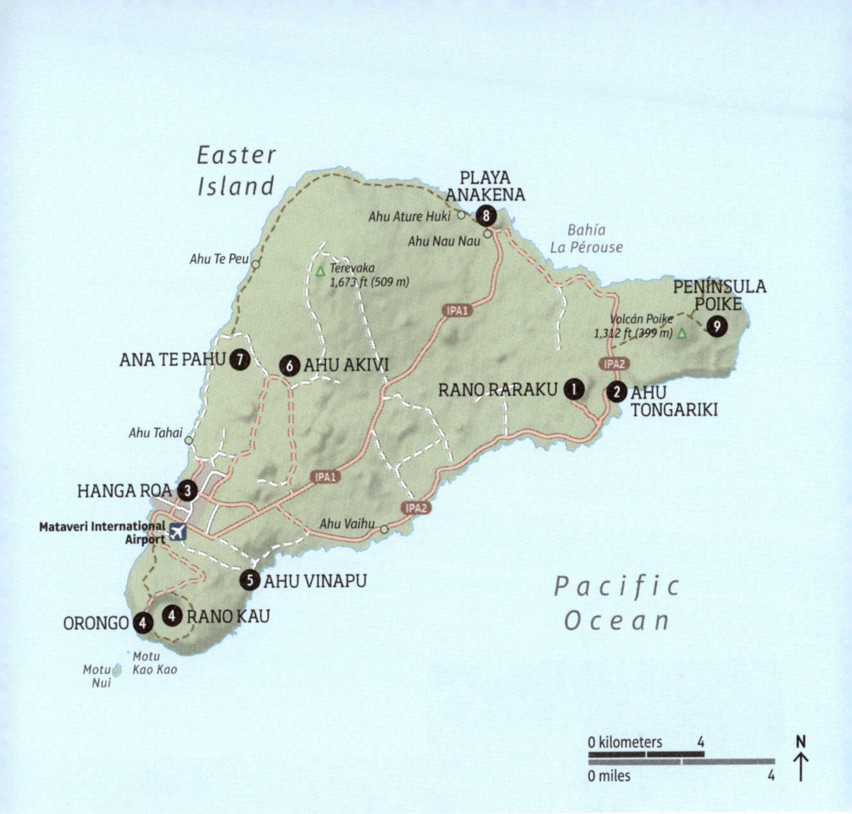

Easter Island
PLAYA ANAKENA
8
Ahu Ature Huki
Ahu Nau Nau
Bahía La Pérouse
Ahu Te Peu
Terevaka 1,673 ft (509 m)
IPA1
PENÍNSULA POIKE
9
Volcán Poike 1,312 ft (399 m)
IPA2
ANA TE PAHU 7
6 AHU AKIVI
RANO RARAKU 1
2 AHU TONGARIKI
Ahu Tahai
IPA1
HANGA ROA 3
IPA2
Mataveri International Airport
Ahu Vaihu
5 AHU VINAPU
Pacific Ocean
ORONGO 4
4 RANO KAU
Motu Kao Kao
Motu Nui
0 kilometers 4
0 miles 4
N

Robinson Crusoe Island
Puerto Inglés
12 CUEVA ROBINSON
Bahía Tres Puntas
MIRADOR DE SELKIRK
11 SENDERO SALSIPUEDES
Cerro Agudo 2,247 ft (684 m)
13
Bahía Cumberland
Fuerte Santa Bárbara
10
Cerro Tres Puntas 1,574 ft (479 m)
PLAZOLETA EL YUNQUE 14
SAN JUAN BAUTISTA
Cerro Centinela 1,033 ft (314 m)
Punta Tunquillax
Bahía Villagra
Cerro Damajuana 2,083 ft (634 m)
Cerro El Yunque 3,001 ft (914 m)
Robinson Crusoe Airport
Bahía Tierra Blanca
Punta Larga
Islote Vinillo
Puerto Francés
Bahía del Padre
Cerro La Piña 1,975 ft (601 m)
Islote Los Chamelos
Playa Arenal
Islote El Verdugo
Punta O'Higgins
Isla Santa Clara
Pacific Ocean
0 kilometers 3
0 miles 3
N

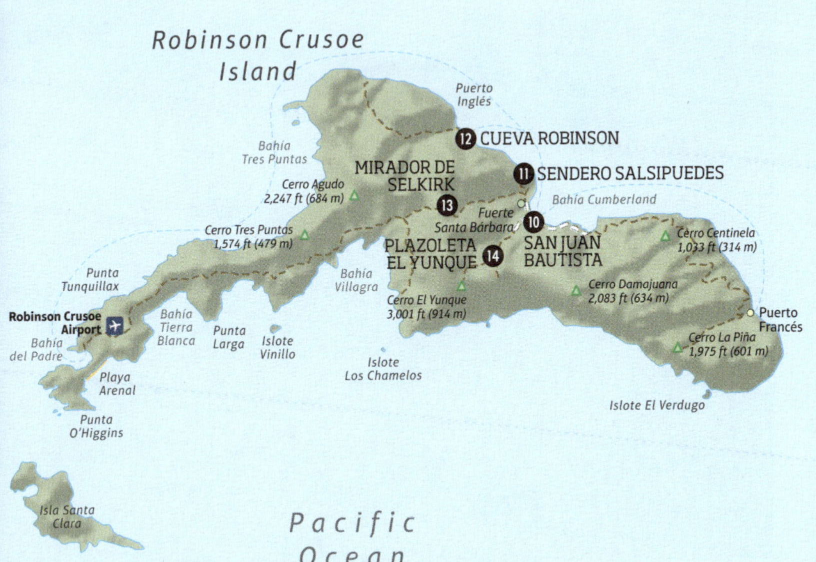

1

RANO RARAKU

11 miles (18 km) E of Hanga Roa Ranger station and rangers on-site: rapanuinationalpark.com

Among Easter Island's most breathtaking features are the *moai*-studded slopes of Rano Raraku; some 400 of the striking monolithic statues built by the Rapa Nui people can be seen here today. The site is also home to Crater Lake, an enormous prehistoric volcanic crater overlooking the Pacific Ocean.

Here, long before the arrival of Europeans, Rapa Nui carvers crafted massive statues from volcanic tuff and, with great effort, freed them from the quarry to be transported across the island. These are seen standing or toppled beside their *ahu* (ceremonial stone platforms). While they differ in detail, they have much in common.

Rano Raraku is one of the most popular sites on Easter Island, so aim to arrive for opening time or stay until closing time. Entry to the site is covered by a general ticket, which you buy at the airport on arrival; you can't book a visit to Rano Raraku ahead of time.

Crater Lake

The vast center of Rano Raraku is occupied by a serene lake. The crater can be reached through a gap in the western end of this site, and the CONAF-built trails around the crater's outer slopes are the only way to explore the area. East of Tukuturi *(p271)* are the basalt foundations of many *hare paenga*, thatched, boat-shaped houses that were reserved for priests.

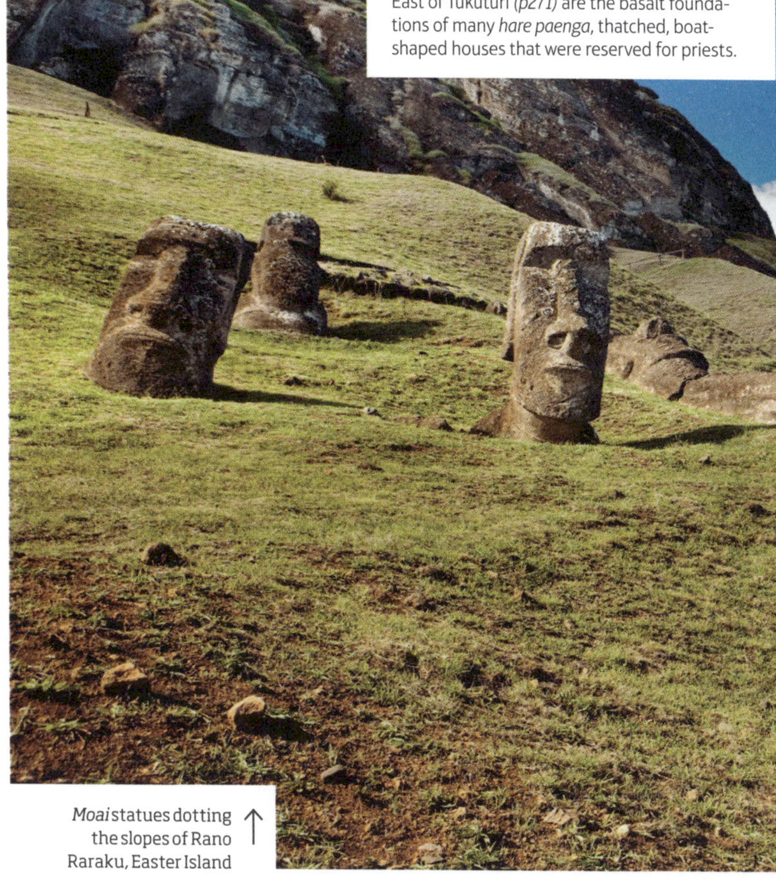

Moai statues dotting the slopes of Rano Raraku, Easter Island ↑

Timeline

c 300,000 years ago

▲ The crater of Rano Raraku is formed by a volcanic eruption.

1200 CE

▼ The first human settlers arrive on Easter Island from Polynesia. They soon start carving *moai.*

1774

▲ Captain James Cook reports that many statues have been toppled. Increasing numbers of *moai* are knocked from their *ahus* over the following years.

1950s

Many of the toppled *moai* are restored to their *ahus.*

MOAI STATUES OF RANO RARAKU

Moai are the highly stylized monolithic statues for which Rapa Nui has become famous. Carved from tuff (compacted volcanic ash), and ranging from 6 ft (2 m) to 65 ft (20 m) in height, there are around 400 completed *moai* on the island today, as well as many others that were never finished, notably at Rano Raraku. They represent important ancestors and were erected to watch over and protect their respective kin-groups. The earliest *moai* are believed to have been carved around 1200 CE.

HINARIRU

Located on one of the lower points of the trail, the much-photographed, 13-ft- (4-m-) high Hinariru is also called the *moai* with the twisted neck, in reference to its bulging base. According to various folktales, Hinariru was the brother-in-law of Hotu Motu'a, legendary leader of the first island settlers, and perhaps also the master who brought the *moai* to the island.

↑ Hinariru with his twisting body and a neighbor in the background

EL GIGANTE

Climbing to the upper slopes of Rano Raraku, the trail reaches El Gigante. As its name implies, at 65 ft (20 m) El Gigante is the largest *moai* ever carved. Unfinished and still attached to the bedrock, its estimated weight is around 270 tons (240 tonnes).

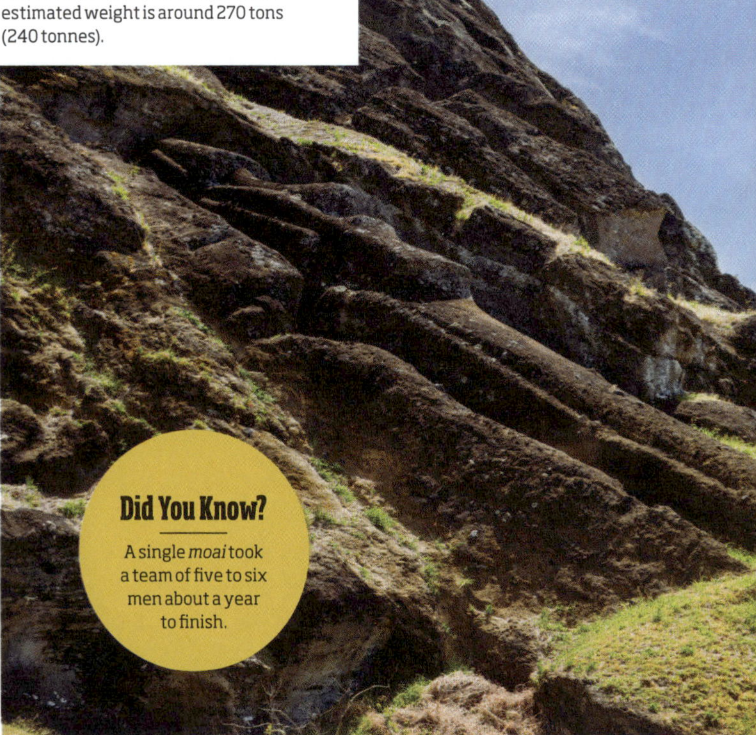

Did You Know?

A single *moai* took a team of five to six men about a year to finish.

PIROPIRO

Just west of Hinariru, on the main path that runs to the quarry, is another 13-ft- (4-m-) high *moai* known as Piropiro. This name means "bad smell" as signified by the *moai* having a prominent nose. About 22 ft (7 m) of its body is buried beneath volcanic soil.

TUKUTURI

The fenced-off Tukuturi is different from other *moai*. It is the site's singular kneeling, bearded *moai* with a complete (if seemingly unfinished) body, and apparently mimics the posture of Polynesian ceremonial singers. According to American archaeologist Joanne van Tilburg, it may be the last *moai* ever made, with links to the Birdman cult.

KO KONA HE ROA

The *moai* known as Ko Kona He Roa, which stands very closely to a second *moai*, bears evidence of European contact in the image of a three-masted sailing ship roughly etched on its trunk. This carving could well depict the sailing ship of Dutch explorer Jacob Roggeveen, who landed at Easter Island in 1722 and reportedly encountered some 3,000 inhabitants.

TAI HARE ATUA

This is understood to be the first *moai* on the island as shown by the statue's rudimentary style. It has been left abandoned, as if the carvers were disappointed with their work.

→ Ko Kona He Roa with petroglyphs showing a ship on his torso

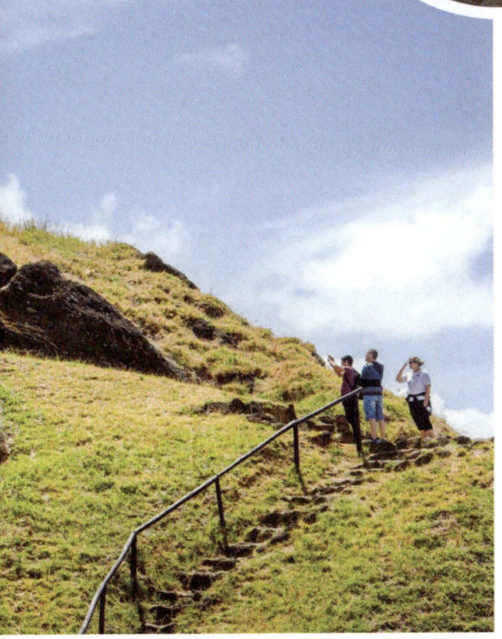

Admiring El Gigante, carved into the rock face, Rano Raraku

THE STATUE-CARVERS

Talented crafters who taught their skills over generations, *maoi* carvers were revered members of society. They were completely dedicated to their craft, exempt from food production and supported by other farmers and fishermen, who provided them with fresh food as payment for their work.

AHU TONGARIKI

12 miles (20 km) W of Hanga Roa **From Hanga Roa**
Dawn–6pm daily **No restrooms or food services for visitors**

On the southeast coast of Easter Island you'll find the iconic and otherworldly Ahu Tongariki. These 15 fascinating and towering *moai* statues are gravely lined up on a 720-ft- (220-m-) long ceremonial platform – or *ahu* – which is the largest platform on the island.

Built between the 13th and 15th centuries, the 15 giant statues at Ahu Tongariki were toppled during the civil wars of the 19th century. The site suffered further damage in 1960 when a 9.5-magnitude earthquake struck the Chilean mainland, triggering a massive tsunami that subsequently hit Easter Island. The *ahu* and fallen *moai* were washed further inland and experienced considerable damage in the process. It was only in 1996, after a five-year restoration project with the help of the Japanese government, that the archaeological site was returned to its former glory and the 15 *moai* were returned to their original positions. The restoration work cost a whopping US$2 million, which was covered by the government of Japan.

Note that this site is part of the Rapa Nui National Park, which covers most of Easter Island. You will pay your park entry fee at the airport on arrival, and this includes entry to all sites.

PICTURE PERFECT
Ahu Tongariki's Maoi

An essential souvenir for anyone visiting Easter Island is a snap of the *maoi* at sunrise (check online for timing). You'll need to be up and out early to get the best vantage point - you won't be the only one with this idea.

The impressive *maoi* of Ahu Tongariki, backed by the Pacific Ocean

1 A rock at Ahu Tongariki includes a petroglyph of a tuna fish.

2 After the tsunami, archaeologist Claudio Cristino sought to return the *maoi* to their rightful place. This photograph shows work taking place at the site in 1992.

3 The site's *maoi* were restored by archaeologists after a tsunami in 1960.

Did You Know?

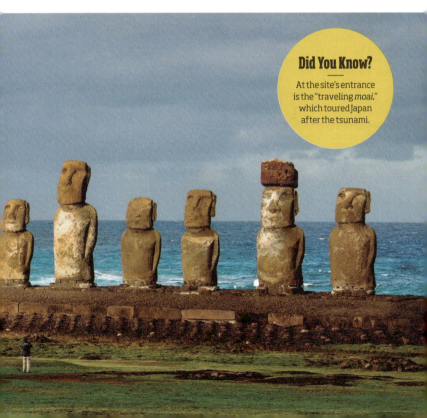

At the site's entrance is the "traveling *moai*," which toured Japan after the tsunami.

EXPERIENCE MORE

Hanga Roa

2,340 miles (3,765 km) NW of Santiago
Avenida Policarpo Toro, at Tuu Maheke; (032) 2100 255

Easter Island's only permanent settlement, Hanga Roa is a sprawling subtropical village housing nearly all of the island's inhabitants. Most of its wide streets are lined with compact homes fronted by gardens. The population is mainly Polynesian but there are also expatriates – from mainland Chile – who participate in the island's growing tourism industry. The village is a hub for visitors who come to enjoy the area's unique attractions, including a sophisticated cuisine that blends various interesting and fresh ingredients with South Pacific touches.

TAPATI RAPA NUI

Easter Island's biggest annual event for the past 30 years, Tapati Rapa Nui, has filled the streets of Hanga Roa with folkloric music, dance, and competitive events. Celebrated during the first two weeks of February, the festival is a chance for islanders to showcase their skills and crafts. Tapati Rapa Nui focuses on tradition and identity, despite the use of imported elements such as drums and guitars.

Rano Kau and Orongo

3 miles (5 km) S of Hanga Roa; Sector Orongo 9am-7pm daily

Part of a national park, the water-filled crater of Rano Kau is Easter Island's most striking natural sight – the panorama from its rim, with the seemingly endless Pacific Ocean on the horizon, is one of the most unforgettable sights on the island. Descending into the crater is no longer permitted, but walking around its rim is a true top-of-the-world experience. On the crater's southwest side, the ceremonial village at Orongo is a complex of 53 houses that were linked to this island's Birdman sect in the 18th and 19th centuries. The sect gets its name from the Birdman, an influential post whose incumbent was chosen each year *(p277)*. Visitors to this historic and fragile site are requested not to leave the marked path or enter the houses, which

← Brightly painted boats lining the wharf in Hanga Roa

consist of overlapping slabs and earth, with doors so low that entering them would require crawling.

Rano Kau and Orongo are reached by a road that passes the west end of Mataveri airport. However, it is also possible to hike there, and back, on the Te Ara O Te Ao footpath that starts at Ana Kai Tangata; this route is closely associated with the Birdman rituals. The admission fee for Rano Kau, collected by CONAF, is also valid for entry to Rano Raraku *(p268)*.

Ahu Vinapu

2 miles (3 km) NE of Rano Kau; Sector Orongo

Ahu Vinapu was once mistakenly held to be proof of South American influence on Easter Island, because its closely fitted stones superficially resemble Inca sites in Peru. The site actually consists of three separate platforms, whose *moai* tumbled over in conflicts during the 18th and 19th centuries. The site is also known for the discovery of fossilized palm, believed to be evidence of island settlement around 1300 CE. Theory holds that the tree became extinct as islanders cleared woods to make space for erecting *moai*.

Ahu Akivi

4 miles (6 km) NE of Hanga Roa; Sector Akivi

With seven standing *moai*, restored in 1960 by American anthropologist William Mulloy and his Chilean colleague Gonzalo Figueroa García-Huidobro, Ahu Akivi is one of few inland *ahu* and, unlike most other *ahus*, its *moai* look toward the sea. They also look toward the platform's ceremonial center and, during both equinoxes, directly into the setting sun.

EAT

Au Bout du Monde
A Belgian restaurant with seafood dishes, homemade pasta, and chocolate mousse.

Policarpo Toro s/n, Hanga Roa (032) 2552 060 Mon, Tue

$$$

DRINK

Te Moana
Enjoy a sunset cocktail or beer (try the Tahitian lager Hinano), in a prime location looking out over the sea.

Avenida Policarpo Toro s/n, Hanga Roa (032) 2551 578 Sun

↑ Standing on the rim of Rano Kau, a spectacular volcanic crater

A tree growing from inside the Ana Te Pahu cavern

Ana Te Pahu

4 miles (6 km) NE of Hanga Roa; Sector Ahu Akivi

Today, much of Easter Island's food is imported from the mainland, but before this became an option, the islanders used lava tube caves called *manavai*, or sunken gardens, to grow their produce. These tunnel-like caves formed when rock solidified around a flowing stream of molten lava, which had resulted from the regular volcanic activity that gave rise to Easter Island in the first place. Ana Te Pahu is one such lava tube cave – the largest cavern on the island.

Owing to the total absence of surface streams on Easter Island's porous volcanic terrain, large-scale agriculture has always been a challenge. The humid microclimate and relatively deep soils in the caves permitted the cultivation of crops; these are still grown in Ana Te Pahu and in similar sites around the island. Visitors can easily descend into the cave to explore with a guide, but a flashlight is necessary.

Playa Anakena

10 miles (16 km) NE of Hanga Roa; Sector Anakena

On the northeastern shores of Rapa Nui, Playa Anakena is the island's only broad, sandy beach and, with its tall palms and turquoise waters, it is almost a caricature of a South Pacific idyll. The beach is a perfect spot for swimming and sunbathing. It also has barbecue pits, picnic tables, changing rooms, and several snack bars that make it the most popular choice with locals for a day's outing.

According to Easter Island's oral tradition, Playa Anakena is the place where the first Polynesian settlers, under chief Hotu Matu'a, landed. Anakena has one thing that no part of Polynesia can match – the seven standing *moai* of Ahu Nau Nau, four of them with *pukao* (headdresses) that were restored in 1979 under the direction of island archaeologist Sergio Rapu. Two of these *moai* are badly damaged, but the remainder are in excellent condition. Also on the same beach, slightly to the south, is the smaller Ahu Ature Huki with a single *moai*. This was re-erected in 1956 by Norwegian explorer Thor Heyerdahl, with the help of a group of islanders.

From Anakena, it is possible to hike around the little-visited north coast, returning to Hanga Roa *(p274)* via two other sites – Ahu Te Peu and Ahu Tahai. However, this is a full day's trip and demands an early start. Since there is an absence of shade along the shore, be sure to carry plenty of water.

Península Poike

13 miles (21 km) NE of Hanga Roa; Sector Poike

The peninsula at the island's eastern end takes its name from Volcán Poike, which

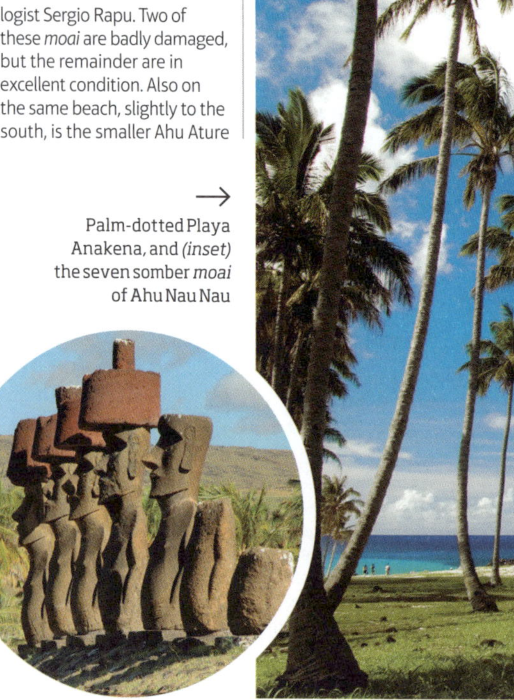

→ Palm-dotted Playa Anakena, and *(inset)* the seven somber *moai* of Ahu Nau Nau

is the oldest volcano on the island and marks this area's highest point. In pre-European times there was a village here, and petroglyphs from the period include a turtle, a tuna fish, and a Birdman. The area also has fascinating landmarks associated with legends of the island. Key among these is a 2-mile- (3-km-) long westerly "ditch," believed to mark a line of defensive fortifications during a war between rival clans.

On the peninsula's southwestern edge is Poike's most stunning asset – Ahu Tongariki *(p272)*. With its 15 *moai*, which stand with their backs to the Pacific Ocean, it is the island's largest platform, and arguably the most important megalithic monument in all of Polynesia.

LEGEND OF THE BIRDMAN

Around the 17th century, Rapa Nui's culture, rooted in ancestor worship, was replaced by a system of beliefs known as *makemake*, named after the creator god. One of this sect's key customs was an annual competition held to elect the Tangata Manu (Birdman), who held a position of power on the island. Each of the contestants would sponsor an islander, a *hopu*, whose task was to scramble down the slope of Rano Kau, swim through shark-infested waters to the islet of Motu Nui, and retrieve the egg of a sooty tern. The sponsor of the first *hopu* to return would become that year's Birdman.

San Juan Bautista

472 miles (759 km) W of Santiago From Santiago From Valparaíso Vicente González 210; comunajuan fernandez.cl

Robinson Crusoe Island's only permanent settlement, San Juan Bautista is nestled on the curving shoreline of the scenic Bahía Cumberland. The waters around it are part of a 187,000-sq-mile (301,000-sq-km) marine reserve that was created in 2015 to protect the area around Robinson Crusoe Island and its neighbors.

Located just south of the village plaza, atop a hill, the small Fuerte Santa Barbara dates from 1770. This stone fort was constructed by the Spanish in response to the presence of the British in the South Pacific. It was rebuilt in 1974, but the fort's several cannons, pointing at the harbor, still stand here.

Next to the fort, the Cuevas de los Patriotas (Caves of the Patriots) was where, in the early 19th century, the Spanish held Chilean leaders who had been fighting for independence. At the village's western end, the Cementerio San Juan Bautista is home to the tombs of early settlers, as well as those of German sailors who stayed on the island after the scuttling of the *Dresden* in 1915. This battleship had been cornered by the British navy in the Bahía Cumberland.

Since the tsunami of 2010, a disaster that was unleashed by a massive earthquake and ultimately claimed eight lives, the **Casa de la Cultura Alfredo de Rodt**, named for an early Swiss settler, shares space with **CONAF**'s national park information office.

Casa de la Cultura Alfredo de Rodt/CONAF

Vicente González 130
8am-1pm & 2-6pm Mon-Fri

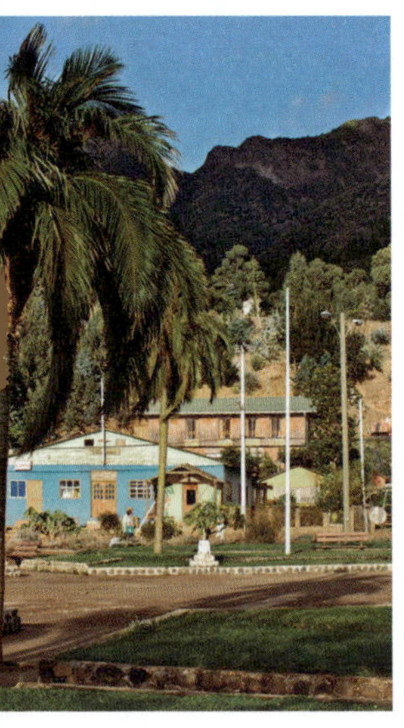

The village of San Juan Bautista on Robinson Crusoe Island

1966

The year that Más a Tierra was renamed Robinson Crusoe Island.

Sendero Salsipuedes

1 mile (2 km) W of San Juan Bautista conaf.cl

Starting at Calle La Pólvora, just west of San Juan Bautista, the Sendero Salsipuedes is a nature trail with multiple switchbacks. The path snakes through dense vegetation and verdant forests of acacia, eucalyptus, Monterey cypress, Monterey pine, and the native murtilla before culminating at the jagged Salsipuedes ridge. The exceptional views from here include sweeping panoramas of San Juan Bautista and of the blue waters of Bahía Cumberland that surround the village.

Cueva Robinson

2 miles (3 km) NW of San Juan Bautista by boat; Puerto Inglés conaf.cl

From the Salsipuedes ridge, a steep pathway descends to the beach at Puerto Inglés

Mirador de Selkirk, with the curve of Bahía Cumberland seen below

and to the Cueva Robinson, claimed to be the site of Alexander Selkirk's shelter *(see box)*. This precipitous approach can be dangerous, and it is necessary to hire the services of a local guide. While there is no clear evidence that Selkirk inhabited this cave, a replica of his supposed refuge dominates the site. Since 1995, American treasure hunter Bernard Keiser has spent several years in this area, searching for a massive, 18th-century Spanish treasure, which is rumored to contain gold, including a necklace belonging to the wife of the last Inca emperor, Atahualpa.

13

Mirador de Selkirk

2 miles (3 km) S of San Juan Bautista conaf.cl

A popular hiking destination, Mirador de Selkirk is the saddle from where the castaway Alexander Selkirk watched for the ship that would rescue him from his lonely exile. The trek to this lookout starts at the southern end of San Juan Bautista's central plaza and climbs steeply through an eroded zone. As the trail gains altitude, it passes through thick endemic rainforest, studded with towering tree ferns, before culminating at the saddle. It is also possible to start the hike from Mirador de Selkirk all the way to the airstrip.

Two metal plaques on the saddle, one placed by the Royal Navy in 1868 and the other by a distant relative in 1983, commemorate Selkirk's exile. The site offers great views over Bahía Cumberland and San Juan Bautista. To the south, the landscape changes dramatically from dense rainforest to desert at Tierras Blancas, where the rugged shoreline provides habitat to the endemic Juan Fernández fur seal (*Arctocephalus philippii*).

14  

Plazoleta El Yunque

2 miles (3 km) S of San Juan Bautista conaf.cl

Starting at San Juan Bautista's power plant, a southbound road turns into a gentle nature trail that leads to the Plazoleta El Yunque, a serene forest clearing with a campground. The site is also the spot where Hugo Weber, a German survivor of the *Dresden* sinking, built a house – the dilapidated foundations of which are still visible today.

There is a steep and challenging hike that begins at the Plazoleta El Yunque and traverses dense forest to reach the saddle of El Camote, which offers sweeping views of the island. Farther ahead, a more strenuous hike culminates at Cerro El Yunque (Anvil Hill), which, at 3,002 ft (915 m), is the highest point on Robinson Crusoe Island, as well as being one of the most visited. Diverse wildlife can be seen here; CONAF organizes guides for those who wish to undertake this hike.

ALEXANDER SELKIRK

Scotsman Alexander Selkirk – who inspired Daniel Defoe's *Robinson Crusoe* (1719) – was abandoned on Isla Más a Tierra in 1704, after he complained about the seaworthiness of his ship, *Cinque Ports*. Selkirk subsisted on feral goats, fish, and plants, clothed himself with animal skins, and stayed hidden from Spanish vessels until his rescue in 1709 by a British privateering ship. As Selkirk had predicted, *Cinque Ports* sank within a month of his being put ashore, and most of its crew drowned.

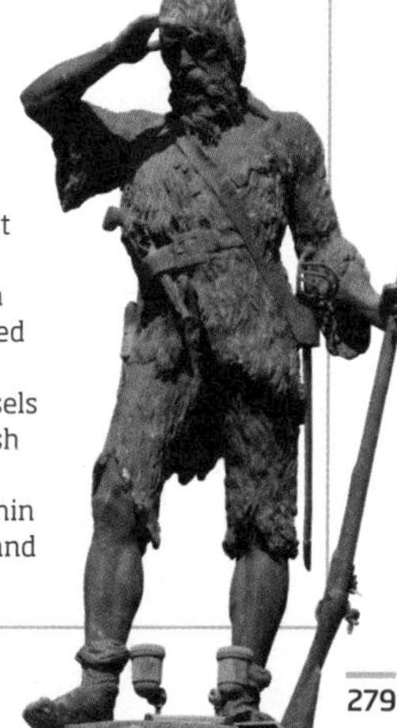

NEED TO KNOW

Winding roads in Parque Nacional Queulat

BEFORE YOU GO

Things change, so plan ahead to make the most of your trip. Be prepared for all eventualities by considering the following points before you travel.

AT A GLANCE
CURRENCY
Chilean Peso (CLP/$)
AVERAGE DAILY SPEND
SAVE $50,000
SPEND $100,000
SPLURGE $175,000+
BOTTLED WATER $1,000
COFFEE $2,800
BEER $4,000
DINNER FOR TWO $50,000
ESSENTIAL PHRASES
Hello — Hola
Goodbye — Adiós
Please — Por favor
Thank you — Gracias
Do you speak English? — ¿Habla inglés?
I don't understand — No entiendo
ELECTRICITY SUPPLY
Standard voltage is 220 volts. Power sockets are type C, fitting two-pronged plugs, and type L, fitting three-pronged plugs.

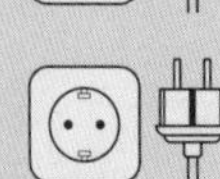

Passports and Visas

For entry requirements, including visas, consult your nearest Chilean embassy or check the **Ministry of Foreign Affairs** website. EU nationals and citizens of the UK, US, Australia, Canada, South Africa, and New Zealand do not require visas for stays of up to 90 days. On arrival, visitors are given a tourist card, valid for 90 days, which can be extended for another 90 days for US$100 and must be surrendered when departing Chile.

Ministry of Foreign Affairs
W chile.gob.cl/chile/en

Government Advice

Now more than ever, it is important to consult both your and the Chilean government's advice before traveling. The **UK Foreign, Commonwealth, & Development Office**, the **US State Department**, the **Australian Department of Foreign Affairs and Trade**, and the Chilean **Gobierno de Chile** offer the latest information on security, health, and local regulations.

Australia
W smartraveller.gov.au
Gobierno de Chile
W gob.cl
UK
W gov.uk/foreign-travel-advice
US
W travel.state.gov

Customs Information

You can find information on the laws relating to goods and currency taken in or out of Chile on the Gobierno de Chile website. Arica, Iquique, and Magellanes have duty-free zones, so there are occasional internal customs checks when visitors are traveling from those regions.

Insurance

We recommend taking out a comprehensive insurance policy covering theft, loss of belongings, medical care, cancellations, and delays, and read the small print carefully.

Vaccinations

It is recommended that travelers are vaccinated against hepatitis A and tetanus.

Booking Accommodation

Chile has a huge range of accommodation, from budget hostels to luxury hotels. Most cities and major tourist areas offer plenty of accommodation, and Chile has many campgrounds in national parks and areas of natural beauty, which should be booked in advance.

Money

Many hotels and tour companies accept US dollars, but it is best to carry pesos, especially if you plan to visit more rural locations. All major credit and debit cards are widely accepted, but some places may only take cash. ATMs are found in major towns and cities and most charge a fee of around $2–3 per transaction.

Tipping is not expected by housekeepers or taxi drivers, but hotel porters and concierge will expect $500 (60 cents) per bag, and waiters 10 per cent of your final restaurant bill.

Travelers with Specific Requirements

While facilities for visitors with specific needs are improving, there is still a long way to go. New public buildings are required to provide wheelchair access but only the larger hotels are likely to be fully accessible or even have lifts. Wheelchair ramps and disabled restrooms are rare and public transportation can be quite complicated, although Santiago is better equipped. Some streetlights have noise-indicated crossings, and national parks and reserves have access ramps, trails with Braille signs, and educational videos with sign language.

The country's official tourism website, **Chile Travel**, has further information on accessible tourism. Operators such as **Accessible Holidays**, **Korke**, and **Wheel the World** are able to make special arrangements should visitors need them.

Accessible Holidays
W disabledholidays.com
Chile Travel
W chile.travel
Korke
W korke.com
Wheel the World
W gowheeltheworld.com

Language

Spanish is the official language, albeit with a distinctive accent and vocabulary that differs from other South American dialects. Some Indigenous people, such as the Mapuche, Aymara, and Quechua, speak their own language but know Spanish too. English is increasing.

Opening Hours

Situations can change quickly and unexpectedly. Always check before visiting attractions and hospitality venues for up-to-date opening hours and booking requirements.

Afternoons Many stores shut from 1pm to 3pm.
Mondays Some museums and attractions close.
Weekends Most stores open for limited hours on Sundays; banks close.
Public holidays Banks and government offices close. Some stores and attractions close early or for the entire day.

PUBLIC HOLIDAYS

Jan 1	New Year's Day
Mar/Apr	Easter
May 1	Labor Day/May Day
May 21	Navy Day
end Jun	Feast of St. Peter & St. Paul
Jul 16	Our Lady of Mount Carmel
Aug 15	Assumption of Mary
Sep 18	Independence Day
mid-Oct	Columbus Day
Nov 1	All Saints Day
Dec 1	Immaculate Conception
Dec 25	Christmas Day

GETTING AROUND

Whether you are visiting for a short city break or rural retreat, discover how best to reach your destination and travel like a pro.

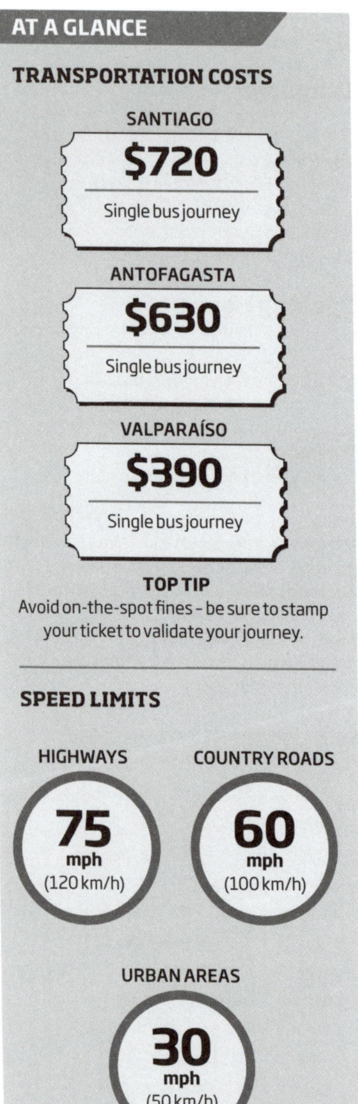

AT A GLANCE
TRANSPORTATION COSTS
SANTIAGO
$720
Single bus journey
ANTOFAGASTA
$630
Single bus journey
VALPARAÍSO
$390
Single bus journey
TOP TIP
Avoid on-the-spot fines - be sure to stamp your ticket to validate your journey.
SPEED LIMITS
HIGHWAYS
75 mph (120 km/h)
COUNTRY ROADS
60 mph (100 km/h)
URBAN AREAS
30 mph (50 km/h)

Arriving by Air

Most visitors arrive at Aeropuerto Internacional Arturo Merino Benítez, 10 miles (16 km) northwest of Santiago. There are connections to the city by bus, shuttle, and taxi, as well as domestic flights. Other airports only receive flights from neighboring countries. Chile's main airline, with direct flights from North America, Australasia, and Europe, is **LATAM**. **Air France**, **Iberia**, and **KLM** operate direct flights from Europe; **American Airlines**, **Delta**, and **Air Canada** fly directly from North America, **United** and **Qantas** from Australia.

Air Canada
W aircanada.com
Air France
W airfrance.com
American Airlines
W aa.com
Delta
W delta.com
Iberia
W iberia.com
KLM
W klm.com
LATAM
W latam.com
Qantas
W qantas.com.au
United
W united.com

Domestic Air Travel

Many travelers move between the regions of Chile by air. Flying is also the only way to reach Easter Island. There are domestic airports, served by LATAM and independent airlines, the biggest of which is **Sky Airline**. Smaller regional airlines, such as **DAP**, which serves parts of Patagonia, often face cancellations due to bad weather during winter in the south.

DAP
W dapairline.com
Sky Airline
W skyairline.com

GETTING TO AND FROM THE AIRPORT

Airport	Distance to city	Taxi Fare	Public Transportation	Journey Time
Santiago	11 miles/17 km	$20,000	Bus	30 mins
La Serena	3 miles/5 km	$6,000	Micro	10 mins
Copiapó	33 miles/52 km	$27,000	Bus	45 mins
Antofagasta	16 miles/26 km	$19,000	Micro	30 mins
Iquique	25 miles/40 km	$40,000	Bus	45 mins
Arica	12 miles/18 km	$10,000	Micro	20 mins
Concepción	3 miles/5 km	$3,500	Bus	15 mins
Puerto Montt	10 miles/16 km	$11,500	Bus	20 mins
Castro	12 miles/18 km	$14,500	Bus	45 mins
Punta Arenas	13 miles/21 km	$10,000	Bus	30 mins
Hanga Roa	1 mile/1.5 km	$7,000	N/A	10 mins

Train Travel

No public services operate north of Santiago. Indeed, the only currently viable services on the state railroad **EFE** run from the capital through the Central Valley to Rancagua, San Fernando, Talca, and Chillán, although there are plans for a high-speed service from Santiago to Valparaíso.

EFE
W efe.cl

Ferry Travel

In Chile's far south, beyond Puerto Montt, a well-developed ferry network negotiates the intricate patchwork of inlets, fjords, and islands that constitute Patagonia, providing a scenic alternative to plane and bus travel. There are also ferry connections along the Chiloé archipelago and the Carretera Austral. Companies such as **Andina del Sud**, **Transbordadora Austral Broom**, **Naviera Austral**, **SOMARCO**, and **Navimag** may prove useful.

Andina del Sud
W empresasandinadelsud.cl

Naviera Austral
W navieraustral.cl

Navimag
W navimag.com

Transbordadora Austral Broom
W tabsa.cl

SOMARCO
W barcazas.cl

FERRY ROUTES

Route	Duration
Caleta Yungay to Puerto Natales	41 hrs
Petrohué to Puella	5 hrs
Puerto Montt to Laguna San Rafael	34 hrs
Puerto Montt to Chaltén	9 hrs
Puerto Montt to Puerto Natales	4 days
Punta Arenas to Porvenir	1 hr 50 mins
Punta Arenas to Puerto Williams	32 hrs
Quellón to Chacabuco	32 hrs
Quellón to Chaltén	5 hrs
Quellón to Puerto Cisnes	12 hrs

Bus Travel

International Bus Travel

A number of bus routes connect Chile with neighboring countries. Connections with Argentina include Valparaíso/Santiago to Mendoza, Puerto Montt/Osorno to Bariloche, Puntas Arenas to Rio Gallegos, and La Serena to San Juan. There are crossings between Chile and Bolivia: Arica via the high Lauca National Park to La Paz, and San Pedro de Atacama to Uyuni on the Bolivian salt flats. The most frequently used and least challenging crossing is from Arica to Tacna in Peru, where connections to Arequipa and other destinations are available.

REGIONAL BUS JOURNEY PLANNER

Plotting the main bus routes according to journey time, this map provides a handy reference for traveling between Chile's main towns and cities. The times given reflect the fastest and most direct routes available.

Key

••• **Main bus routes**

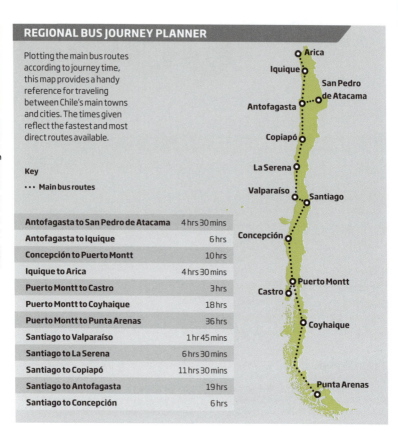

Antofagasta to San Pedro de Atacama	4 hrs 30 mins
Antofagasta to Iquique	6 hrs
Concepción to Puerto Montt	10 hrs
Iquique to Arica	4 hrs 30 mins
Puerto Montt to Castro	3 hrs
Puerto Montt to Coyhaique	18 hrs
Puerto Montt to Punta Arenas	36 hrs
Santiago to Valparaíso	1 hr 45 mins
Santiago to La Serena	6 hrs 30 mins
Santiago to Copiapó	11 hrs 30 mins
Santiago to Antofagasta	19 hrs
Santiago to Concepción	6 hrs

Regional Bus Travel

With an extensive network of routes operated by private companies, the bus is the most efficient and used means of transportation. **TurBus** and **Pullman Bus** are the big nationwide companies, complemented by regional operators.

Standards are quite high, with three classes offering increasing comfort levels: the *clásico* has normal semireclining seats; the *semicama* offers more legroom and the seats recline farther; and the *salon cama* contains wider seats, which recline almost horizontally. All have on-board restrooms and the more luxurious usually offer free water, soft drinks, and the occasional light snack.

Prices are relatively low because of intense competition – tickets cost around $1,500–2,000 per hour of travel on a basic bus, with luxury services costing up to four times more. Booking in advance is advisable, especially on popular routes. Visitors can book using comparison sites such as **Recorrido**, the bus company's own website, and at bus stations. Cities and larger towns often have several bus stations, with dedicated depots for larger companies, while other towns have huge integrated terminals.

Pullman Bus
W pullmanbus.cl
Recorrido
W recorrido.cl
TurBus
W turbus.cl

Public Transportation

The main form of public transportation is local buses. Only Santiago has a developed subway system, although there is a single-line overground train between Valparaíso and Viña del Mar. In Santiago, when using the **Red Metropolitana de Movilidad**, you must use the electronic Tarjeta Bip! card, which you can buy and top up at machines or ticket windows in stations and major bus depots. Outside Santiago, local transportation is paid for with cash. Many buses have a plastic box to deposit money, so you need to have the exact fare, while others have a conductor on board.

The **Ministerio de Transportes y Telecomunicaciones** is the Chilean government's transport authority. Safety and hygiene measures, timetables, ticket information, transport maps, and more can be obtained from the ministry's website.

Ministerio de Transportes y Telecomunicaciones
W mtt.gob.cl

Red Metropolitana de Movilidad
W red.cl/en/

Subway

The **Santiago Metro** network consists of seven intersecting lines covering major hubs (excluding the airport). Trains run 6am–11pm weekdays, 6:30am–11pm Saturday, and 7am–11pm Sunday.

Santiago Metro
W metro.cl

City Buses

Santiago has an extensive bus network that is useful for reaching places not covered by the metro. Buses are modern and comfortable but can get crowded during rush hour.

Colectivos

These shared taxis ply set routes for fixed fares that are often not much higher than local bus fares. The destination is usually displayed on a board on the roof, and taxis depart when full. Mainly used for travel within urban areas, they sometimes connect outlying towns and villages.

Micros

Local bus services are supplemented by these numbered minibuses – useful for reaching places not covered by the official network.

Taxis

Taxis are found in all Chilean cities and towns. They are black with yellow roofs; a light in the windshield's top right-hand corner indicates availability. Fares are low, at $130 per 655 ft (200 m) on top of the initial $450 charge. Radio taxis are more expensive, with a $2,000 call-out charge, followed by a quote for each destination. Taxi apps, such as Uber and Beat, are popular in Santiago. Small-town and rural taxis are rarely metered, so get an idea of the going rate and be prepared to bargain; although not frequent, overcharging unsuspecting tourists does occur.

Driving

Most visitors use planes or buses to get around the country, but the public transportation network to areas of natural beauty is limited or nonexistent. To avoid an organized tour, rent a car.

Driving in Chile

There is currently a four-lane highway from La Serena in the Norte Chico to Puerto Montt at the top of Patagonia, and well-surfaced roads in all but the most remote parts of the country. The main highways are all toll roads and around Santiago they require an electronic or daily fee permit, which can be bought online at **Servipag**.

Driving the country's famed Gringo Trail will take you through spectacular scenery on sometimes narrow but well-paved roads. Much of the southerly Carretera Austral has loose gravel and blind curves in places, so care is required. Parts of the Atacama Desert, most national parks, and the high-altitude altiplano are best negotiated in a locally rented jeep or 4WD vehicle.

Servipag
W servipag.com

Car Rental

International rental companies such as Avis and Hertz have affiliates in all major cities and some smaller towns. Local companies, including **Lys** and **RecaSur**, offer cheaper rates. Unlimited mileage is the rule but prices are generally higher than in the US or Europe.

Drivers must be at least 21 years old and have a valid driving license, passport, and credit card. In theory an international license is required but that is hardly ever enforced, although it can help avoid bureaucratic problems if you are stopped by the police. The rental company must provide the vehicle's ownership documents. Insurance policies have deductibles as high as 20 per cent of the vehicle's value. Crossborder rentals need power of attorney and additional insurance.

Lys
W lys.cl

RecaSur
W recasur-rac.com

Rules of the Road

Driving is on the right and passengers are required by law to wear seat belts. There are strict penalties for drunk driving. On the Carretera Austral, drivers must carry warning triangles, a fire extinguisher, and a first-aid kit.

Cycling

Bikes can be rented in most towns and tourist centers but those intent on some serious cycling are advised to bring their own cycle, a repair kit, and spares. Wear a helmet; it is illegal not to. The greatest danger comes from careless drivers, so luminous and reflective gear is essential.

Walking

Chile is a great place to explore on foot. Walking around the cities is a good way to get a feel for different neighborhoods. Hiking holidays are very popular in Chile, and most ntional parks have trails to suit all levels and abilities.

PRACTICAL INFORMATION

A little local know-how goes a long way in Chile. Here you will find all the essential advice and information you will need during your stay.

AT A GLANCE

EMERGENCY NUMBERS

MARITIME SEARCH AND RESCUE	AMBULANCE
137	**131**

FIRE DEPARTMENT	POLICE
132	**133**

TIME ZONE

CST/CLST. Daylight saving time runs from the first Sunday in September to the first Sunday in April.

TAP WATER

Unless otherwise stated, tap water is safe to drink in Chile, apart from in the Atacama Desert region.

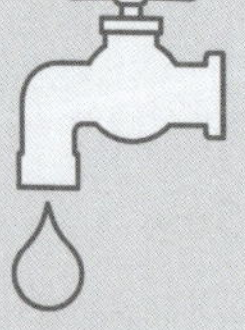

WEBSITES AND APPS

CONAF
The best resource for national parks information, albeit only in Spanish *(conaf.cl)*.

Chile 360°
This app offers incredible 360-degree images, videos, and maps of sights.

Recorrido
A handy app for comparing bus companies and booking tickets.

Personal Security

Chile is one of the safest countries in South America, where violent crime is extremely rare. However, petty theft does take place, especially in parts of Santiago, Valparaíso, and transit towns such as Arica, Calama, and Puerto Montt, where extra vigilance is advisable. Use your common sense, keep your belongings close, and be alert to your surroundings. If you have anything stolen, report the crime within 24 hours to the nearest police station and take your passport with you. Contact your embassy if your passport is stolen, or in the event of a serious crime or accident.

Homosexuality was legalized in Chile in 1999, with same-sex civil unions following in 2015. Gender transition is legal, and since 2019, those over the age of 14 can change their gender in documents without prohibition. Nonetheless, due to the somewhat conservative nature of Chilean society, public displays of affection by same-sex couples are viewed unfavorably outside of Santiago. However, the government has passed strict anti-discriminatory laws, and there is very little chance of encountering homophobic violence. Santiago has a vibrant gay scene – centered in the Bellavista neighborhood – and a Pride parade is held every June.

Health

Chile has high standards of public health and excellent hospitals in the larger towns and cities. There are no endemic diseases to be concerned about. There have been very few cases of tourists developing infections from diseases such as dengue fever, Chagas disease, and hantavirus disease, which have occasionally broken out. Given the wealth of adventure activities on offer, trauma injuries are the most common cause for requiring medical treatment. It is therefore wise to take out travel insurance.

Emergency medical care is given at hospitals and medical facilities; you will need to show your medical insurance documents. Private hospitals are expensive; keep receipts to reclaim the cost from your insurance company later. Note that facilities on Easter Island – where there is only

one hospital – are limited, and you will likely be taken by air ambulance to mainland Chile. If you need medicinal supplies or advice about minor ailments, seek out a pharmacy.

As the northern and central Andes contain some of the highest elevations in the Western Hemisphere, be aware of the danger of altitude sickness (AMS). Symptoms include headaches, nausea, fatigue, dizziness, and dehydration. The best precaution is to acclimatize by gradually increasing altitudes; and if you do start showing symptoms, retreat to lower ground immediately.

Alcohol, Smoking, and Drugs

A range of alcohol is available throughout Chile, which is unsurprising for a country renowned for the quality of its red wine and signature *pisco* sour. Consequently, it is part of the culture, although you do not generally see people drinking to excess, and public inebriation is generally frowned upon.

A fairly high percentage of Chileans smoke tobacco but the laws banning the habit from all enclosed public areas, including restaurants and bars, are strictly adhered to. Almost all recreational drugs are illegal as well as socially unacceptable. There's a confusing statute that small amounts of cannabis can be consumed in private homes but not in any public places, including hotels. This effectively renders the practice impractical to travelers and it is best to refrain, as penalties can be harsh.

ID

Both Chilean nationals and foreigners are officially required to carry ID, so it's advisable to keep your passport with you at all times.

Responsible Travel

The delicate ecosystems of Chile and Easter Island are under threat. Water scarcity is a particular issue in the north, so use water responsibly. Deforestation has caused havoc in the national parks and Patagonia; paying the entrance fees ensures you contribute to the maintenance of these landscapes. Visiting local communities is the best way to learn about the country's ecology, and parks offer opportunities to stay on traditional ranches or take tours with local workers. Campfires are illegal in many of Chile's parks due to wildfires.

Cell Phones and Wi-Fi

Local SIM cards can be purchased within the country, although you need to register online first if you plan on staying for more than 120 days; the Spanish-only **Multibanda** site has more information. Pre-paid phone cards offer the most competitive rates for international dialing, and are best bought in the larger cities and tourist centers.

Multibanda
W multibanda.cl

Post

Post offices, easily identified by the blue Correos sign, are generally open 9am–7pm during the week, with some large branches operating longer hours and on Saturday.

Visiting Churches and Cathedrals

Dress modestly when visiting churches and other places of religious significance – no shorts or skirts above the knee, and no sleeveless tops.

Local Customs

Chile is a moderately conservative country and the Catholic Church still exerts influence here. Chileans value courtesy and are polite in their dealings with strangers, so rudeness does not go down well.

Taxes and Refunds

Chile has a tax called IVA, equivalent to VAT, of 19 per cent on all goods and services. This is included in the quoted price, with a couple of exceptions. Some hotels don't include IVA in their room prices, instead adding it at the end. Tourists are exempt from IVA if paying for rooms in US dollars but may need to ask for the discount. Car rental companies rarely include IVA in their prices.

Discount Cards

Valid youth and student ID cards allow visitors discounted or free entry to museums and other tourist sites. Santiago's **Costanera Center** offers foreigners an easily obtainable discount card.

Costanera Center
W costaneracenter.cl

INDEX

Page numbers in **bold** refer to main entries.

A

B

C

D

I

J

K

L

M

N

O

P

Q

R

S

T

PHRASE BOOK

Chileans themselves sometimes apologize for speaking bad Spanish, and anyone who has learned the language elsewhere may find it a challenge. Still, it is fairer to say that, given the country's geographical isolation, Spanish simply developed differently here. Additionally, because of Mapuche influence, there are many non-standard words, and pronunciation can also be difficult.

Chileans often omit the terminal "s," making it difficult for outsiders to distinguish singular from plural, and sometimes even the internal "s." On the tongue of a Chilean, for instance, *las escuelas* (the schools) may sound more like "la ecuela." Similarly, Anglicisms such as "show" sound more like "cho" in local speech.

In everyday informal speech, Chileans may also use non-standard verb forms. For instance, second-person familiar verbs often end in an accented "í," as in "¿Querí?" (Do you want?) rather than the conventional "¿Quieres?."

SOME SPECIAL CHILEAN WORDS

carrete	**kahrehteh**	*party*
chupe	**choopeh**	*a seafood stew*
completo	**kohmplehtoh**	*Chilean hot dog*
copa	**kohpah**	*glass (of wine)*
galería	**gahlehree-ah**	*shopping mall*
oficina	**ohfeeseenah**	*office; in the Atacama nitrate-mining towns*
parcela	**pahrsaylah**	*country home or small farm*
parrilla	**pahreeyah**	*grill restaurant*
paseo	**pahsayoh**	*pedestrian mall*

IN AN EMERGENCY

Help!	**¡Socorro!**	*sokorro*
Stop!	**¡Pare!**	*pareh*
Call a doctor!	**¡Llamen un médico!**	*yamen oon mehdeeko*
Call an ambulance	**¡Llamen a una ambulancia**	*yamen a oona amboolans-ya*
Police!	**¡Policía!**	*poleesee-a*
I've been robbed	**Me robaron**	*meh robaron*
Where is the nearest hospital?	**¿Dónde queda el hospital más cercano?**	*dondeh keda el ospeetal mas sairkano*
Could you help me?	**¿Me puede ayudar?**	*meh pwedeh a-yoodar*

COMMUNICATION ESSENTIALS

Yes	**Sí**	*see*
No	**No**	*no*
Please	**Por favor**	*por fabor*
Pardon me	**Perdone**	*pairdoneh*
Excuse me	**Disculpe**	*deeskoolpeh*
I'm sorry	**Lo siento**	*lo s-yento*
Thanks	**Gracias**	*gras-yas*
Hello!	**¡Hola!**	*o-la*
Good morning	**Buenos días**	*bwenos dee-as*
Good afternoon	**Buenas tardes**	*bwenas tardes*
Good evening	**Buenas noches**	*bwenas noches*
Night	**Noche**	*nocheh*
Morning	**Mañana**	*man-yana*
Tomorrow	**Mañana**	*man-yana*
Yesterday	**Ayer**	*a-yair*
Here	**Acá**	*aka*
What?	**¿Cómo?**	*komo*
When?	**¿Cuándo?**	*kwando*
Where?	**¿Dónde?**	*dondeh*
Why?	**¿Por qué?**	*por keh*
How are you?	**¿Cómo está?**	*komo estah*
Very well, thank you	**Muy bien, gracias**	*mwee byen gras-yas*
Pleased to meet you	**Encantado/a/ mucho gusto**	*enkantad o/a/ moocho goosto*

USEFUL PHRASES

That's great!	**¡Qué bien!**	*keh b-yen*
Do you speak English?	**¿Habla usted Ingles?**	*abla oo-sted eenglehs*
I don't understand	**No entiendo**	*no ent-yendo*
Could you speak more slowly?	**¿Puede hablar más despacio?**	*pwedeh ablar mas despas-yo*
I agree/okay	**De acuerdo/bueno**	*deh akwairdo/ bweno*
Let's go!	**¡Vámonos!**	*bamonos*
How do I get to/ which way to...?	**¿Cómo se llega a...?/¿Por dónde e va a...?**	*komo se llega a/por dondeh seh ba a*

USEFUL WORDS

large	**grande**	*grandeh*
small	**pequeño**	*peken-yo*
hot	**caliente**	*kal-yenteh*
cold	**frío**	*free-o*
good	**bueno**	*bweno*
bad	**malo**	*malo*
sufficient	**suficiente**	*soofees-yenteh*
open	**abierto**	*ab-yairto*
closed	**cerrado**	*serrah-do*
entrance	**entrada**	*entrada*
exit	**salida**	*saleeda*
full	**lleno**	*yeno*
right	**derecha**	*dairehcha*
left	**izquierda**	*eesk-yairda*
straight on	**derecho**	*dehrehcho*
above	**arriba**	*arreeba*
quickly	**rápido**	*rahpidoh*
early	**temprano**	*temprahno*
late	**tarde**	*tardeh*
now	**ahora**	*a-ora*
soon	**pronto**	*pronto*
less	**menos**	*menos*
much	**mucho**	*moocho*
in front of	**delante**	*delanteh*
opposite	**enfrente**	*enfrenteh*
behind	**detrás**	*detrahs*
second floor	**segundo piso**	*segoondo peeso*
ground floor	**primer piso**	*preemair peeso*
bar	**bar**	*bar*
discotheque	**boliche**	*bohleecheh*
lift/elevator	**ascensor**	*asensor*
bathroom	**baño**	*ban-yo*
toilet paper	**papel higiénico**	*papel eeh-yeneeko*
bribe	**coima**	*koyma*
girl/woman	**mina**	*meena*
women	**mujeres**	*moohaires*
men	**hombres**	*ombres*
child (boy/girl)	**niño/niña**	*neen-yo, neen-yah*
camera	**cámara**	*kamara*

batteries	**pilas**	*peelas*
passport	**pasaporte**	*pasaporteh*
visa	**visa**	*beesa*
tourist card	**tarjeta turística**	*tarheta tooreesteeka*
driver's license	**licencia de conducir**	*leesensyah de condooseer*
thief	**ladrón**	*lahdrohn*
cop	**carabinero**	*ka-ra-bin-air-oh*
money	**dinero**	*deenehroh*
lazy	**flojo**	*flohoh*
mess	**lío**	*lee-oh*
shanty town	**callampa**	*kayahmpah*
to eat	**comer**	*koh-mehr*
to steal	**robar**	*rohbahr*
to back away	**arrugar**	*ahroogahr*
to put up with	**soportar**	*sohportahr*
No way	**¡De ningun manera!**	*Day neengoonah manehra*

HEALTH

I don't feel well	**No me siento bien**	*No meh s-yento been*
I have a stomach ache/ headache.	**Me duele el estómago/ la cabeza**	*meh dweleh el estohmago/ la kabesa*
He/she is ill	**Está enfermo/a**	*esta enfairmo/a*
I need to rest	**Necesito decansar**	*neseseeto deskansar*

POST OFFICES AND BANKS

I'm looking for a... bureau de change	**Busco una... casa de cambio**	*boosko oona kasa deh kamb-yo*
What is the dollar rate?	**¿A cuánto está el dólar?**	*a kwantoh esta el dohlar*
I want to send a	**Quiero enviar una**	*k-yairo en-vyar-oona*
letter	**carta**	*karta*
postcard	**postal**	*postal*
stamp	**estampilla**	*estampee-ya*
withdraw money	**sacar dinero**	*sakar deenairo*

SHOPPING

I would like...	**Me gustaría...**	*meh goostaree-a*
I want...	**Quiero...**	*k-yairo*
Do you have any...?	**¿Tiene...?**	*t-yeneh*
How much is it?	**¿Cuánto cuesta?**	*kwanto kwesta*
What time do you open/close?	**¿A qué hora abre/ cierra?**	*a ke ora abreh/ s-yairra*
May I pay with a credit card?	**¿Puedo pagar con tarjeta de crédito?**	*pwedo pagar kon tarheta deh kredeeto*
expensive	**caro**	*karo*

SIGHTSEEING

beach	**playa**	*pla-ya*
castle, fortress	**castillo**	*kastee-yo*
guide	**guía**	*gee-a*
hamlet	**aldea**	*ahdayah*
motorway	**autopista**	*owtopeesta*
neighborhood	**barrio**	*bahreeoh*
road	**carretera**	*karretaira*
street	**calle**	*ka-yeh*
tourist bureau	**oficina de turismo**	*ofeeseena deh tooreesmo*
town hall	**municipalidad**	*mooneeseepaleedad*

GETTING AROUND

When does it leave?	**¿A qué hora sale?**	*a keh ora saleh*
When does the next train/bus leave for...?	**¿A qué hora sale el próximo tren/ autobús a...?**	*a keh ora saleh el prokseemo tren/ owtoboos a*
Could you call a taxi for me?	**¿Me puede llamar un taxi?**	*meh pwedeh yamar oon taksee*
departure gate	**puerta de embarque**	*pwairta deh embarkeh*
boarding pass	**tarjeta de embarque**	*tarheta deh e embarkeh*
customs	**aduana**	*adwana*
fare	**tarifa**	*tareefa*
insurance	**seguro**	*segooro*
car hire	**alquiler de autos**	*alkeelair deh owtos*
bicycle	**bicicleta**	*beeseekleta*
gasoline station	**estación de servicio**	*estas-yon deh serveeseeoh*
garage	**garage**	*garaheh*
I have a flat tire	**Se me pinchó un neumático**	*seh meh peencho un nayoomahtikoh*

STAYING IN A HOTEL

I have a reservation	**Tengo una reserva**	*Tengo oona rresairba*
Is there a room available?	**¿Hay habitación disponible?**	*I ahbitahseeohn deesponeeble*
single/double room	**habitación single/ doble**	*abeetas-yohn senglay/dobleh*
twin room	**habitación con camas gemelas**	*abeetas-yon kon kamas hemelas*
shower	**ducha**	*doocha*
bathtub	**tina**	*teenah*
I want to be woken up at...	**Necesito que me despierten a las...**	*neseseeto keh meh desp-yairten a las*
hot water	**agua caliente**	*agwa lak-yenteh*
cold water	**agua fría**	*agwa free-yah*
soap	**jabón**	*habohn*
towel	**toalla**	*to-a-ya*
key	**llave**	*yabeh*

EATING OUT

I am a vegetarian	**Soy vegetariano**	*soy behetar-yano*
fixed price	**precio fijo**	*pres-yo feeho*
glass	**vaso**	*baso*
cup	**taza**	*tahsah*
cutlery	**cubiertos**	*koob-yairtos*
Can I see the menu, please?	**¿Puedo ver la carta, por favor?**	*pwedoh vair la carta, por fabor*
The check, please	**la cuenta, por favor**	*la kwenta por fabor*
I would like a glass of water	**Me gustaría un vaso de agua**	*meh goostaree-a oon baso deh agwa*
breakfast	**desayuno**	*desa-yoono*
lunch	**almuerzo**	*almwairso*
dinner	**cena**	*saynah*

MENU DECODER

parrillada	*pahreeyada*	mixed grill
lomo	*lohmoh*	beefsteak
lomo a la pimienta	*lohomo ah la peemee-entah*	pepper steak
lomo vetado	*lohmoh vehtadoh*	ribeye
lomo liso	*lohmoh leesoh*	sirloin
barros luco	*bahros lookoh*	beef sandwich with melted cheese
cazuela de vacuno	*kahswaylah de vahkoonoh*	beef and vegetable stew
cazuela de ave	*kahswaylah de ahvay*	chicken and vegetable stew
centolla	*sentoyah*	king crab

pebre	*pehbray*	Chilean salsa
chorizo	*chohreezoh*	pork sausage
choripán	*choreepan*	pork sausage in a bun
churrasco	*choorrasko*	thin boneless steak on bread
cola de mono	*kohlah de mono*	aperitif of coffee, milk, and liqueur
curanto	*kooranhntoh*	stew of shellfish, meat, and potatoes
lúcuma	*lookoohmah*	eggfruit
mollejas	*moyehas*	sweetbreads
pastel de choclo	*pahstel deh chohcloh*	corn pie
plateada	*plahte-ahda*	stewed beef and vegetables
terremoto	*tairehmohtoh*	cocktail of white wine, Fernet, and pineapple ice cream
humita	*oomeeta*	mashed sweet corn mixed with onion and milk
arroz	*arrohs*	rice
atún	*atoon*	tuna
azúcar	*asookar*	sugar
bacalao	*bakala-o*	cod
camarones	*kamarones*	shrimp
carne	*karneh*	beef
cebolla	*sebo-ya*	onion
chirimoya	*cheereemoyah*	custard apple
huevo	*webo*	egg
jugo	*hoogo*	fruit juice
langosta	*langosta*	lobster
leche	*lecheh*	milk
mantequilla	*mantekee-ya*	butter
marisco	*mareesko*	shellfish
pan	*pan*	bread
papas	*papas*	potatoes
pescado	*peskado*	fish
pimienta dulce	*peemee-entah doolsay*	sweet pepper
pollo	*po-yo*	chicken
postre	*postreh*	dessert
roseta	*rroseta*	bread roll
sal	*sal*	salt
salsa	*salsa*	sauce
sopa	*sopa*	soup
té	*teh*	tea
vinagre	*beenagreh*	vinegar
zapallito	*sapa-yeeto*	squash

TIME

minute	**minuto**	*meenootoh*
hour	**hora**	*ora*
half an hour	**media hora**	*med-ya ora*
quarter of an hour	**un cuarto**	*oon kwarto*
Monday	**lunes**	*loones*
Tuesday	**martes**	*martes*
Wednesday	**miércoles**	*m-yairkoles*
Thursday	**jueves**	*hwebes*
Friday	**viernes**	*b-yairnes*
Saturday	**sábado**	*sabado*
Sunday	**domingo**	*domeengo*
January	**enero**	*enairo*
February	**febrero**	*febrairo*
March	**marzo**	*marso*
April	**abril**	*abreel*
May	**mayo**	*ma-yo*
June	**junio**	*hoon-yo*
July	**julio**	*hool-yo*
August	**agosto**	*agosto*
September	**septiembre**	*sept-yembreh*
October	**octubre**	*oktoobreh*
November	**noviembre**	*nob-yembreh*
December	**diciembre**	*dees-yembreh*

NUMBERS

0	**cero**	*sairo*
1	**uno**	*oono*
2	**dos**	*dos*
3	**tres**	*tres*
4	**cuatro**	*kwatro*
5	**cinco**	*seenko*
6	**seis**	*says*
7	**siete**	*s-yeteh*
8	**ocho**	*ocho*
9	**nueve**	*nwebeh*
10	**diez**	*d-yes*
11	**once**	*onseh*
12	**doce**	*doseh*
13	**trece**	*treseh*
14	**catorce**	*katorseh*
15	**quince**	*keenseh*
16	**dieciséis**	*d-yeseesays*
17	**diecisiete**	*d-yesees-yeteh*
18	**dieciocho**	*d-yes-yocho*
19	**diecinueve**	*d-yeseenwebeh*
20	**veinte**	*baynteh*
30	**treinta**	*traynta*
40	**cuarenta**	*kwarenta*
50	**cincuenta**	*seenkwenta*
60	**sesenta**	*sesenta*
70	**setenta**	*setenta*
80	**ochenta**	*ochenta*
90	**noventa**	*nobenta*
100	**cien**	*s-yen*
500	**quinientos**	*keen-yentos*
1000	**mil**	*meel*
first	**primero/a**	*preemairo/a*
second	**segundo/a**	*segoondo/a*
third	**tercero/a**	*tairsairo/a*
fourth	**cuarto/a**	*kwarto/a*
fifth	**quinto/a**	*keento/a*
sixth	**sexto/a**	*seksto/a*
seventh	**séptimo/a**	*septeemo/a*
eighth	**octavo/a**	*oktabo/a*
ninth	**noveno/a**	*nobeno/a*
tenth	**décimo/a**	*deseemo/a*

ACKNOWLEDGMENTS

This edition updated by
Contributor Carol King
Senior Editor Dipika Dasgupta
Senior Art Editor Stuti Tiwari
Project Editor Anuroop Sanwalia
Project Art Editor Ankita Sharma
Editors Ekta Chadha, Alex Pathe
Assistant Editors Sarah Mathew, Pankhoori Sinha
Proofreader Debra Wolter
Indexer Helen Peters
Assistant Picture Research Administrator Manpreet Kaur
Senior Picture Researcher Nishwan Rasool
Deputy Manager, Picture Research Virien Chopra
Publishing Assistant Simona Vellikova
Jacket Picture Researcher Laura O'Brien
Senior Cartographer Mohammed Hassan
Cartography Manager Suresh Kumar
Pre-production Coordinator Tanveer Zaidi
Pre-production Manager Balwant Singh
Production Controller Kariss Ainsworth
Deputy Managing Editor Dharini Ganesh
Managing Editor Beverly Smart
Managing Art Editor Gemma Doyle
Senior Managing Art Editor Priyanka Thakur
Editorial Director Hollie Teague
Art Director Maxine Pedliham
Publishing Director Georgina Dee

DK would like to thank the following for their contribution to the previous edition: Shafik Meghji, Stephanie Dyson, Nick Edwards, Wayne Bernhardson, Declan McGarvey, Kristina Schreck, Hilary Bird

The publisher would like to thank the following for their kind permission to reproduce their photographs:

Key: a-above; b-below/bottom; c-center; f-far; l-left; r-right; t-top

123RF.com: Antonio Abrignani 45clb.

4Corners: Guido Cozzi 192–3b.

akg-images: 46cr; Album / Oronoz 45tr; 46tl; historic-maps 45tl.

Alamy Stock Photo: age fotostock / Tolo Balaguer 221tr, 225cl, 226t, / Gábor Kovács 200–201t, / Dave Stamboulis 235; Albertoloyo 178–9b; All Canada Photos / Wayne Lynch 34bl, Sally Anderson 67clb; Arco Images GmbH / G. Lacz 189crb; Al Argueta 25tr, 68t; Sven Arved 27t; Krys Bailey 238cr; Joao Barcelos 234br; Norman Barrett 156bl; Aaron Beck 164tl; Hal Beral / VWPics 270cra, 271ca; Bildagentur-online / Begsteiger 181br; BIOSPHOTO / Jean-Claude Malausa 33cl, 133tr, 137b; Blickwinkel / Hummel 237br; Tibor Bognar 55t, 69bl, 72tl, 84–5; Michele Burgess 24tl, 41crb, 157br; byvalet 24cra, 70b; Cal Sport Media 108–9t; Cannon Photography LLC / BrownWCannonIII 27br, 268–9b; Blanca Saenz de Castillo 204–5t; Cavan / Aurora Photos / Tim Martin 16c, 50–51; Chris Schmid Photography 272–3b; Jan A. Csernoch 167tr; Cultura Creative Ltd / Ben Pipe Photography 20t; Ian Dagnall / Graffiti by Gabriel Eduardo Maulen Muñoz 105tr; Danita Delimont / DanitaDelimont.com / Walter Bibikow 172–3b, 224cra, / Fredrik Norrsell 246–7b; David Noton Photography 148bl; Chile DesConocido 124tl; Design Pics Inc / Destinations / Deddeda 26–7b, / Peter Langer 94cr; DGB 279br; Doleesi 161tr; Reiner Elsen 76tl; Everett Collection Inc / © Sony Pictures Classics / Ron Harvey 61br; FerrizFrames 32br; Constanza Flores 8clb; Florilegius 45cr, 47cb, 269tr; Folio Images / Felix Oppenheim 10clb; Galopin 43tr; Jorge Garrido 56cr; David Gee 259br; Diego Grandi 104b; Granger Historical Picture Archive / NYC 47tr, 105br; Mark Green 11br; Marcel Gross 10ca, 34–5t; Have Camera Will Travel | Central & South America 59br; hemis.fr / Walter Bibikow 171cra, / De Winter - Van Rossem 184–5t; Hemis.fr / Hughes Hervé 58-59b; Heritage Image Partnership Ltd / Index 44bc, / Werner Forman Archive / N.J Saunders 269tl; Cindy Hopkins 22cla; Ian Dagnall 12–13b; Image Professionals GmbH / Enno Kapitza 208t; imageBROKER / Christian Handl 192t, / Christian Heinrich 233tr, / Martina Katz 43crb, / Karol Kozlowski 40–41b, / Michael Runkel 27cl, / Stefan Schurr 129t, / Harald von Radebrecht 243bl; incamerastock / ICP 45cla; John Warburton-Lee Photography / Paul Harris 59tr; Jon Arnold Images Ltd 20bl, / Walter Bibikow 158–9b, 224–5b, 255t; Paul Kennedy / *Street Art Bellavista Sunflower Energy* by Gonzalo Matiz Salinas 30–31b; Keystone Press / Keystone Pictures USA 48tl; Russell Kord 17tl, 109bl, 114–15; MARKA / maurizio virgili 167ca; Daniel Korzeniewski 245t; Stefano Politi Markovina 38–9t; mauritius images GmbH / Cyril Gosselin 88-89t, mauritius images GmbH / Stefano Paterna 55bl, 83tl, 98–9, / Jutta Ulmer 212b; mikecranephotography.com 213t; MJ Photography 274–5t; Ashot Mnatsakanyan 89br; Raquel Mogado 241tl, 242t; Gianni Muratore 43tl; National Geographic Image Collection / Babak Tafreshi 11t; National Geographic Image Collection / Nigel Hicks 216br, / Maria Stenzel 18cb, 228–9, / Dave Yoder 160tl; The Natural History Museum 46br, 137tr; Nature Picture Library / Merryn Thomas 25cla; Francisco Negroni 211br; Niebrugge Images 72–3b; M. Timothy O'Keefe 110tl; Panther Media GmbH / braeumer 276bc; Stefano Paterna 254br; Pictorial Press Ltd 48cb; Maurizio Polese 28bl; Porky Pies Photography 257bl; Prisma Archivo 46–7t; Hoberman Publishing 138; Mauricio Quevedo 179tr; Ricardo Ribas 164–5b; Jeremy Richards 278–9t; Robertharding 168–9b, / Jordan Banks 56crb, / Geoff Renner 273tr, / Yadid Levy, 78b; Pep Roig 236bl; Grant Rooney 119cr, Francisco Javier Ramos Rosellon 130t; RP

Images / SrA Sarah Mattison 136cra; Michael Runkel 135br; Philip Scalia 36tr, 60–61t; David South 180tc; South America 226cra; Marina Spironetti 20crb,
183br; Jose Luis Stephens 56t, 97tr; Johnny Stockshooter 122bl; Keren Su / China Span 184bl; Sueddeutsche Zeitung Photo / Jose Giribas 40t, 41cla, 89cl, 90b, 125crb; Tetra Images / Henryk Sadura 256t; Markus Thomenius 162–3t; Toniflap 67crb; travelbild.com 278bl; Universal Images Group North America LLC / DeAgostini / DEA Picture Library 31crb; UPI 49clb; Lucas Vallecillos 23tr, 66–7t, 160–61b, 177br; Simon Vine 203tr; Shiona Webster 203cra; WENN Rights Ltd 49bc; Leon Werdinger 26tl; Andreas Werth 13br, 233cra; Westend61 GmbH / Stefan Schütz 32–3t, 239tl, 246tl; Karin De Winter 167cra; Wim Wiskerke 67br; Xinhua / © Jorge Villegas 42cla; Alessandro Zappalorto 182cra; Zoonar GmbH / Barbara Boensch 170bl.

AWL Images: Walter Bibikow 187t; Karol Kozlowski 2–3, 25tl, 56bl, 71t, 79tr, 92t, 276tl; John Warburton-Lee 275br; Alex Robinson 260–61t.

Bocanáriz: Katherine Hidalgo 28-29t

Bridgeman Images: Archivio Arici / Graziano Arici 38bl; Sophie Bassouls 39cla; Look and Learn 45crb; Photo Josse 46clb.

Depositphotos Inc: pierivb 4; tjalex4life@gmail.com 17cb, 150–51; Toniflap 215b.

Dorling Kindersley: Demetrio Carrasco 31cla.

Dreamstime.com: Hernan Perez Aguirre 132b; Hoang Bao Nguyen / *Street Art* by Aibar 22–3ca; Albertoloyo 176–7t; Antonella865 182t; Pierre-yves Babelon 122–3t; Rui Baião 42cr; Bigapplestock 125b; Lukas Bischoff 54c, 62–3; Larisa Blinova 210–11t; David Brooks 58tr; Byvalet 39b; Dmitry Chulov 176bl; Ionut David 19t, 248–9; Francisco Javier Espuny 96b; Marcelo Vildosola Garrigo 188tl; Diego Grandi 8–9b, 22tl, 36–7b, 42cl, 77b, 91tl, 102–3t, 106–7b, 118–19t, 120–21b, 130–31b, 139tr; Mario Gyss 219br; Ildipapp 29ca; Burt Johnson / *Street Art* by Sammy Espinosa 37tr; Jesse Kraft 80–81b, 178tl; Marabelo 136t; Maximoangel 205cb; Andres Morales 42crb; Oksanabratanova 175br; Pabloborca 217tr; Pattilabelle 120cla; Kseniya Ragozina 12t, 166–7b, 169br; Jeremy Richards 42clb, 154bl, 180bl, 227bl; Rodolfosteck 146–7b; Martin Schneiter 37clb, 174c, 174–5t, 198bc; Patrick Silveira 82bl; Sonechka 19bl, 264–5; Stuart456 37b; Tifonimages 18tl, 75br, 194–5, 222t; Vladgalenko 261br; Wastesoul 74–5t.

Getty Images: AFP / Martin Bernetti / *Street Art* by Sammy Espinosa 126–7t, / Martin Bernetti 13t, 43cr, 59cl, 142bl, 186–7b, 238–9b, / Rodrigo Buendia 206bl; Agencia Makro 207br, Anadolu Agency / Muhammed Emin Canik 48–9t; Corbis Historical / Julio Donoso 12clb; De Agostini Picture Library / DEA Picture Library 269ca, / W. Buss 42cra, / V. Giannella 33br, / G. Nimatallah 277tr: Michael Duva 154–5t; FIFA / Alex Grimm 145t; Gamma-Rapho / Yves Gellie 273cra; Hulton Fine Art Collection / Heritage Images 44t; imageBROKER / Ulrich Reichel 237c; LatinContent WO / Marcelo Hernandez 20cr, / Alejandro Zoñez 207t; Keith Levit 253clb; The LIFE Picture Collection / Carl Mydans 48bl; LightRocket / SOPA Images / John Milner / *Street Art* by Gonzalo Matiz Salinas 60b; Lonely Planet Images / John Elk III 180–81t, / Aaron McCoy 198cra, / Witold Skrypczak 209b; Moment / Marco Bottigelli 112–13, 262b,/ DircinhaSW 190–91b, / Ruben Earth 24tr, / Fotografías Jorge León Cabello 198clb, 199, / Claudio Sepúlveda Geoffroy 210bl, / Image by Nonac_Digi for the Green Man 22–3t, / Pakawat Thongcharoen 202–3b, / Traumlichtfabrik 11cr, / Yongrong Yu 263tl; Moment Open / florentina georgescu photography 220b, / Foto por Juan Cristóbal Hurtado 203cb, / Ganagafoto 276–7b, / Joy Ride By Taylor 214tr, / Photography by Jessie Reeder 13cr; Moment Select / Niall Corbet @ www.flickr / photos / niallcorbet 157t; NurPhoto / Fernando Lavoz 43clb; Ignacio Palacios 259t; Photodisc / Andrea Pistolesi 240b; Robertharding / Bruno Barbier 273tl; David Silverman 205br; Universal Images Group / Hoberman Collection 23cla, 140t, 141br, 149tr, / Insights 94–5b, / PHAS 44crb, / Universal History Archive 47bl; Westend61 8cla, 232–3b.

Getty Images / iStock: abriendomundo 189b; Ampueroleonardo 129cra; Claudio Arriagada 143t, 144bl; Neil Bowman 143cra; Agustina Camilion 236–7t; Christhilf 274bc; E+ / AscentXmedia 216bl, / Andrew Peacock 280–81; EAQ 170–71t; Alexis Gonzalez 147crb; iFerol 203br; leonardospencer 110–11b; miralex 270–71b; NataliaCatalina 258b; Taku_S 218–19t; Tituz 43cl.

Museum of Contemporary Art Santiago © Colección MAC: Post 90 Exhibition. MAC; Parque Forestal. March 31 – September 10., Artworks from the Contemporary Art Museum., Arts Faculty; Universidad de Chile. / Luna Quezada 61cla, 80tl.

naturepl.com: Kristel Richard 35ca.

Robert Harding Picture Library: 8cl; Jordan Banks 6–7; Antonio Busiello 35clb; Robert Francis 203cr; Christian Handl 29crb.

Shutterstock.com: AP / Victor R Caivano 49t; Luiz Barrionuevo 89cra; Birdymeo 252–3t; Christina Fink 233tl; Guaxinim 234clb; Cristian Aravena Jara 93b; Maurizio De Mattei 30-31t; Sergey-73 134t; Sunsinger 244b; Warehouse of Images 203tl.

Unsplash: Loïc Mermilliod / @loacfr 10–11b.

Front flap images
Alamy Stock Photo: Marcel Gross c; Philip Scalia cla; **Dreamstime.com:** Diego Grandi cra; bl; Kseniya Ragozina br; **Unsplash:** Loïc Mermilliod / @loacfr t.

Cover images
Front and Spine: **Getty Images / iStock:** E+ / DieterMeyrl.
Back: **Alamy Stock Photo:** Cannon Photography LLC / Brown W CannonIII c; **Dreamstime.com:** Francisco Javier Espuny cl; **Getty Images:** Marco Bottigelli tr; **Getty Images / iStock**: E+ / DieterMeyrl b.

Mapping
The maps of Santiago are derived from © openstreetmap.org and contributors, licensed under CC-BY-SA; seecreativecommons.org for further details.

Illustrators: Chinglemba Chingtham, Surat Kumar Mantoo, Arun Pottirayil, T. Gautam Trivedi.

First edition 2011

Published in Great Britain by Dorling Kindersley Limited, 20 Vauxhall Bridge Road, London SW1V 2SA

The authorised representative in the EEA is Dorling Kindersley Verlag GmbH. Arnulfstr. 124, 80636 Munich, Germany

Published in the United States by DK Publishing, 1745 Broadway, 20th Floor, New York, NY 10019

25 26 27 28 10 9 8 7 6 5 4 3 2 1

A CIP catalog record for this book is available from the British Library.

A catalog record for this book is available from the Library of Congress.

ISSN: 1542 1554
ISBN: 978 0 2417 5680 5

Printed and bound in Malaysia.

www.dk.com

This book was made with Forest Stewardship Council™ certified paper – one small step in DK's commitment to a sustainable future.
Learn more at **www.dk.com/uk/information/sustainability**

A NOTE FROM DK

The rate at which the world is changing is constantly keeping the DK travel team on our toes. While we've worked hard to ensure that this edition of Chile and Easter Island is accurate and up-to-date, we know that opening hours alter, standards shift, prices fluctuate, places close and new ones pop up in their stead. So, if you notice we've got something wrong or left something out, we want to hear about it. Please get in touch at travelguides@dk.com